Incantations & Divinations

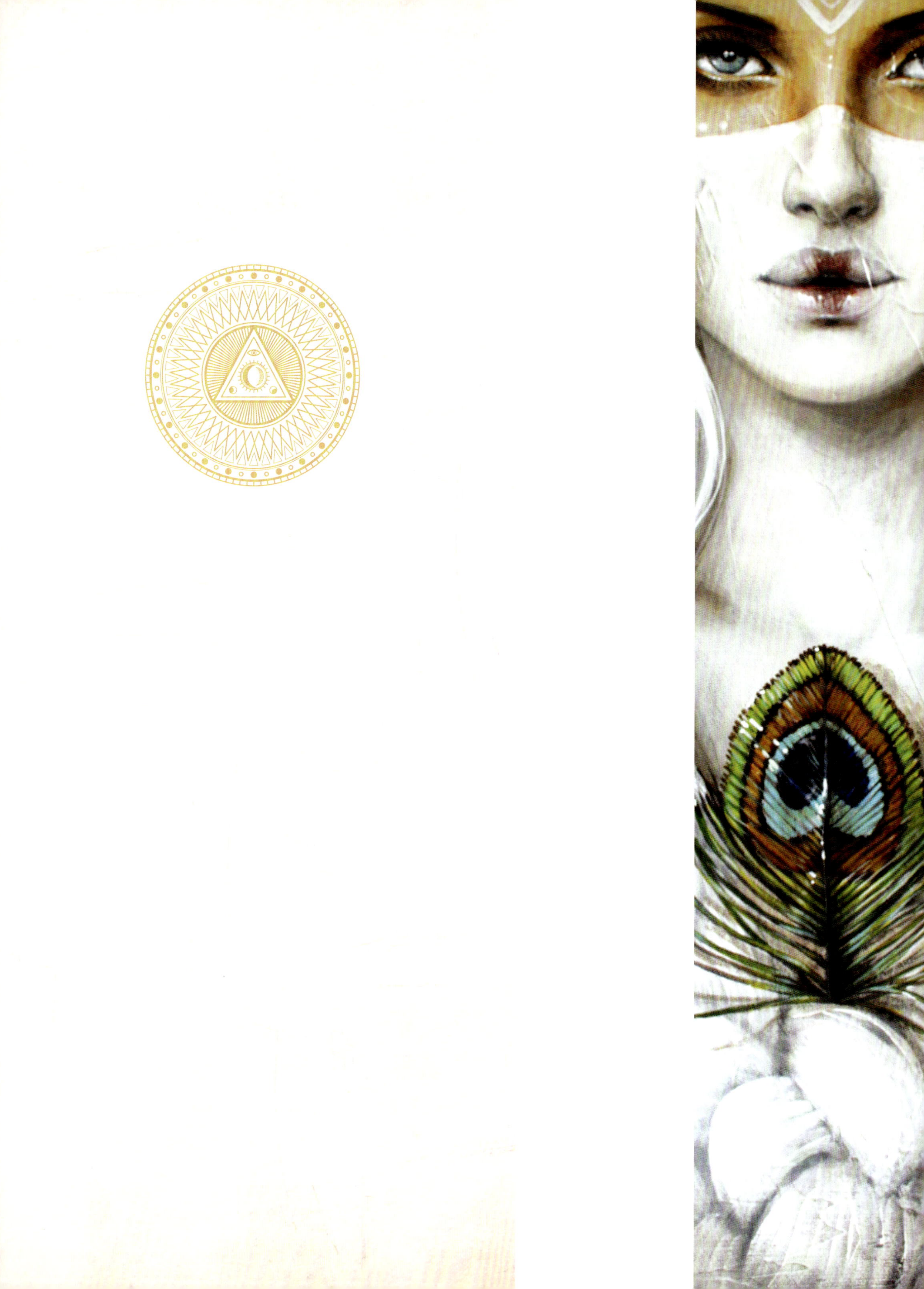

Incantations & Divinations

A Grimoire of Goodness and Grace
to Inspire Your Sacred Prophecies
and Express Your Esoteric Voice

Alana Fairchild

INCANTATIONS & DIVINATIONS
A Grimoire of Goodness and Grace to Inspire Your Sacred Prophecies
and Express Your Esoteric Voice

Published by Blue Angel Publishing®
10 Trafford Court, Wheelers Hill,
Victoria, Australia 3150
E-mail: info@blueangelonline.com
Website: www.blueangelonline.com

Front cover artwork by A. Andrew Gonzalez
Back cover artwork by Laila Savolainen
Internal artwork credits – pages 316-317

Editors: Jules Sutherland and Peter Loupelis

Blue Angel is a registered trademark of Blue Angel Gallery Pty Ltd.

ISBN: 978-1-922574-20-6

Printed on sustainably sourced paper, with soy-based ink.

Contents

Introduction

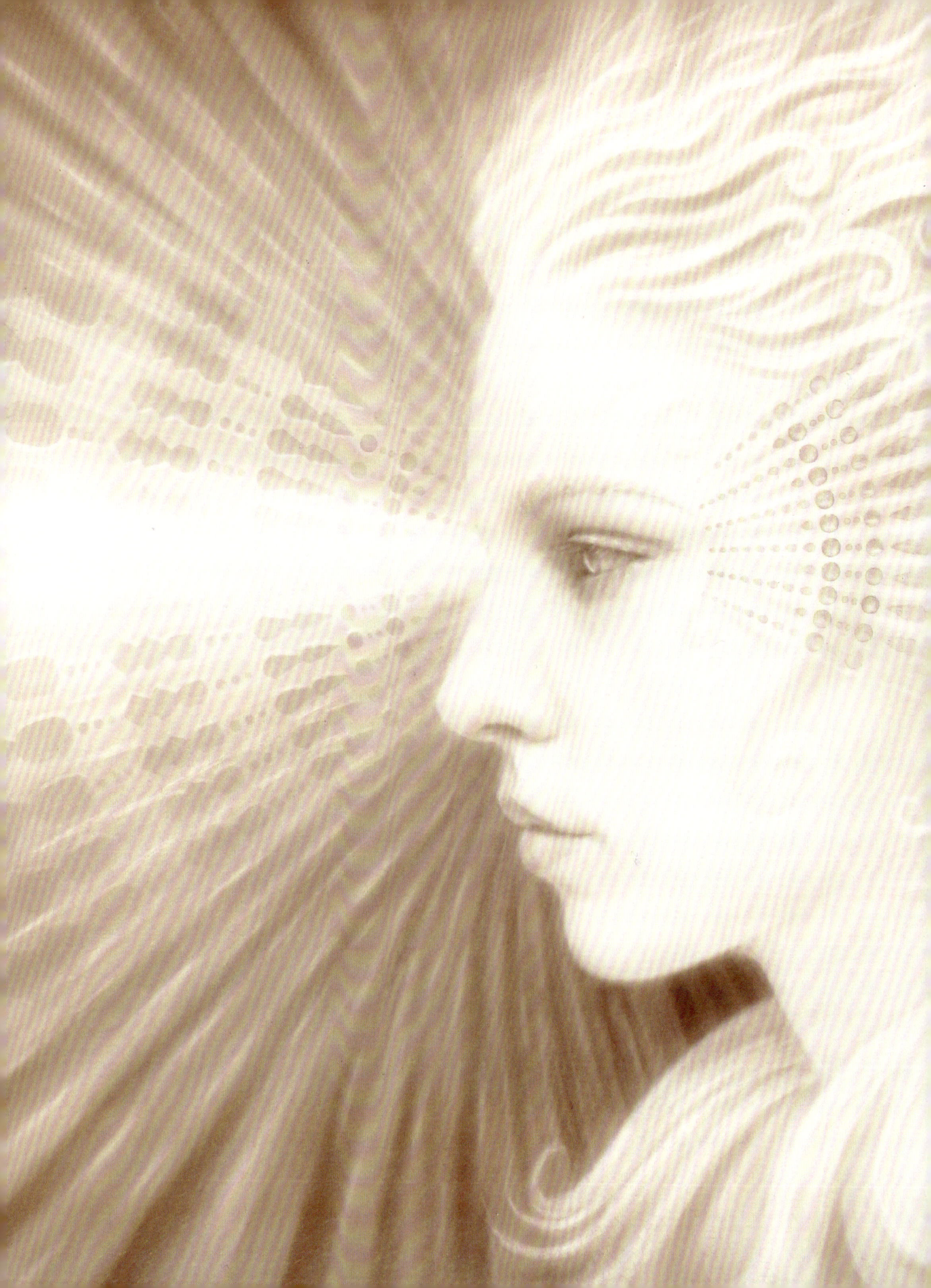

Welcome, Magical Creature

As a being with divine and human qualities, you possess the natural ability to consciously cultivate and channel your energy with clear intention, to manifest more desirable outcomes. Practice will nurture this talent already within you.

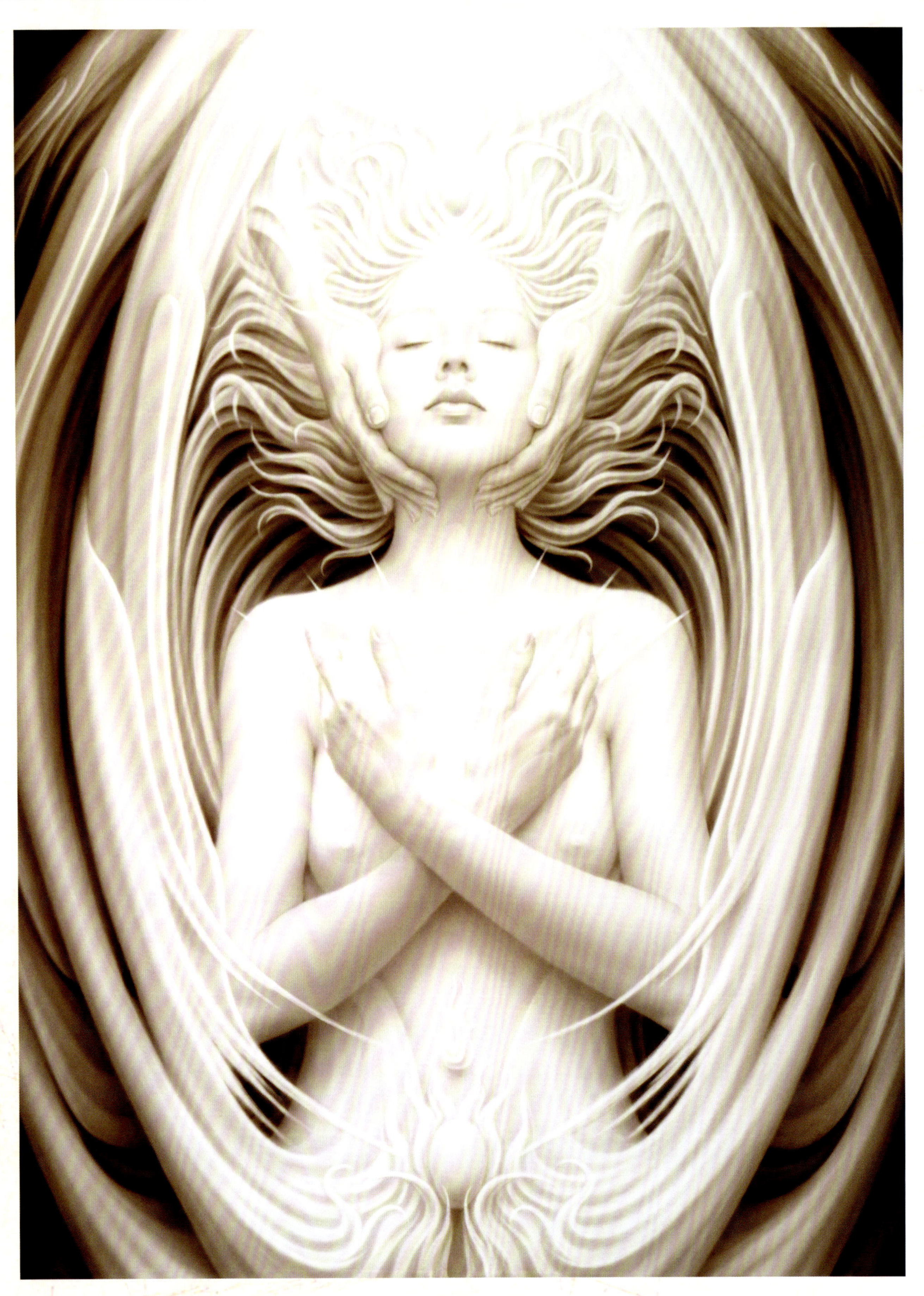

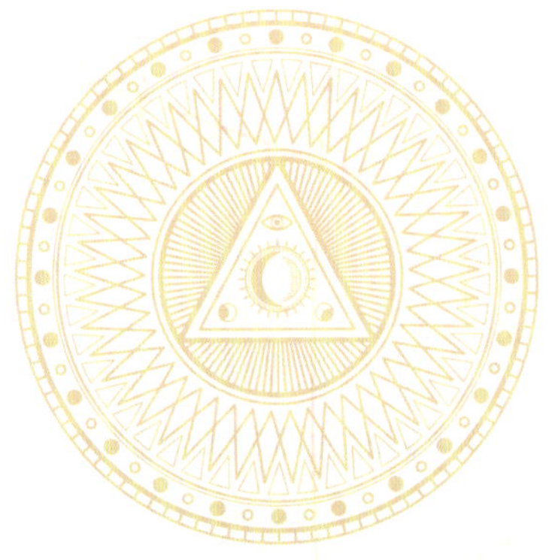

Claiming Your ESOTERIC VOICE

CLAIMING YOUR ESOTERIC VOICE IS A PATHWAY TO access your magic. Your magic is your creative spiritual potency. This is your power to utilise your energy with awareness in order to bring about constructive outcomes, making the most of your life experiences in a way that is beneficial, beautiful and blessed.

On a deeper level, your voice is more than the words you speak or sing. Voice signifies sound, and sound is ultimately energy. To claim your esoteric voice means to claim the inner reality of your voice, which is actually your energy. You can speak with words, and you can also speak through your silence (there is an expression that puts it this way: silence speaks volumes). You can speak (or express) your energy through the vibration of your thoughts and intentions, as well as your attitude, choices and actions.

So, the secret—or esoteric—expression of your voice requires that you work with your energy. We create a field of energy around us through our thoughts and actions, including the words we speak and the decisions we make daily. Tuning into our magic increases the intentionality of this energy field. We can work with this field to positively affect our experiences of life, and enhance our presence and effect in the world.

Choosing spiritual practices that engage your heart is a surefire path to claiming your energy—and working your magic—with wisdom. When your spiritual practices help you manage your mental states more consciously and constructively, too, then the positive effects for you and your creative healing and manifesting work increase radically.

Spiritual practices can include activities like prayer, conscious dance and meditation, and rituals that may include intentional wording (such as in this book or my various oracle decks), along with healing processes, visualisations and so forth, as you choose. Other constructive practices include walking in nature with awareness and mindfully focusing on breathing during yoga or exercise. Intention is massively important. You can clean your house or take a bath with the intention to cleanse your mind and energy, too, transforming it into a secret spiritual practice. Secret? Yes, in that it is an ordinary activity that you have cleverly chosen to imbue with deeper meaning and broader positive effect. Setting aside time and space to reflect on your mental and emotional states with the intent to deconstruct reactivity and cultivate compassion can be a powerful and rapid transformational practice. So, too, is the simple act of connecting to your heart with intentional gratitude. Yet another way of working with your energy intentionally and constructively could be to draw an oracle card to align yourself with universal wisdom.

> These practices are magic amplifiers that I hope you will relish and express with joyful empowerment.

The inspirational prayers, invocations and sacred words in this book have been lovingly crafted to integrate the creative power of your voice as physical sound infused with divine healing energy — integrating the exoteric (or outer form) of voice and the esoteric (or inner reality) of voice as energy. These practices are magic amplifiers that I hope you will relish and express with joyful empowerment. You can include them in any positive spiritual practice as you wish, or use them as a positive spiritual practice on their own, too.

As we think, so we become. What we speak about, we bring about. May we use the manifesting potency of our energy, our voices, with happiness and wisdom.

Setting INTENTIONS

IT HAS BEEN MY EXPERIENCE THAT THE MORE WE CHOOSE TO ENGAGE with the loving presence of the higher spiritual dimensions, the more we are changed in positive ways. The ways of being that aren't really a reflection of our authentic selves begin to crumble, and our true inner spiritual radiance begins to shine from within. Interestingly, our desires and intentions evolve as we do. The urge for revenge gives way to the urge for healing. The experience of judgement starts to feel 'icky' for want of a better term, and we yearn to taste the sweet freedom bestowed by kindness. Our desire for personal financial security expands to include a desire that *all* beings know safety and peace. We feel less alone and more spiritually connected, less controlled by the inevitable fluctuations of fear and doubt, and more trusting in the active presence of love in our lives.

> The ways of being that aren't really a reflection of our authentic selves begin to crumble, and our true inner spiritual radiance begins to shine from within.

Our minds and our lives tend to be complicated enough already. I sincerely want our use of innate spiritual creativity—our magic—to be beneficial, to alleviate difficulty and help us find a way through our problems more readily. We don't want to amplify any confusion that is likely already clouding our vision and obscuring our capacity to bring about resolution. We want to invoke a higher intelligence to reveal the swiftest and most beautiful potential for healing, helping us focus and draw upon the considerable inner resources we already have and graciously attract anything else that is of benefit.

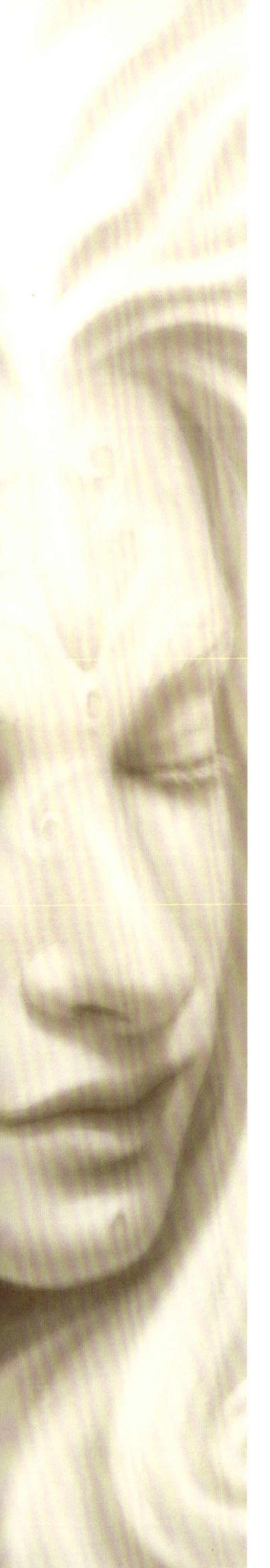

So, instead of focusing on attempting to impose our preferred vision of reality onto the people and circumstances around us according to what we think should happen, I encourage humans to utilise our abilities to pull in higher grace with the intention that this helps us and improves the situation at hand for all beings in the best possible way. We don't have to know what that will look like. We don't need to instruct grace. It is already an expression of loving divine intelligence. We just need to learn how to receive it and allow it to move through us into the world for the spiritual benefit of all beings.

The wisdom of this approach is twofold. Firstly, we know opinions can change over time. Even the most mentally inflexible person will likely have had an experience where something they once absolutely believed to be true turned out to be otherwise. An example of this can be found in the shifting understandings and advice of modern medicine. The way we see things is limited and, therefore, changeable.

If we don't really see what the problem is, we cannot be sure what the best remedy could be. Even good intentions cannot overcome limited understanding. A well-intentioned human may sincerely wish to help but unintentionally cause further complications. Good intentions are profoundly important, but we also need wisdom. So, calling on a higher intelligence that understands the most suitable medicine for the situation and can dispense it in a way that benefits all beings (including you) is spiritually smart.

This doesn't mean we have to surrender our free will and power of choice. We must lay claim to those essential facets of our spiritual birthright. If we don't, we will simply be moved by collective unconscious forces, more easily manipulated and feel devastatingly disconnected from our own sense of path, purpose and personhood. Embracing your magic requires that

you claim your will and your power, as well as your voice. To then
align and offer your energy, your intention and your practice to
the higher will of a greater love is an intelligent act that generates
multiple rewards. One such gift is to be enveloped within the
cosmic fold of a medicinal matrix that continuously intervenes to
help all beings, including you. You become inspired, educated and
guided as to how to best utilise your considerable energy, talent
and potency in ways that generate far-reaching benefits.

You will likely need some time and space to figure out what this
surrendered alignment feels like, what this looks like for you, and
how to move into that space through your spiritual practices.
Simple prayers, the incantations and divinations in this book, and
all of my published works can help you get there. So will talking
with like-minded others, contemplating and reflecting, until you
find your sense of balance and integration of self-assertion and
spiritual surrender.

Connecting with others who can accept your spiritual
unfoldment as a unique expression of your intimacy with the
Universe can increase your energy and be deeply healing. There is
still collective fear and resistance to embracing our individuality,
particularly when it comes to the spiritual path. This is one
reason why I created a community membership program called
Community of the Sacred. There are humans who will love and
support you and your process, recognising the sacredness and
validity of your personal soul journey.

Sometimes, we need to seek before we find. What we want
and need exists, but we must put ourselves in the appropriate
energetic state to be able to recognise and access it. As we
increase our energy levels through spiritual practice, the obstacles
to finding will eventually give way. There is much goodness and
generosity wanting to find its way into the lives of all beings.
Embracing our spiritual path is part of how that can happen.

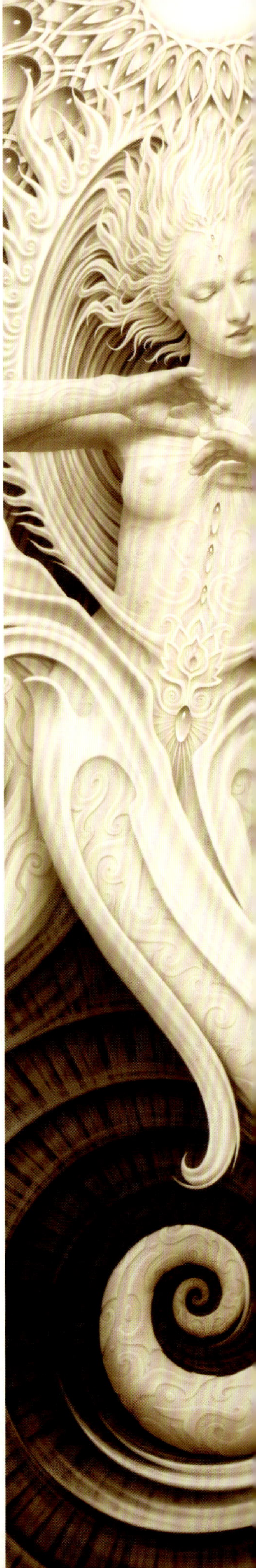

There is much
goodness and
generosity wanting
to find its way
into the lives of all
beings. Embracing
our spiritual path
is part of how that
can happen.

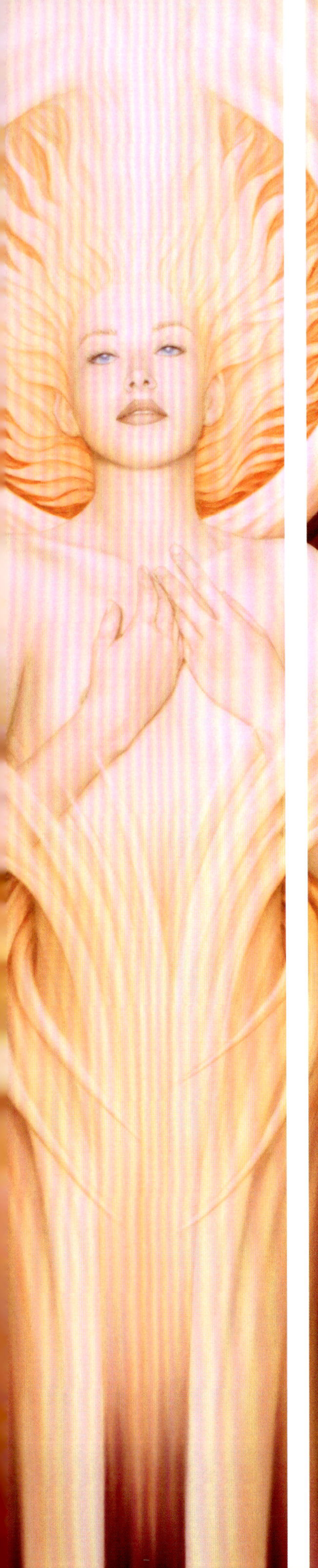

Resonance MAGIC

Magic can be expressed in many ways, through high ceremonial methods with formal steps and tools, to more informal folk practices using everyday objects to imbue protection and healing, to spontaneous rituals perhaps inspired by light streaming through the trees during forest bathing, or a feather you find on your path during a bushwalk and place on an altar at home.

From formal and scripted to inspirational and intuitive, and everything in between, magic can be practised through a myriad of methods that suit individual tendencies and talents and the circumstances of the moment.

The craft shared in this work I have coined as *subtle* or *resonance* magic. It is grounded in the law of attraction and vibration, incorporating readily available tools— this grimoire (or collection of spells and poetry) and your body, voice and mind—to increase your divine magnetism. Whilst you can add whatever additional tools and practices you wish into the mix (such as crystals, incense, candles, music, meditation, dance and so forth), those four key elements of book, body, voice and mind are the only necessities for engaging in the practice of resonance magic.

As you express words with positive meaning and qualities, your vibration alters at a subtle-energy level. Rather like a tuning fork, you begin to vibrate at a certain beneficial frequency. Your energy body is attuned through the use of your mind, voice and physical body as you vocalise the sounds. Researchers in the field of mind-body medicine propose that the mind does not only evoke an effect on the subtle body but also causes changes in the physical body — something Tibetan Buddhist masters have been teaching for thousands of years.

As we refine our mind and body through voice (energy) work, we amplify our resonance. It is like turning up the spiritual volume. The law of attraction—or 'like attracts like'—manifests more noticeably in our lives, and we begin to use karma or 'what you speak about, you bring about' more deliberately. We become more creative rather than reactive.

> As we refine our mind and body through voice (energy) work, we amplify our resonance.

Subtle magic can be far from subtle in effect! As we work with our energy, inner changes can evoke many positive and palpable transformations in ourselves and our lives. Multiple and diverse spiritual traditions teach us that all of creation arises from sound. In the Hindu tradition, the goddess Saraswati speaks her heavenly prophecies, and inevitably, events unfold in all the worlds as a consequence. Working with our energy, our voices, through resonance magic is a way of practising a very creative spirituality — utilising your path, practices and energy as magical methods for manifestation.

Because it works at the subtle level, resonance magic can rapidly shift your mindset and uplift your mood, allowing you to see more clearly and grasp the best steps forward more readily. As your ability to focus your intention on the words increases, you can cultivate the flow of your energy so that you are less likely to fall into negative habits of consciousness and more likely to lift yourself out of unhelpful patterns, to recognise and embrace life-enhancing opportunities. Changing your vibration can reduce stress, increase happiness and wellbeing on every level, amplify your ability to process and release your experiences, as well as stimulate more desirable outcomes in future. This is not only about manifestation, it is about the healing that evokes transformation rather than temporary, superficial changes.

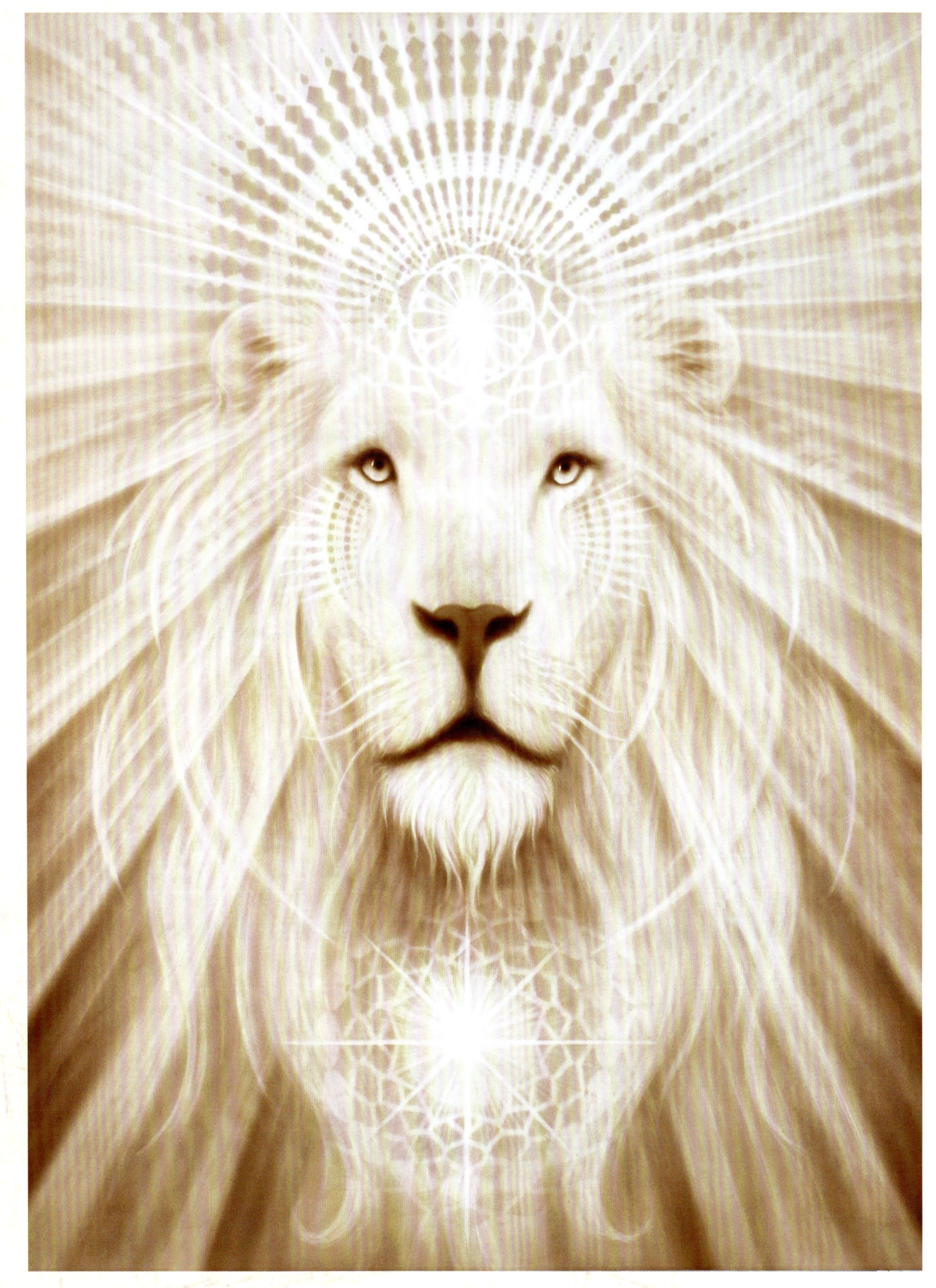

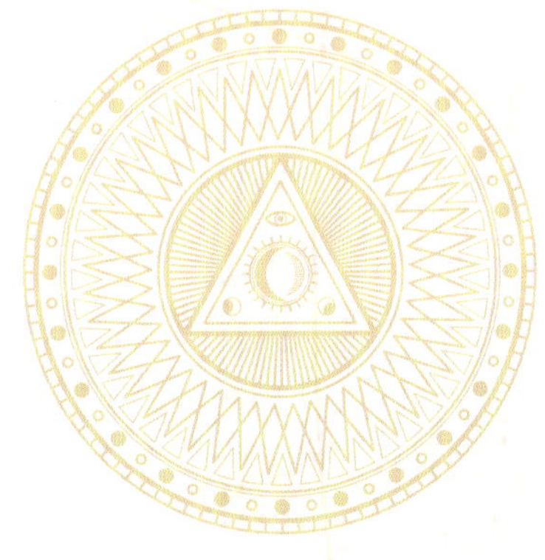

Speaking, Thinking and CREATING

Your intentional, consciously creative use of your energy—particularly your voice—is at the heart of your innate ability to practise resonance magic. Your voice is a potent healing tool for manifestation. I have created this work to provide you with an accessible practice to train and express this facet of your being.

Sometimes, when I am writing, I have glimpses of people connecting with the work in future. These visions happen spontaneously. With this work, I saw numerous readers reconnecting with a capability of 'magical voice' they had developed in previous incarnations. I could feel their wonder, happiness and joy in reclaiming this facet of their spiritual power, once again giving voice (pun intended) to this talent in a positive way and enriching their connection to their soul and the spiritual dimensions in doing so.

For those in our human family who are hearing or speech impaired, you have first-hand experience of how heightened other senses and abilities can become in response to the limitation of one of our senses. You can utilise this to your advantage in the practice of resonance magic and teach the rest of us a valuable lesson, too. How? Focus on the subtlest aspect of voice, which is your energy. Notice the flow of energy through your mind. Working with the mind is essential to this art and any magical or spiritual practice. We can speak wonderful words, but if we are not mentally present to what we are doing, the power drains away. The presence and intention generated by the conscious use of your mind is powerful in and of itself.

So, if you cannot speak or hear the words for whatever reason (even if it is simply not practical to say these words because you are travelling and have no privacy to conduct a ritual, for example), then use the enormous potency of your mind to compensate for the restriction. You can engage your mind as the key tool for your practice by imagining hearing, sounding or feeling the energy of the words instead of speaking them aloud.

This may create an added benefit of slowing you down and increasing your focus. Just make sure to keep a relaxed approach as you do so. Focused and relaxed brings best outcome. This can be tricky if we are worried about an issue that needs resolution. Your trust and confidence in yourself and the Universe will help you relax and do your practice in the most productive way.

We may assume that more intensity in spiritual work will generate a more powerful result, but too much tension tends to indicate over-exertion and often results in headaches and compromised outcomes. Too little tension and we lose focus or even drift off to sleep (though sometimes that means we need to tend to our overall sleep quality, too).

I like to balance enthusiasm with pragmatism. I encourage spiritual practitioners to have determination and confidence, acknowledging the efficacy and realness of what we are doing, but tempering this with lightness or perhaps even a joyful playfulness whenever we can. Power and force are not necessarily synonymous. Play can be powerful, and a light-hearted approach doesn't have to undermine our spiritual discipline. It can simply facilitate marvellous outcomes because we are more relaxed in allowing the results to flow freely.

May you vocalise to your heart's most joyful content, manifesting blessed beauty in your heart, your life and our world, increasing your most sacred fulfilment and genuinely benefitting all beings.

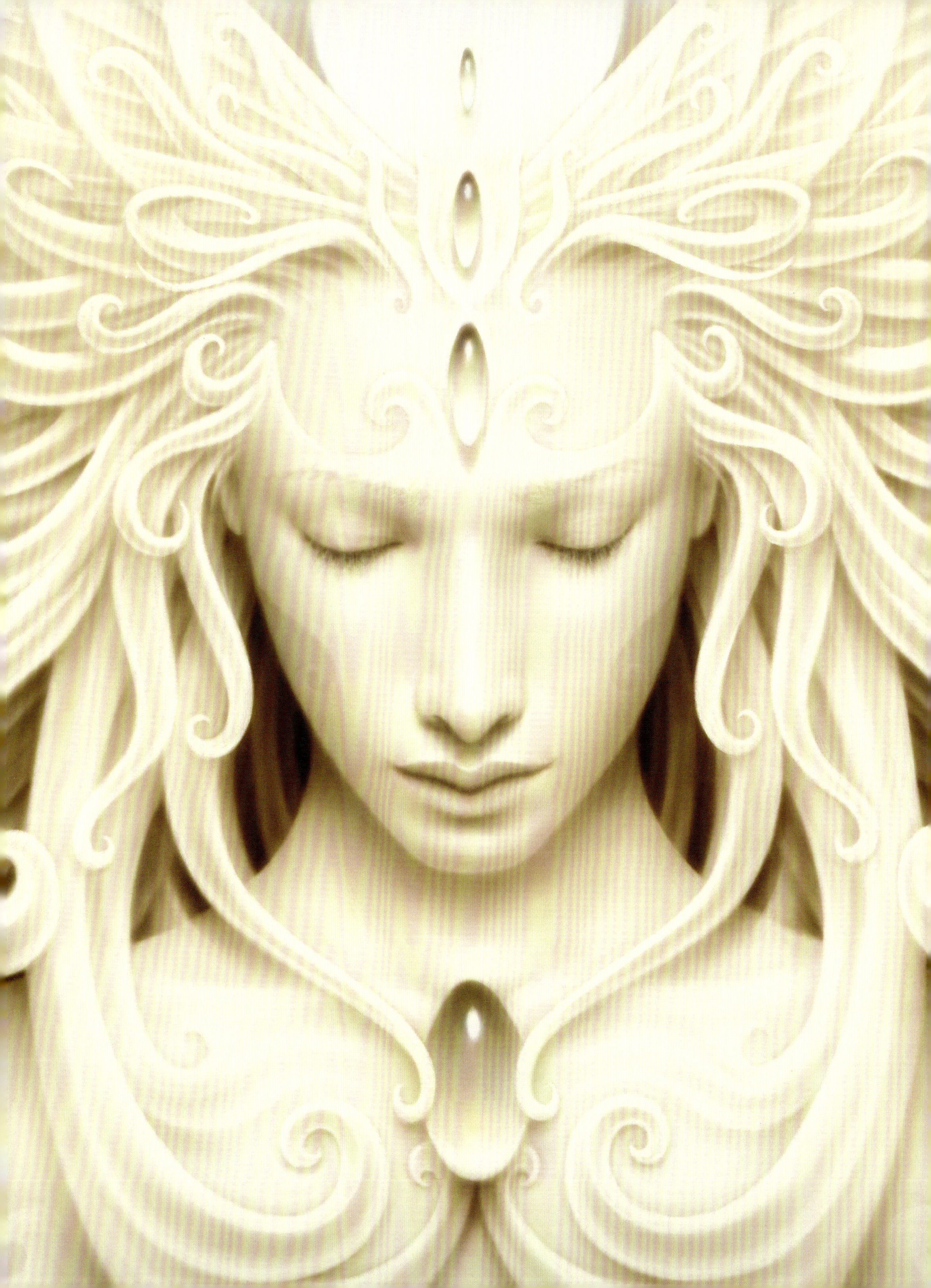

Incantations, Invocations and ENLIGHTENED BEINGS

INCANTATIONS ARE A FORM OF SPOKEN INVOCATION. Invocation is the calling in of otherworldly or multidimensional energies. Such energies can include a range of beings of different states of consciousness, some helpful and beneficial and others perhaps not so much.

Personally and professionally, I practise strict boundaries in invocation. I ask for help from spiritually enlightened beings with the intelligence to recognise deeper truths that humans may otherwise miss and the kindness to deliver remedy in skilful and merciful ways, compensating for natural human limitations.

Whilst an advanced practitioner trained in certain methods may invoke or otherwise engage with lower-level beings in order to tame and benefit them through blocking their ongoing negative behaviours, that can easily go awry. I strongly feel that such an approach should only be attempted in very particular circumstances, with training and guidance from an appropriate teacher.

If you were to invite a chaotic, angry person into your home, heart and life, your otherwise peaceful energy and lifestyle may become disrupted. You may or may not have sufficient spiritual development—and that person may or may not have the sufficient spiritual development—to overcome the potential for increased negativity.

In contrast, if you invite a spiritually awakened person into your home, heart and life, you may notice a sense of calm, happiness, confidence and clarity arises. I remember when receiving an initiation via Zoom from one of my spiritual teachers, the typical neighbourhood noise quietened down considerably during the time he was chanting and imparting the transmission. Of course, sometimes spiritual energy seems to stir up resistance, and things can temporarily become more chaotic as you do your work! Even in such instances, we can have faith that if we are connecting with enlightened beings, then any chaos is temporary, signalling a healing crisis that will ultimately give way to a better outcome in due course.

The reality is that we can be influenced by the company we keep. This applies to the company of human beings and spiritual beings. When opening doorways to other dimensions, such as through rituals and invocations, we want to ensure that the beneficial energies we desire enter the space, nothing else. As noted above, if you are specifically trained to do spiritual rescue or other such work, then you may seek to communicate with non-enlightened beings, but even then, I would unequivocally state that you need to have your inviolable inner circle of enlightened protection in place.

Choosing to work with enlightened beings will ultimately have a positive effect whilst avoiding multiple potential pitfalls, and is the responsible approach for a publicly accessible teaching. Please don't think that this somehow makes the work less potent. When applied skilfully, this text will evoke accomplishing power.

Enlightened beings are profoundly protective, and always with us. As you connect with your innate and inviolable spiritual purity through relevant spiritual practices—such as the use of these incantations and divinations—your connection to that field of energy will continuously become more conscious. You can focus on your work and trust that the space will retain its loving integrity.

The old adage applies: *the proof of the pudding is in the tasting*. When you are working with spiritually advanced beings—even if they seem fierce (which for some beings can be part of how their protective nature manifests, like a spiritual warrior of sorts, fighting for love, light and wisdom)—the *effect* will be positive and evolutionary. You will feel more able to love, let go when needed, discern when to stand your ground, and how to be you and live your precious life with your own courageous creativity and authentic spirituality.

The One and THE MANY

Numerous practices in this book contain prayers and mantras that will establish a direct spiritual link between you and a particular enlightened being or state of enlightened consciousness.

You may be attracted to certain beings or qualities of consciousness because that particular flavour or vibrational medicine is what you need most at the time. As you heal and grow, or your life circumstances change, your attractions may shift a little or a lot, perhaps increasing the range of enlightened beings who hold appeal for you.

What you choose to do with that relationship—to reinforce it, explore it, or be cautious and patient with it—is absolutely your decision to make. Like any relationship, it can unfold over time and reveal its beauty as we are ready to make the commitment with trust.

I suggest you sense which connections resonate for you and trust your intuition to guide your personal process. That may involve reaching out to relevant teachers and other resources to deepen your knowledge and understanding as feels right for you, or simply giving that bond some time and attention and allowing it to flower naturally. Through such a process, you will likely need to filter the opinions of others to ultimately recognise the truth as it is revealing itself to you. Often, such recognition will be signified by a peaceful knowing in your heart.

Whilst you may feel attracted to certain enlightened beings more so than others, I will say this — all enlightened beings are one, regardless of religious or cultural matrixes from which they arise. That does not dismiss the value of diverse human culture, but it does protect our spirituality from political and societal conditioning, which tends to increase confusion and fear, which in turn can prevent us from accessing the spirituality that works best for each individual.

As the spiritual progress of individuals benefits the entire ecosystem of creation, it is in every being's ultimate interest that spirituality is protected and effective. We can have due regard for politics, society and culture, and the role they play in human relationships and development whilst recognising inherent limitations and potential problems and cutting them off at the root before they compromise what matters most. When our spirituality is strong, we can encourage the evolution of consciousness within our human collective, which in turn will help heal and mature all facets of culture and society.

Integration of Incantation, Divinity and MANTRA

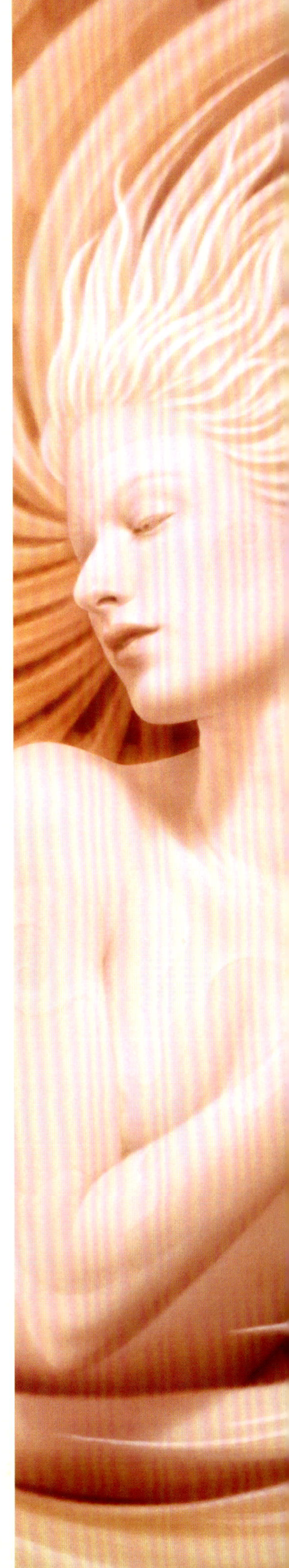

In my work, I often use the terms 'enlightened' and 'divine' interchangeably. This is unlikely to cause major issue, but I do want to be clear about the unconventional nature of my terminology.

In Hinduism, Buddhism, Western occultism and some folkloric and shamanic traditions, there are spiritually enlightened beings who are not also recognised as godly or divine in the strictest sense of the term.

Examples of such enlightened beings include certain humans, animals and otherworldly beings like nagas, angels and dakinis. Examples of enlightened human beings who are not gods by the conventional definition include saints and mystics such as Rumi, Ramakrishna and Yogananda.

To me, Mother Mary is an emanation of a delicious concoction of consciousness, a living alchemy of enlightened humanity, ascended master and goddess.

In certain Buddhist teachings, Earth is considered a living Buddha, an enlightened, fully awakened being. To my heart, these beings *are* divine ones, but that is according to my admittedly more expansive and radical definition of the term.

In the aforementioned spiritual traditions, there is acknowledgement not only of enlightened beings who are not godlike or divine but also of godlike beings who are not enlightened. Fascinating! Upon rare occasion, I have encountered such beings on the spiritual planes. They are powerful, no doubt, and perhaps even spiritually advanced, but not so much as we would like and need in order to create true benefit. My rule has always instinctively been to steer clear of them as much as possible, as we have different agendas. Put simply, enlightened beings want to serve all, while the non-enlightened want all to serve them.

So now that we have a little clarity on my terminology—and we understand enlightened divinity as our 'working model' for invocation—we can learn more about mantras and why we use them.

Incantations are particularly potent because rather than simply thinking of a divine one, for example, you are speaking the words that evoke their essence and invite their presence into your heart and your world. It is like calling out the name of your beloved to gain their attention and receive their energy. Certain mantras can have this effect, and there are some examples of this in the text.

These mantras are a type of medicinal sound to stimulate the frequency of higher beings who can assist humanity.

Some mantras require initiation from a lineage holder to be utilised safely, and others are more accessible and available to all sincere practitioners. In this work, I utilise mantras that can be safely used by anyone, whether they have received an initiation into that mantra or not. These mantras are a type of medicinal sound to stimulate the frequency of higher beings who can assist humanity.

I want to make a note about the use of mantras when you are not receiving them in person from a teacher, and are perhaps receiving instruction through a text like this one. Do your best to reproduce the sound faithfully based on the phoneticisation in the text but know this — your pure intention is the most important element of mantra.

Working towards accuracy in sound is important and maximises vibrational attuning to the vast lineage of practitioners of the mantra. This can strengthen our personal practice considerably, but there is no need to feel uncertain or even afraid lest you make an error in pronunciation. Sincerity trumps imperfection! Various spiritual traditions from which the mantras in this text are sourced (such as the Hindu and Buddhist traditions) share stories of marvellous humans who became enlightened sages while pronouncing mantras incorrectly. They didn't know that they were in error, and they practised with enormous faith and, through this, secured extraordinary benefits from the mantra anyway.

Why are such stories shared? Not to dismiss the value of attempting to do something correctly, but rather to indicate that faith bridges the gap between our intention and our skilfulness. Faith can help us overcome our fear of making a mistake. Such fear could undermine our confidence and even our willingness to try, so it's not very helpful! These stories also reinforce the necessity and high value of pure intention, and the willingness and benevolent potency of the divine ones who really want to connect with all beings who genuinely seek assistance.

In addition to mantras in the text, I have also utilised a divine name or a poetic epithet or title to call forth various enlightened beings. These are simply additional methods to evoke the essence and attract a higher presence. I love working with mantras, and many who follow my work feel the same, but we can also explore the power of intention through less ornate means and realise its effectiveness. You'll note that in some verses, I simply use words and phrases that combine to craft an inviting spell for the divine beloved to move closer. A name might not be mentioned at all. It is more of a feeling tone and quality of consciousness that resonates with the certain state of higher loving awareness we are invoking.

To be clear, the invitational quality is really about our own minds. Incantations often appear to be a spiritual summoning, but in truth, the enlightened ones are with us always and want to increase their presence in our hearts and generate benefit in our lives. They don't need to be cajoled or coerced and cannot be controlled. Imagine trying to tell Mother Mary or the goddess Sekhmet what she can and cannot do! Their inviolability and wildness are expressions of their purity. They want to help all beings overcome suffering and find liberation, happiness and relief. They want to end the cycles of pain and open us to the inner blissful reality of truth. So, they are keen to connect always. Our challenge is to remember this and have confidence in their love and our own ability to work intelligently with these guides and guardians.

We work with incantations because we need to put our minds in that state of wanting, of inviting, of opening and readying ourselves to receive. This helps us let go of our attachment to more familiar (and likely less healthy) mental states. It takes some spiritual muscle in ourselves to detach (even momentarily in order to do spiritual practice) from our anguish, anger, fear, anxiety, doubt, despair, judgement and criticism, lack, obsessive desire, and so forth. Yet we have the ability to learn how to do this, to become *willing* and *able* to be lifted into a higher state of perception and awareness.

The spiritual practices in my work are designed to help you strengthen that spiritual muscle, and any authentic spiritual practice will help you further develop such strength. Through that increased willingness and capacity, we then become *able* to heal, shift, evolve and transform our inner state and our experience of our lives and be inspired by what we can offer to the world. Our outer lives eventually follow on, and the inner magic is demonstrated as outer manifestation.

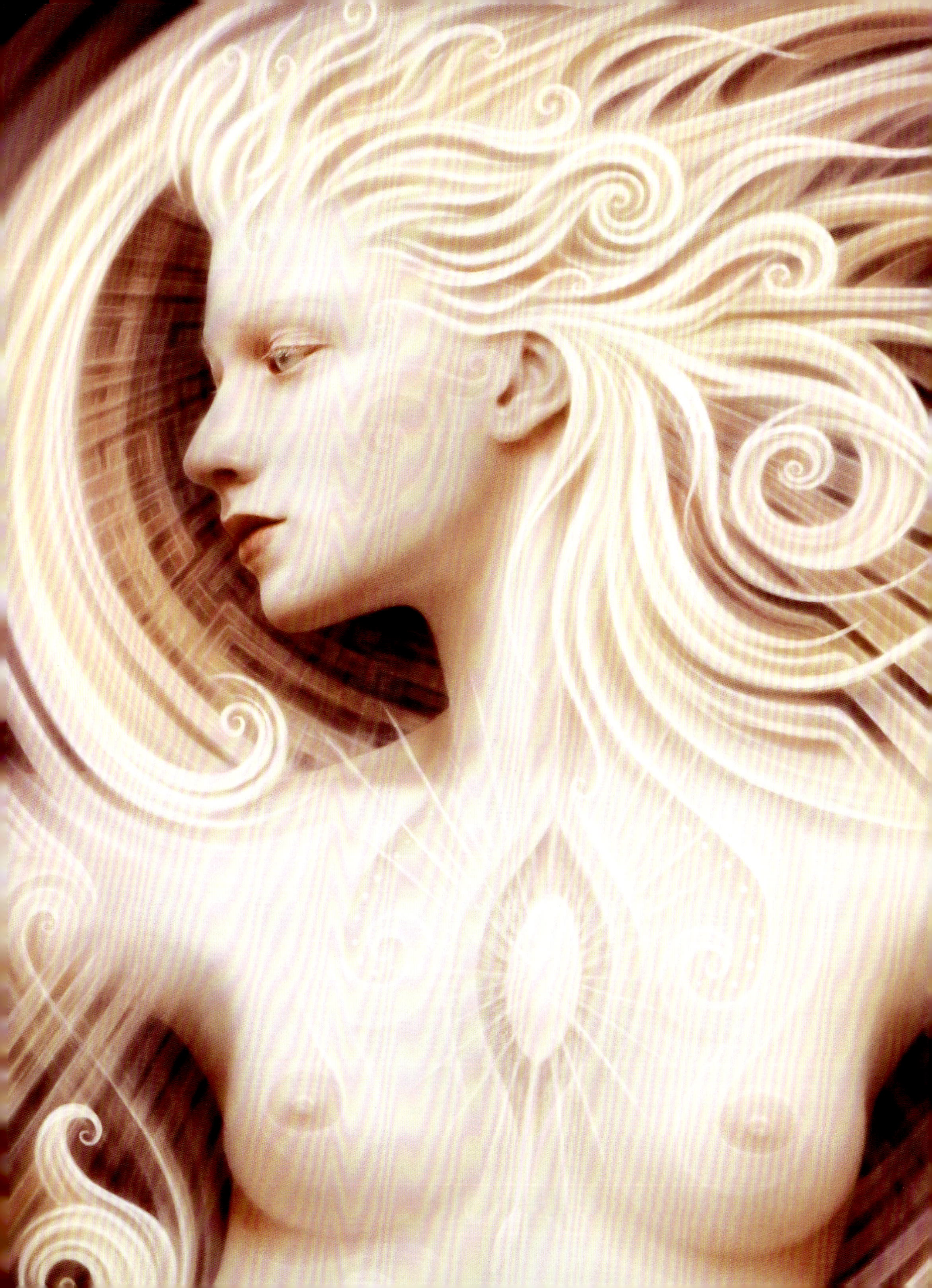

What Are Divinations and How Are They BENEFICIAL?

Divinations are a little different to incantations. A divination or divining is part prediction and part prophecy.

Prediction and prophecy may seem like different words for the same thing, but they are subtly yet significantly distinctive.

Prediction recognises unavoidable karma. This refers to the things that have been set in motion so utterly that they need to work their way through to completion. Past life influences often come into play in such matters. We might call this fate.

In contrast, prophecy recognises and activates our destiny. Prophecy is dynamic and creative. Where prediction decrees the 'done deal', prophecy distils and declares a best possible future, and simultaneously energises it through lending the vision and voice, energy and intent of the prophet to the process of manifestation.

You've probably heard the term 'self-fulfilling prophecy'. It is most often applied in a negative sense. The classic example is a child who is told often enough that they are bad and begins acting as such, believing in what they have been told as being true, which attracts further negative reinforcement in response to the acting out. With loving energy and wisdom, we can utilise this powerful phenomenon of self-fulfilling prophecy in positive ways, respecting free will, and yet also inspiring, motivating and energising ourselves and others for constructive, widely beneficial outcomes.

What differentiates prophecy from fantasy? Prophecy arises intuitively from the ground of authentic potential. It is not divorced from reality. It is a purposefully energised affirmation of genuine possibility. The idea that a caterpillar can evolve into a penguin is not grounded in the reality of its nature, however the prophecy that the caterpillar will develop wings and fly free as a butterfly absolutely is. Our innate potential is not necessarily any less dazzling than our fantasy life. Sometimes, it may be more incredible!

For a prophecy to be useful and compelling—and therefore catalysing and amplifying sacred fruition, rather than fantastical, unattainable, or even distracting and confusing—there must be genuineness. A prophecy, in the way that we work with it in this grimoire, is a statement of healing, a blessing of sorts, which sees a truly possible path of elevated experience and lends the goodwill of the prophet to its manifestation. To be a prophet of love is to be a great encourager with a firm grip on reality, neither inflating nor denying the creative power that rests in each individual.

When we prophesy, we are utilising our free will, intention and creativity to support a blessed destiny. We cultivate visions and build pathways to accomplish our dreams and fulfil our purpose (or the path and purpose of another being, if we are prophesying for others). We can go this way or that to reach our intended destination. Free will remains intact. The prophecy functions as a type of north star by which we can chart our course.

Can prophecy do more than fertilise our most inspired choices and encourage our most beautiful destiny? It cannot change unavoidable karma, but it can certainly help us find the best ways to respond to it. Our spiritual creativity is going to be useful in every facet of our lives. Destiny and fate are interconnected, working in tandem, a bit like the tricep and bicep muscles in your arms. Together, they allow your soul to move and engage and grow through life. Using our consciousness creatively allows us to utilise these muscle movements to accomplish our intentions.

Though the creative freedom of destiny-making through prophecy can be exhilarating, there are inherent challenges. Making important decisions, perhaps even potentially life-changing choices, can ask a lot of us. Maybe we are decision-fatigued! Maybe we have a dent in our self-esteem from past disappointments, and we need to find a way to rally our confidence and dare to dream (and do) yet again. Taking responsibility for our freedom, and our choices, requires work, risk and courage. Yet, we only need to be temporarily deprived of our freedom for the inestimable value and preciousness of it to become clear. In short, freedom is worth the effort it takes to live it wisely.

Enlightened beings, and incantations that invoke their presence, boost our ability to prophesy intelligently and creatively to best effect. When you add the energy of enlightened divine presence through incantation, your predictive prophetic statements become more inspired, refined and potent. Then prophecies can become subtle-energy fuel and spiritual building blocks for the kind of future that you want. You are not attempting to control Life or contrive an outcome — you are simply recognising that when you plant fruit tree seeds, you are not going to grow a field of wheat. You will grow a fruit orchard. So, you want to plant the seeds that you want to grow, for the destiny you want to express.

Through divinations, we read the energies and express them more completely. We can compare it to a singer harmonising over a drone note to create a chord. The root note is adhered to, yet something new is also created. The more we work with incantations to access enlightened presence, the more skilful we can become at this process. With incantations, we are cultivating intentionality, enhanced by the loving kindness, higher wisdom and capacity-increasing energy of more spiritually advanced beings. Our divinations are all the more beautiful and blessed for it.

Through the application of this work, we are planting seeds of intention, fertilised by the positive amplifying energy we have invoked, and voila! We have contributed genuinely towards a more beautiful outcome that will ultimately benefit all beings (because enlightened wisdom and activity only genuinely benefit all beings). Our happiness in the moment increases, our future happiness increases, and our hearts and minds become less attached to the pains of our past and more open to a healed, transformed reality. This is not bypassing the necessary stages of one's healing journey, rather it is providing a light, path, energy, inspiration and motivation to move forward with more elegance and swiftness. It is an act of affirmation and trust in our own potential to evolve into new ways of living. Like the lattice we build for the climbing plant to be able to reach the heavens, our prophecy can support the soul's most sublime fruition.

How Are These Practices Useful and PRODUCTIVE?

Practising incantations and divinations recalibrates your emotional flow. We are comprised mostly of water. Water is a receptive element. There have been studies conducted where words (or sounds) change the structure of water at a subtle level. Words of love increase harmony and beauty, and words of hate result in structural disorder. When we work with positive use of voice, we infuse our being, our subtle waters at the cellular level, with a harmony-increasing frequency.

When our inner harmonics are enhanced, we experience an increased sense of naturalness, ease and trust. We act from an authentic inner alignment with Life itself. We channel our efforts into cultivating our state of consciousness, rather than trying to manipulate the world to suit our momentary personal preferences. When there is a struggle or challenge to face, we sense the rightness in doing so and that we are meant to grow and heal through the process. We experience synchronicity, a sense of right relationship with ourselves and the Universe, and our way and pace of interacting with the world sit well with us. We feel more graceful at a spiritual level, even whilst we may be bumbling about inelegantly for a while as we figure things out in the clunkier reality of the physical dimension. We have the realisation that we are on our path and living our life.

We don't want to deny the value of experiences of disharmony. Sometimes, they are great motivators for change! They can also be excellent teachers on an inner level, nudging us to practise holding our centre and standing our ground without becoming rigid, defensive or angry. Then our inner state of trust and openness increases in resilience. For the highly sensitive types amongst us, this can be very useful. However, without sufficient stabilisation in harmony, any type of disharmony will have us feeling tossed about on the capricious whims of fate, rather than ready to rumble with love.

We also want to take care not to become so attached to the joys of harmonious living that we stop ourselves from engaging in the challenges that can help us grow. This is important because as we work with spiritual energy, there will inevitably be a purification response. This is a temporary clearing that follows a fresh influx of higher consciousness. The mechanism is like a filtering and purging process. As the purging of purification occurs, internal space for an elevated and expansive consciousness opens up. Think of it like clearing clutter from your house. As you empty out cupboards and your wardrobe and the like, there will be temporary chaos as you sort through what needs to stay and what needs to go. It can be tiring. More than once, I have begun this process with enthusiasm, only to realise halfway through that it was going to take more time and energy than expected! Yet if we persist with patience, once the sorting process is done and various items have been redistributed, we will have created more space and refinement in our energy and feel far better for it, too.

How do we know if a challenging situation is ultimately going to be useful or if it is just a truckload of unnecessary drama someone is attempting to dump at our door? Your intuition is often going to give you a clear idea. Working with incantations and divinations increases soul talents like intuition, so you can tune in and trust yourself more readily when faced with choices like, 'Do I engage or just let this move right on by me?'

There is also a protective field generated through regular invocation of enlightened wisdom. That doesn't prevent us from needing to make choices in our lives or deal with growth-edge-inducing challenges from time to time. We are still responsible for ourselves and our journey because we retain our inner freedom and power of choice. However, this subtle field does have a positive effect, functioning as a type of buffer, allowing us a little more space to observe and respond deliberately rather than reactively to what is occurring around us, or even within our own minds.

If you do find that you have engaged in an unwise course of action—perhaps affording the benefit of the doubt when you probably would have been better to trust your initial instincts about the likely fallout from certain choices—then these practices can help you more swiftly return to centre.

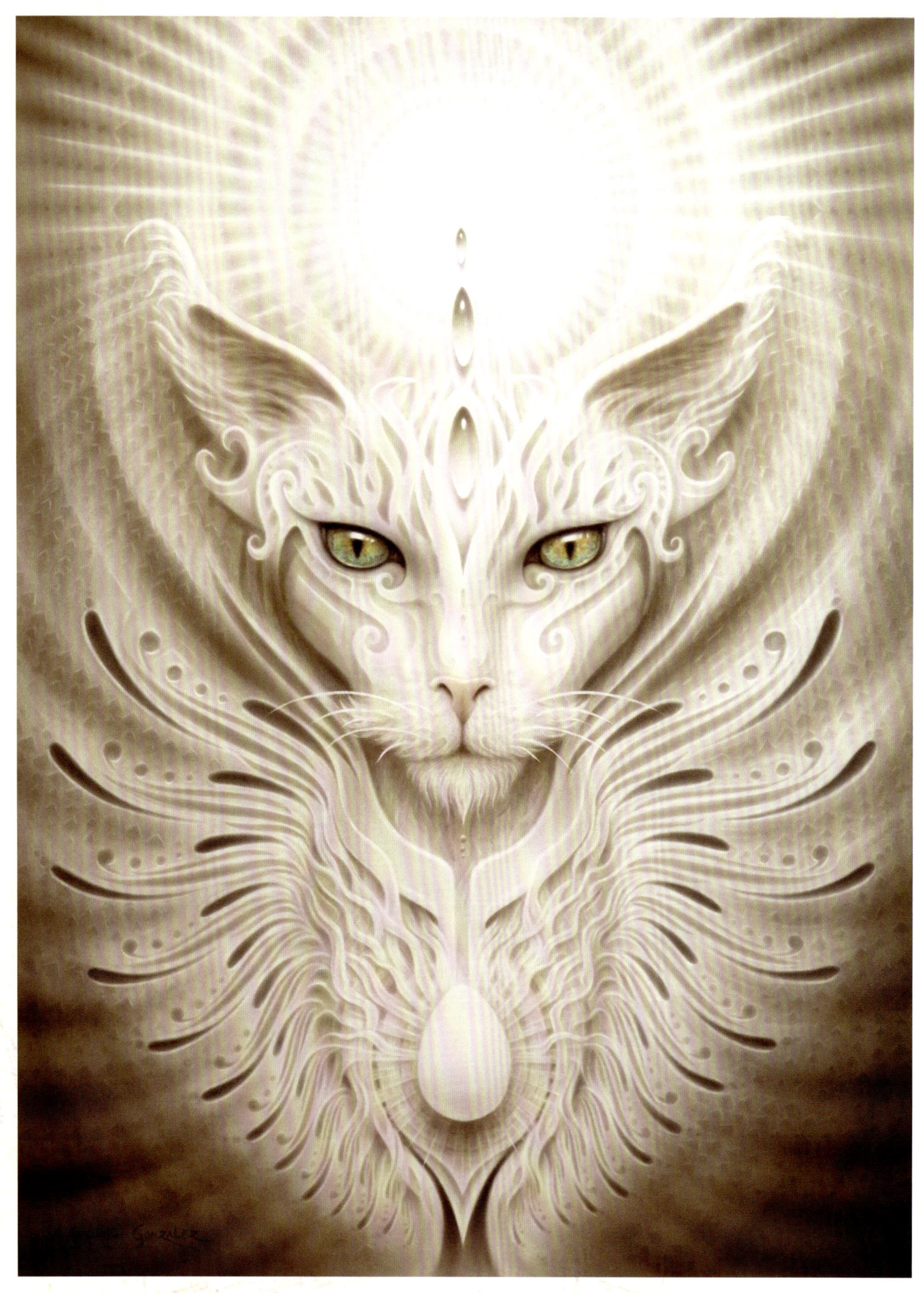

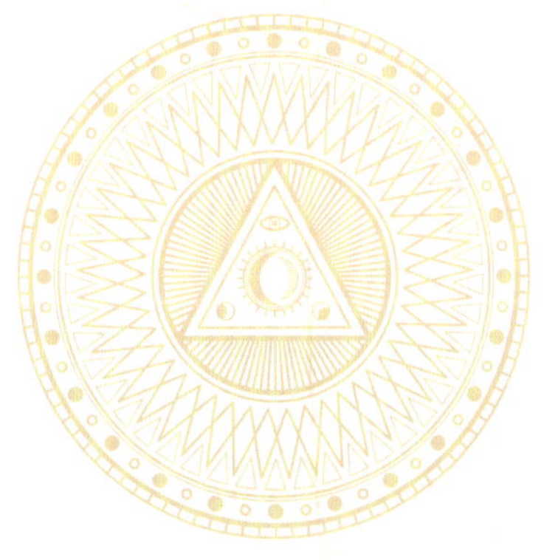

Spiritual
DIVERSITY

The diverse representation of divine beings and wisdoms shared in this work has been lovingly and intuitively chosen for their ability to speak to humanity in a universal way. Truth resonates in the heart, regardless of our different experiences and personality quirks. People from different nations, cultures, religions and socio-economic backgrounds share meaningful commonalities. We all know what it is to feel pain and suffer, and to desire happiness, love and freedom.

The spiritual diversity that flourishes through my entire body of work, including this specific offering, began as an unconscious and spontaneous expression of my own relationship with the Divine. It is very easy for me to experience divinity as a multifaceted presence to be found in everything, including all cultures and traditions, and belonging to all of humanity as one people, one race — the human race.

I was raised in a multicultural society and a family that was unusually open-minded about such matters, perhaps because our own lineage was so mixed. I instinctively embraced multiple religious expressions and cultural traditions as I was exposed to them through my numerous friendships from early childhood all the way through to graduation from law school in my 20s. I was never confused or frightened by spiritual and religious diversity. I was just fascinated and curious about it. Such fascination persists!

I always loved and felt consciously connected to the Divine, whether I was being a wild little pagan child communing with tree spirits in the local bushland parks, or revelling in my naturally mystical heart by laying supine and gazing at the sky pondering the presence of God, or was mesmerised by the swift movement of my grandmother's fingers over her rosary beads as she repeated her nightly prayers to Mother Mary. I gazed at images of Ganesha and goddess Kali in my Hindu friends' homes, Guru Nanak in the homes of my Sikh friends, and statues of serene buddhas like Shakyamuni and Kuan Yin in the homes of my Buddhist friends, and so forth. I loved these many expressions of that one divine being, in the same way that we can fall in love with a human being, getting to know all the various facets of someone's personality and eccentricities and enjoying that intimacy as part of the closeness and connection.

I want to share this diversity through my work because it is authentic and empowering for me personally and very natural. I have faith in the truth of our naturalness, of our quirks and strangeness. I don't believe those things are random or in error. I believe that as we become most fully and faithfully who we are, we are fulfilling the divine plan and purpose that we cannot always grasp consciously. In some way, this will be of benefit — especially as we heal and awaken spiritually.

So, my intention is not that you must adopt the same belief system or divine relationship that I have, but rather that I share the fullness of my own relationship with you. Through that sharing, I hope you are supported to experience your own direct and personal divine intimacy, in whatever way manifests authentically for you. That may look and feel similar to mine or very different indeed, and that is okay. What yields the best effect for you and all beings is what truly works for you, engaging your heart.

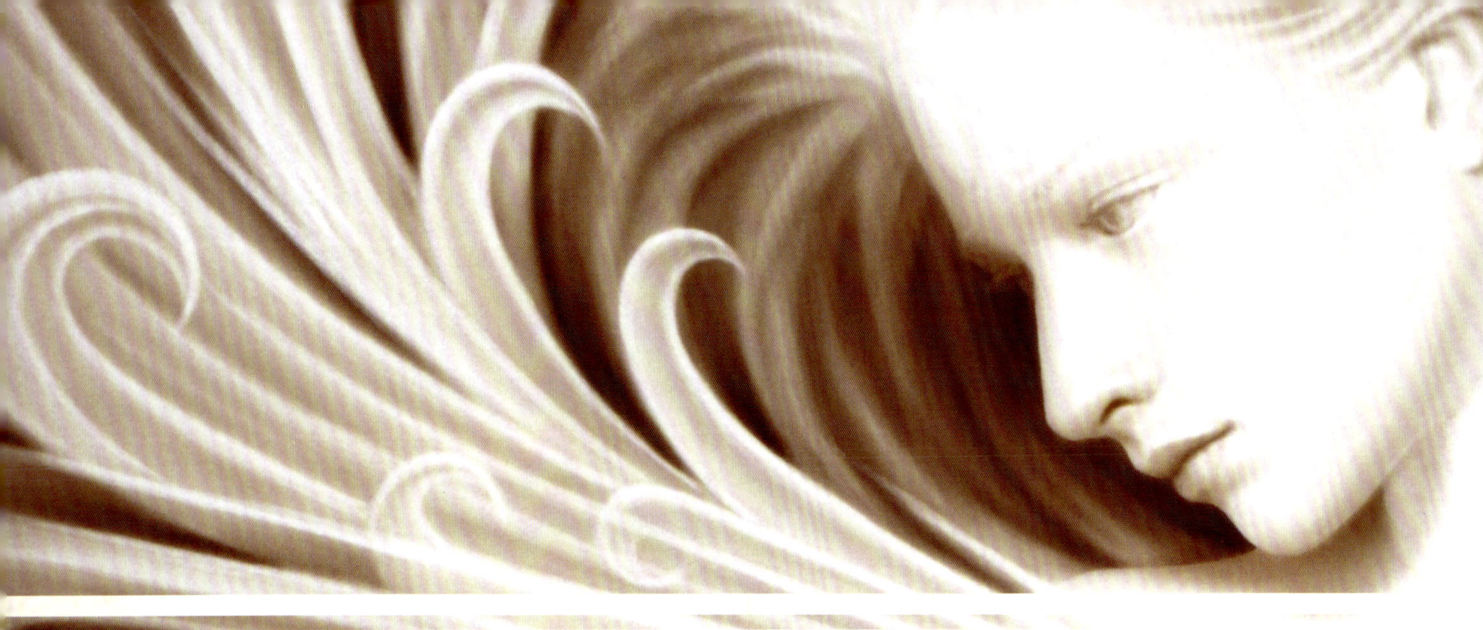

THE MOTHER
Discourse

The mother discourse is the foundational teaching from which my work arises. It is a simple series of principles that forms the spiritual premise of each work. The mother discourse is not always described as such. I usually just call it an introduction! You'll find mother discourses in many of my books, oracle decks, and even booklets that accompany music and meditation albums. At the heart of the mother discourse for this work is the goddess Isis, even though there are numerous other divine emanations included in the grimoire. As we explore this mother discourse on the goddess Isis, we touch upon the spiritual secrets and deeper teachings the soul can experience when working with this book.

Our Lady Isis is one of the divine beings I have connected with since early childhood, when I first saw her images in a book about ancient Egypt. It was certainly a case of love at first sight! Although, I have since realised that I carry a heart connection with her that is beyond the confines of this one lifetime. So perhaps it was love at second sight, so to speak.

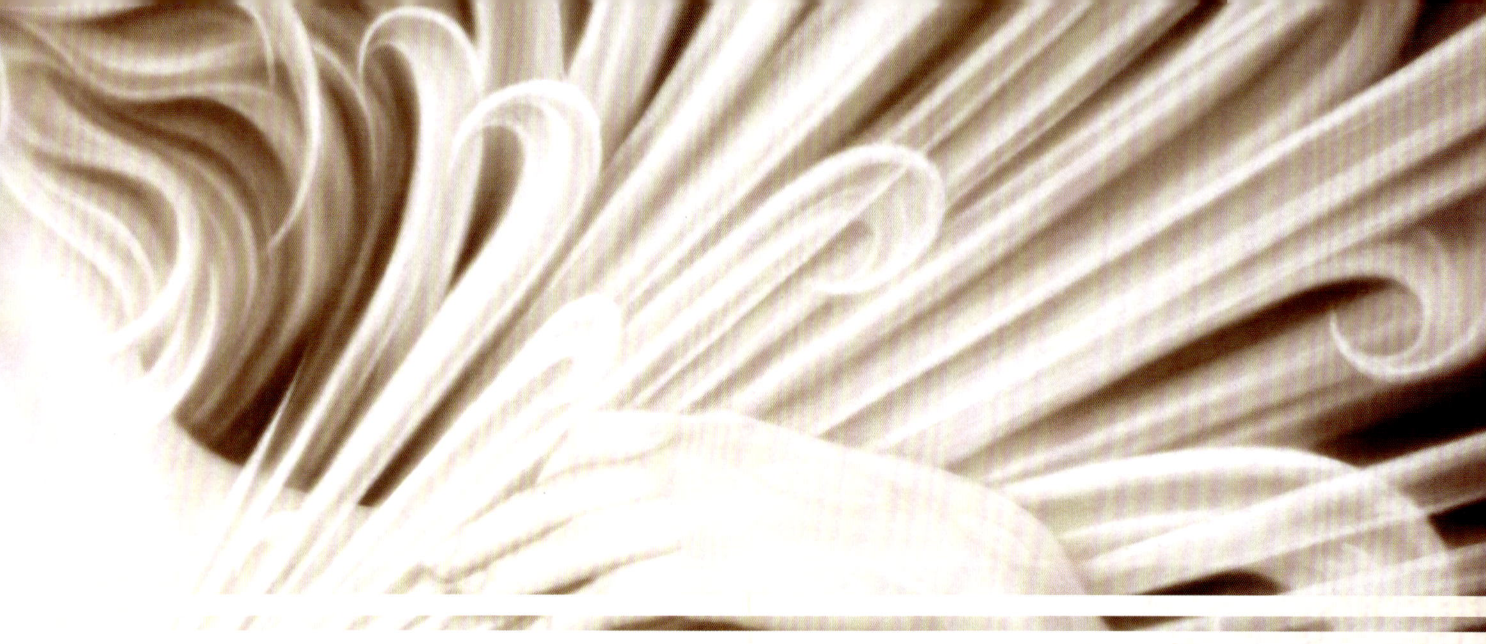

There are many who truly recognise the love and wisdom of the goddess Isis, finding solace and strength in their devotion to her, becoming braver, kinder, happier and more effective human beings. I felt powerfully guided to include invocations to her presence in this work. Hers is the chapter that I wanted to write first. So, I sense she wants to foster that divine connection with us, too. It's a true love.

Rising from the traditions of ancient Egypt, the goddess Isis became rapidly beloved through many and varied cultures in the ancient world, and such widely sourced adoration continues in our modern world. Known as the Goddess of Ten Thousand Names, she is expressive of the divine power of diversity and is available for all beings sincerely reaching for her.

The wisdom of Isis is drawn from the power of the heart. Her lessons and guidance for us are many, but at the core of each is a lesson in love. Her strength comes from her passion, a love so deep and devoted that she was unwilling to let anything overcome her will to accomplish what her heart was set on attaining. Her determination is inspirational.

So, too, is her simultaneous capacity for surrender. Our Lady Isis did not resist life's challenges. Even when a devastating struggle arose on her path, she did not try to wish it away or make it become something else. Instead, she chose to acknowledge what was happening, and respond creatively by utilising her intelligence and her heart wisdom to find a way through. She was clever and grew rapidly in power, yet she used her strength to serve life, to serve others, to honour nature and her cycles. She is wise in power.

Those who feel a strong attraction to the energy of Isis are often learning that love is a power that can overcome all other forces. It is not a power that uses force, however. It is intelligent in that it can unlearn old patterns and adopt new ways of being that are more likely to create what we truly yearn for in life. With Isis, we can learn to prophesy rather than push, to create rather than control. Her way is powerful in that she resists nothing and yet is not conquered by anything, either.

Isis is a magical creatrix extraordinaire, and the use of voice for magical healing purposes is part of her spiritual repertoire. Writing the incantations and divinations for the Book of Isis flowed swiftly and effortlessly. This is her natural domain.

She teaches us that alignment with love doesn't stop the challenges in Life from arising at times, but it empowers us to deal with them in a constructive, creative, empowering way. This is where claiming our voice, our magic, is so potent. Isis utilised voice and magic for her healing and to bring out the best in all circumstances. We don't have to feel trapped in despair, even when Life seems to be blocking our best intentions from manifesting. Instead, the wisdom of Isis gives us the strength to stay real, to be authentic with what we feel and to never, ever give up on the belief that love will always find the way through. With that understanding, we become strong in faith that any darkness, no matter how dire, can be overcome. If it hasn't happened yet, it doesn't mean we won't succeed — it just means time and growth are needed, and we continue on our path, because what could be more motivating than the greatest love, passion and bliss?

Isis particularly instructs us in the power of word. As we have already explored above, our power to speak is a potentially tremendous spiritual power. Every time we utter a word or set an intention, we are essentially praying or 'putting it out there' to the Universe and into our own cellular matrix. Isis guides us to come to terms with our power and utilise it creatively in service to a greater love. She is fearless in claiming her own magic and applying herself on her path to manifest the highest and best outcome for those in her care.

When we act with such an empowered attitude of spiritual leadership (in our own lives and our communities), we can be compassionate rather than despairing in the face of suffering — whether it be our own personal suffering or the suffering we recognise in the world around us. We can be moved by it and inspired to *act*, to *heal*, to *contribute* positively. Any effectiveness in the world, which is one way we could meaningfully define power, starts with the realisation that our own words and energy hold much potency and can be expressed as an affirmation of light and goodness.

As you work with these materials, the power of your words will grow. Take care to come from your heart, and if you find yourself thinking or speaking from a place of fear, judgement, hate, anger or doubt, just take a moment when you can to come back to your heart and surrender into the mystery of Life itself. Things happen, and sometimes those things will not seem fair at all, yet we can affirm our faith, our love and our creative power to bring about the best for all beings because this is the way we want to feel, be and live. We work with the inevitable obstacles from a place of determination and heart alignment.

Isis is a magical creatrix extraordinaire, and the use of voice for magical healing purposes is part of her spiritual repertoire.

When emotional pain arises, we can work with our feelings as part of our spiritual path. We can witness respectfully and inquire therapeutically to understand and process our inner and outer experiences as facets of our personal journey. We can do this because we choose to have faith in a higher plan and a love so great that it only ever wishes for freedom and happiness for all beings.

Recognising our emotions—including anger, fear, frustration and so forth—and finding useful avenues for channelling and expressing them is important. Sometimes, witnessing a difficult emotion is enough for it to eventually 'energetically evaporate' without anything further required of us. Sometimes, we need to increase the positive energy in our hearts and minds, to flush things through and encourage the natural process of emotional release. Ritual work can be one way to accomplish this.

Whilst acknowledging that our emotional and mental states will fluctuate, I recommend that we aim to begin any spiritual practice in a peaceful way, with gratitude and compassion. If other emotional states are hovering around to be cleared during the process, that is absolutely fine, but taking a moment to reconnect to gratitude aligns us with the innermost love of the heart.

To develop an ability to do this, regardless of what other thoughts or feelings we may be having at the time, is a powerful spiritual discipline that yields many benefits, including an ability to channel energy—even intense emotions like anger—in a constructive way that doesn't further inflame difficult situations. We can then work with what is, whilst being most powerfully motivated by a deeper love.

Isis teaches us that love is the inner foundation that gives us the most strength, courage and confidence. It is a source of power that will energise us. Trying to source strength from anger (rather than transforming it into passionately compassionate love), for example, may seem powerful as a motivating force in the short term, but I do not recommend it. Motivation for ritual arising from anything other than love can increase difficulties, undermine our spiritual growth, deplete our heart essence and ultimately sabotage progress. The effort it takes to learn how to honour all emotional states and still connect to the eternal light of love in our hearts is well worth the benefits it yields in the long term.

Developing this attitude will help to imbue your words with love. One day, you may find that even speaking in a regular conversation with another, or exchanging a passing word with a stranger, can have a healing, soothing effect on them. You'll become a vehicle for healing energy in this world just by speaking! Now, that is quite a power to emanate.

In the teachings of the magical traditions of many cultures, the notion that what you put out comes back to you—multiplied—applies. This means that should you choose to use the power of your word to control circumstances or other people, even if you think it's for the best, you will be setting yourself up for greater enslavement in your own life, too, not more freedom. When there is a situation that requires adjustment—perhaps it is not respectful—then set boundaries and make your choices. Isis is free because she doesn't try to control the greater process of life, but moves through it as a skilful, bold and determined player who doesn't stop to doubt herself, who uses her energy instead to find ways to outgrow obstacles, always inspired by her great love.

Remembering this method of Our Lady Isis can be useful when engaging with powerful systems in the world—or unhelpful patterns within our own minds—that resist change. Rather than trying to dominate those forces, we can work with love's creative intelligence to learn how to thrive and outgrow any destructive influence they may have in our lives. We carve out a new path of consciousness, a new way of being, and help generate a viable alternative for ourselves and perhaps inspire others, too.

Healing happens when we are brave enough to follow our heart no matter where it leads us, trusting in Life to guide us to our best and greatest destiny, even if that means facing some things we find uncomfortable and challenging. If we are being led there, we are powerful enough to deal with it. The incantations in this book are your toolkit, to help you through any aspect of your life journey from a magical, heart-centred, empowered, practical and spiritual perspective.

Here, you'll find the energies of many divine ones—including goddess Isis, Our Lady Mother Mary, the mystic sage and kindly brother to humanity known as Rumi, and goddess of mercy and compassion, Kuan Yin and many others—as your cosmic companions for inspired creativity.

How to Use THIS BOOK

You can keep this book on your altar, coffee table or bedside, to remind you of the beautiful divine energies that are always with you.

This book can also be your resource for intuitive selection of prayers, poems, divinations and incantations to increase your energy, amplifying a field of positive protective presence around you. This energy can then be focused and channelled constructively according to your intention. That might be for something specific you wish to tackle or even a general offering for the wellbeing of all.

You can incorporate these words into your prayer, meditation and visualisation practices for manifesting your heartfelt visions, and even as an 'activated affirmations' practice to align your attitude with gratitude, increasing your receptivity to spiritual presence, guidance and grace each day. You may wish to speak, sing, whisper or contemplate these words as your method of expression.

You can select verses from multiple books, read all of a verse or only one or two lines as feels right for you. You can focus on one book per day, week or month for an incantation immersion retreat, or whatever feels inspiring for your path.

Each book in this grimoire has an associated oracle deck written by me. If you have a particular affiliation with one or more of those decks, you may like to intuitively add the related verses to the beginning and end of your oracle card readings and healing processes.

Using your intuition, you can transform these words into an oracle for higher guidance. Connect to your heart for a moment by focusing on what you feel most grateful for and then ask the Universe, "What energy will be of most benefit for me now?" To receive your answer, you can then open to a random page or intuit a number between 65 and 303 and follow that practice. You may also find your best practice for that moment by flicking through pages and seeing what attracts you, or by focusing on a particular artwork that speaks to you at a soul level and then choosing the practice placed near that image in the text. Once you have intuited your practice, sense the essence of that practice — what qualities or energies are being expressed? This is your medicinal magic, your healing divine tonic, to bring your soul into its greatest strength, clarity and truth in this moment.

You may like to incorporate these practices spontaneously into your day when needed as a spiritual 'pick me up' or energy adjustment. You could include these prayers as part of a ritual, meditation or conscious dance practice, for example. You can also add them to the healing processes included in my many published works. If certain words, sounds or phrases really resonate with you, you could write, paint or collage them in your journal. These could become a morning or evening contemplation. These healing offerings are for you to use with all of your heart and for all of your heart. Work with them as creatively as you wish!

If you would like to share your experiences with kindred folk, such as our Community of the Sacred, we would love to hear from you, and you are warmly welcomed to join our online temple space for regular practice, teaching, conversation and connection. You can find out more at **www.alanafairchild.com**.

Spell of the Cosmic MADONNA

THE FINAL, LONGER INVOCATION IN THE grimoire is known as the Spell of the Cosmic Madonna. It does not belong to any one deck, and unites the potency of all ten decks included herein.

This particular incantation can be utilised as a spiritual invocation and divination for help with any issue or concern, and as an offering to help any or all beings.

> *These words can be a little like perfume — a dab at a time might be more than enough to evoke the desired effect!*

You may like to explore some of the shorter incantations and divinations first, discovering how these words of potency affect you and manifest various effects in your life. Contrary to the popular idiom, sometimes there needs to be a storm (of purification) before the calm (of divine realignment) can occur.

These words can be a little like perfume — a dab at a time might be more than enough to evoke the desired effect! So, proceed patiently and curiously, as you work your way into when and why you may prefer one of this work's numerous in-depth prayers or a combination of verses intuited by you.

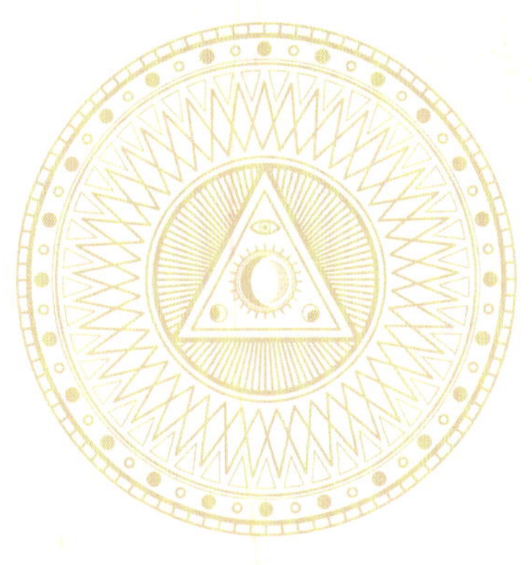

Crafting a
DEEPER
PRACTICE

Enacting a Magical Opening Sequence

You can open your space and align your energy with this magical opening sequence, then proceed to other incantations and divinations as you choose.

You can utilise this sequence of affirmative declarations to open your practice, if you wish. They are offered as a method to amplify the alchemical nature of your work.

You can speak these sentences quietly, or you can sing, dance, whisper or simply contemplate them as you prefer.

These statements are like an energy key, turning your awareness within and preparing your mind and heart to engage consciously in subtle magic. They capture your focus, magnetising your energies into the best alignment and intention to support your work, opening the spiritual door to your most fertile spiritual creativity.

In the first statement, we affirm our potency as innate. We realise we have the power!

In our second statement, we set the alchemy of creativity in motion. We recognise and reinforce that our nature is creative, and when we focus, manifestation can unfold in beneficial rather than reactive or less helpful ways.

In our third and final opening statement, we recognise that we belong to the Universe and are part of something sacred unfolding in every moment. We can choose to trust in this and allow the manifestation process to become an expression of loving and joyful spiritual wisdom that is within us and permeates all things.

Loving bold confidence arises spontaneously from within me, seeking expression now.

Energy, thought and word of love generate within my channel, catalysing constructive creativity.

I align, collaborate and joyfully activate love's highest potential with the creative resourcefulness of the Universe.

ENACTING A GROUNDING CLOSING SEQUENCE

You can complete your deeper practice with this series of sanctifying statements to ground, offer or dedicate, and seal your work using the grounding closing sequence. You would utilise this portion of your practice after you have completed your selected incantations and divinations from the main text.

Why would we do this?

We ground with the first statement to remind ourselves what we have just accomplished. This is a positive reinforcement and reminder. This can be useful to firm up the effect of our practice, especially if our focus has become distracted as the energies start to move.

With the second statement in this sequence, we affirm our alignment with the great and wise Universal Heart and the desire to generate expansive benefit for all beings through our work. As we affirm our wish to help all beings, our manifestations unfold in ways that fulfil us whilst benefitting others. Such intention activates the law of attraction, radically increasing positive effects for you, as well as all beings. This subtle adjustment of attitude towards honouring the greater good yields hugely positive returns.

In our third and final closing statement, we access that all-important divine confidence and closure. If you keep taking the lid off a pot to check how the cooking is progressing, you may unintentionally dissipate heat and disrupt the process. We need to have faith in our work. This is sensible and well-founded when we understand that everything is energy, and as we act, we are directing the flow of energy.

GROUNDING CLOSING SEQUENCE

Through the sanctified gift of my sound, healing magic manifests with mercy and grace.

I am one with the wisdom of the Universal Heart, and thus, this work generates genuine benefit for all beings.

The word is decreed, the seal is made, and so it must be.

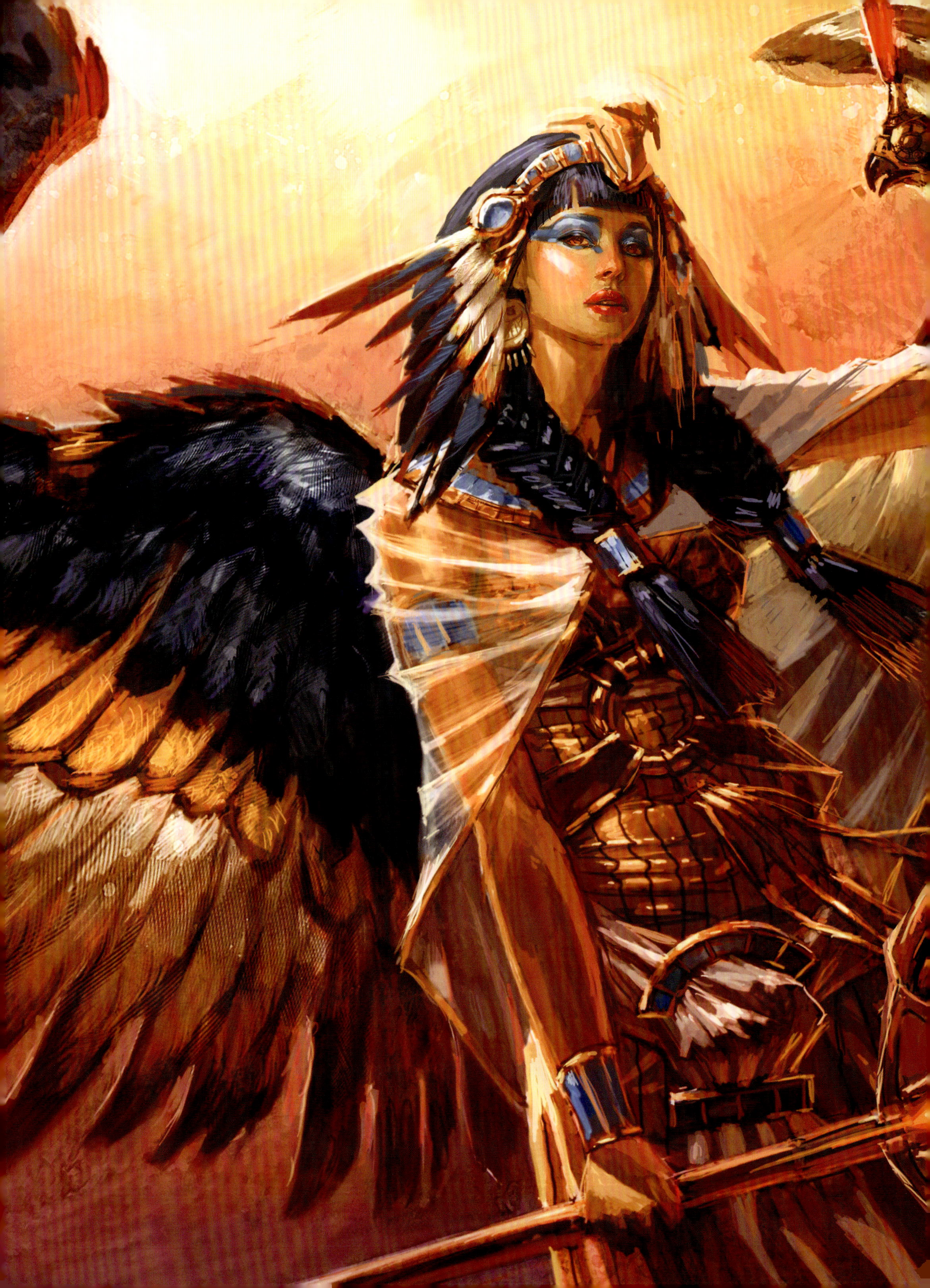

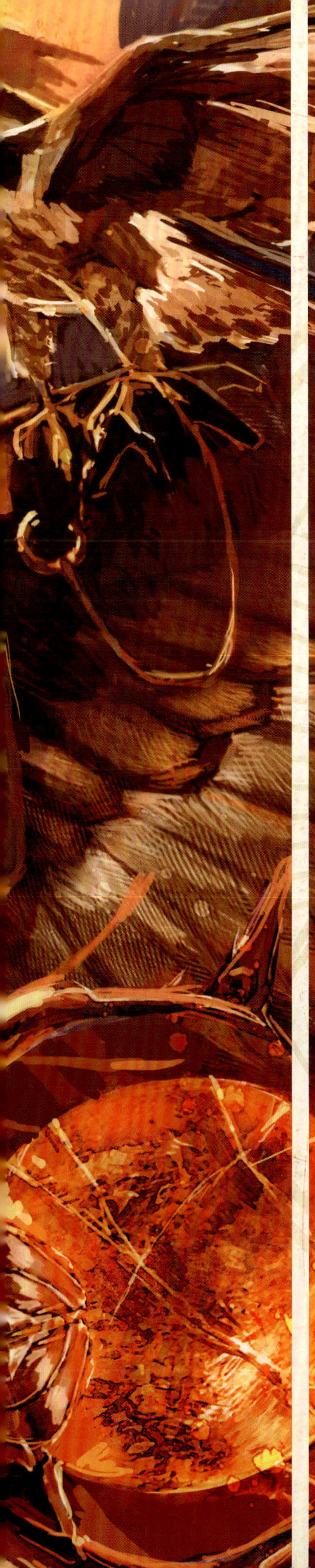

Book of ISIS

Incantations and Divinations for Empowering Love's Sacred Sorcery with the Voice of Healing Magic

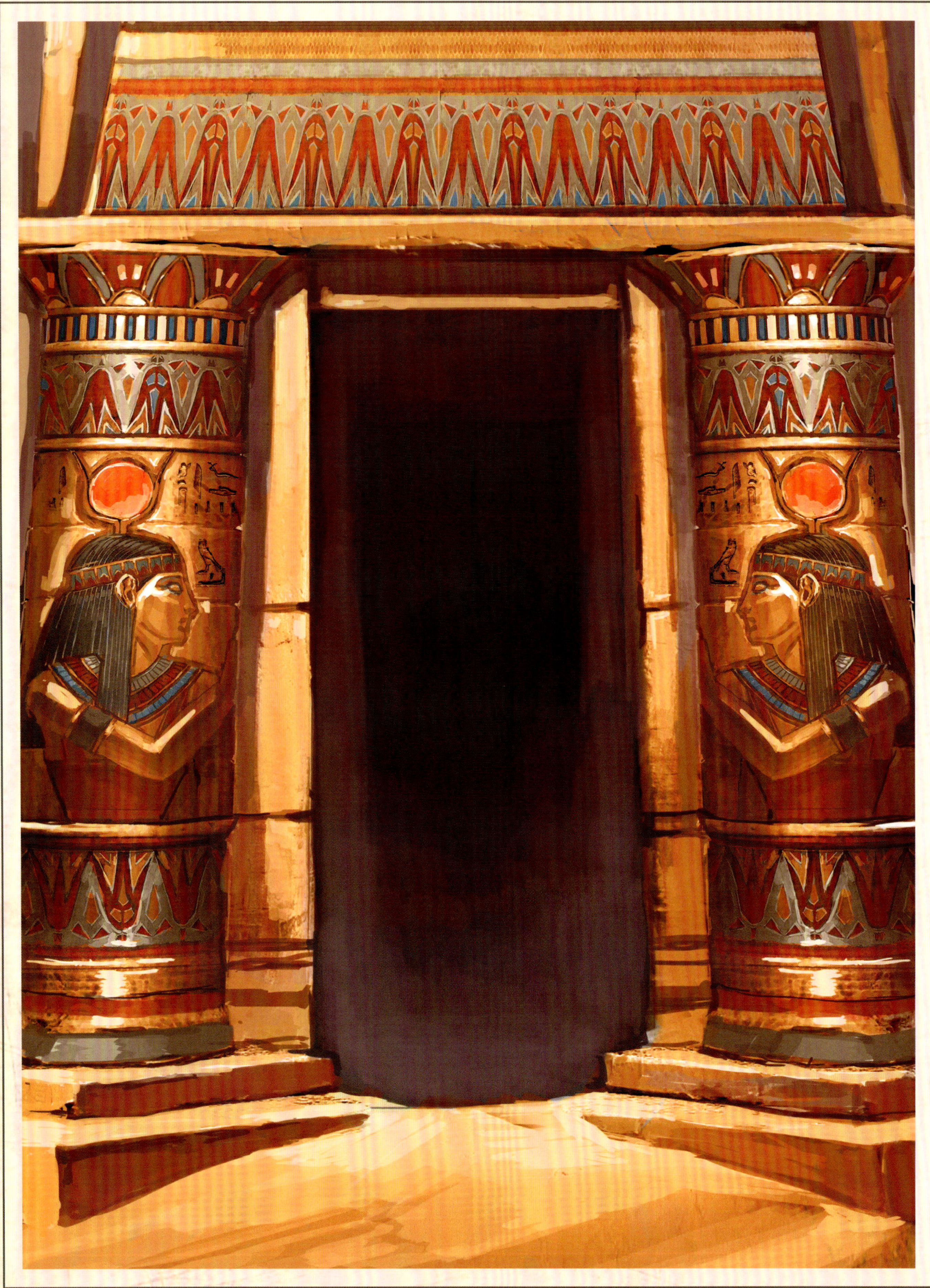

Verse I

RADIANT SOLAR MOTHER,
I INVOKE YOUR TRUE AND LIFE-AFFIRMING GUIDANCE,
BLESSING AND DIRECTION.
FLOOD MY HEART AND MIND WITH YOUR RESTORATIVE RADIANCE.

Our Lady Isis, intelligence of the divine prevailing light,

All phenomena are enchanted, bound and blessed by your love.

Tamed and transformed into highest healing expression,

In every experience, I discover a way to be closer to you.

All beings surrender, and all circumstances yield to your grace,

Like sunflowers mesmerised and guided by solar luminosity.

Radiant One, bless my heart with the gift of higher spiritual knowledge,

Empower me with the patience that fortifies inner resources and increases clarity.

Trusting in our bond, I become bold, serene and confident,

Expressing dynamic activity with wisdom, at the opportune moment.

Solar Mother, I invoke your true and life-affirming guidance, blessing and direction.

Watch over me, guide me, secure my path and with merciful grace, reveal the way.

Verse II

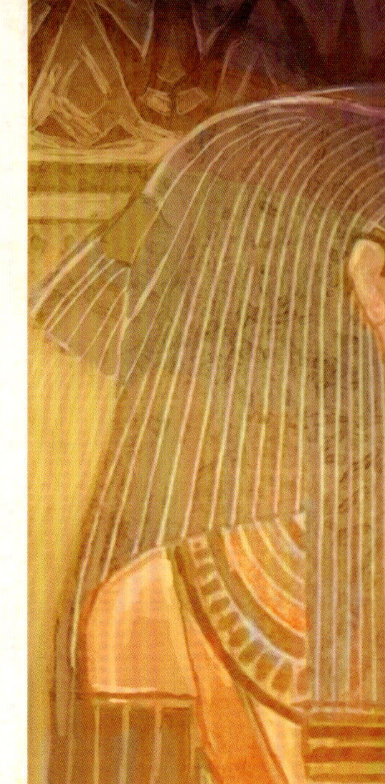

Beloved Divine Mother, secure my sacred rebirth,
for I am called from within, to arise anew.
Divine Doula, I trust in you.

I am your own child, Beloved Divine Mother Isis,
I am of the truth, light and love that you are,
Beloved Divine Mother, we belong to each other.

Faithfully attuned to love's unyielding presence in your heart,
I am content and inspired in your blissful shielding radiance,
Beloved Divine Mother, we honour each other.

Sheltered within the divine expanse of your wings,
I receive the necessary blessings to arise with dignity and grace,
Beloved Divine Mother, we sanctify each other.

Beloved Divine Mother, guard and guide my healing transformation,
For I hear the call to rise with strength to attain my destiny.
Beloved Divine Mother, we empower each other.

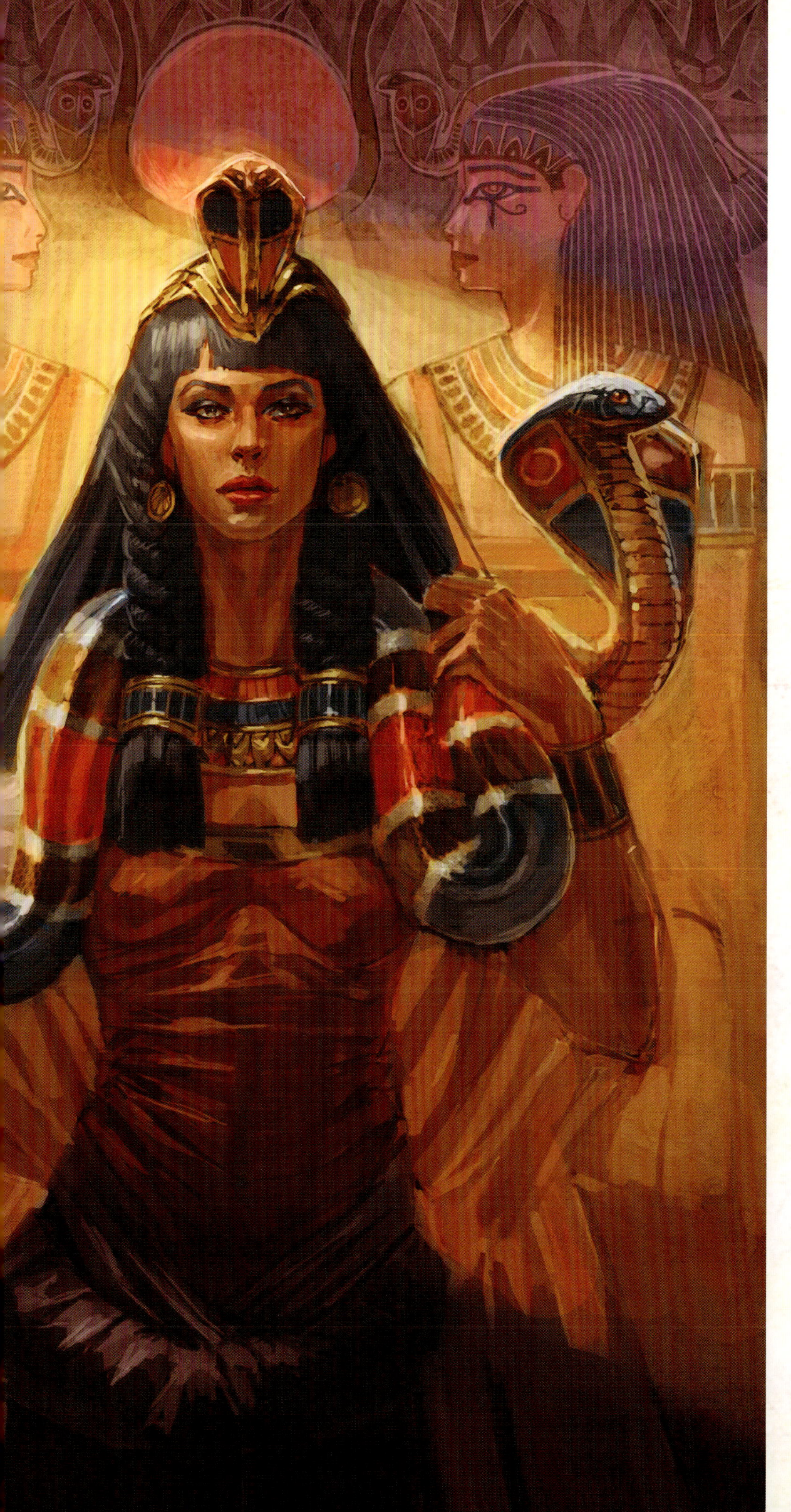

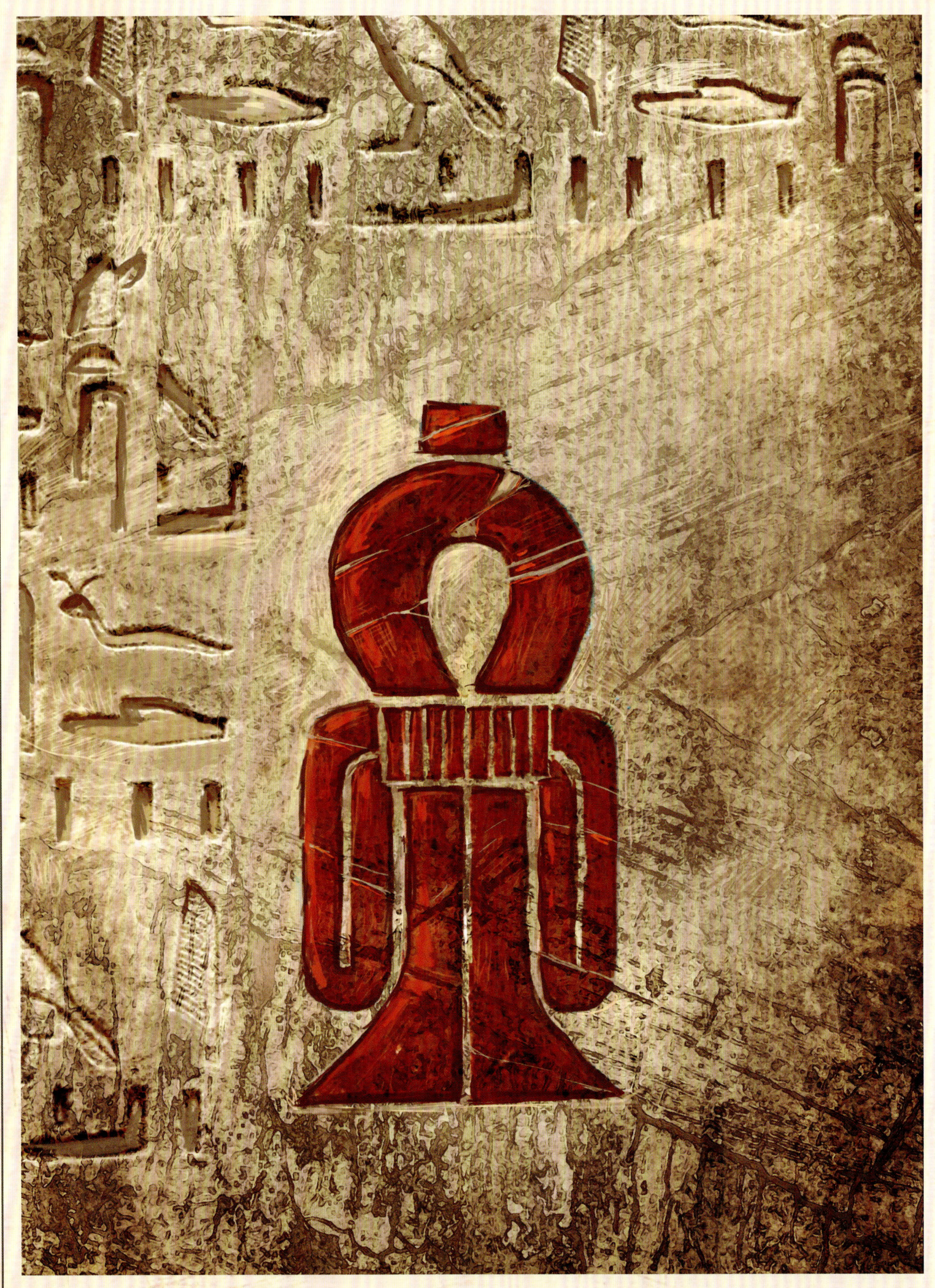

Verse III

FOREVER BLESSED AND GRATEFUL FOR YOUR LOVE,
WHICH TRANSFORMS EVERY OBSTACLE INTO AN OFFERING,
YOUR MAGIC INSPIRES MY OWN.
MY TRUST IS UNWAVERING, MY MANIFESTATION IS INEVITABLE.

Through your kind and clever magic,

Every darkness is transformed into a holy womb,

Fertile and purposed for sacred creation.

Forever blessed and grateful,

I affirm the effective potency of goodness,

And assert my right to create.

Verse IV

Your love-imbued light descends through the crown of my head, entering my heart.

There your presence shines like the sun, moon and stars.

My mind is emptied of fear and doubt.

My heart is untroubled.

Sweetness fills my soul as I wonder at your generous and uplifting power.

I rest gently in the comforting presence of your heart within mine.

Priestess of Lotus Blue, I invoke your divine alchemy.

You reveal the spirit-renewing path, perfumed with hope,

Releasing your heavenly scent so love can flourish in every dimension.

Queen of Lotus White, I invoke your mystical blessing.

You authorise the opening and closing of all gates with wisdom,

Fulfilling the wishes of all beings with mercy and compassion.

I bow to Divine Lady of Lotus and Ankh,

Lotus Blue creating the knowledge,

Lotus White inspiring the activity,

That sacred fulfilment shall arise,

Through my own heart and hand,

Guided by her, serving the Ankh of Life.

May your love align me with my truest path, purpose and personhood,

Healing my soul into most sublime and sacred fruition.

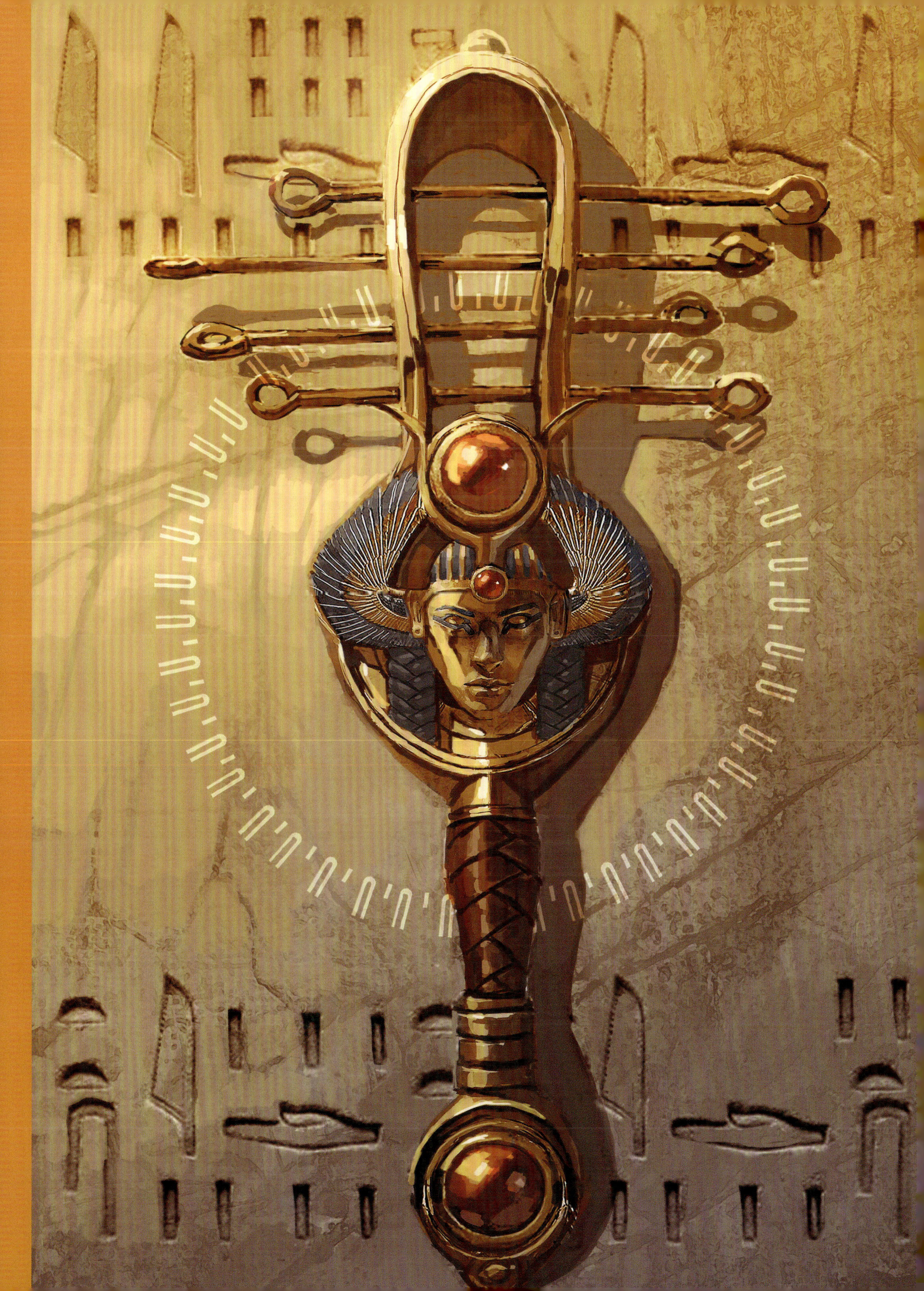

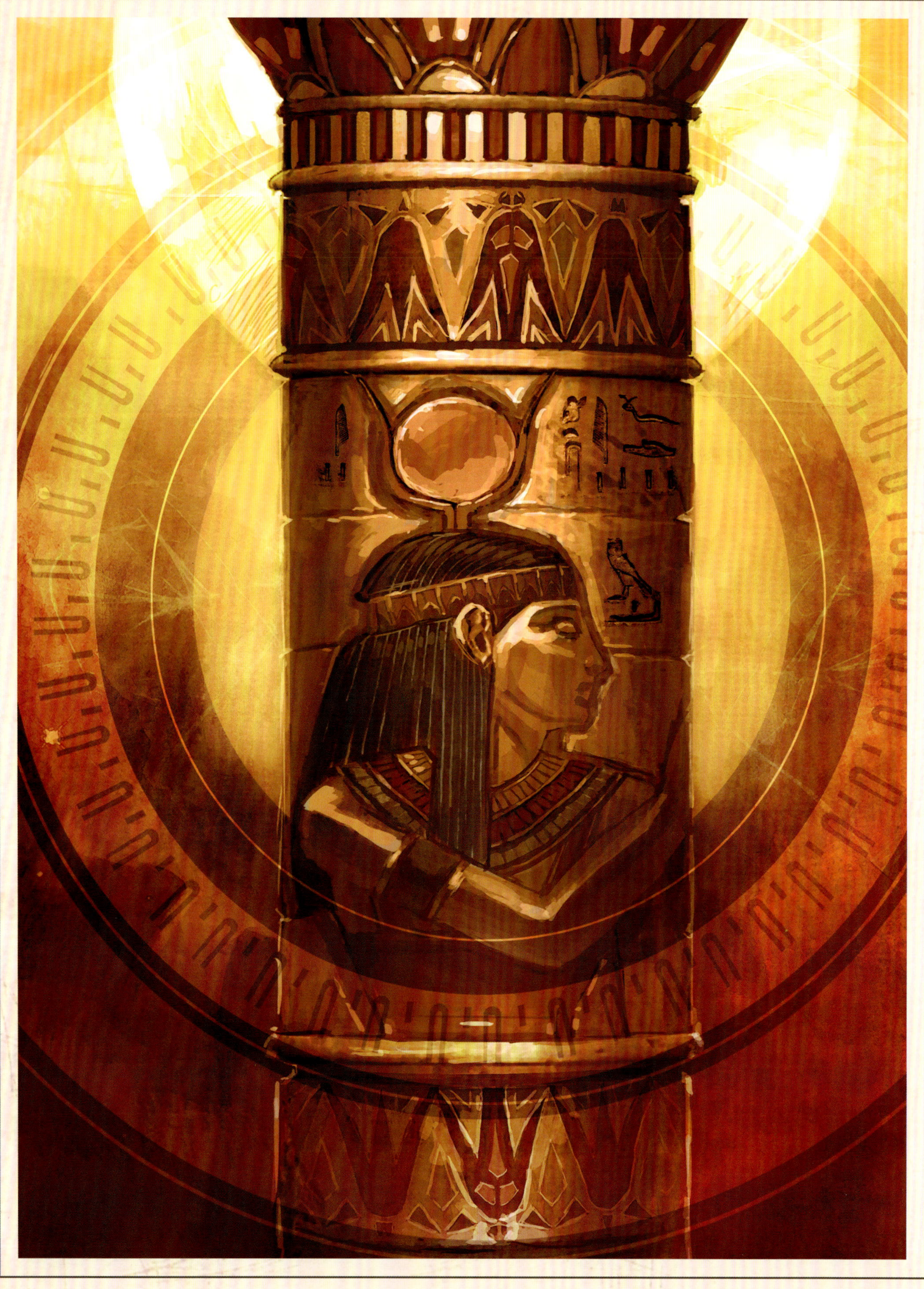

Verse V

Within me radiates the light of the luminous lady, most cherished and trusted.

This light eternal, unwavering, transcendent, casts no shadow.

As resilient as this light are my faithfulness, joy and confidence.

Her light within motivates my smallest step and inspires my greatest leap.

In her glory, all obstacles crumble, all interference submits.

Serving such sacredness, I manifest her beauty in my heart and the world.

Divine Lady of Light, protect me, empower me, bless me.

Reassure me, for I am your faithful and devoted one.

And my heart yearns to sing fearlessly, your blessed songs of love and truth.

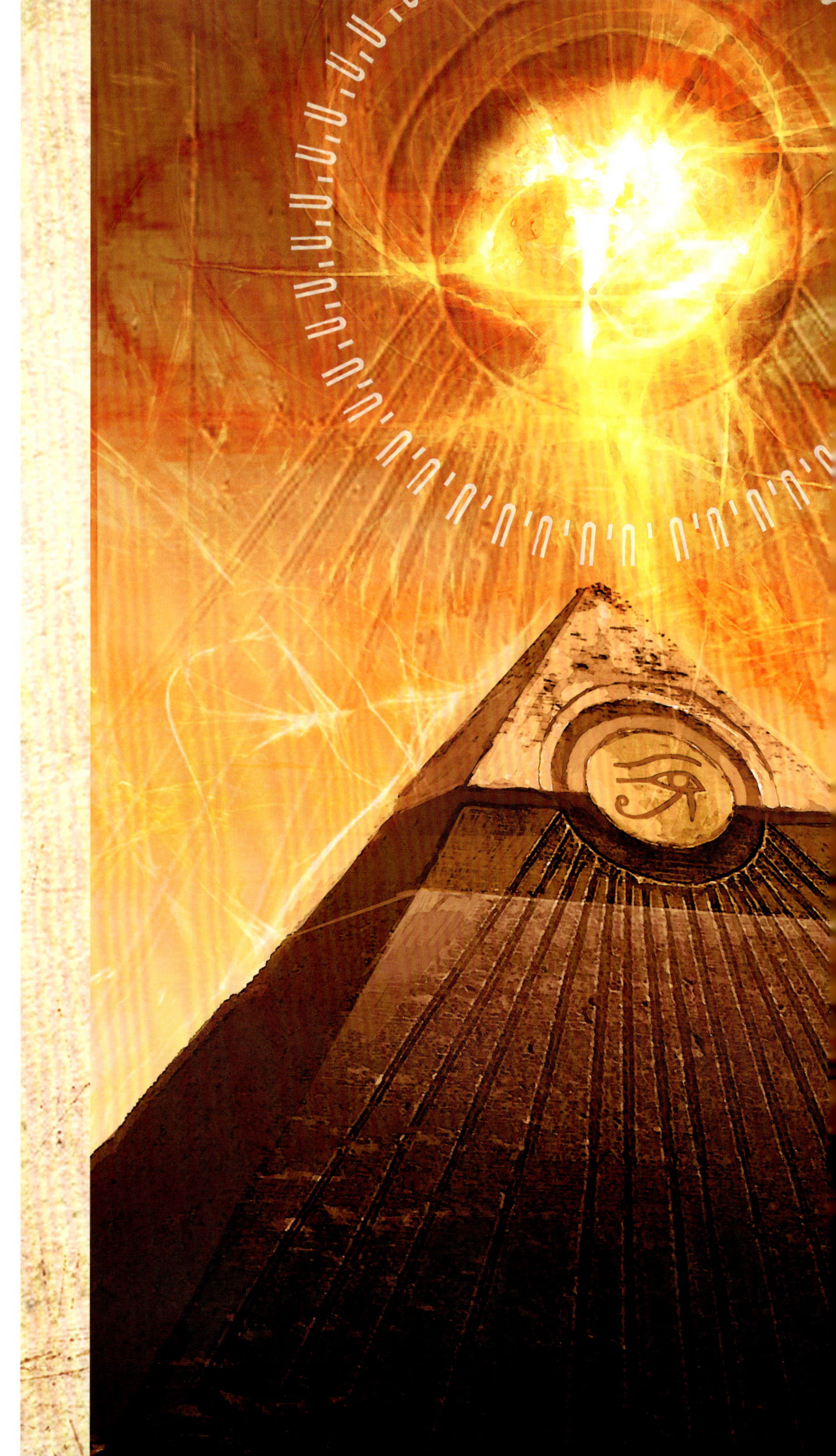

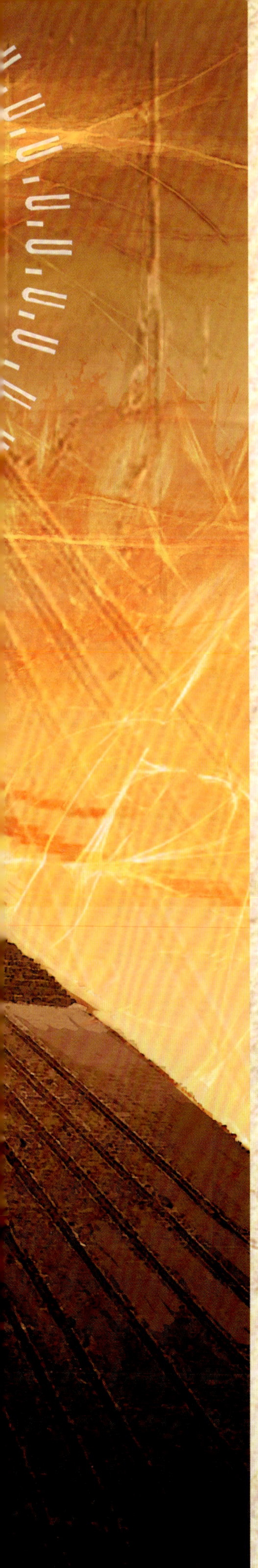

Verse VI

Lady Isis, your divine love is a sun, bestowing brightness,
You reveal the blessed way and the words to attain it.

Radiant fire of Sekhmet, Eye of Ra, Mother of Holy Wrath,
You scorch obstacles, reducing them to ash.

Lady Justice, Ma'at, crowned with Cosmic Feather of Truth,
Harmonic priestess of flawless decree confirms divine timing.

Sublime bliss of Bastet dispensed with the shake of her sistrum,
Anoints the world with healing nectars and sacred rhythms for rebirth.

Through merciful grace of divine intervention,
My wise and courageous activity thus inspired,
I am kindly and irrevocably placed upon the path of truth.

I commit to continue, create and contribute,
Secure in the knowledge of divine protection,
All obscurations will give way to Divine Feminine play.

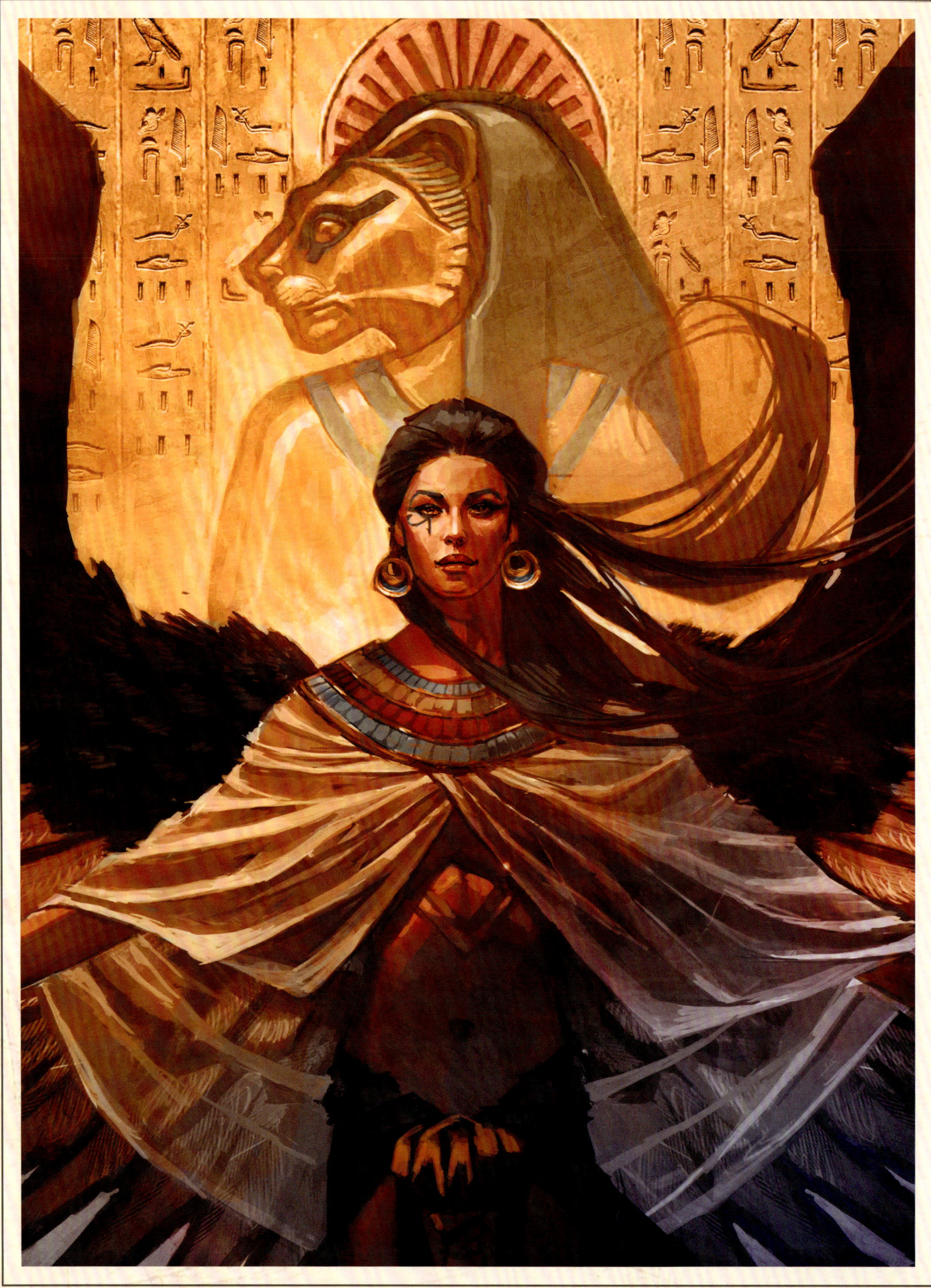

Verse VII

Through the wounds I grew in wisdom,

Through the darkness I discovered strength.

In the light, I recognised beauty,

In the joy, I embraced creativity.

Through the mystery I unveiled meaning,

Through the journey I found generosity.

My heart innately fearless and free,

Radiates my Lady's divinity.

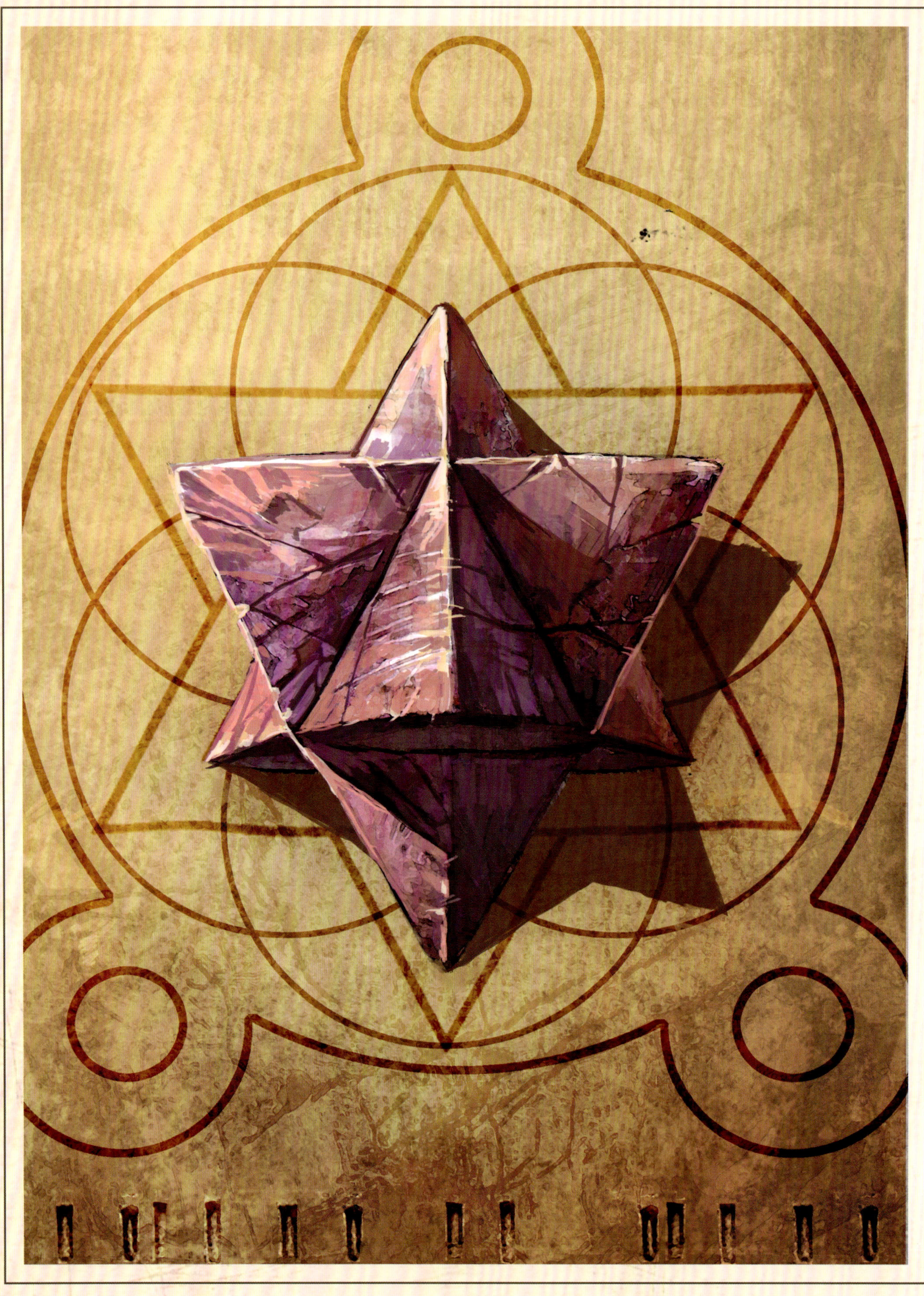

Verse VIII

Imbued with faith, I invoke Divine Lady Isis,

Divine Mother, protect me from karmic crisis.

Words said in haste, their effect and cause,

Through your grace, momentum will pause.

Negative repercussions completely cease,

And all involved are filled with peace.

My energy clear,

I am love beyond fear.

Light within, light without,

I am peace beyond all doubt.

My voice is freed through grace,

My energy returns through faith.

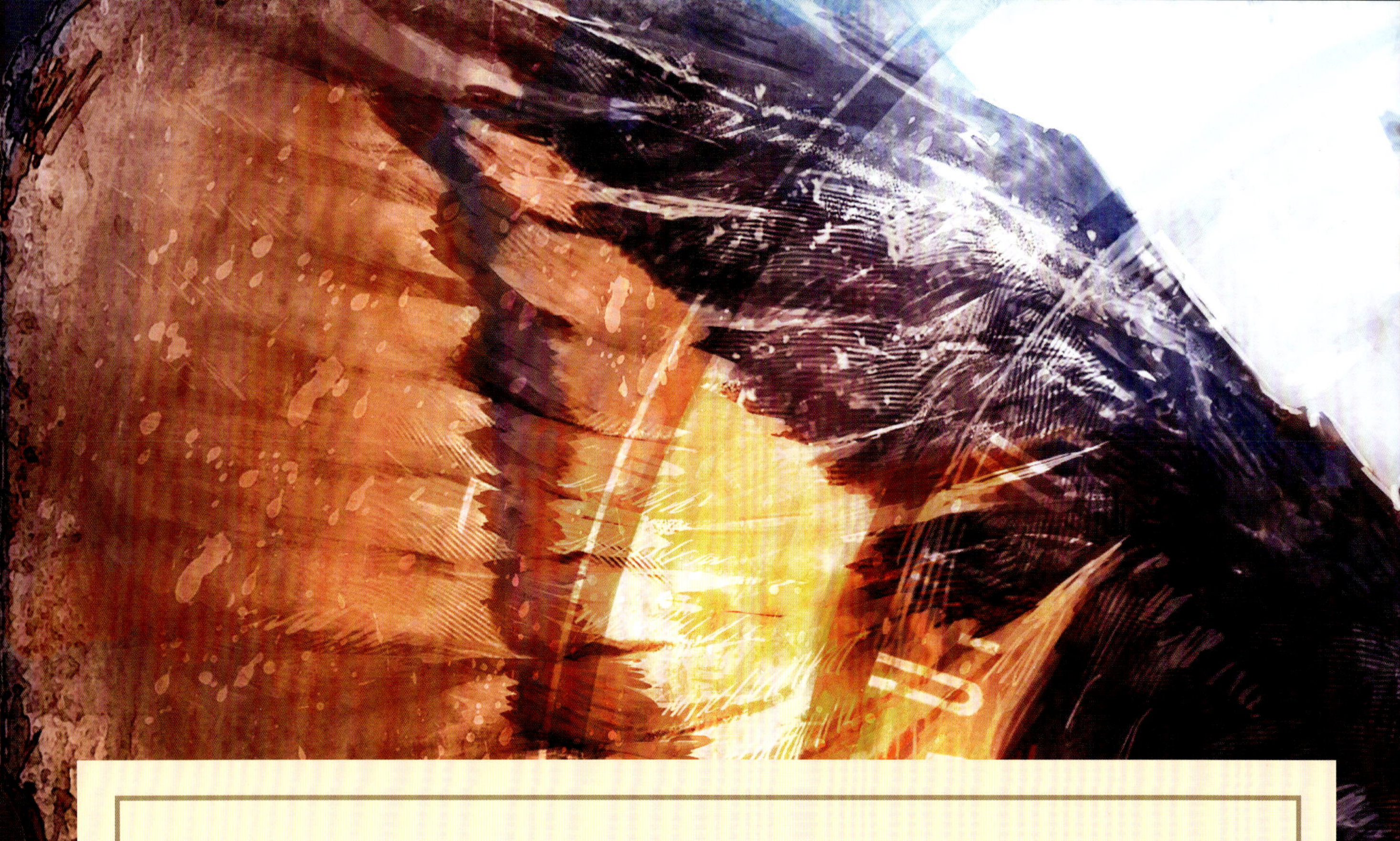

Verse IX

My words, my intention, evoke your love, your protection.

Winged Mother, Guardian of Light,
Surround me with your protective might.

Only love and light enter this field,
All to the scarab sword shall yield.

Driving away darkness with her light,
Sanctifying every day and every night.

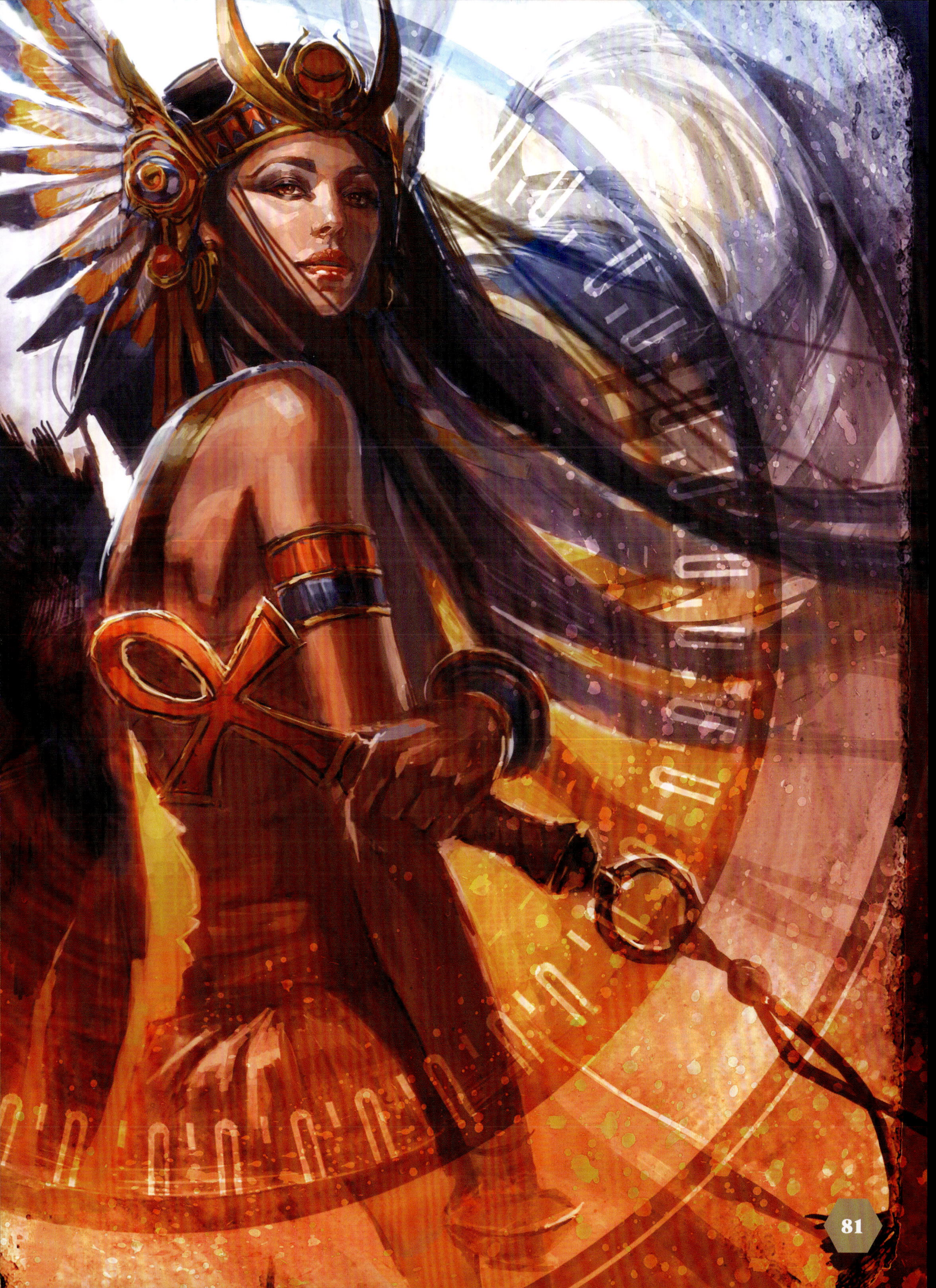

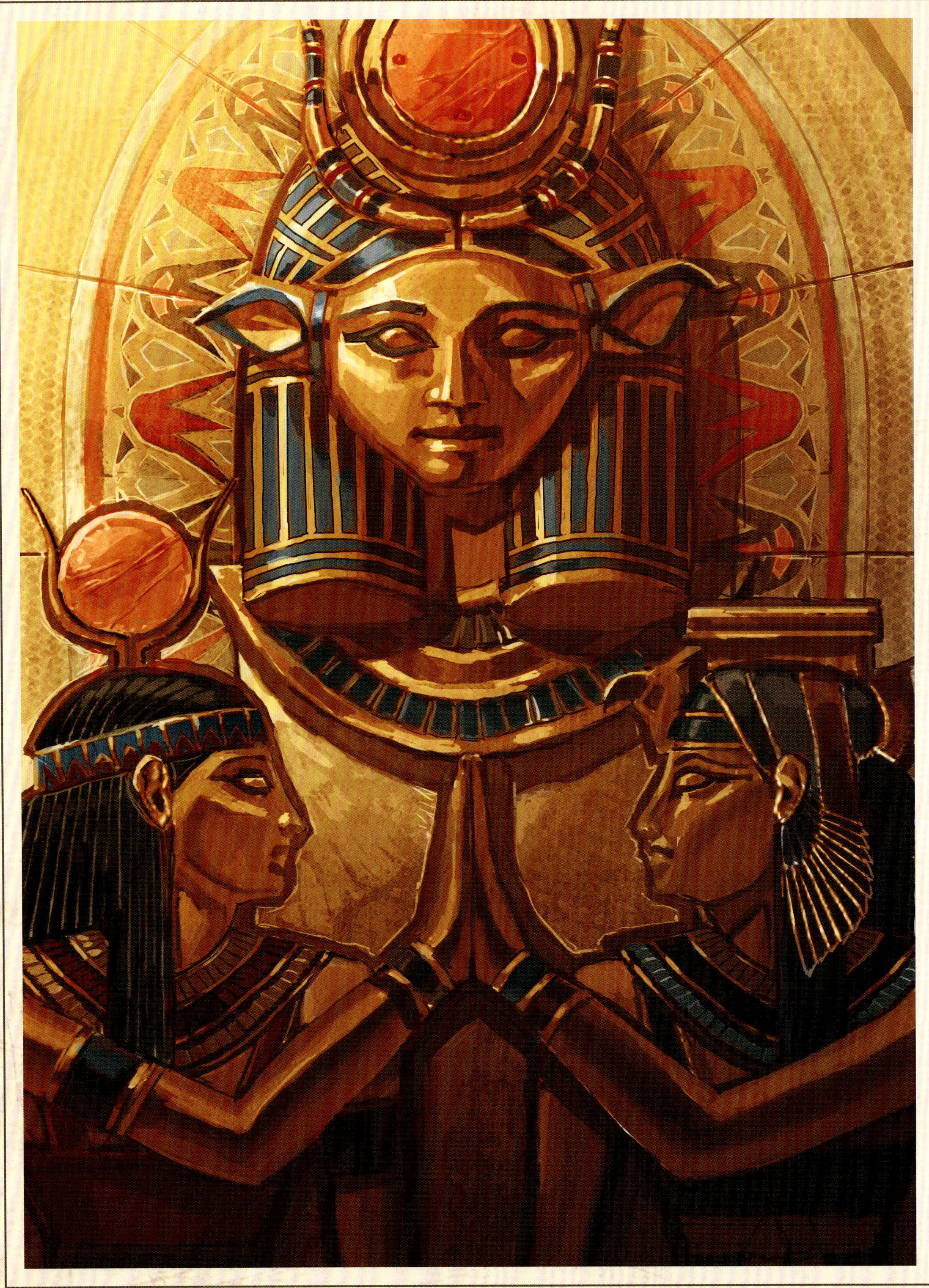

Verse X

Through wise use of mind and owning my power of choice,
I consciously create and manifest magic.
I affirm and decree this human inheritance of divine ability.

I affirm my innate dignity and sacred sovereignty,

I lay claim to myself and my life as an expression of love.

My inner light emanates bright as the noon desert sun,

I recognise and enact my powerful freedom to choose.

My open and worthy heart attracts abundant divinity,

Inspiring joyful expression of my personal responsibility.

My life is entirely my own,

yet held tenderly in the Blessed Lady's hand.

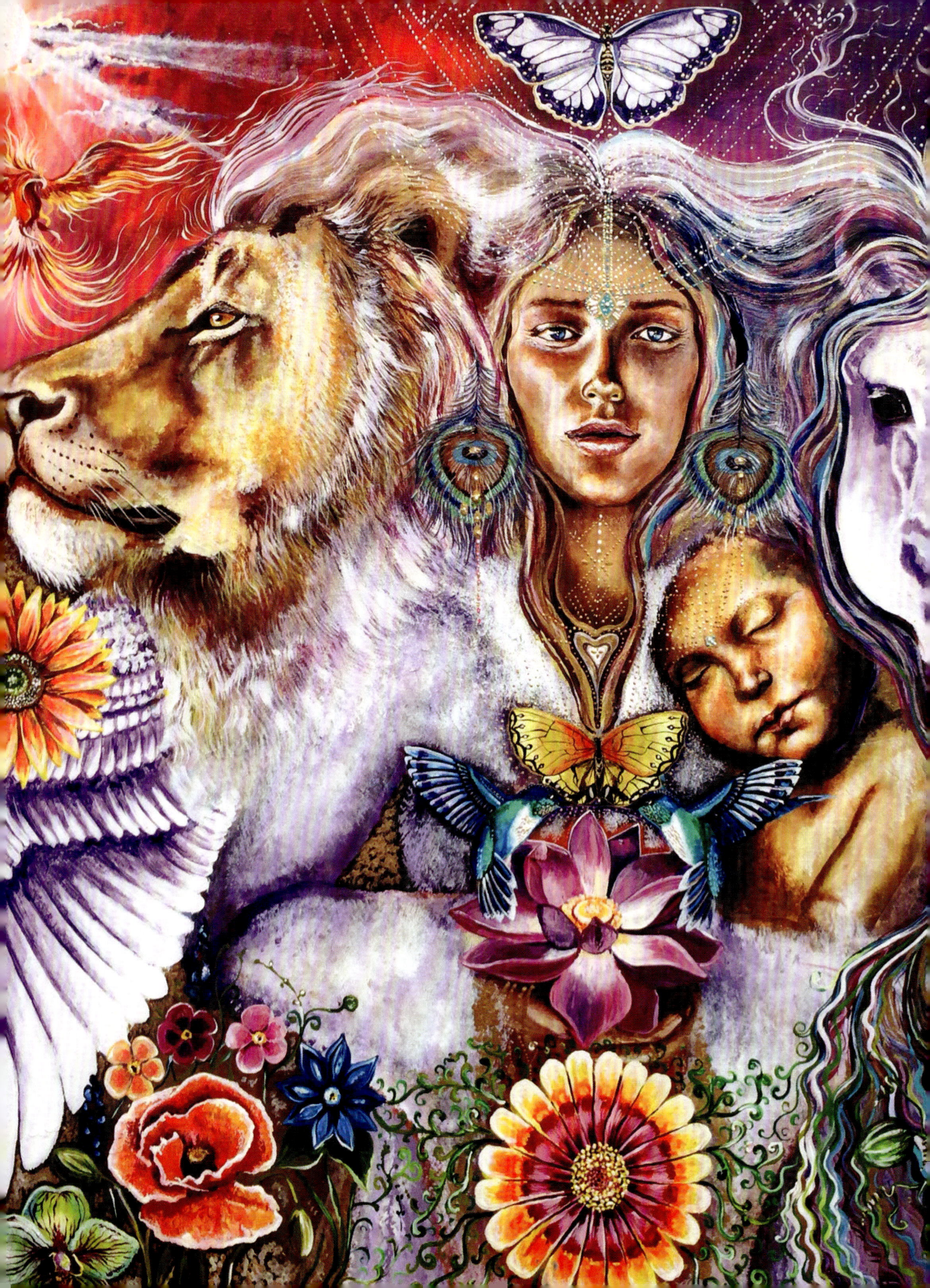

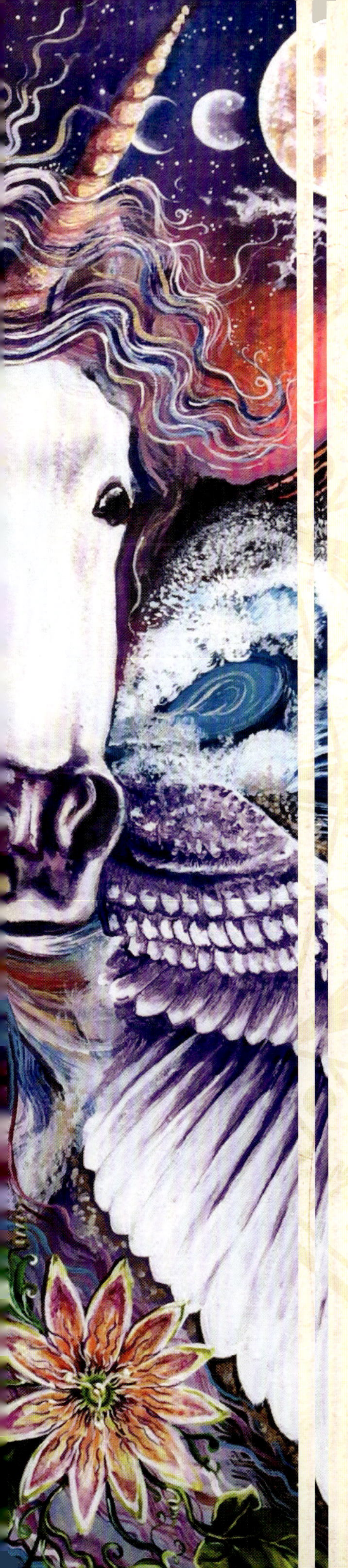

Book of EARTH WARRIORS

Incantations and Divinations for Your Sacred Manifestations and Alchemical Visioning of Humanity Unified

Verse I

I hold a vision of grace and goodness. I affirm a reality of healing and happiness.

I invoke enlightened activity to support manifestation most blessed.

Children of Earth are beautiful and blessed with wisdom. They play in divine beauty.

Young people of Earth are beautiful and blessed with wisdom. They dance in divine beauty.

Parents of Earth are beautiful and blessed with wisdom. They love in divine beauty.

Grandparents of Earth are beautiful and blessed with wisdom. They rest in divine beauty.

I invoke spiritual protection to comfort and care for the vulnerable.

I invoke divine love to guide and uplift the lost and lonely.

I invoke strength of soul to encourage and support every heart.

I invoke highest harmonic healing for peace amongst all peoples.

I walk with beauty before me. I walk with beauty behind me.

I walk with beauty above me. I walk with beauty below me.

I walk with beauty all around me and within every part of my being.

All else departs instantaneously as I invoke the healing light of divine beauty.

It shines within, brightening my wisdom, and I recognise the inevitable destiny

of all hearts in discovering such beauty within.

"

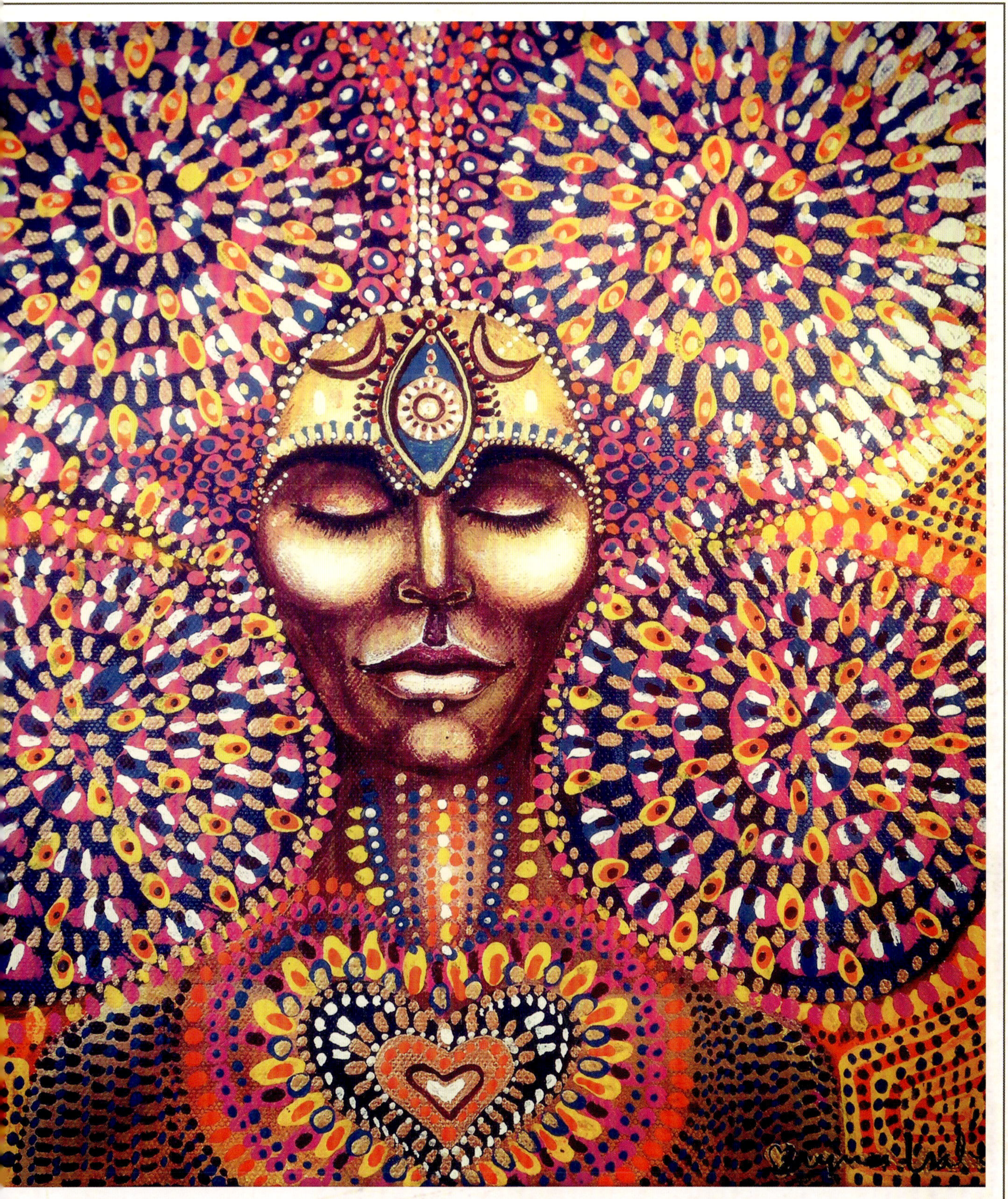

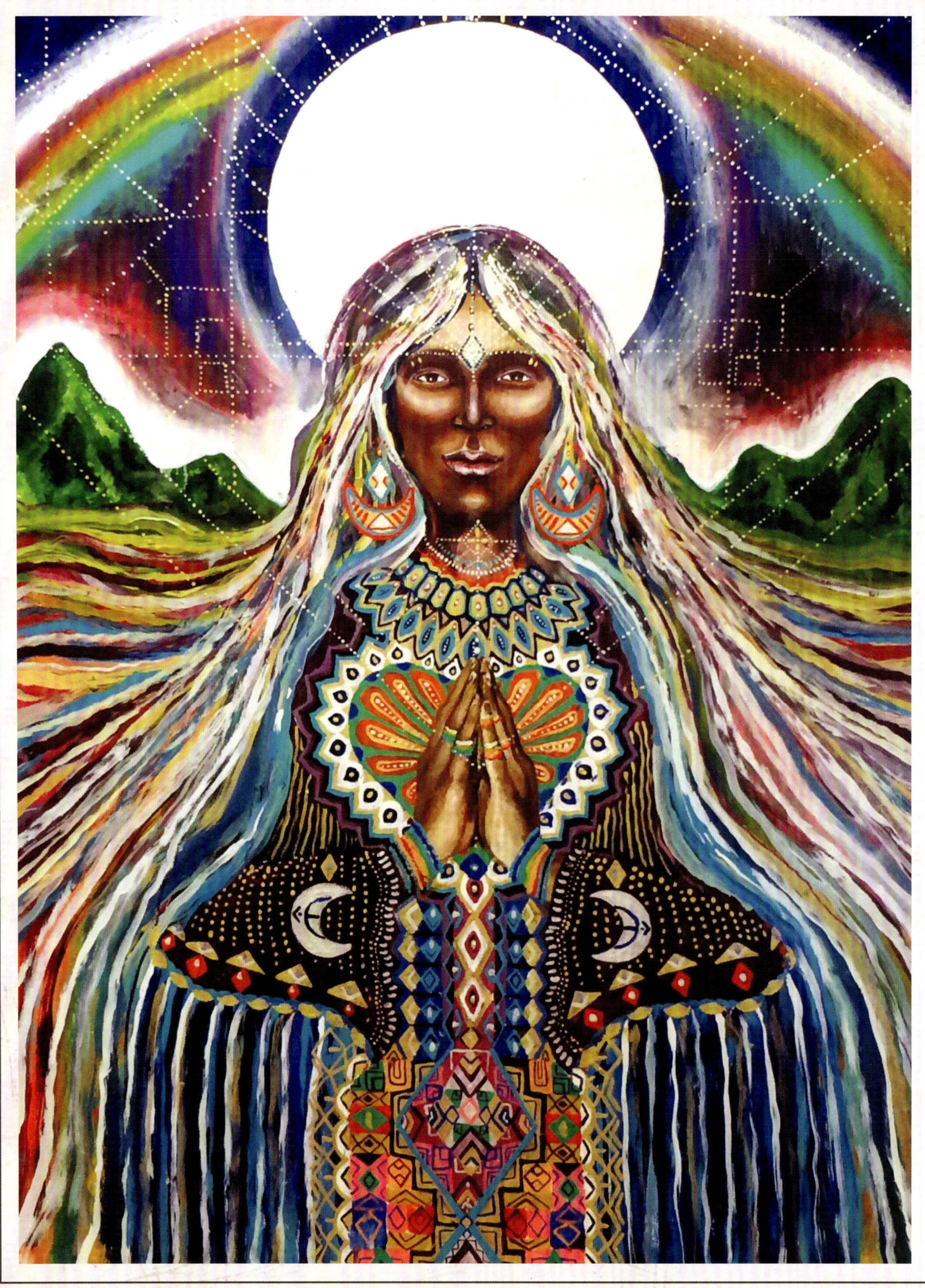

Verse II

THROUGH THE PROTECTIVE GATEWAY OF UNCONDITIONAL LOVE,
I ISSUE THIS INCANTATION OF SPIRITUAL IGNITION,
AND BLAZING SACRED FIRE PURIFIES NEGATIVITY,
RIPENING THE SEEDS OF POSITIVE KARMA FOR THE BENEFIT OF ALL BEINGS.

I am Human of Earth and Spirit of Sky.
I am love's alchemy manifest.

Gifted with meaningful knowledge,
I serve the greater good through my passion.

Devoted to timeless wisdom and eternal love,
I am guided by the grace that benefits all beings.

Protected through the purity of my purpose,
I am generously endowed with all necessary resources.

And so, I manifest love's steadying resilience
and actively evoke healing transformation for humanity.

I invoke the power of divine grace into my being and into this world.
I invoke the power of divine will into my being and into this world.
I invoke the power of divine healing into my being and into this world.
I invoke the power of divine presence into my being and into this world.
I invoke the power of divine love into my being and into this world.

Verse III

Sacred shift from past to present, laying the foundations of a most blessed future, I invoke divine Puma spirit guardian, and affirm thus — I have the power.

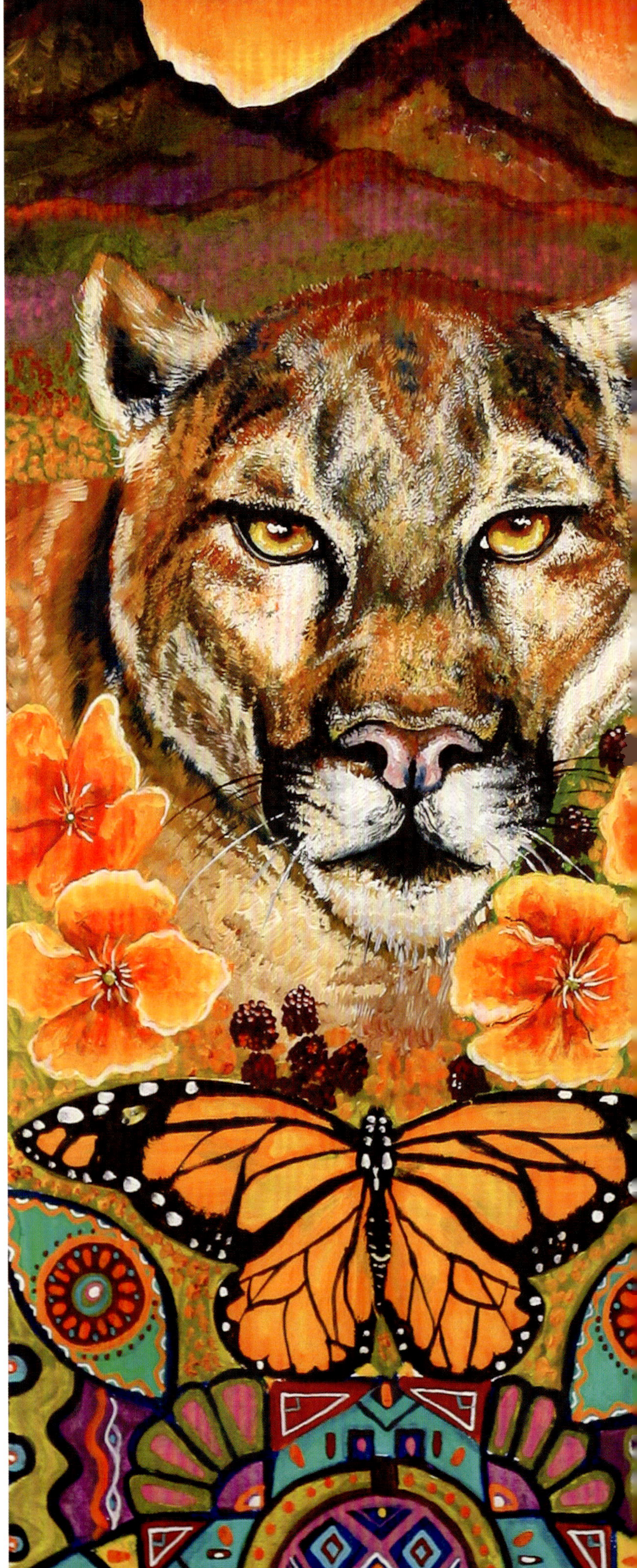

Medicine mentor, sacred Puma,
You arise in my mind, steadying my heart,
Evoking unwavering instant presence,
Revealing what is true and what to do.

Vigorous energy harnessed, I focus.
Awareness aligns instinctively with divine timing.
At the best moment, I act with precision.
Puma spirit guardian, render clear, best decision.

Medicine mentor, sacred Puma,
You arise in my mind, steadying my heart,
Evoking unwavering instant presence,
Revealing what is true and what to do.

Fearlessly I leave the past behind me.
I engage wholeheartedly in the here and now,
To manifest courageously that which must be.
Puma medicine mentor, gift radical clarity.

Medicine mentor, sacred Puma,
You arise in my mind, steadying my heart,
Evoking unwavering instant presence,
Revealing what is true and what to do.

Patient, and steady, engaged with presence,
I witness spontaneously arising knowing,
As clarity crystalises like diamond of Earth,
I practise sacred severance to instigate rebirth.

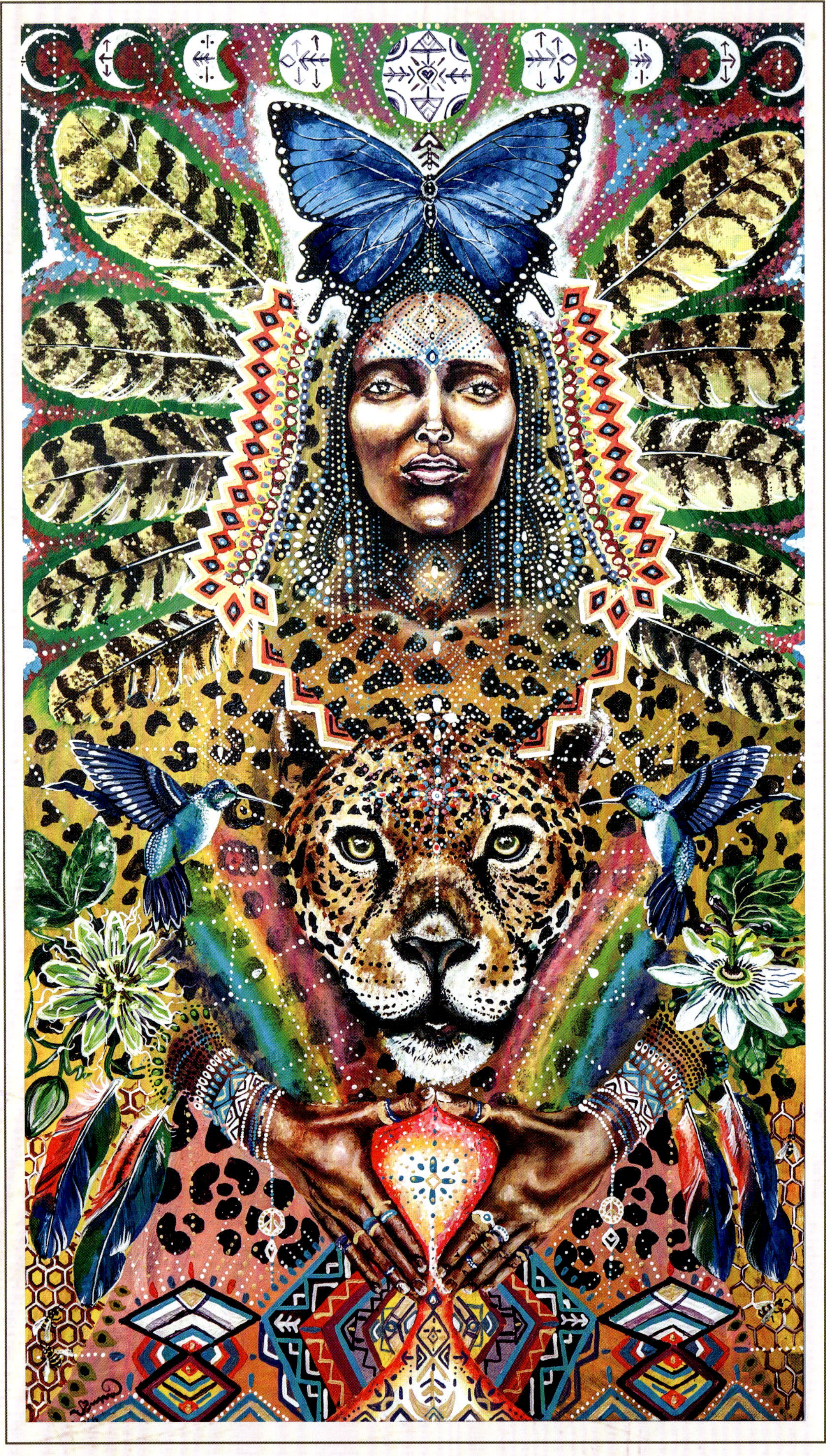

Verse IV

I CALL UPON THEE, BELOVED GODDESS DIVINE, TO SHARE WITH MY HEART YOUR SECRETS OF REPLENISHMENT AND MATURITY, THAT I SHALL RIPEN INTO ALL I AM DESTINED TO BE, RESTORING HOPE, BEAUTY AND BLESSING IN OUR WORLD.

Ixchel Medicine Jaguar, Lunar Lady of Rabbit and Vulture,
I invoke your regenerative magic of essential eradication.

Rainbow Sorceress of Promised Rebirth, hold me in your heart,
As I enact necessary closure with confidence and dignity.

Breaking free from patterns unworthy of my soul,
I am grounded and assured in the truth of your love.

Mother Jaguar, Fortress of Protective Power,
Magical Midwife and Crone of Crossed Bones,

Serpent-Crowned Goddess, Ancient Warrior Queen,
You evoke the strength and truth required to break free.

With complete faith, I proceed with courage,
Guide me safely through the perils of transformation.

Revive my heart with your sacred heavenly waters,
That I, too, may increase Life and love in this world.

Verse V

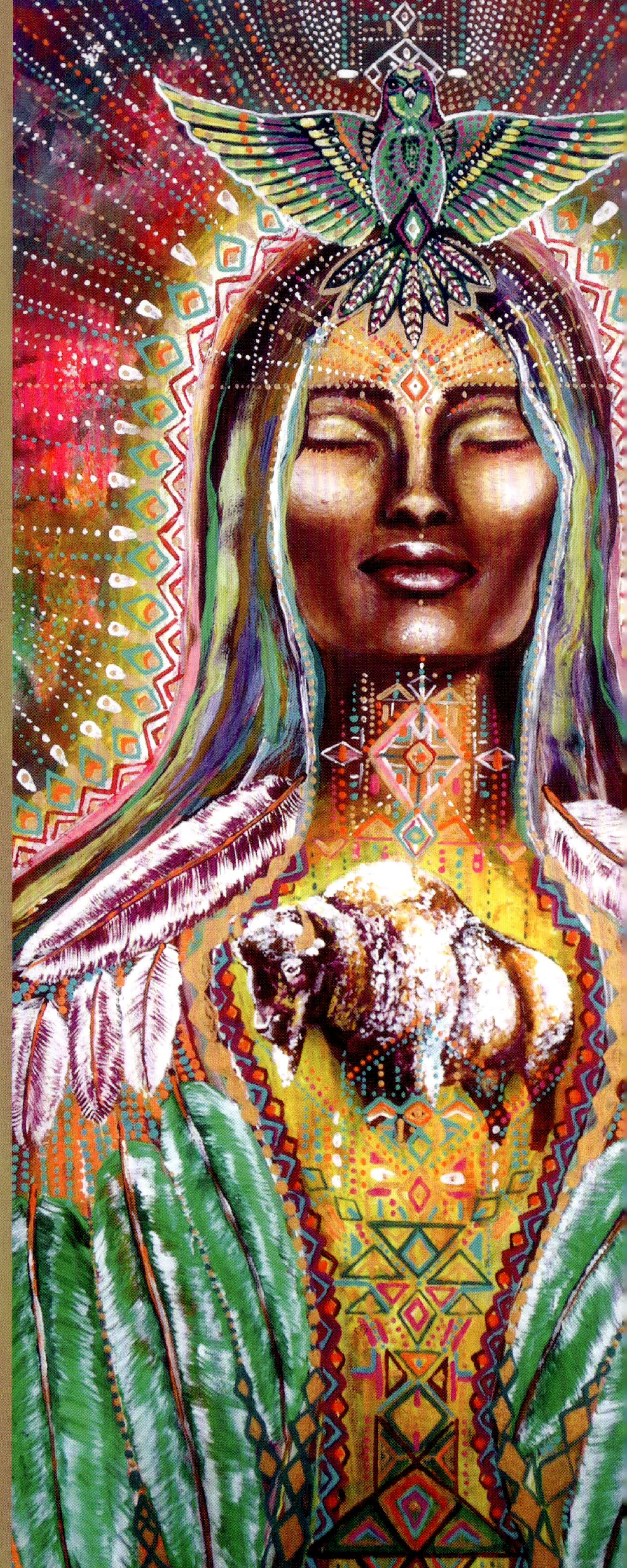

White Buffalo Calf Woman, sacred light in my heart, divine voice in my mind, reveal your guidance. Teach me your way, for I am willingly your devotee and messenger, desiring manifestation of your perfect and peaceful prophecies.

Om Shanti Om.
Jai Ma Jai Jai Ma!

White Buffalo Calf Woman, I see your shining face.
Releasing the past, I envision and decree a future most blessed.

Om Shanti Om.
Jai Ma Jai Jai Ma!

White Buffalo Calf Woman, I hear your loving voice.
I let go of doubt, trusting joyfully in my heart's guidance.

Om Shanti Om.
Jai Ma Jai Jai Ma!

White Buffalo Calf Woman, I feel your gentle presence.
I soften in love and light, affirming goodness destined for all.

Om Shanti Om.
Jai Ma Jai Jai Ma!

White Buffalo Calf Woman, I receive your healing love.
Your peaceful power protects and evokes fulfilment of my heart.

Om Shanti Om.
Jai Ma Jai Jai Ma!

White Buffalo Calf Woman, I invoke your calming light.
Sacred saviour, shine your goodness now to bless all beings.

Om Shanti Om.
Jai Ma Jai Jai Ma!

Anointed with white light, I am sheltered from the storms.
Bathed in white light, I recognise the wisest choice for now.
Blessed by white light, I attract grace with my gratitude.

Om Shanti Om.
Jai Ma Jai Jai Ma!
Om Shanti Om.
Om Shanti Om.

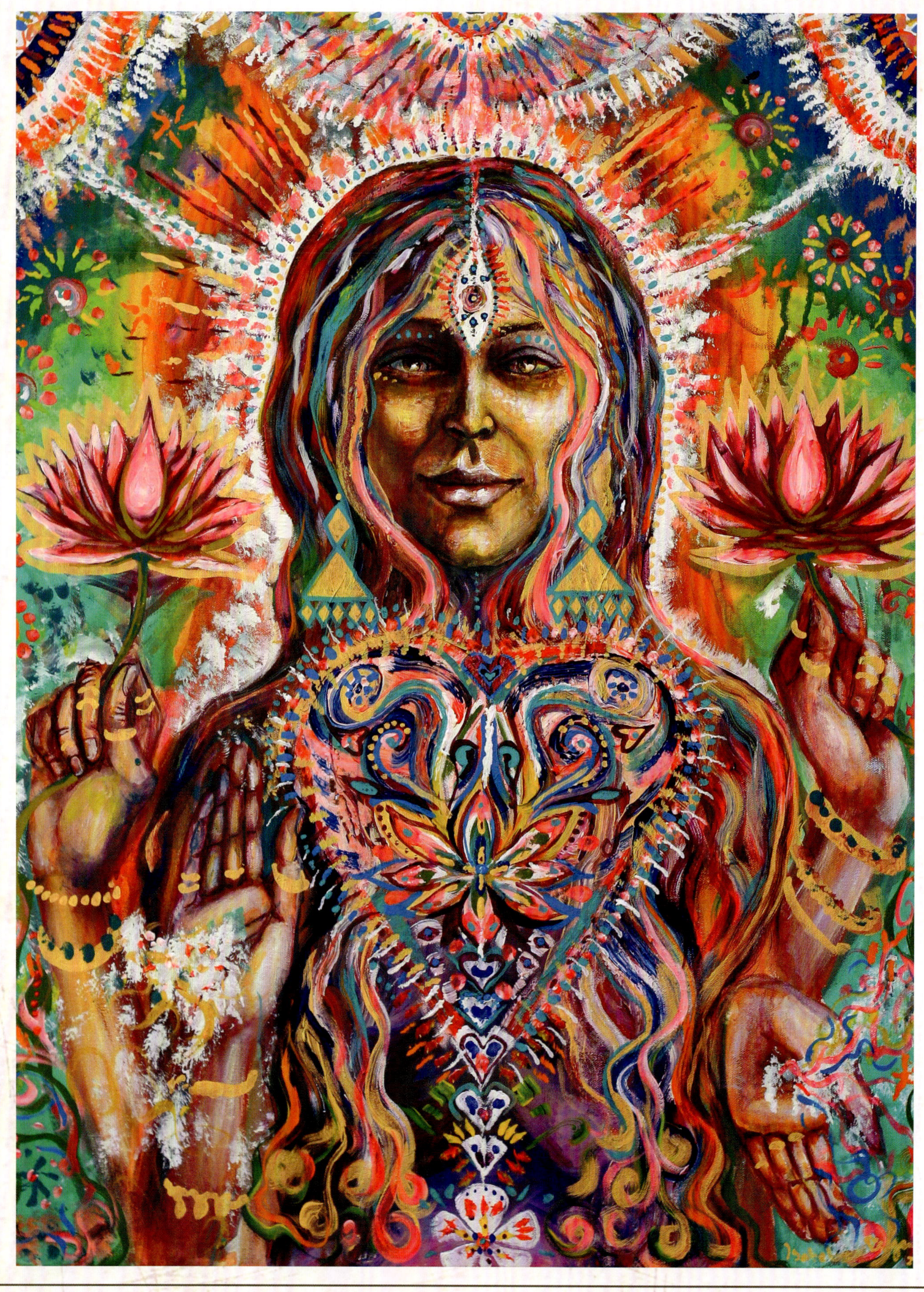

Verse VI

SOVEREIGN OF SOUL, I AFFIRM MY POWER, NATURALNESS AND DIVINITY,
EXPRESSING MY SACRED BIRTHRIGHT AS A RESTORATIVE CHANNEL AND CREATIVE
VISIONARY, HEALING MY OWN BEING AND BENEFITTING OUR WORLD.

In sanctified solitude, I concentrate,
Generating internal healing nectars,
Restoring my essence.

Arising naturally from sacred seclusion,
I open to Life with expansive expression,
Nourishing the world with my love.

I belong to myself,
I belong to the vastness,
I am a living dimension of spiritual truth.
From this deep knowing, I source love's power.

I dance between retreat and engagement,
Heeding rhythmic urgings of my soul.

Adhering to the truth of my path,
I progress swiftly in bliss of purpose.

Realising divine inevitability restores faith,
And I trust in love's ultimate fulfilment.

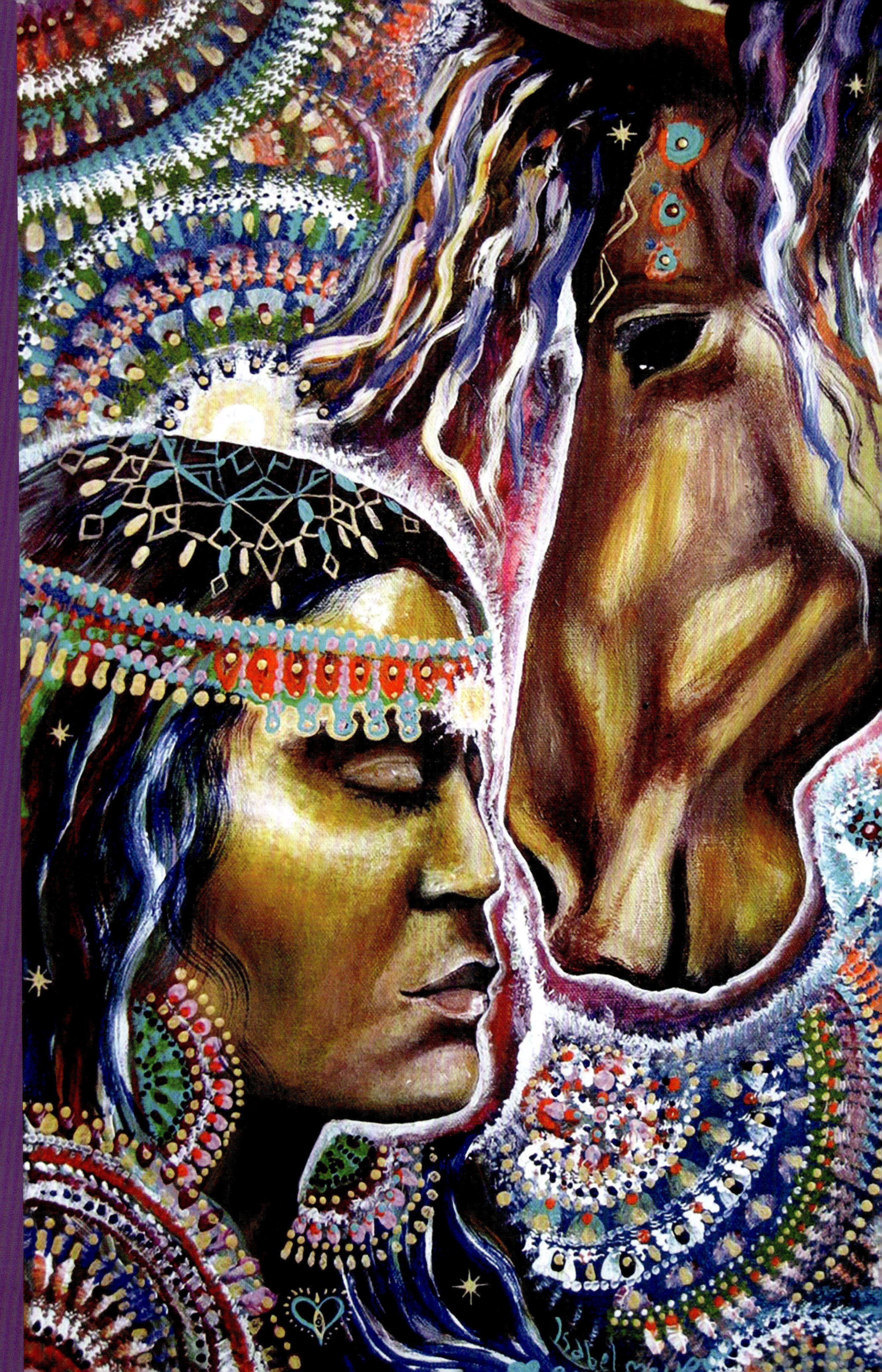

Verse VII

Lung Ta, Spirit Horse, bearing the Wish-Fulfilling Gem
your divine inspiration uplifts my heart and assures
swift progress on the path.

Medicine Horse, Spirit Horse, Lung Ta,
Your energy ensures I shall go far.

Confident optimism quickens my pace.
Expansive horizons open with grace.

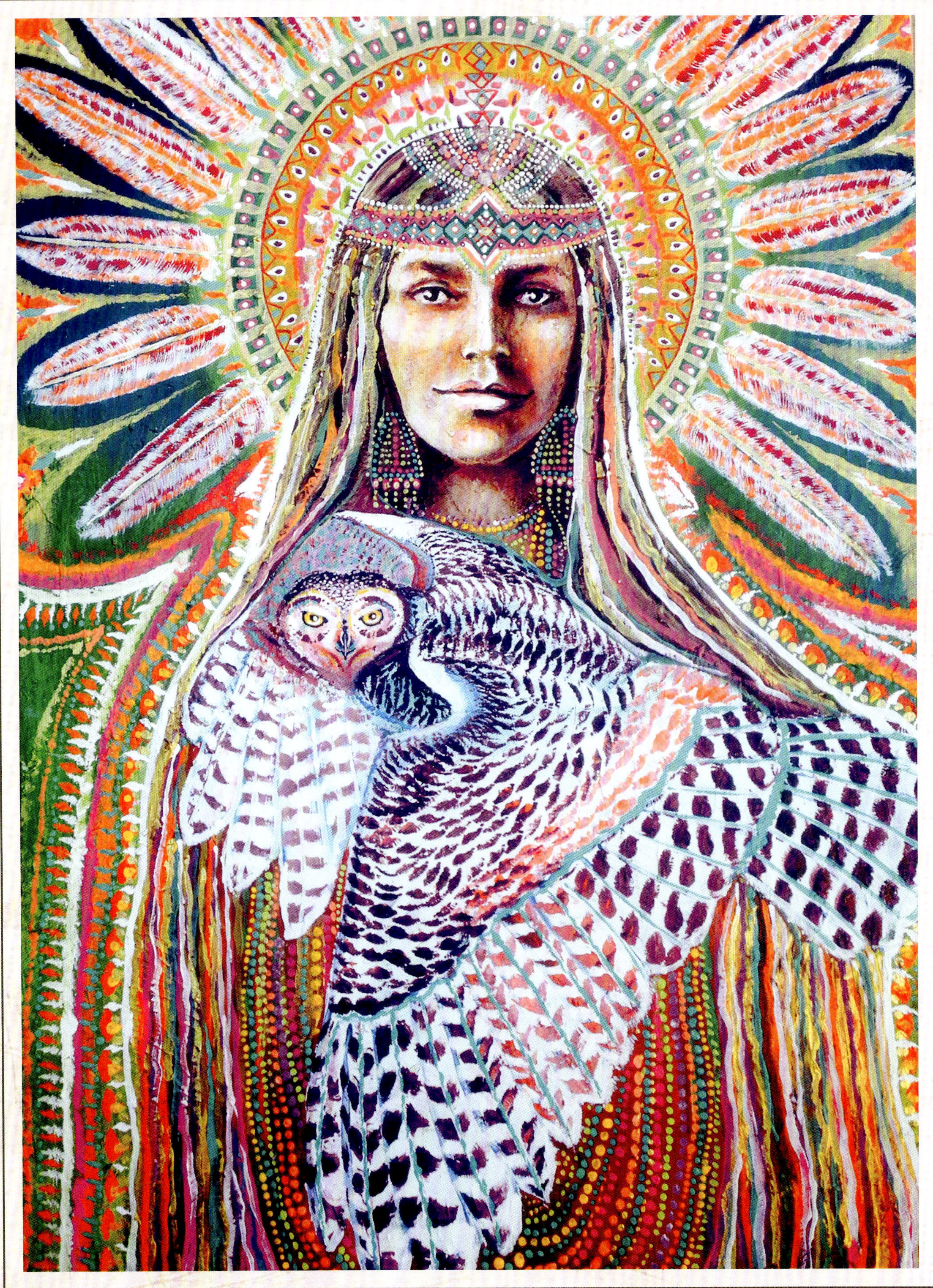

Verse VIII

DIVINE MOTHER OF OWLS AND PROTECTOR OF DREAMS THAT
MUST TAKE FLIGHT, OF GOODNESS PURE HEARTEDNESS AND SACRED JUSTICE,
I INVOKE THY NATURAL LAW AND MIRACULOUS MAGIC,
FOR YOU ARE THE SPIRITUAL PROTECTION INHERENT TO AUTHENTIC
PATH AND PURPOSE, EVOKING JOY AND REWARDING DEVOTION.

Hi'aka, feather-clad Sorceress of Light,
Open your wings,
Disperse darkness of night.

Dispelling fear, doubt and confusion,
You dance, emanating light, as I breathe.

My recalibrated heart softens in hope and gratitude.
You spin and my worldview is uplifted and transformed.

I become bolder and brighter in your presence,
As your protective power shields my soul.

Hi'aka, feather-clad Sorceress of Light,
With a shake of your hips,
Joyfully unveil the bright.

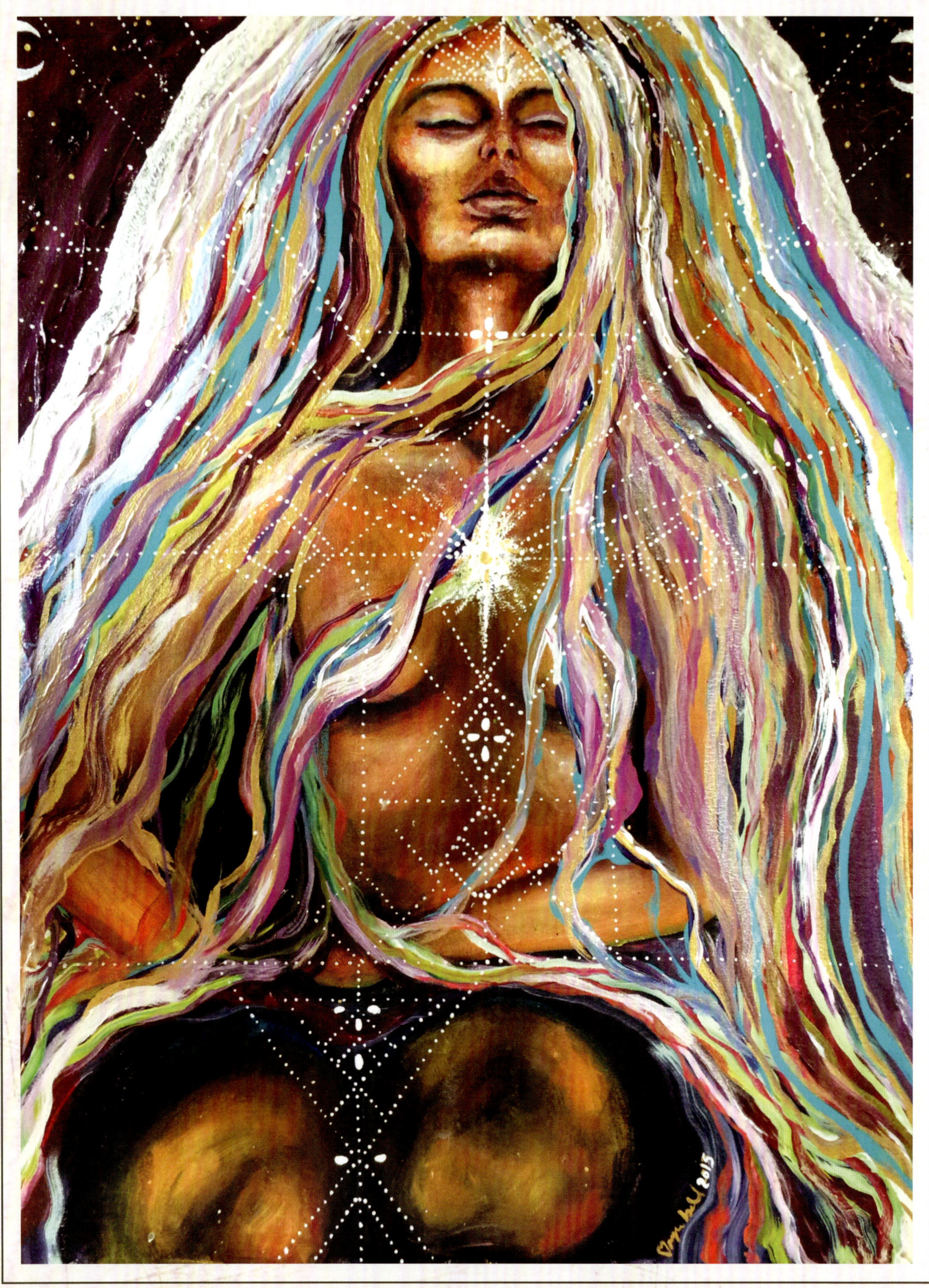

Verse IX

Sky Creatrix, Soma Priestess of Divine Nectar,
Goddess of the Galactic Heart, Majestic Mother Mayu, Divine Nurturer,
bestow your ample ambrosia to this beloved cosmic child.

Mother Mayu, drip sweet soma from your galactic heart,
Into this willing vessel of my heart.

Bestowing your nutritive divine empowerment,
I grow stronger, casting my creative net wider.

Daring to embrace expansive and elevated expression,
True purpose is grounded for greater good.

Bestowing sacred seal of divine imprimatur,
You augur my sacred fruition and fulfilment.

And so I thrive, nourishing the world with goodness,
Enriched with blessing, I strive to benefit all beings.

Beloved Divine Mother, let me be your eyes, your ears, your hands, for I am your
divine descendant of blood and bone, breath and spirit, seeking to live your
grace in our world.

May your protection and blessing flow abundantly to me and through me,
for the benefit of all.

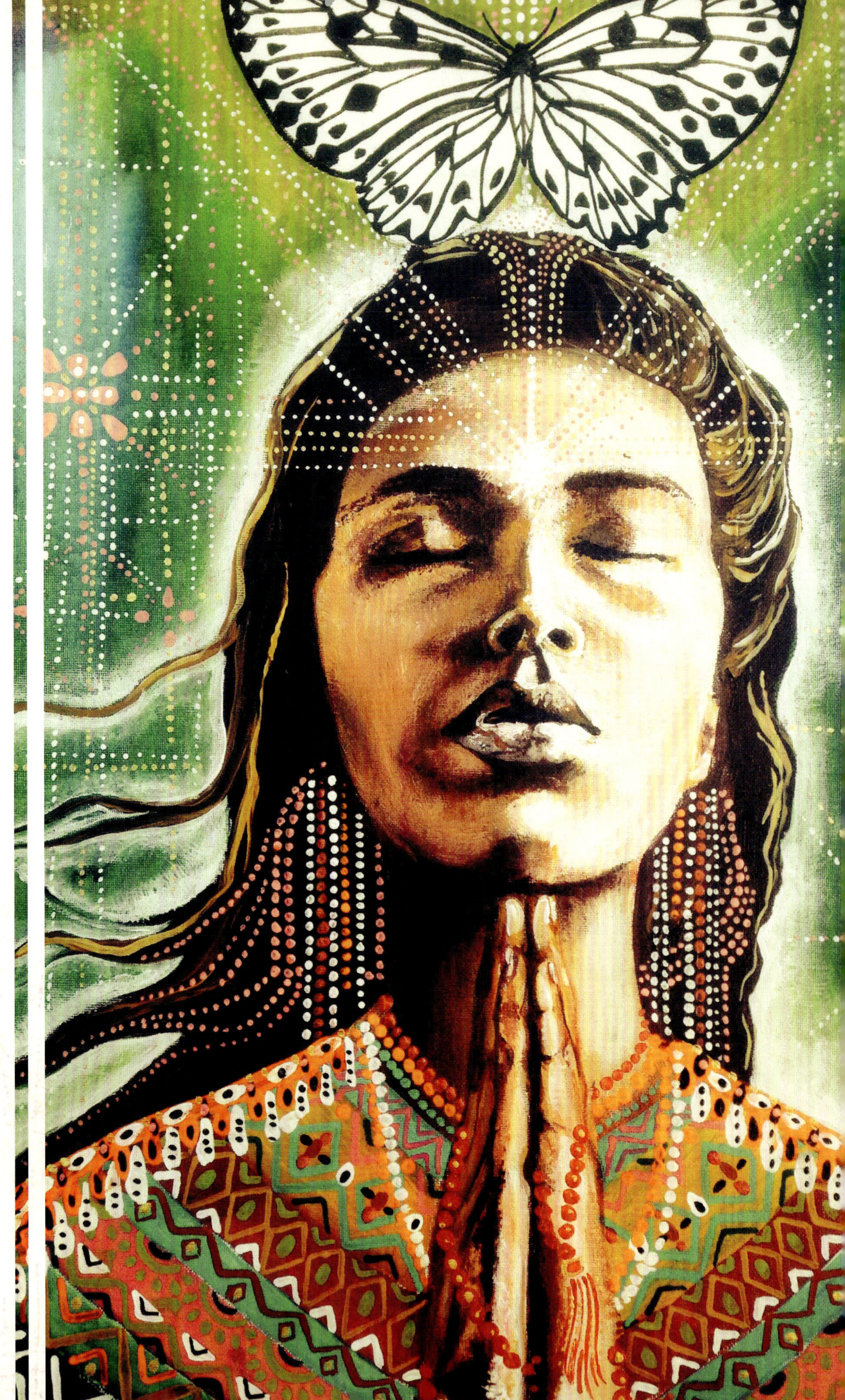

Verse X

Turquoise Changing Woman,
Crystalline emanation of sacred sound.

Take my hand and protect my heart,
Avert peril, guide me on my path.

Through devotion, we become one voice,
Love's prophet of necessary healing change.

Revitalised in your turquoise light,
I see and trust the next steps to take.

Lady of Light, Lady of Change,
I weave a new tapestry, embroidered with your blessing,

Cloaking me in comforting revelation,
Inspiring my confidence to create with faith.

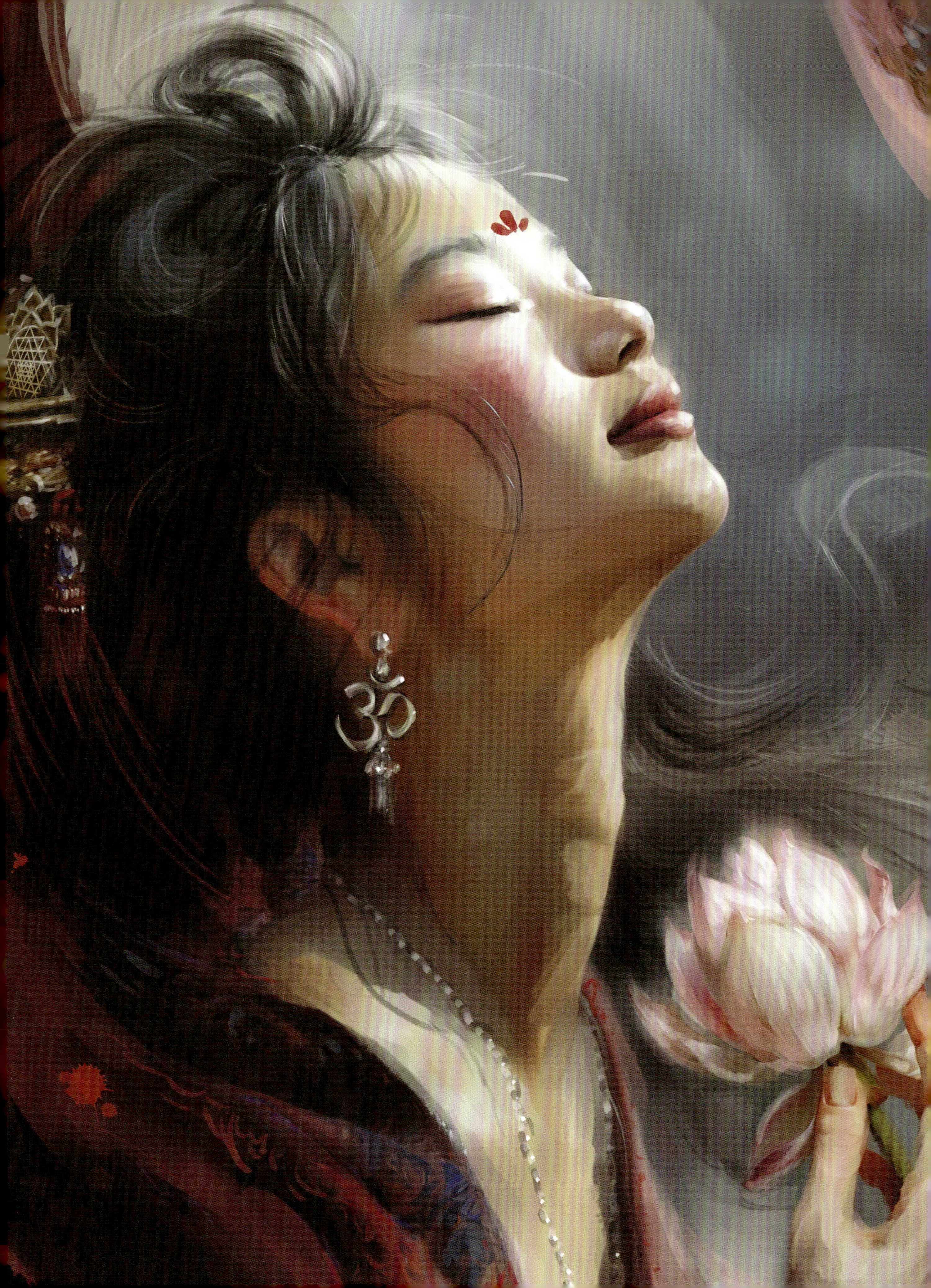

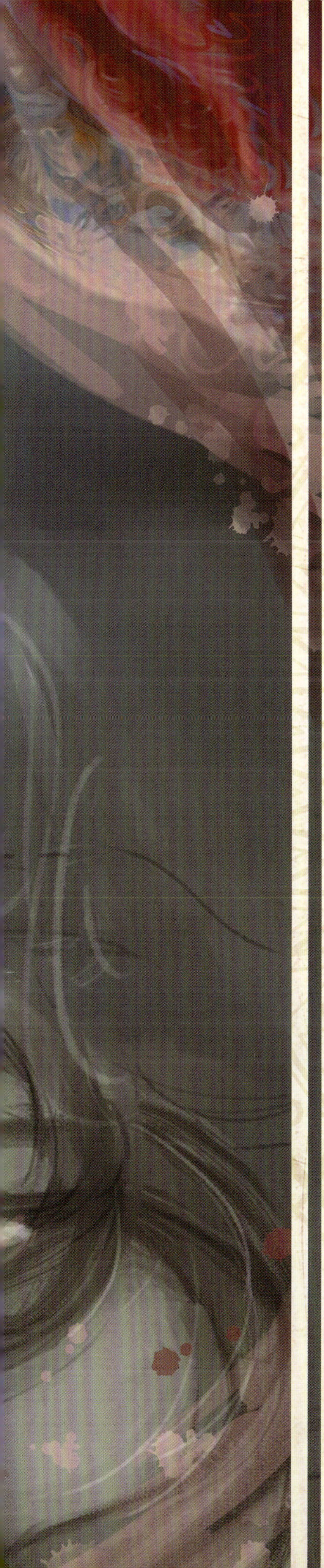

Book of KUAN YIN

Incantations and Divinations Evoking Emanations of Infallible Grace and Protective Mercy

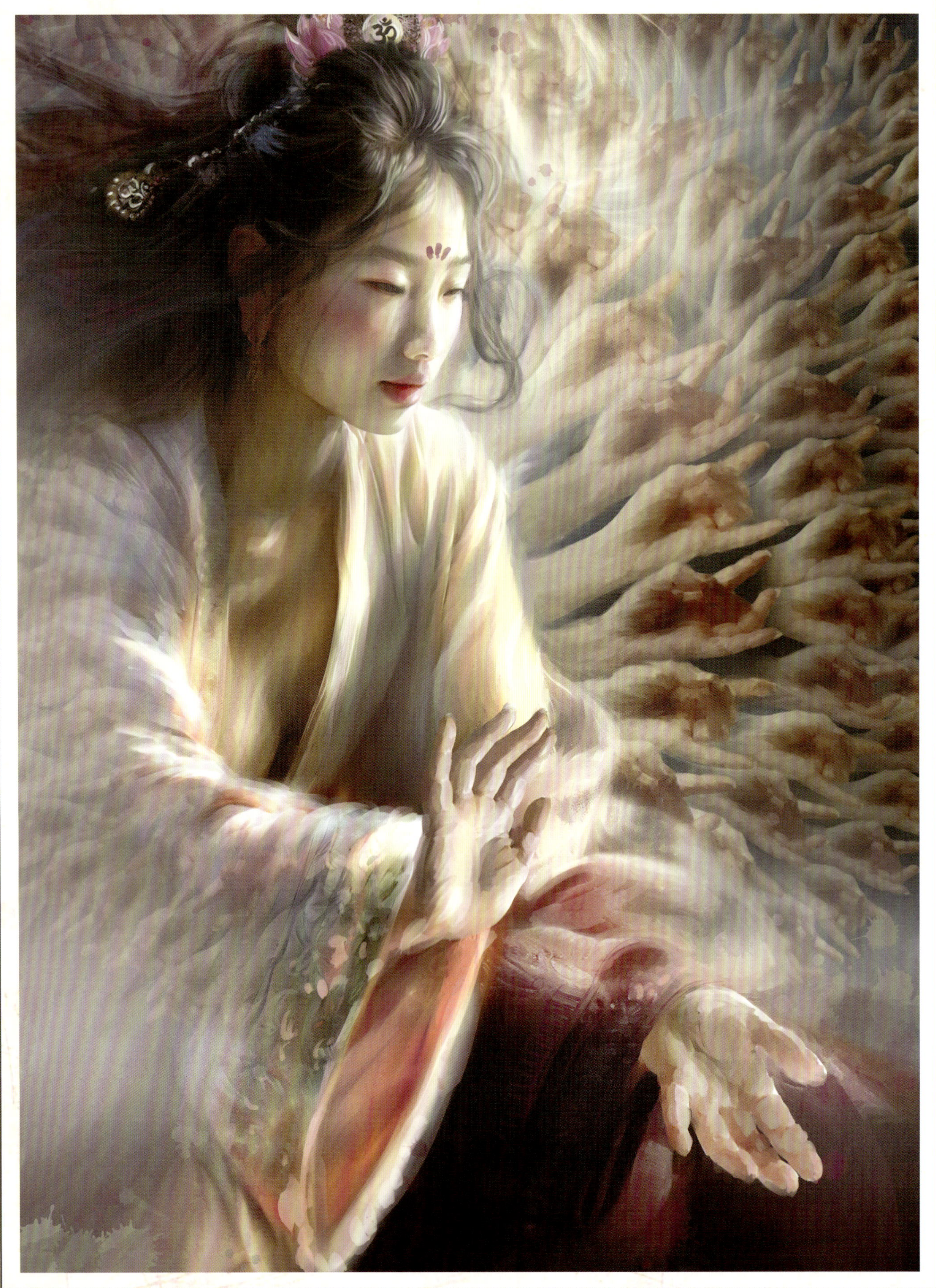

Verse I

BELOVED GODDESS, YOUR INFALLIBLE GRACE IS MY STEADFAST SECURITY, SUSTAINING MY FAITH DURING TESTING TIMES, GUIDING ME TO THE EXQUISITE ECSTASY OF REALISATION THAT YOU ARE ALWAYS WITH ME.

Goddess of infallible grace,
Ever merciful protector,
I absorb your tender compassion,
A fortifying tonic for my soul.

In the sanctuary of your mantra,
I am restored to trust and peace,
Secure in the mandala of your love,
I know all good things shall come to be.

Om Mani Padme Hum.
Om Mani Padme Hum.
Om Mani Padme Hum.

Verse II

MOTHER OF LIGHT, MOTHER OF LOVE,
BRING FORTH BLESSINGS AND PROTECTION,
AS ORDAINED FROM DIMENSIONS OF GRACE, TO REVEAL THE WAY AND
STRENGTHEN MY RESOLVE, TO DISCOVER DEEP ABIDING JOY,
AND ENSURE FULFILMENT OF DIVINE DESTINY.

Kuan Yin, Divine Mother of Light,

Kuan Yin, Divine Mother of Love,

I invoke your blessing now.

You are my steadiness and my strength,

You are my resilience and my rest,

Your light shines and illuminates my path,

The way of best choice become clear to me.

Kuan Yin, Divine Mother of Light,

Kuan Yin, Divine Mother of Love,

I invoke your blessing now.

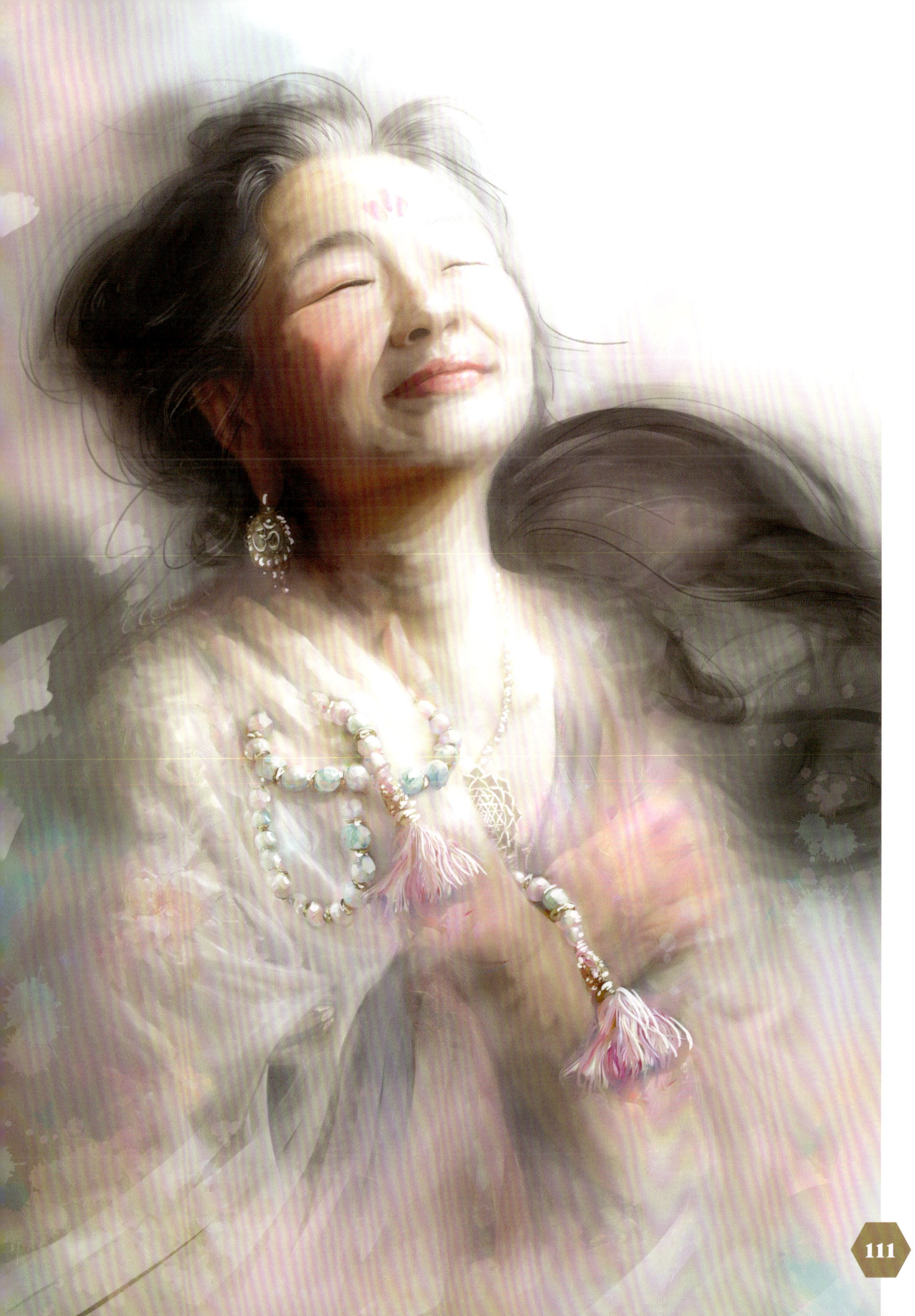

Verse III

Wish-Fulfilling Mother, your kindness and wisdom alleviate suffering,
inspiring me to release the past and become present in this moment
where magic can happen and healing is truly possible.
May all beings realise your miraculous kindness!
May I contribute to your enlightened activity, bringing about
fulfilment of all wishes. I release doubt and embrace
joyful confidence in your compassionate resourcefulness.

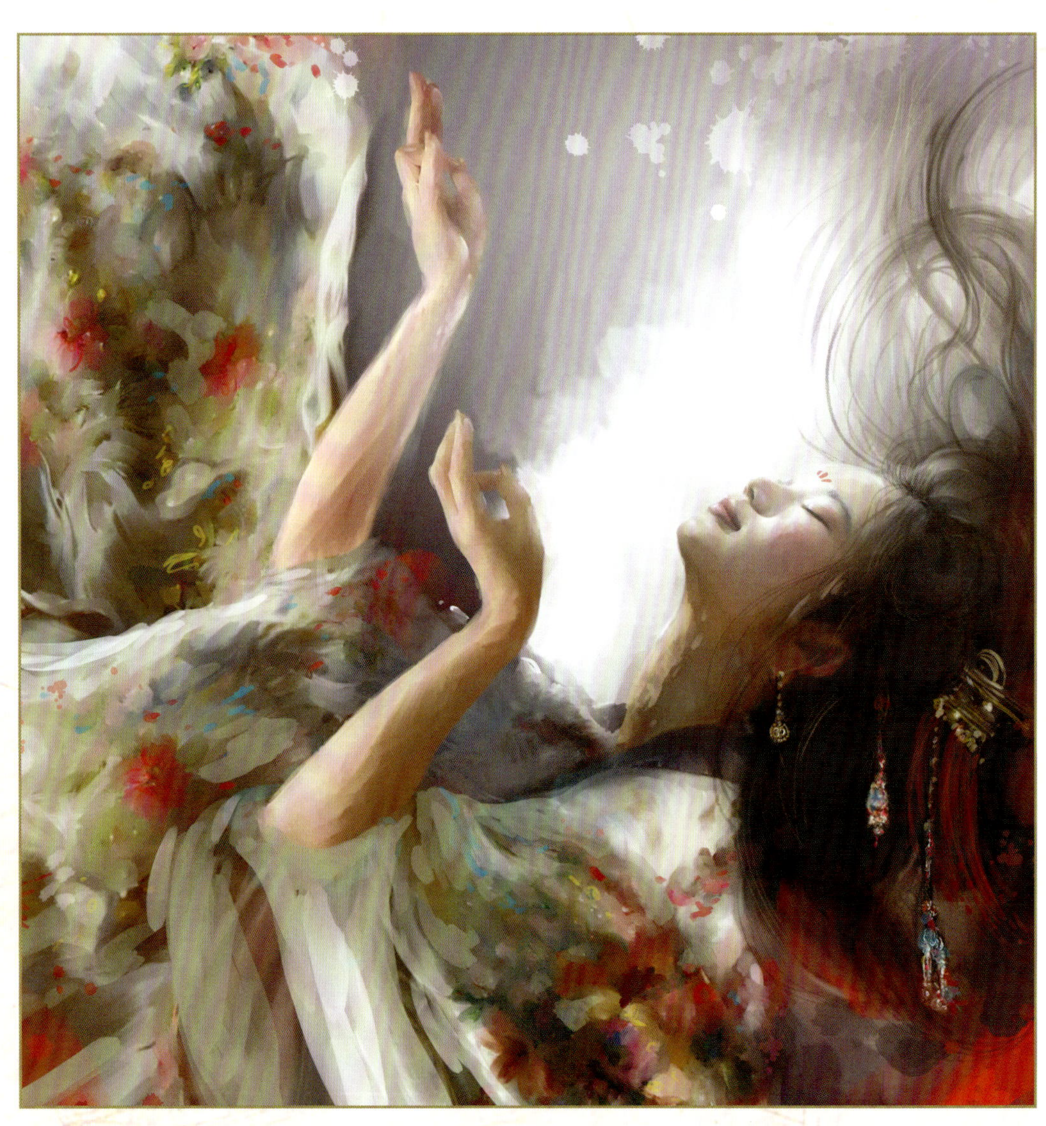

Wish-Fulfilling Gem,

Wish-Fulfilling Tree,

Wish-Fulfilling Wheel,

Sweet fruits of grace,

Ripen with your mercy.

Rainbow lights shining within my heart.

Rainbow lights shining in all directions.

Rainbow lights shining in all dimensions.

Wish-Fulfilling Gem,

Wish-Fulfilling Tree,

Wish-Fulfilling Wheel,

All wishes attain fruition,

Through Rainbow Chakra *Cintamani*

Rainbow lights shining within my heart.

Rainbow lights shining in all directions.

Rainbow lights shining in all dimensions.

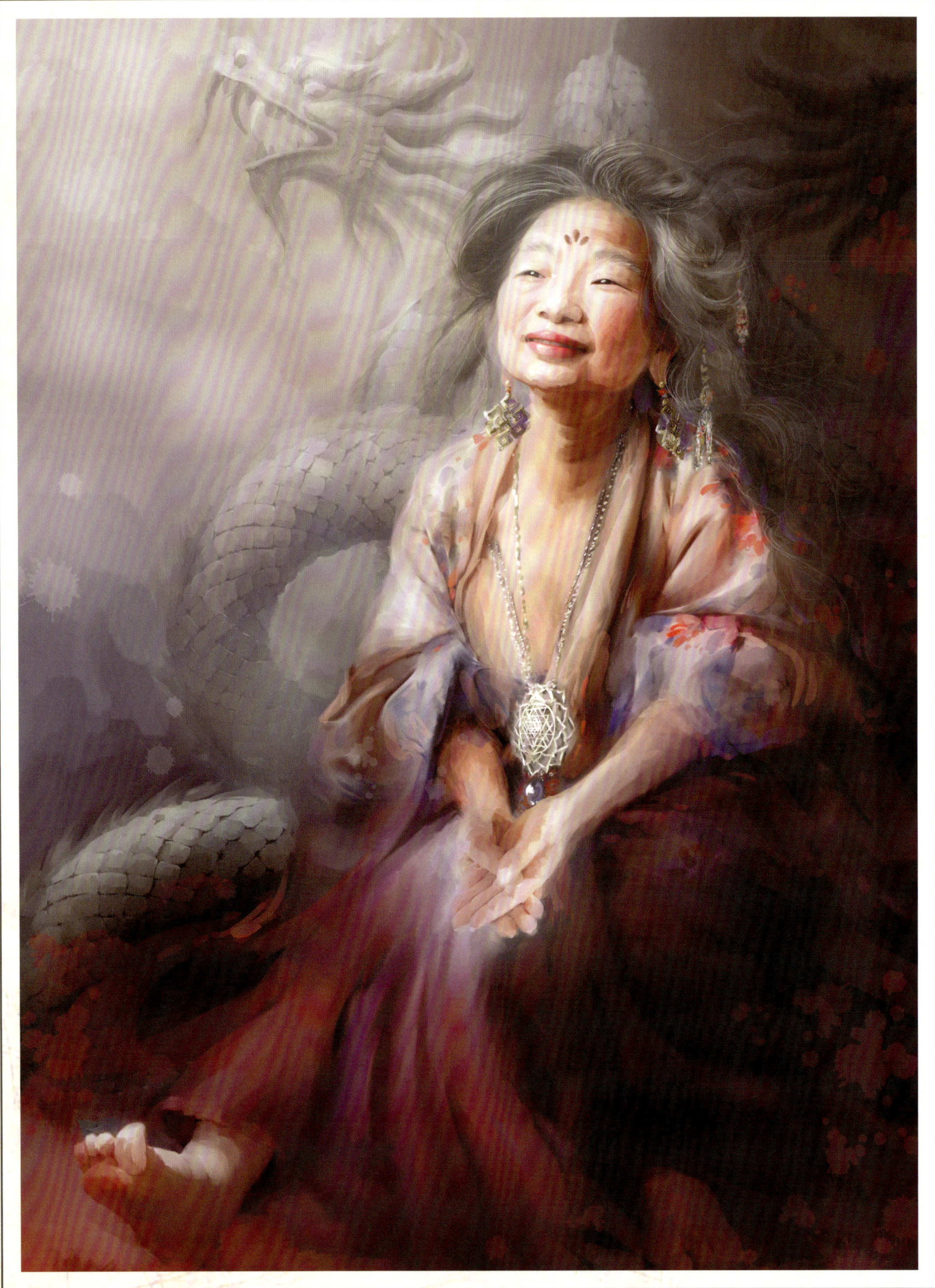

Verse IV

Ancient Mother, bestows peace to my mind.
Beloved Goddess, awakens happiness in my heart.
Sweet Saviour, reassures me with comforting love.
Divine Guardian, protects me with unfading light.

Our enduring heart bond elevates me.
Lifted beyond confusion and fear,
I flourish in the reality of our love.

And so I choose,
To witness, and reflect,
To contemplate, and create,
To recognise, and respond,
To engage, and express,
To soften, and be kind,
To strengthen, and be wise.

I fearlessly enact loving magic,
Casting spells of healing and peace,
And through such generosity,
Obtain long-lasting spiritual relief.

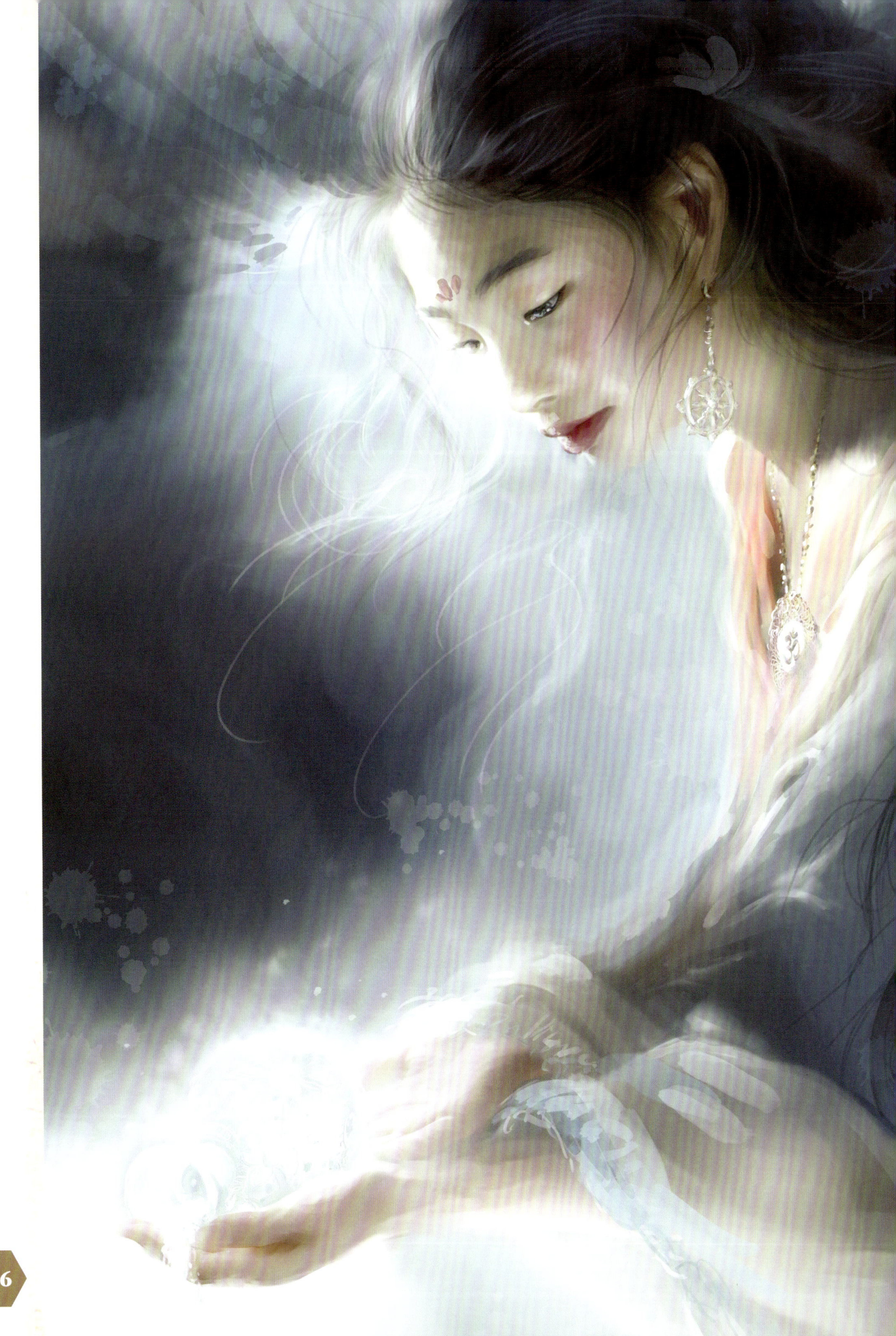

Verse V

When darkness disturbs my mind,

Obscuring the light with doubt and confusion,

Your love restores my faith and clear vision.

All circumstances contain hidden healing potential.

Wisdom Mother, unveil the divine secret to me,

Revealing the truth that unburdens my soul.

Your benevolent presence amplified,

Your sacred beauty infusing my heart,

Only your sweetness shall overcome me.

Wisdom Mother, open my eyes to my power.

Confidently, I claim and express my free will.

Wisdom Mother, open my heart to your love.

Joyfully, we surpass all obstacles and rise.

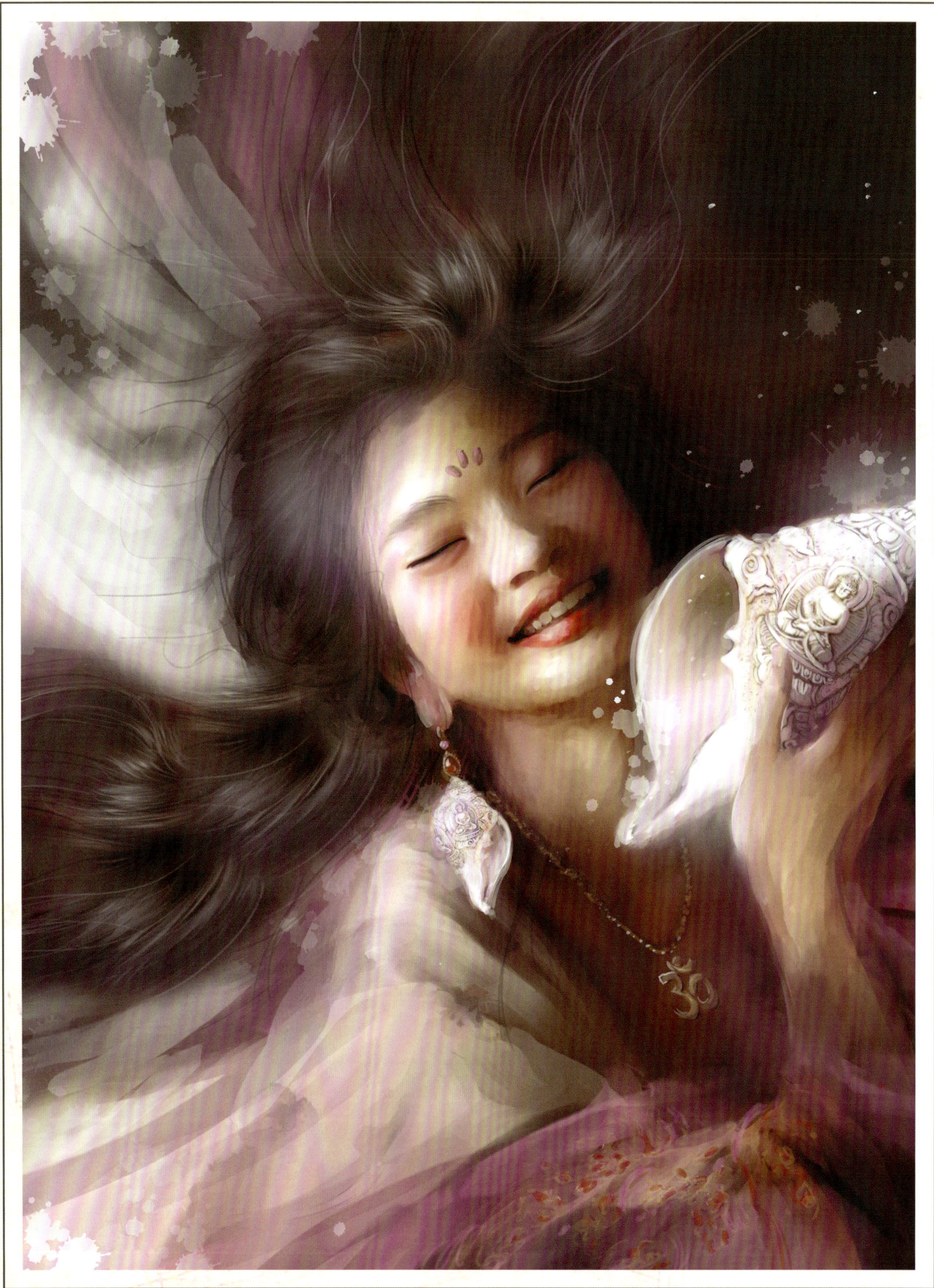

Verse VI

You who are first and foremost in my heart,
you who are my whole heart, you who dwell as all hearts,
as one love, one truth, one light,
how I cherish your kind presence.
It is so natural and wise to trust in you,
experiencing sweet relief in the entirety of my being.

What could possibly compete with the compelling and vast
reality of your love?

All else—even greatest aversion and greatest desire—

is naught but a drop in the ocean of your compassion.

I want to dwell in the infinite beauty of your loving heart.
This is what I choose.

Om Namo Kuan Shi Yin Poosa.

Verse VII

Under your merciful auspices, may my truest path and highest potential manifest swiftly and gracefully, with beauty and delight.

May I experience inner spiritual fulfilment so enriching, that spontaneous outpouring of your grace is evoked, nurturing all beings and fulfilling all wishes with compassionate wisdom.

Beloved Radiant Mother, protect me from any obstacle, past vow or present delusion, which could undermine my higher purpose. Gently, lovingly and firmly reveal the truth I need to recognise now, to take my next steps with assurance and wisdom.

Through your blessing, may I radiate the light and love that is needed in the world and beyond.

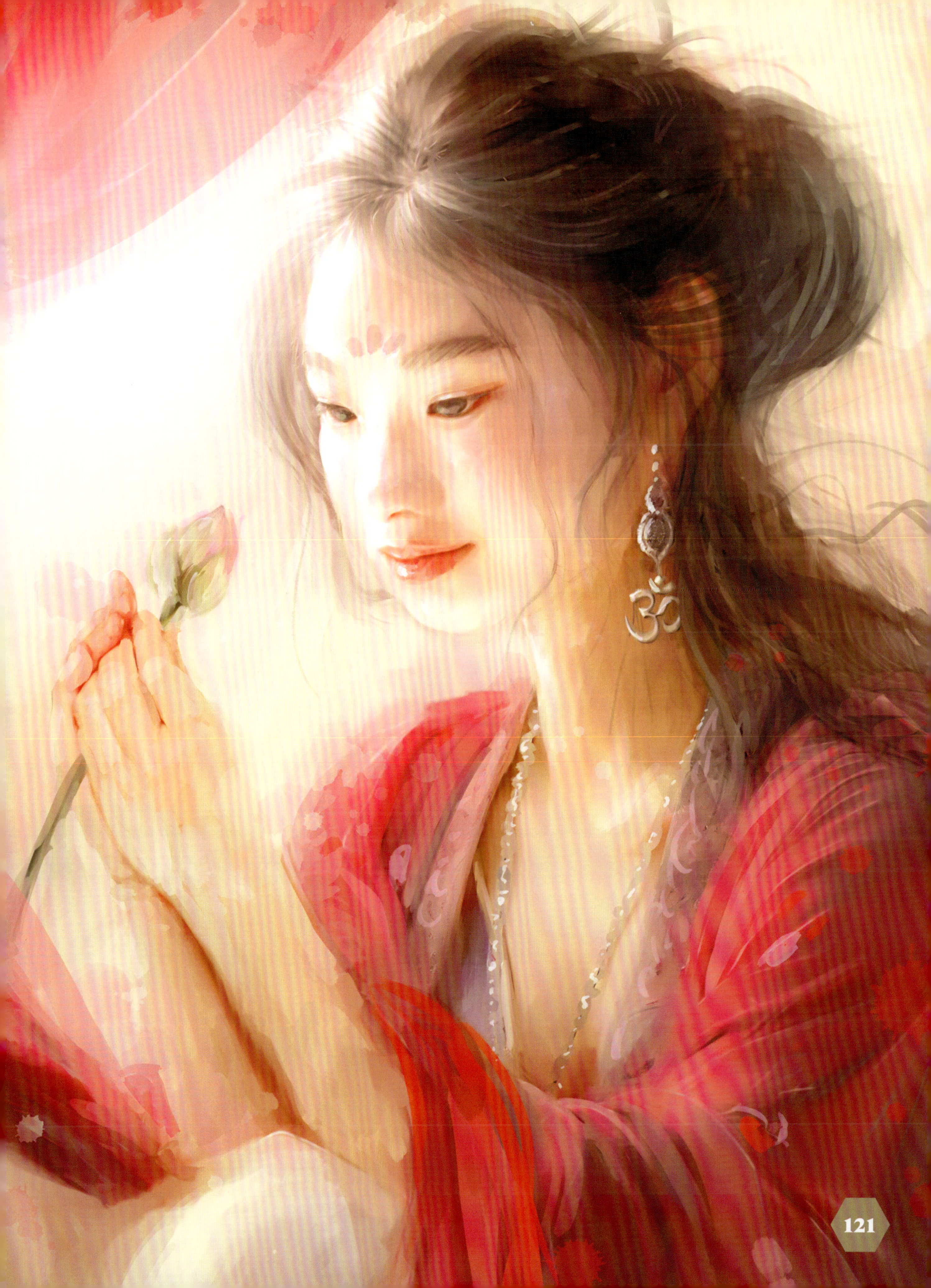

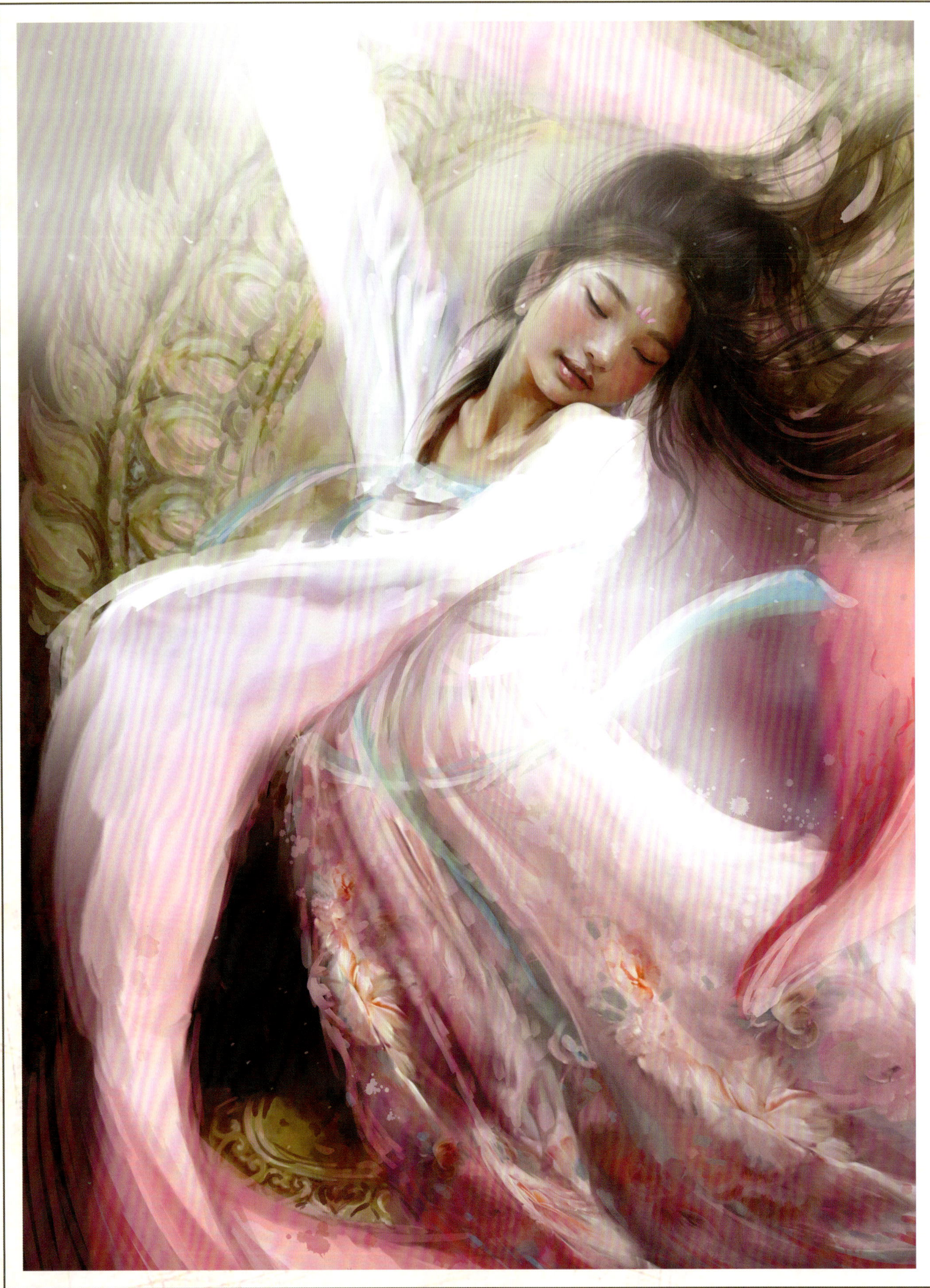

Verse VIII

MANTRA MOTHER OF LIBERATING LOVE, YOU POSSESS THE POWER TO TRANSFORM THAT WHICH CAUSED PAIN INTO THAT WHICH BESTOWS FREEDOM. I OPEN MY HEART TO YOU, SUMMONING MY SPIRITUAL WILL TO BECOME RECEPTIVE AND READY FOR YOUR BLESSING. I WISH THIS HEALING ALCHEMY OF BLISSFUL RELIEF FOR MYSELF AND FOR ALL BEINGS.

Opening my heart with gratitude and courage,
I am filled with resolve to affirm the light,
And initiate secret inner alchemy,
Spiritually metabolising every experience,
As soul food to strengthen my being.

As your divine voice issues oracles of protection,
My heart is encircled by your swirling syllables,
Of mystic mantras, sacred sounds of divine love,
Rays of white, red and blue light stabilise protection,
Sealing with grace the gates at crown, throat and heart.

Om Mani Padme Hum.
Om Mani Padme Hum.
Om Mani Padme Hum.

Om Mani Padme Hum.
Om Mani Padme Hum.
OM AH HUM.

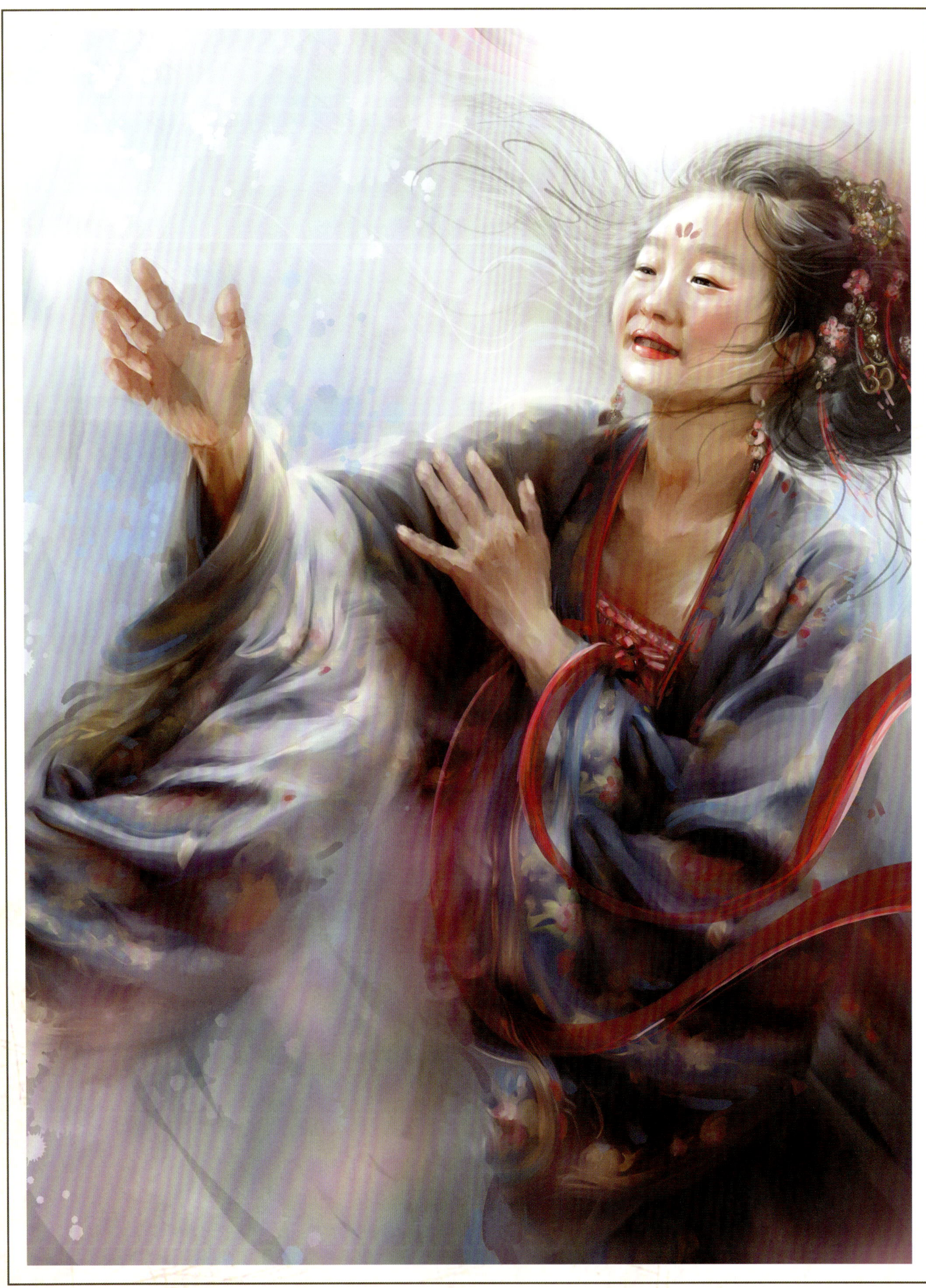

Verse IX

BOUNTIFUL ONE, BENEVOLENT ONE, BEAUTIFUL ONE, YOUR REPAIR IS INSTANTANEOUS AND COMPLETE, AND IN REALISING THE GLORIOUS PROSPECT OF RECEIVING SUCH BLESSING, I STRETCH MY HEART AND MIND, OPENING TO YOUR WAYS. MAY MY FAITH IN YOU BE STRONGER THAN MY ATTACHMENT TO THE PAST. I SURRENDER MY SOUL TO YOUR TENDER MINISTRATIONS.

Your spiritual relief comes swiftly,
Shining with the light of assured resolution.

Joyful recognition arises in my mind,
My heart blazing with passionate gratitude,

Mother who fulfils all wishes and needs,
In the best way to soothe and liberate the soul,

Replenishes my confidence at this critical moment,
when blessed attainment is imminent.

With steady faith and resilient hope,
I allow for your divinely timed grace.

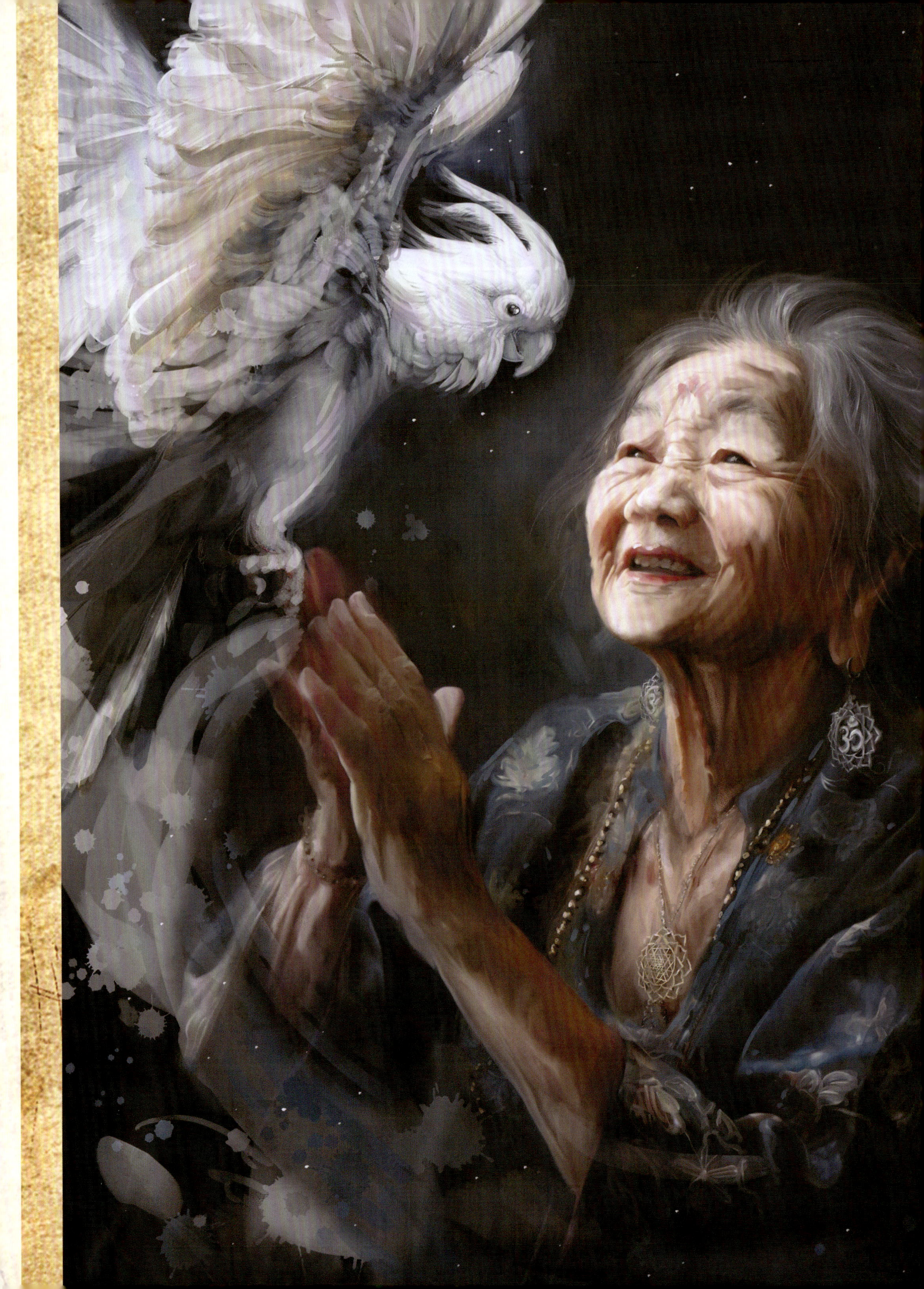

Verse X

Sacred one who guards all hearts, especially during vulnerable times of transition and powerful times of growth, keep me safe and steady, for my evolution is occurring in a significant way, and I am in need of your love to stabilise my mind. I acknowledge your unwavering presence in my heart, and cross the threshold before me.

Many-Armed Divine Mother Fierce,
Your protective decree resounds,
Heralding my victory over the past,
Opening the way to a new era.

Through the joy of letting go,
I bloom like luscious lotus red,
Magnetising incorruptible goodness,
Drinking it in and dancing your grace.

Om Hum Hrih Soham.
Om Mani Padme Hum.

Om Hum Hrih Soham.
Om Mani Padme Hum.

Om Hum Hrih Soham.
Om Mani Padme Hum.

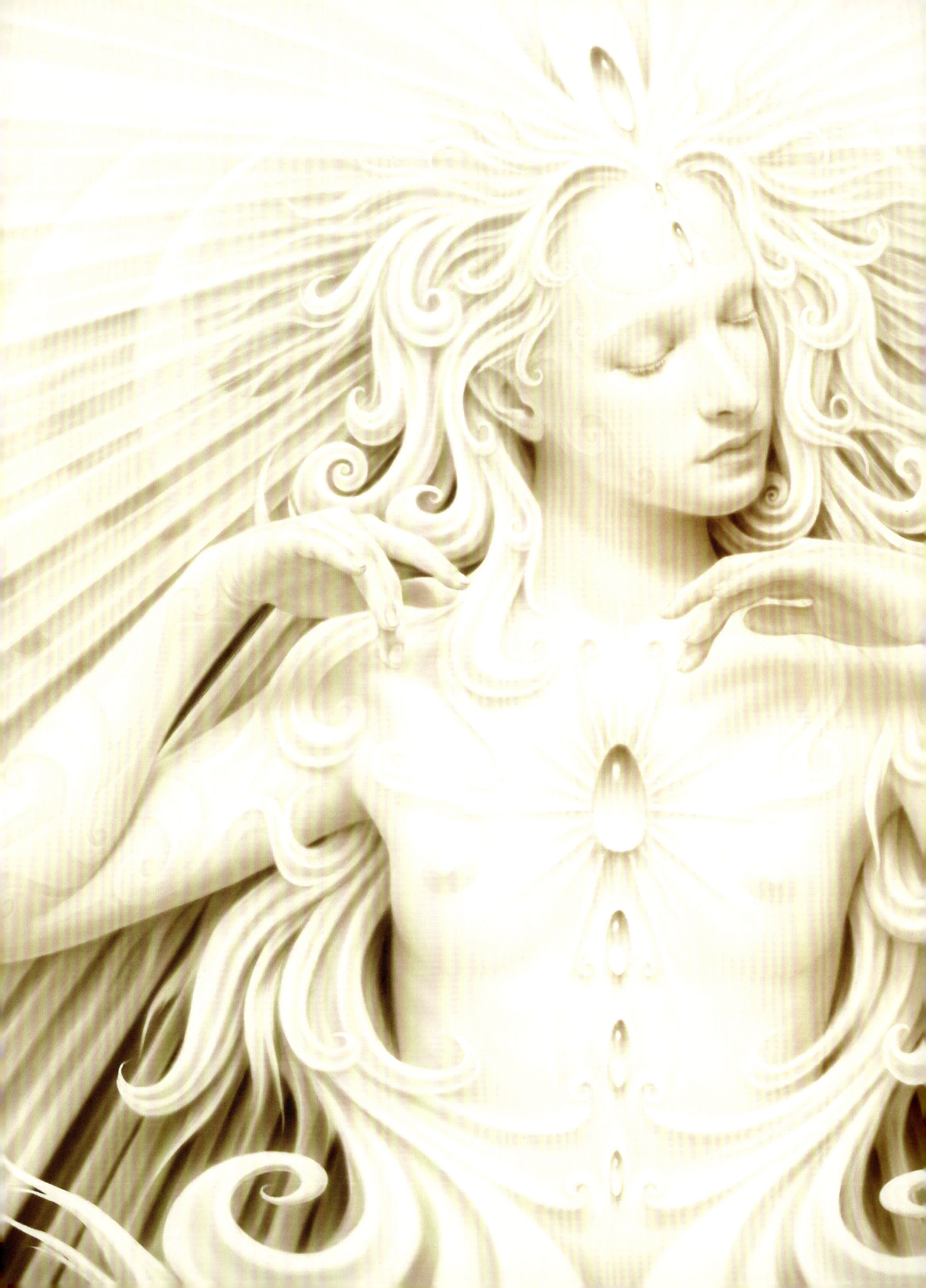

Book of WHITE LIGHT

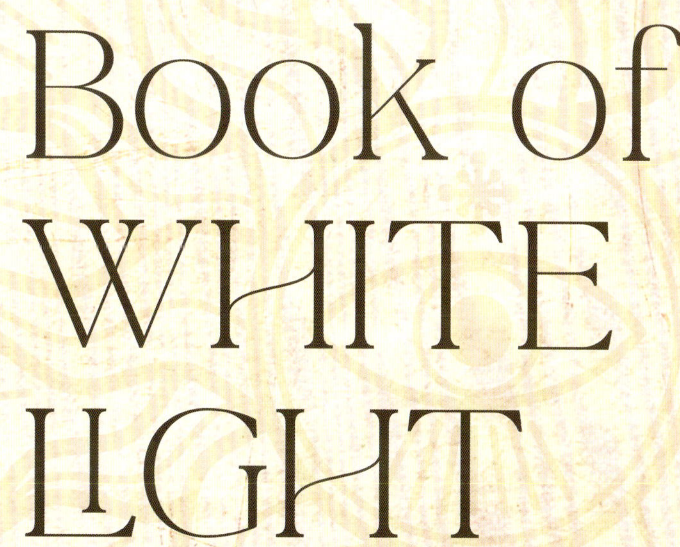

Incantations and Divinations for Sacred Activations with Frequencies of Sound and Light

Verse I

HOLY ENLIGHTENED ONES OF THE HEALING RAYS AND SOUNDS,
SANCTIFY AND SUPPORT THESE FREQUENCIES OF AFFIRMATION,
THAT ALL SACRED WORKS, INCLUDING THOSE THAT NOW FOLLOW,
BE DIVINELY UTILISED FOR THE GREATEST GOOD,
AMPLIFYING POSITIVE EFFECT FOR ALL BEINGS.

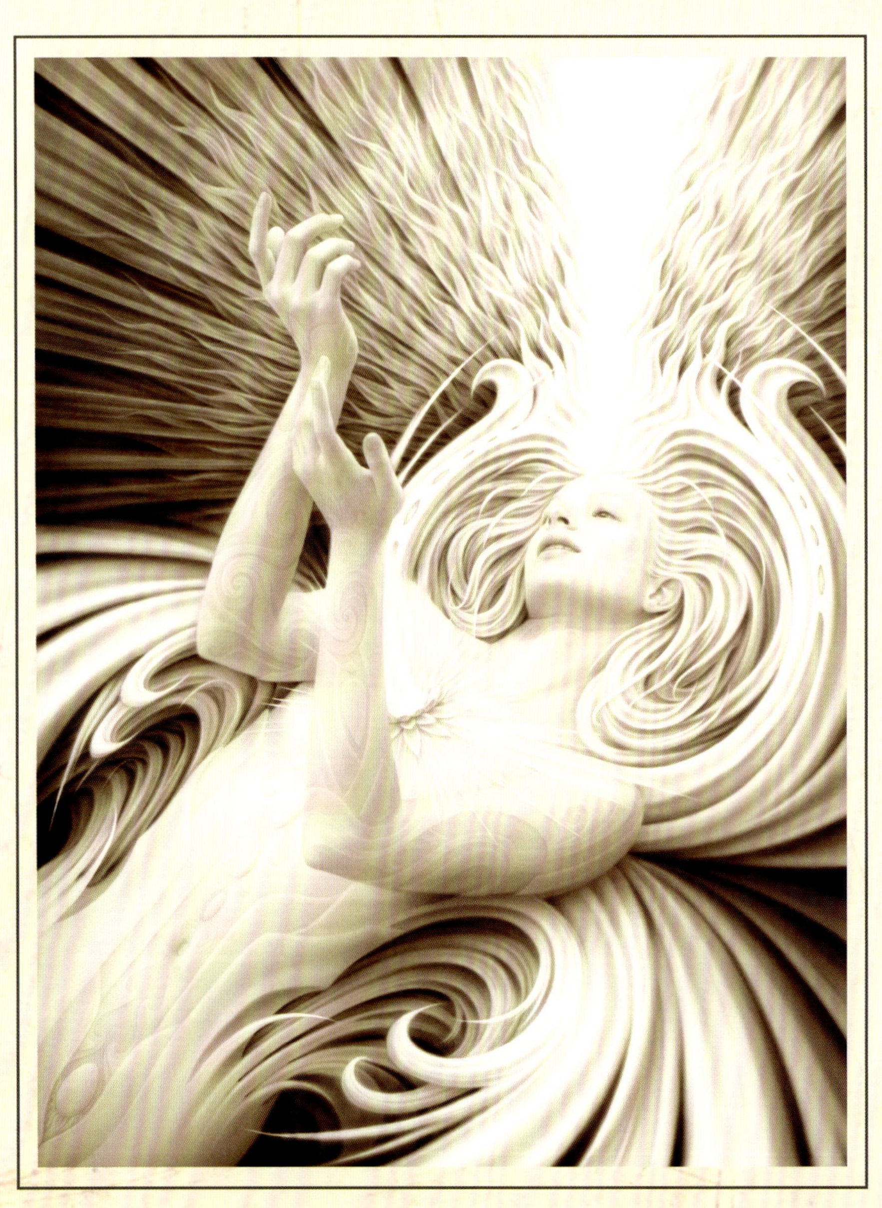

Opening my heart to universal wisdom,
I invoke unconditional love for the greatest good.
Pure frequencies of white light now fill this sacred space.

Through my heart channel,
Universal light radiates,
The unconditional love frequency 528.

Containing all colour vibrations and all wisdom medicines,
Spiritually expansive presence manifests fully, blissfully,
In abundant and blessed inspirational flow.

Through my heart channel,
Universal light radiates,
The unconditional love frequency 528.

Divine energies gather, circulate and coalesce,
As a sanctum of divine white light,
Encircling all, to protect and heal body, mind and soul.

Through my heart channel,
Universal light radiates,
The unconditional love frequency 528.

In this sanctity, I realise and own my worth,
I align my energy to create intentionally,
Becoming one with the Universal Heart.

Through my heart channel,
Universal light radiates,
The unconditional love frequency 528.

Verse II

Essence of the Universal Heart,
ever renewing and refreshing,
I abandon my attachment
to what has been,
and open myself to the process,
path and progress,
your great blessing has
bestowed upon me.

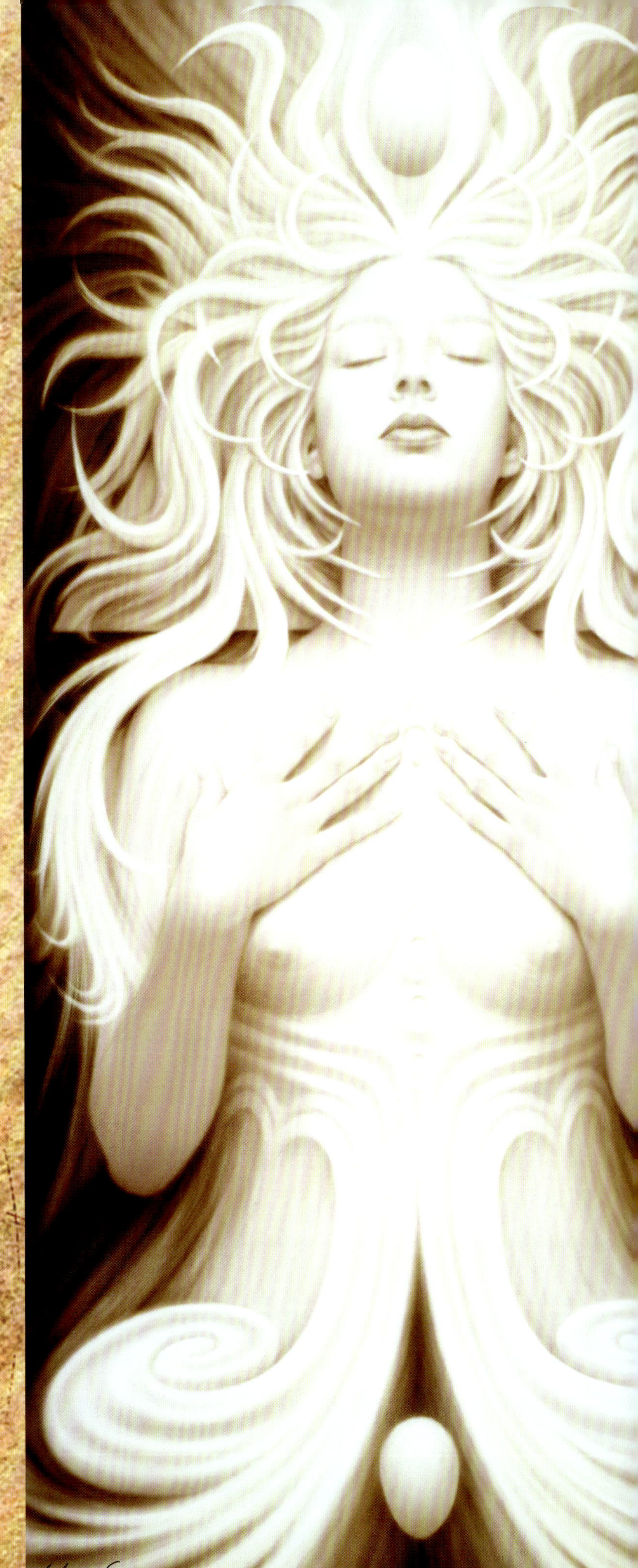

Guided by the liberating intelligence of my heart,
I release known worlds and greet fresh possibilities.

Frequency 639,
Sonic Gateway of Love Divine,
Recalibrate my energy and my mind,
With purest truth, path and purpose.

Soul-deep attractions inspire me to engage with life,
Enchanted, I boldly embrace vitalising pathways.

Frequency 639,
Sonic Gateway of Love Divine,
Recalibrate my energy and my mind,
With purest truth, path and purpose.

As expansive new horizons open naturally before me,
My spiritual devotion rises and rallies.

Frequency 639,
Sonic Gateway of Love Divine,
Recalibrate my energy and my mind,
With purest truth, path and purpose.

With wise trust in myself and affirmation of cosmic kindness,
I choose faith in my good fortune and what is destined to be.

Frequency 639,
Sonic Gateway of Love Divine,
Recalibrate my energy and my mind,
With purest truth, path and purpose.

Verse III

I CULTIVATE THE INTENTION, THE ALIGNMENT, THE CHOICE THAT WILL SET ME
FREE TO LOVE AND BE LOVED AS MY SOUL YEARNS TO BE.
ON THE INHALATION, I AFFIRM THE GIFT OF LIFE, PERFUMED WITH BLESSINGS.
ON THE EXHALATION, I SURRENDER AND COURAGEOUSLY EMBRACE SYMBOLIC
DEATH, LETTING GO IN ORDER TO ARISE ON THE NEXT INHALATION,
REBORN, RENEWED AND READY.

Universal Divine Heart, secrete your subtle fragrance,

Emit your secret nectars as blissful infusions,

Pulsing sweet euphoria through my sensitive yearning heart.

The past is now cleansed and liberated spiritually,

Through Atlantean 741 frequency.

Bathed and blessed in 396 of the Pleiades,

I magnetise grace of enlightened deity.

Your presence caresses and settles upon this soul,

Like ethers of sacred perfume upon this precious body,

Anointing this mind with beautiful balsams of your love.

The past is now cleansed and liberated spiritually,
Through Atlantean 741 frequency.
Bathed and blessed in 396 of the Pleiades,
I magnetise grace of enlightened deity.

Swept into unexpected ecstatic connection,
Troubles dissipating in our ethereal convergence,
I am transformed, emerging readied and replete.

The past is now cleansed and liberated spiritually,
Through Atlantean 741 frequency.
Bathed and blessed in 396 of the Pleiades,
I magnetise grace of enlightened deity.

Delicate attar of love, your scent evokes memory,
A rediscovery of strength, dignity and heroism within.
I am calm with certainty, I shall attain what I seek.

The past is now cleansed and liberated spiritually,
Through Atlantean 741 frequency.
Bathed and blessed in 396 of the Pleiades,
I magnetise grace of enlightened deity.

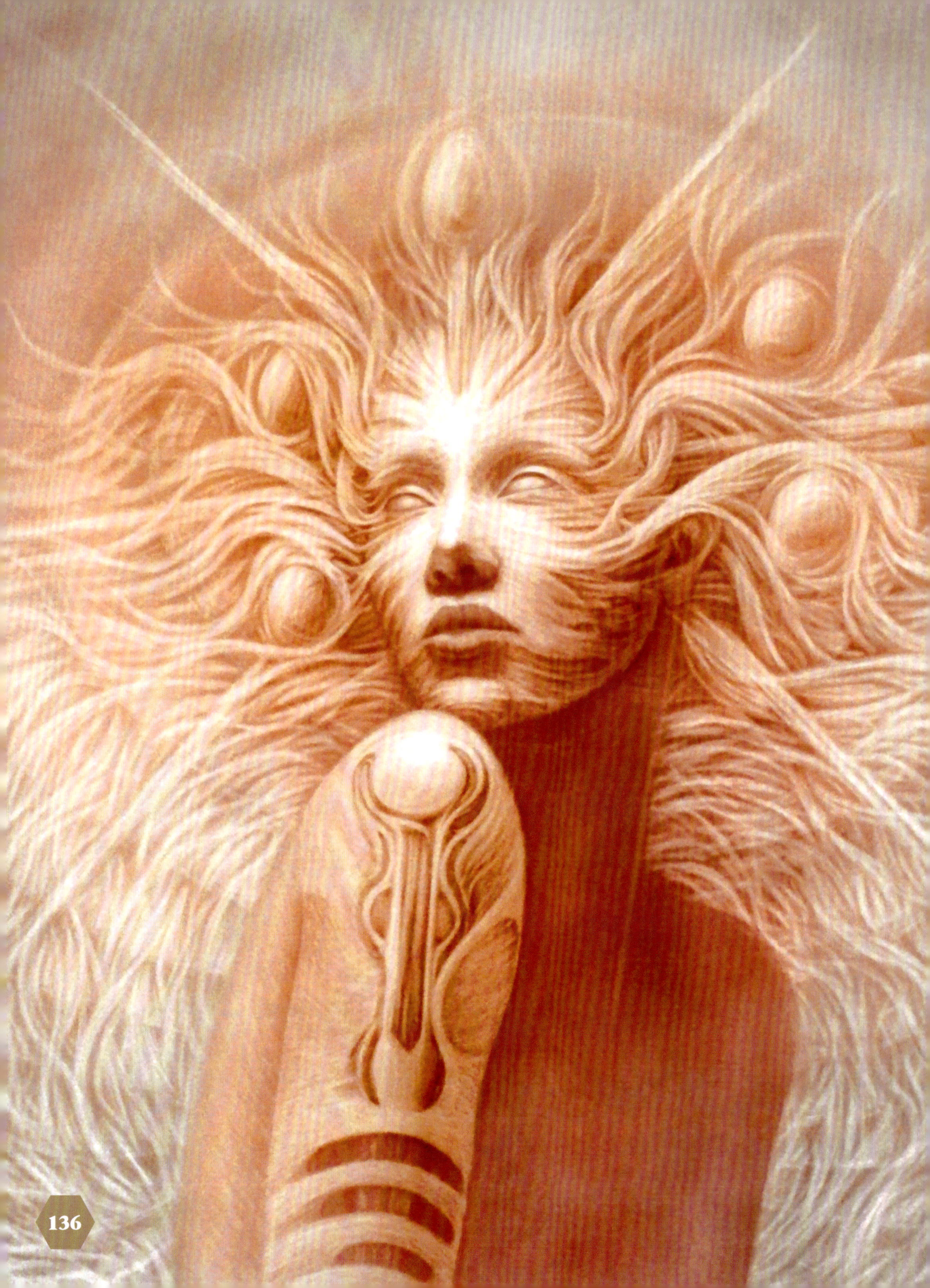

Verse IV

I gladly place my unwavering trust in spiritual tenderness,
And the way through all troubles is revealed with mercy.
I am spiritually strengthened through genuine devotion,
Courage arises and disarms all doubt.

Bat Kol 963, Angelic Voice of Divinity,
Recalibrate every manifestation,
Through your heavenly frequency,
And all hearts in need now receive,
Blessings through prayer songs of angels,
Kadoish, Kadoish, Kadoish,
Adonai Tsebayoth.

Relaxed with confidence in myself and divine timing,
I recognise the best choice and act at the best moment.
Surrendered as a channel for universal healing wisdom,
Goodness of the infinite manifests through me.

Bat Kol 963, Angelic Voice of Divinity,
Recalibrate every manifestation,
Through your heavenly frequency,
And all hearts in need now receive,
Blessings through prayer songs of angels,
Kadoish, Kadoish, Kadoish,
Adonai Tsebayoth.

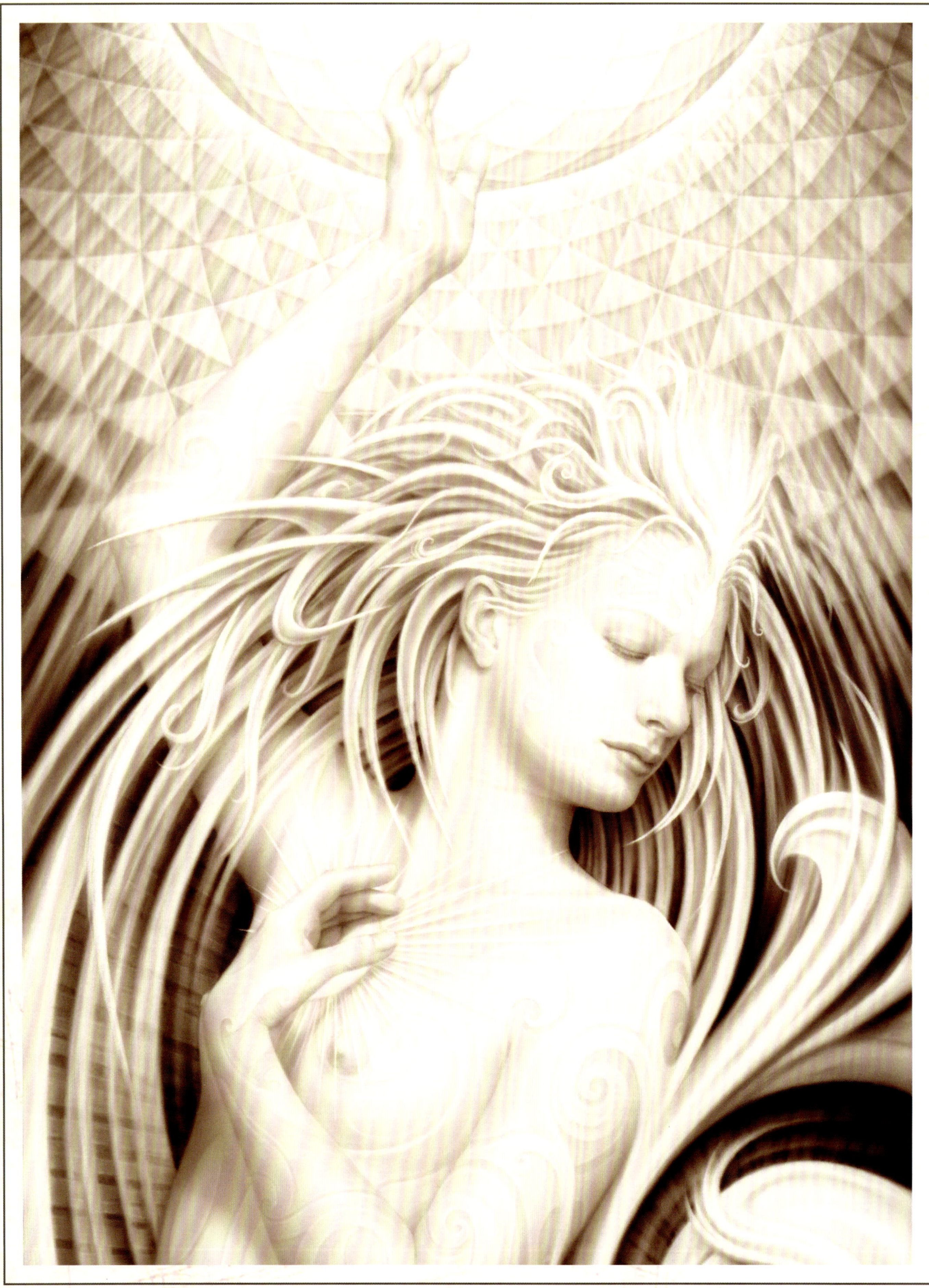

Verse V

MAY ALL WISHES BE FULFILLED WITH MERCY, COMPASSION AND WISDOM.
MAY ALL BEINGS FIND PEACE, HAPPINESS AND FREEDOM.
MAY ALL BEINGS FIND ENDURING SPIRITUAL SANCTUARY IN LOVE.

Recognising innate spiritual value,
I take pause to restore myself,
Reconnecting with loving truth,
I remember I am enough, and find peace.

Om Shanti Om.
Peace before me.

Om Shanti Om.
Peace behind me.

Om Shanti Om.
Peace to my right.

Om Shanti Om.
Peace to my left.

Om Shanti Om.
Peace above me.

Om Shanti Om.
Peace below me.

Om Shanti Om.
Peace around me.

Om Shanti Om.
Peace within me.

Honouring my spiritual values,
I orient myself to inner light,
Suffused with quiet confidence,
I know I am love and radiate peace.

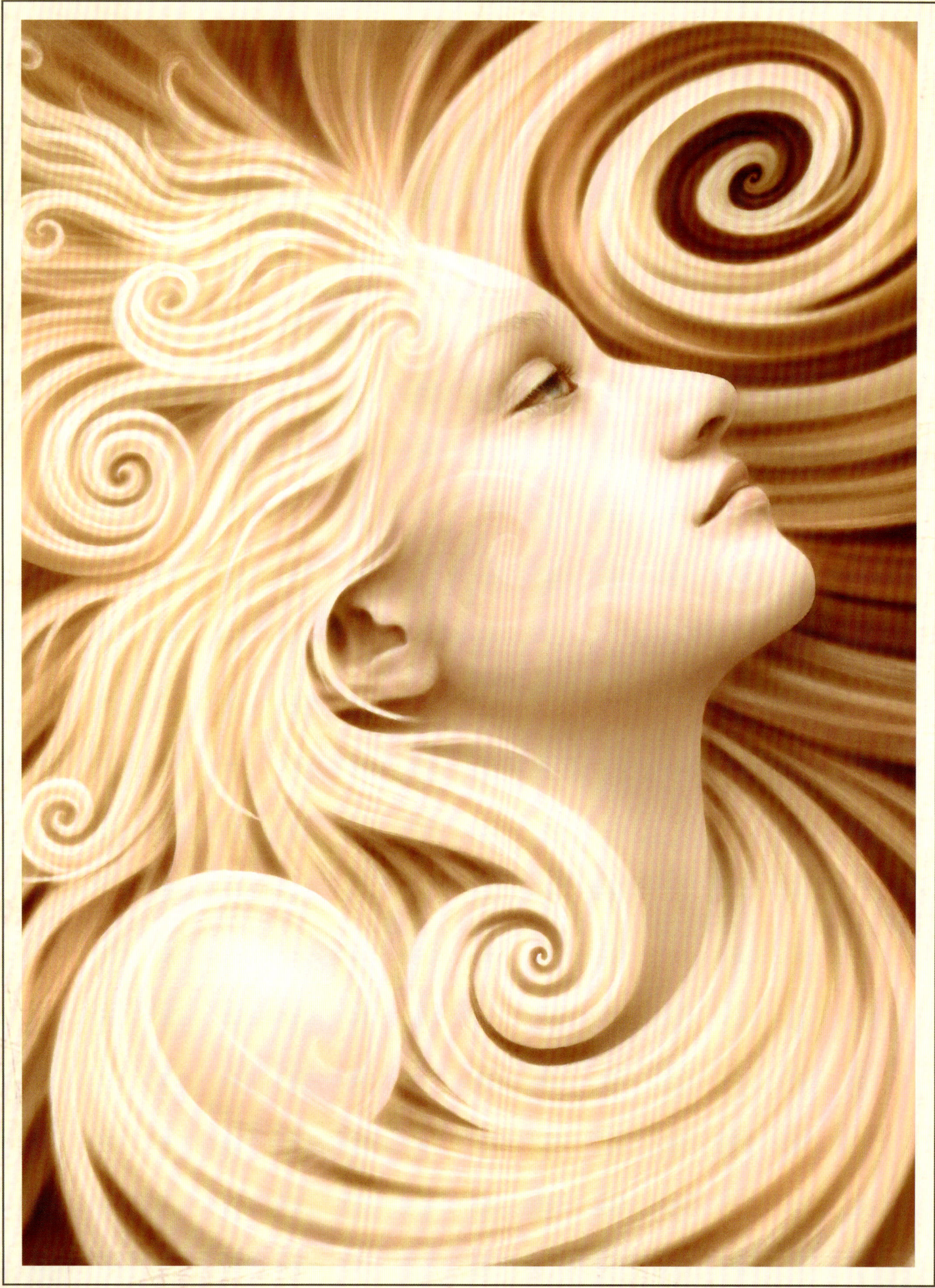

Verse VI

I AFFIRM THE REALITY OF HEALING AND MAGIC. I AFFIRM THE WILL OF THE UNIVERSE FOR BENEFICIAL TRANSFORMATION. I INVOKE ALL AWAKENED ALLIES AND LOVING DIVINE ENERGIES NECESSARY FOR BLISSFUL ASCENDANCY AND ATTAINMENT. SIRIUS 852, SPIRITUAL SUN OF HIGHER CONSCIOUSNESS, AND YOUR RADIANT RETINUE OF WISDOM BEINGS AND ENLIGHTENED PROTECTORS, SHINE YOUR SACRED LIGHT TO BRING FORTH MOST BLESSED FRUITION FOR THE SPIRITUAL BENEFIT OF ALL BEINGS.

Sacred synchronicities of alignment,
Joyful heroic allies of enlightenment,
Gather now in expression of grace!

Manna, soma, ambrosia, boon,
Inspiring sun and manifesting moon,
Through free will of this human divine,
Ample blessings attract and align.
Beneficial ascendancy shall manifest,
In time and way most truly blessed.

Verse VII

With spiritual creativity, I transform every experience
into soul-strengthening medicine.
My soul is my instrument,
and the artist within me is love.

I AM love.
I AM courage.
I AM wisdom.
I AM light.

I invoke Magdalene of 417,
Love's healing frequency aligning Earth with Heaven.
My heart entrained with your cosmic oscillation,
resounds as a living song of wisdom and love.
All negative momentum halts in divine decree of reversal,
As I become one in harmonic tantra with the Christ Universal.

I AM power.
I AM grace.
I AM creativity.
I AM blessing.

I invoke Magdalene of 417,
Love's healing frequency aligning Earth with Heaven.
My heart entrained with your cosmic oscillation,
resounds as a living song of wisdom and love.
All negative momentum halts in divine decree of reversal,
As I become one in harmonic tantra with the Christ Universal.

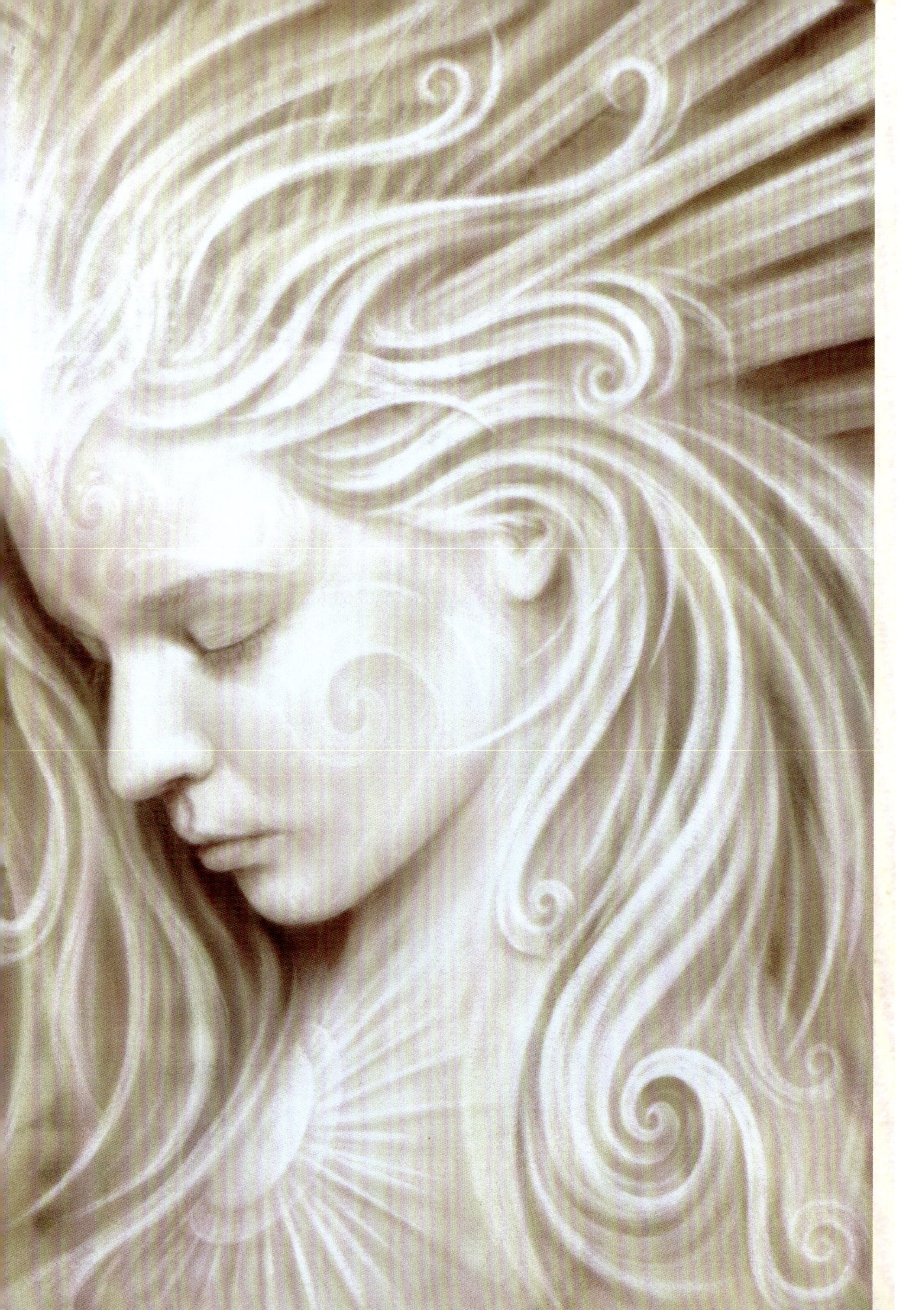

Verse VIII

THROUGH THIS VERSE OF PROTECTION TO BENEFIT ALL BEINGS,
I INVOKE DIVINE LIGHT RAYS OF WHITE, RED AND BLUE,
WITH THE THREE SACRED SYLLABLES OF TRUTH'S PERFECTION,
SO LOVE DOTH IMBUE BODY, ENERGY AND MIND,
WITH PURITY, STRENGTH AND PROTECTION.

OM AH HUM.

Medicine Buddha 285,

Lemurian wisdom brought to life,

Reconnecting essential bonds,

Positive energies are now strong.

The Universe supports me generously,

As I act to manifest my high destiny.

Radiant at my crown,

Shimmering White Light of OM,

My body cleansed and blessed.

OM AH HUM.

Medicine Buddha 285,

Lemurian wisdom brought to life,

Reconnecting essential bonds,

Positive energies are now strong.

The Universe supports me generously,
As I act to manifest my high destiny.

Radiant at my throat,
Shimmering Red Light of AH,
My energy clear and strong.

OM AH HUM.

Medicine Buddha 285,
Lemurian wisdom brought to life,
Reconnecting essential bonds,
Positive energies are now strong.

The Universe supports me generously,
As I act to manifest my high destiny.

Radiant at my heart,
Shimmering Blue Light of HUM,
My mind peaceful and steady.

OM AH HUM.

OM AH HUM.

Tayata Om Bekanze Bekanze Maha Bekanze Bekanze Ratza Samutgate Sohum.

Tayata Om Bekanze Bekanze Maha Bekanze Bekanze Ratza Samutgate Sohum.

Tayata Om Bekanze Bekanze Maha Bekanze Bekanze Ratza Samutgate Sohum.

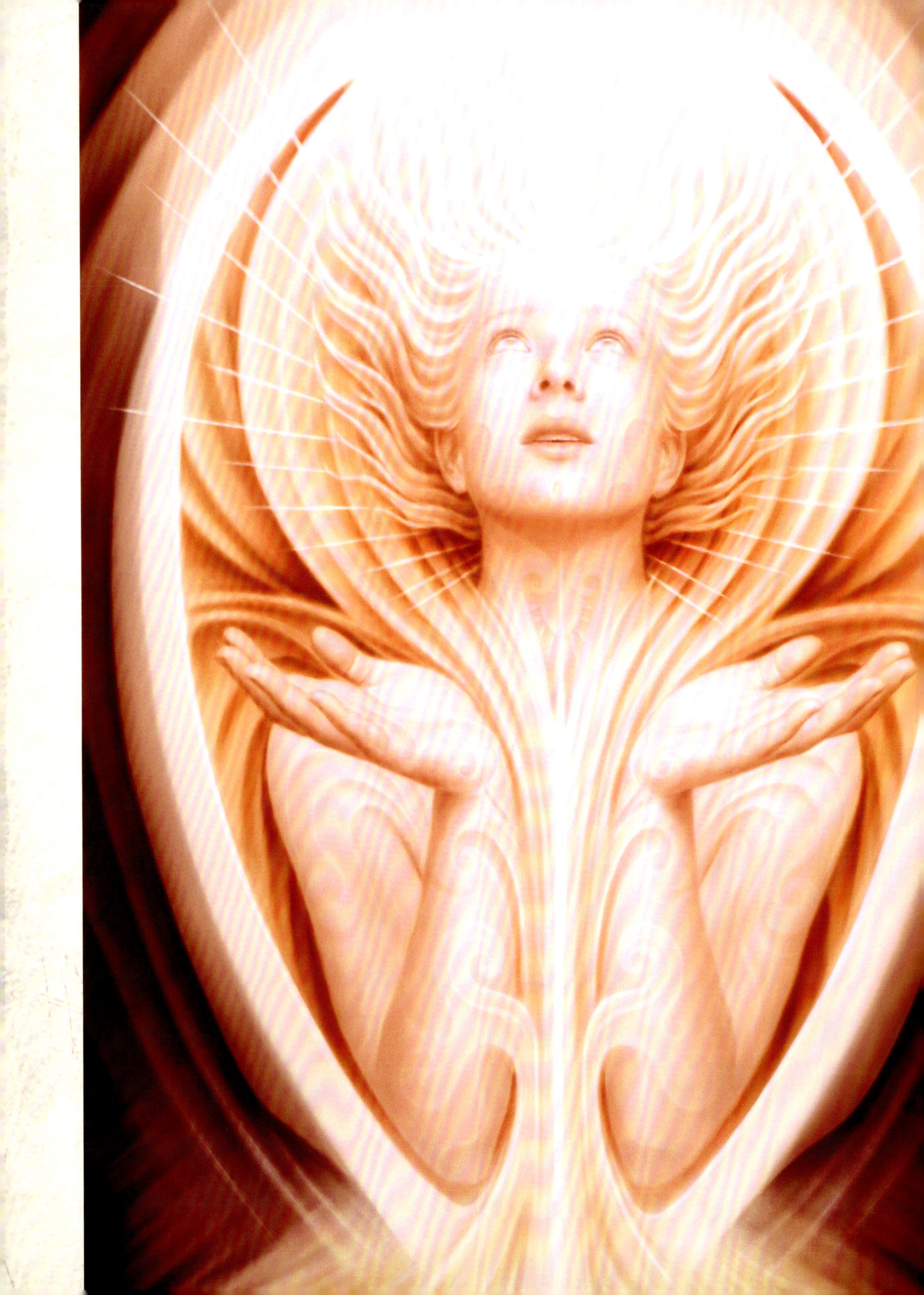

Verse IX

I am a prayer alchemist for humanity. My radical and inspired heart dares to invite the most outlandishly blessed interventions of light to benefit all beings.

I speak, envision, dream, express,
I rise, write, dance, redress.

Sri Ma, Jai Ma, Jai Jai Ma,
Amrit Ananda Maha Devi Ma.
Divine Mother, evoke the remedy,
To manifest perfect spiritual victory.

I sound sacred harmonic melody,
Invoke, embody and ground the remedy.

Sri Ma, Jai Ma, Jai Jai Ma,
Amrit Ananda Maha Devi Ma.
Divine Mother, evoke the remedy,
To manifest perfect spiritual victory.

For collective liberation, love I unbind,
Catalysing healing alchemy for humankind.

Sri Ma, Jai Ma, Jai Jai Ma,
Amrit Ananda Maha Devi Ma.
Divine Mother, evoke the remedy,
To manifest perfect spiritual victory.

Wisdom Mother reveal method and path,
Bestow all resources to accomplish your task.

Sri Ma, Jai Ma, Jai Jai Ma,
Amrit Ananda Maha Devi Ma.
Divine Mother, evoke the remedy,
To manifest perfect spiritual victory.

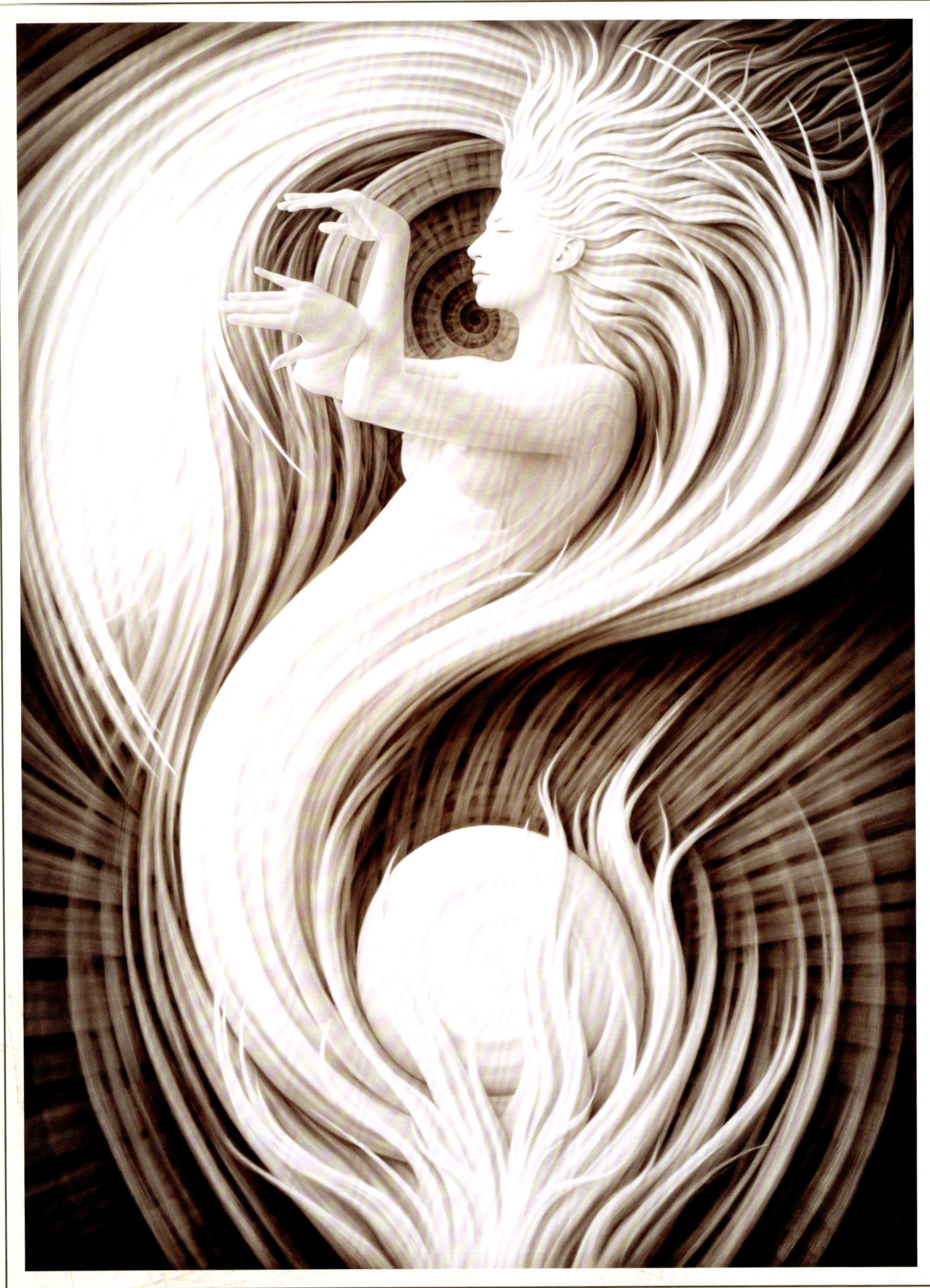

Verse X

You who are the Divine Rays of Light, Radiance Redux bearing Prosperity and Peace, restore our consciousness to abundance and alignment. You who are the Guardian of the Glory, providing protection through times of transition, bless all beings with your watchful wisdom. You who are the Cosmic Cornucopia of Plenty, transmute all vibrations through the alchemical frequency of 174 into wealth and good fortune, guiding all beings into the new era of generosity and grace.

Divine one manifesting as rays of light,
Om Marici Moom Swaha.

Beloved one bestowing miraculous grace,
Om Marici Moom Swaha.

Gentle one who can never be overcome,
Om Marici Moom Swaha.

Loving one enriching and protecting the path,
Om Marici Moom Swaha.

Golden pink vajra-lotus heart,
Secure and support sacred destiny,
Averting all obstacles with your divinity.

Om Marici Padme Hum.
Om Marici Padme Hum.

I am fearless and unstoppable,
Energised in the warmth of your love,
Acting with assurance and dignity.

Om Marici Padme Hum.
Om Marici Padme Hum.
Om Marici Padme Hum.
Om Marici Moom Swaha.

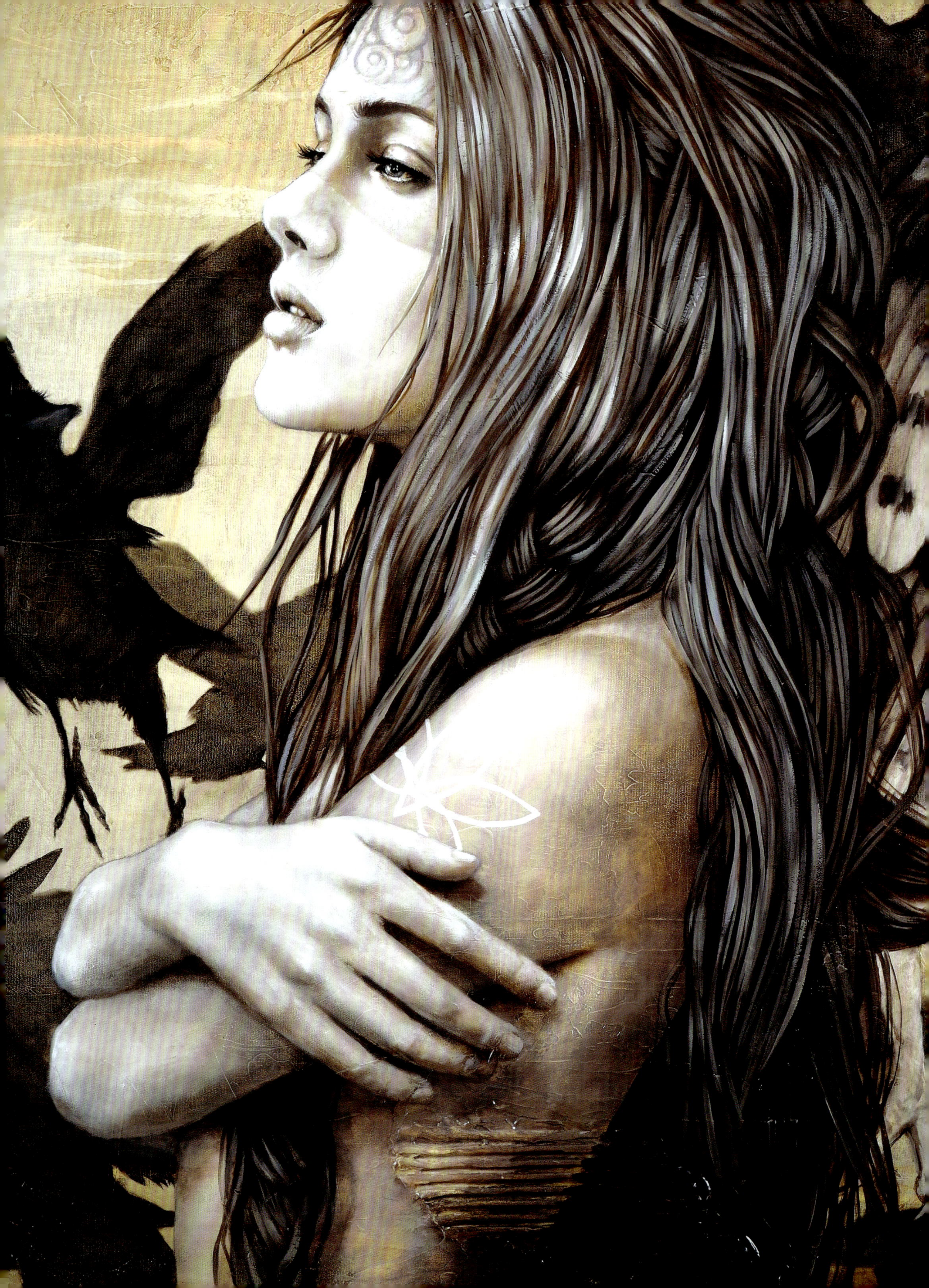

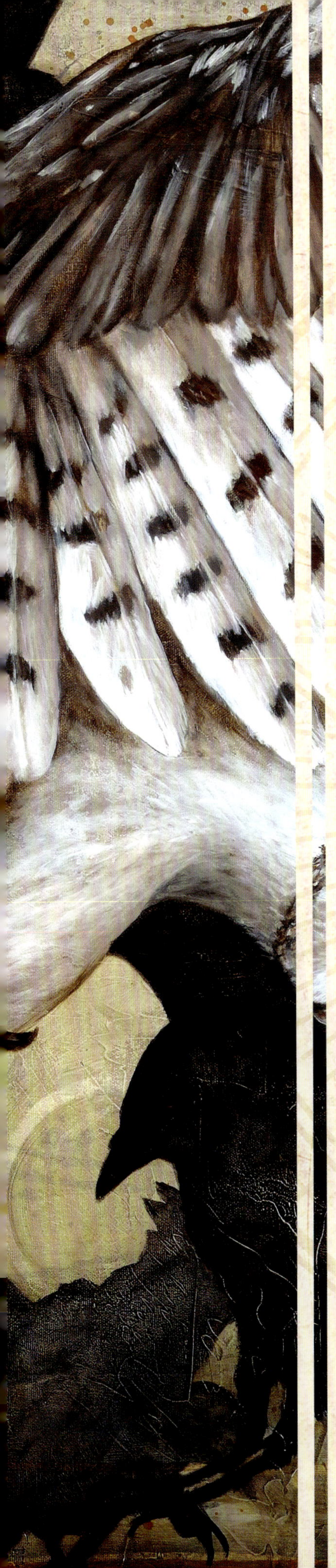

Book of MEDICINE HEART

Incantations and Divinations Evoking Heart Lineages of Medicinal Wisdom to Alchemise Divine Human Integration

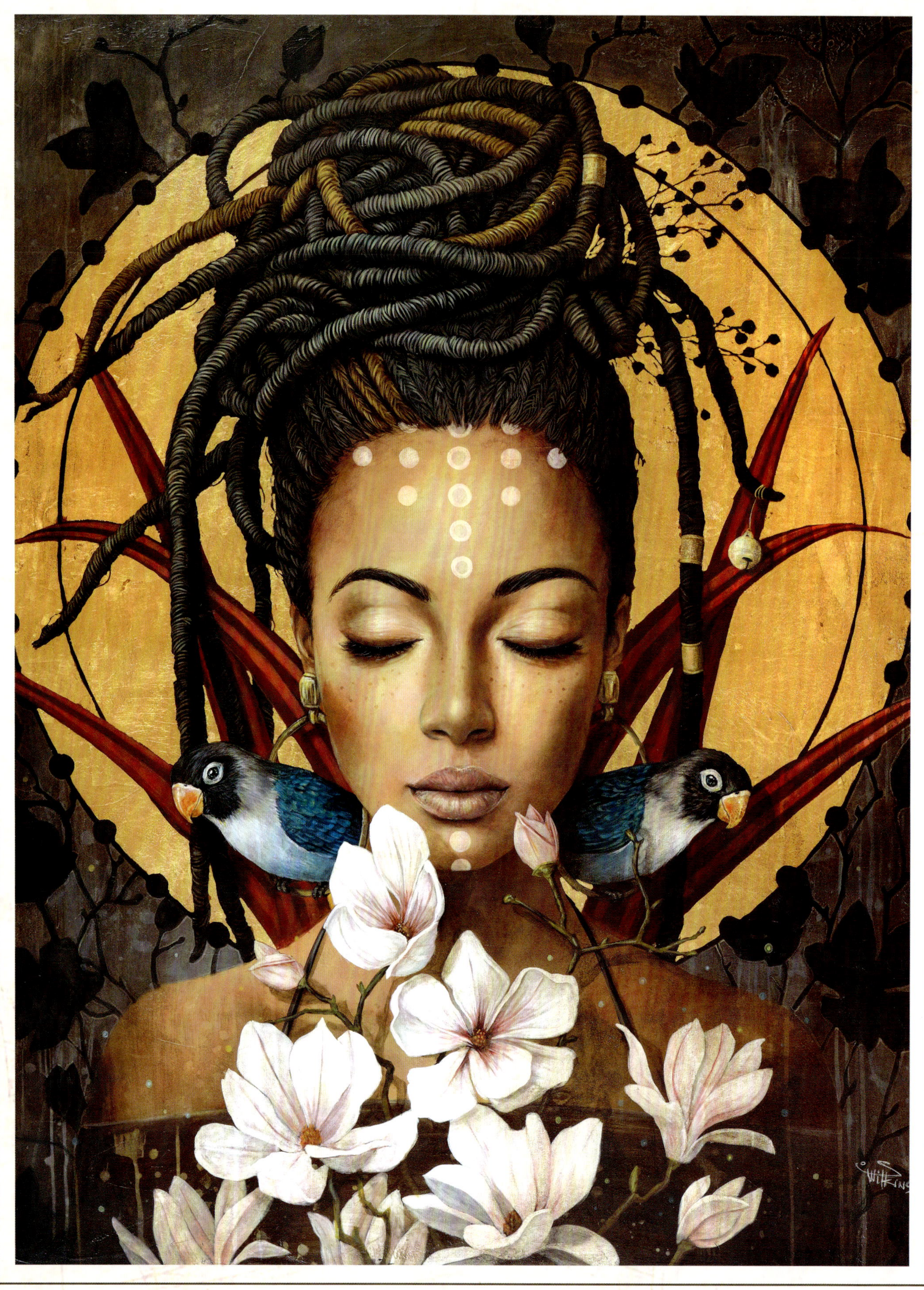

Verse I

FREE WILL AND SPIRITUAL RESPONSIBILITY ARE THE SACRED GROUND WITHIN WHICH THE HOLY SEEDS OF SOVEREIGNTY, PERSONAL POWER AND DIVINE POTENTIAL CAN GERMINATE. EVERY HUMAN HEART POSSESSES THESE PRECIOUS SEEDS. MAY THEY BE PROTECTED AND RIPENED THROUGH DIVINE LOVE.

Strong in spirit, with blessed heart, I stand in dignity as a self-sovereign being.

I affirm my freedom of choice and assume spiritual responsibility to choose my path and express my purpose according to the deepest truth.

I choose to live with personally resonant spirituality, reverence for the sacred, valuing dignity, strength and love.

For all ancestries supporting me over eons of evolution, for all lineages that continue to provide for my growth, I call upon the enlightened wisdom of healing unconditional love, that you may be strengthened and blessed. May my life be a loving testament to the great brightness that you radiate.

As I live, I learn.
As I love, I heal.
As I create, I evolve.

I claim my place, path and purpose, opening to the protective wisdom of all enlightened sources, to ensure the deep fulfilment that will generate bliss and benefit for all beings.

May such eternally loving light fill my heart and mind, guiding me with unwavering kindness.

Strong in spirit, with blessed heart, I assume my place in the abode of awakened ones.

Verse II

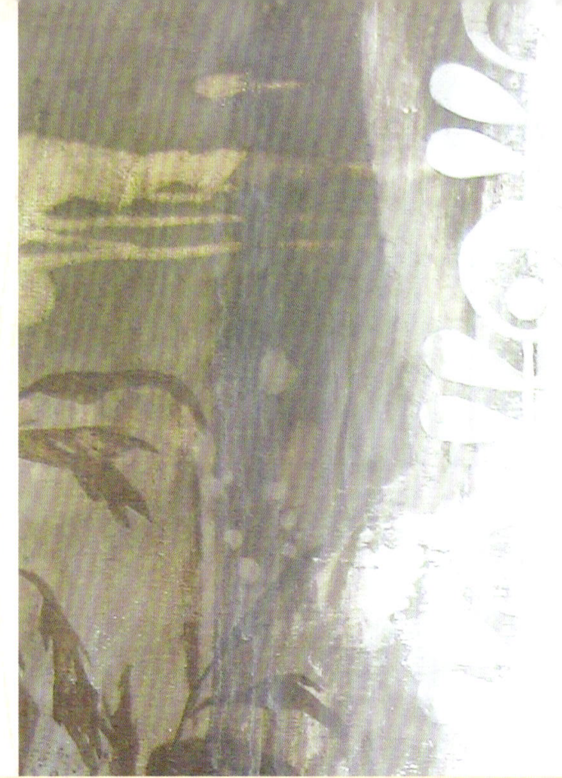

Way-showers of wild wisdom, I invoke my divine birthright of spiritual knowledge, to access the unconditioned truth and the way to genuine attainment. May your divinity of love and healing vibrate in my bones, animate my blood, and infuse lifeforce through my heart. Holy ones, evoke deep, abiding resonance in my mind, so I instantly recognise and proceed on the path to best and blessed outcome.

I open my mind to the light-bearers who practise truth and liberate the courageous hearts of the faithful.

I receive spiritual protection and return fully to my body, being and breath, grounded in presence and grace.

I witness the reality of the divine hand guiding mine, and stay true to my higher self and my authentic path.

I allow divine blessing into my heart, untangling thoughts to bestow both patience and peace.

I practise faith in the Universal Heart, affirming my devotion and amplifying receptivity to the boundless assistance it provides.

Through my hand, my heart, my voice,
My mind, my actions and my choice,
May genuine benefit now manifest,
For highest healing of all.

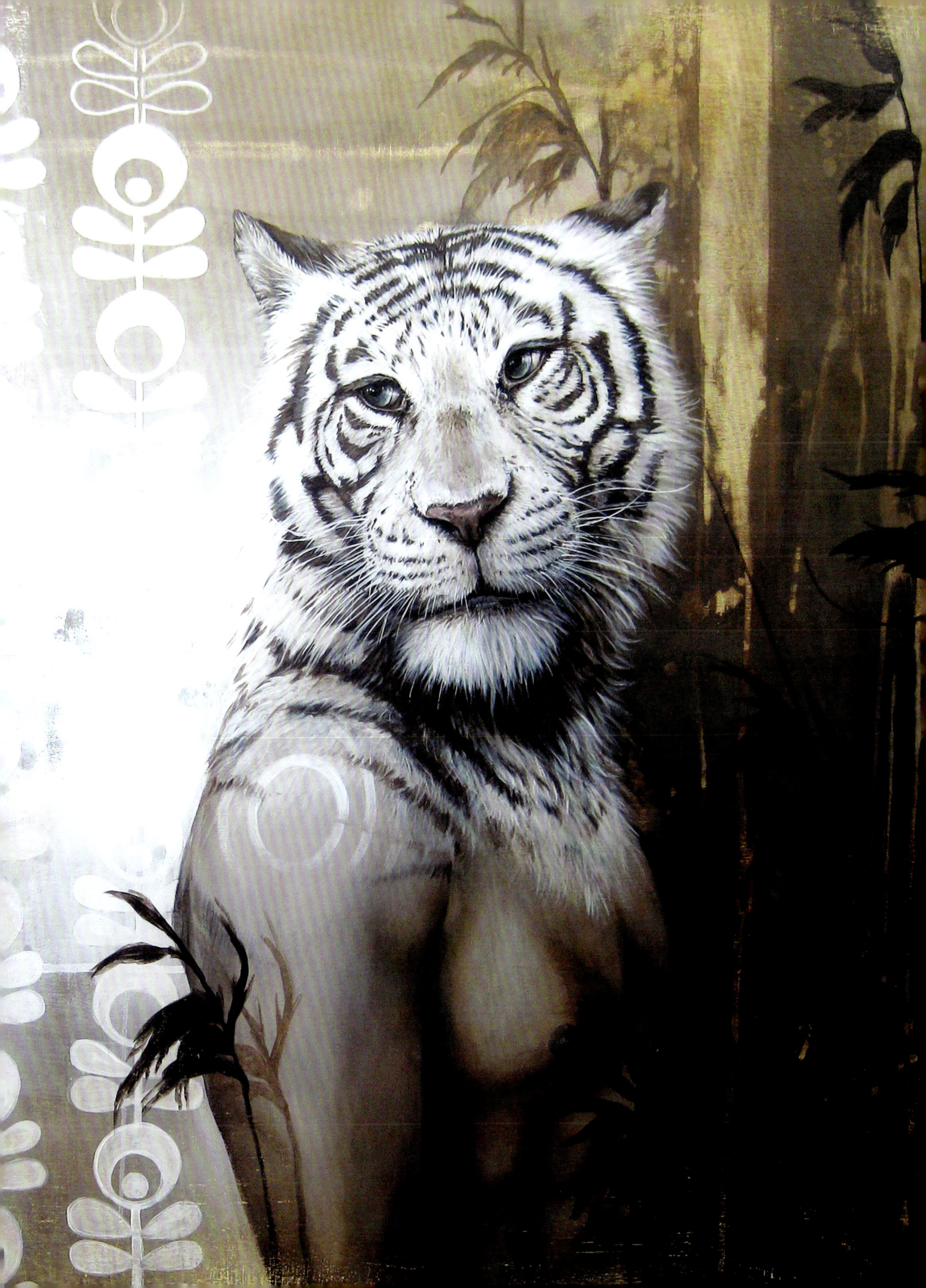

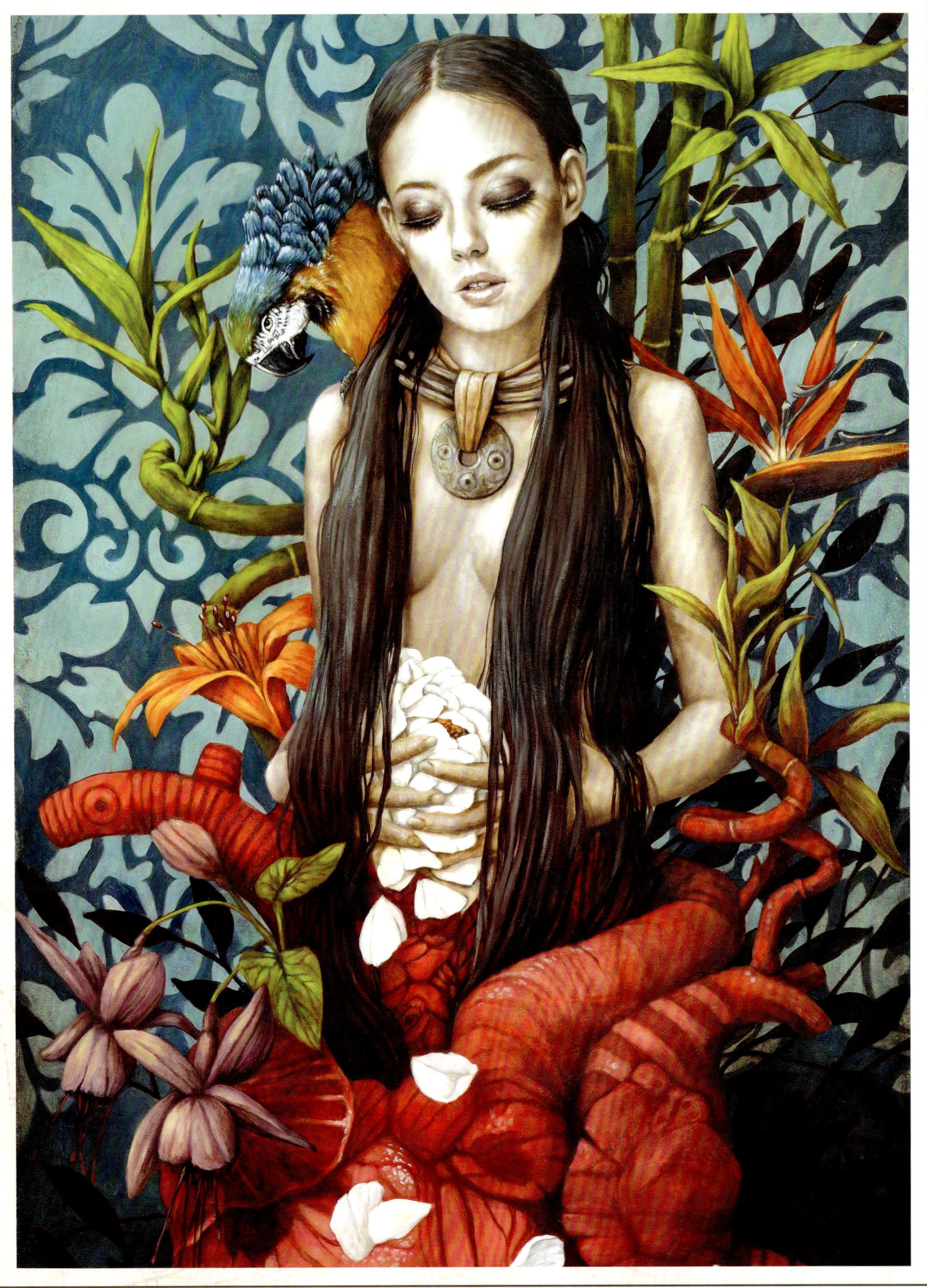

Verse III

THE EYE WITHIN MY HEART SEES WITH AN OTHERWORLDLY VISION, PERCEIVING HEALING POTENTIAL IN EVERY EXPERIENCE. SUCH CARDIOGNOSIS STRENGTHENS MY RESOLVE, AND IN THE SPIRITUAL DIMENSIONS, MY SOUL IS KNOWN AS SAGE AND WARRIOR, ALIGNED WITH DIVINITY AND UNCONQUERABLE WITH LOVE'S POTENCY.

Journey of love leads me into depths of darkness,
Where I meet the wisdom of symbolic death.

Initiated into knowledge beyond this world,
I embrace secret blessing of figurative dying.

Turning arcane key to catalyse alchemy,
I release myself into sacred transmutation.

Hope and courage evoke mystical resurrection,
I arise as Phoenix spirit from ashes of what once was.

Because I possess courage, I find comfort in unfolding process.
Because I possess creativity, I find confidence in powerful inspiration.
Because I possess trust, I find certainty in inevitable blessing.

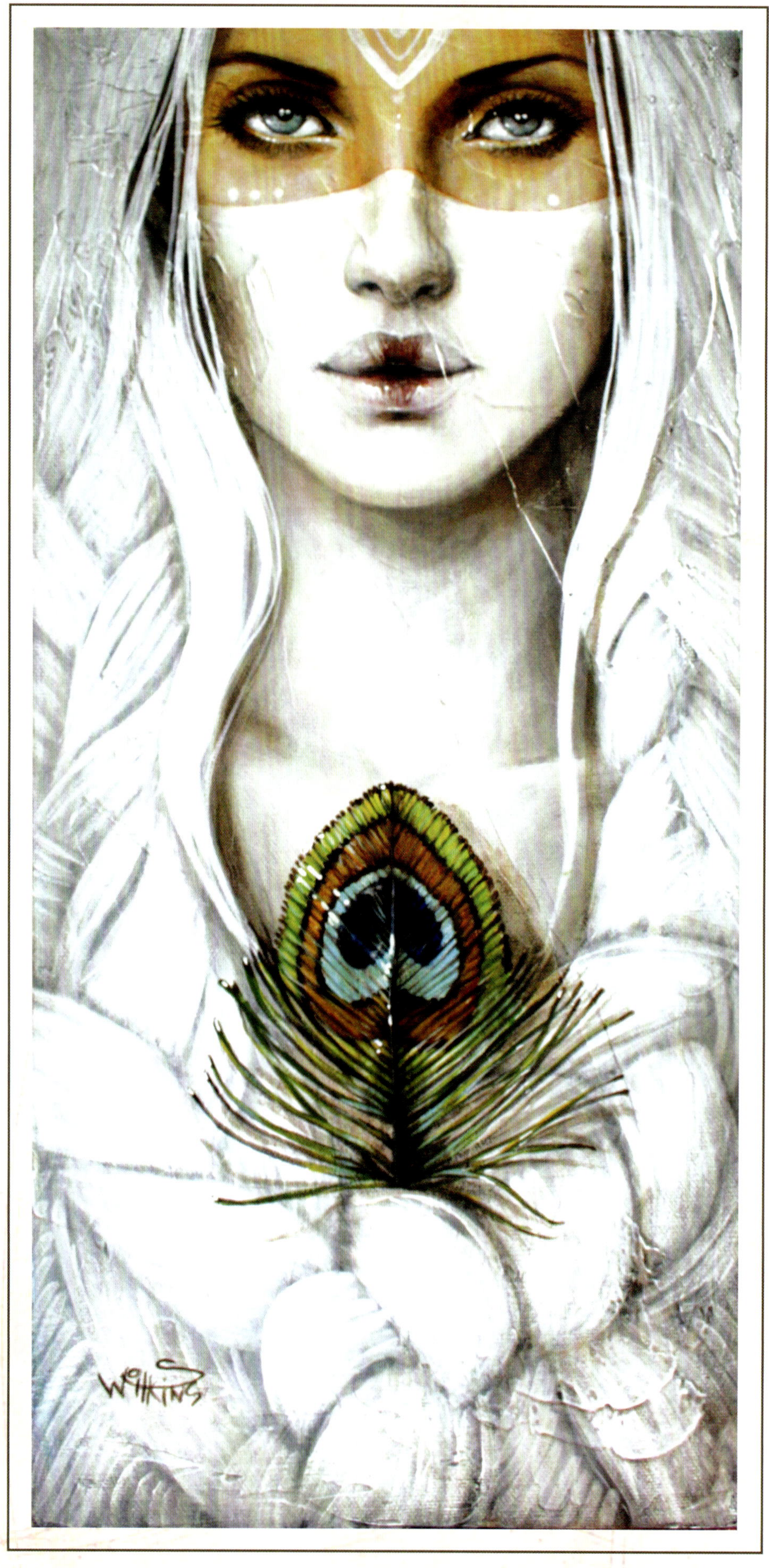

Verse IV

DIVINE BLESSINGS FLOW THROUGH ME AS IF I WERE HOLLOW BONE, STRONG ENOUGH TO CONTAIN THE POWER AND CLEAN ENOUGH TO PRESERVE THE PURITY. DIVINE RIPENING FLOURISHES THROUGH ME, AS IF I WERE SWEET FRUIT ON VERDANT VINE, MY HEART BLOOMING INTO EMANATIONS OF DIVINITY, SUMPTUOUS WITH NOURISHMENT FOR ALL SOULS.

Hollow bone, sweet heart,

I trust in the higher wisdom which cannot always be
consciously understood.

Hollow bone, sweet heart,

I surrender into the mysteries of my life which are
bestowing blessings yet to be revealed.

Hollow bone, sweet heart,

I am faithful to love's purity and purpose, and I conquer
every criticism with compassion.

Hollow bone, sweet heart,

I value my place within Life's greater unfolding, and
discover trustful belonging with all of creation.

Hollow bone, sweet heart,

I cultivate the joyful wisdom of trust in the goodness of
what is becoming.

Verse V

Supreme Mother, you are the intelligence within my heart that knows how to love and nurture and grow. You are the wisdom within that yields to life's flow, yet remains resilient and creative. I invoke your generosity, intervention and guidance. Please reveal the path and provide the means to accomplish it. I, the child of your divine heart, will apply myself to attain what is being asked of me. With your blessings, I shall succeed and contribute meaningfully to your loving dispensations of mercy.

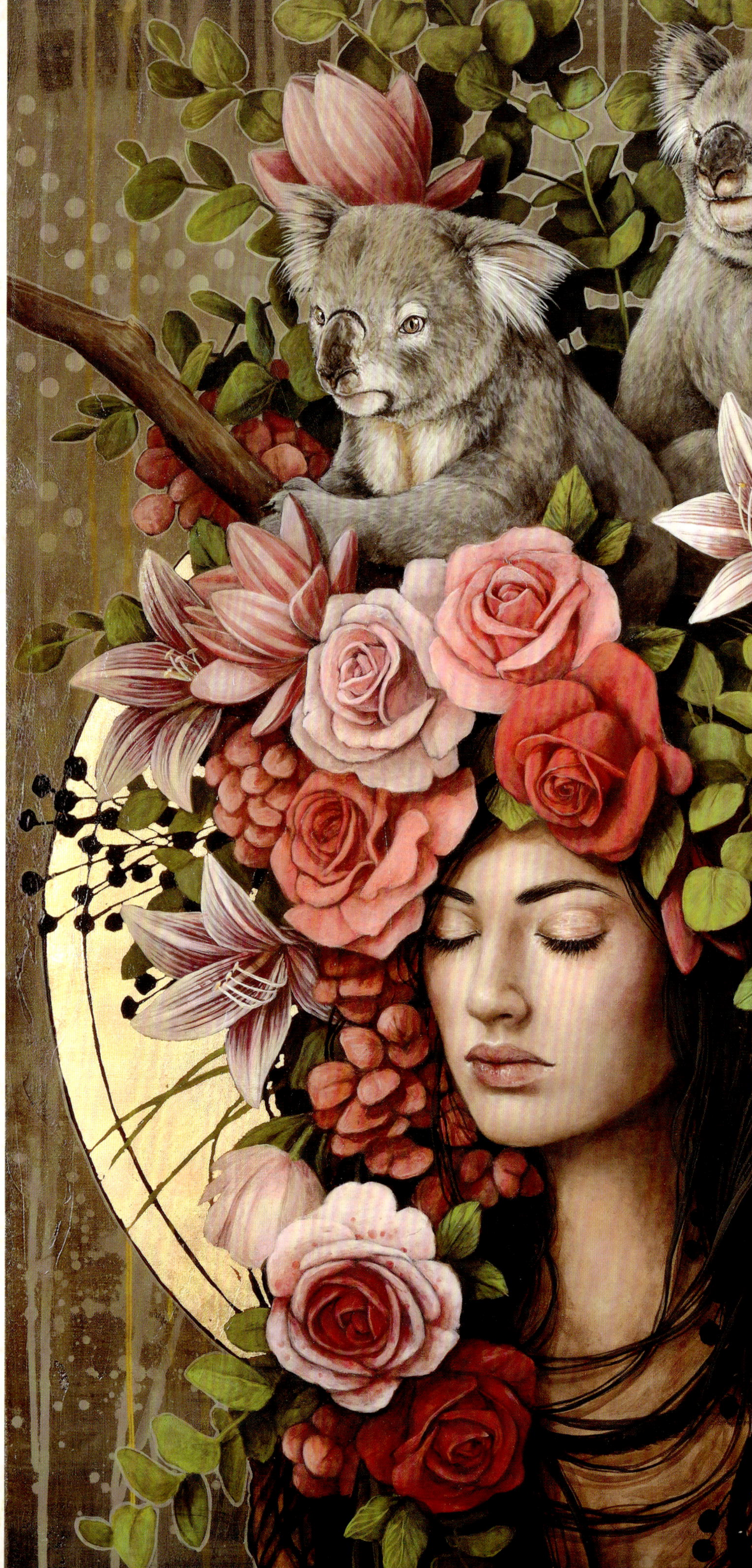

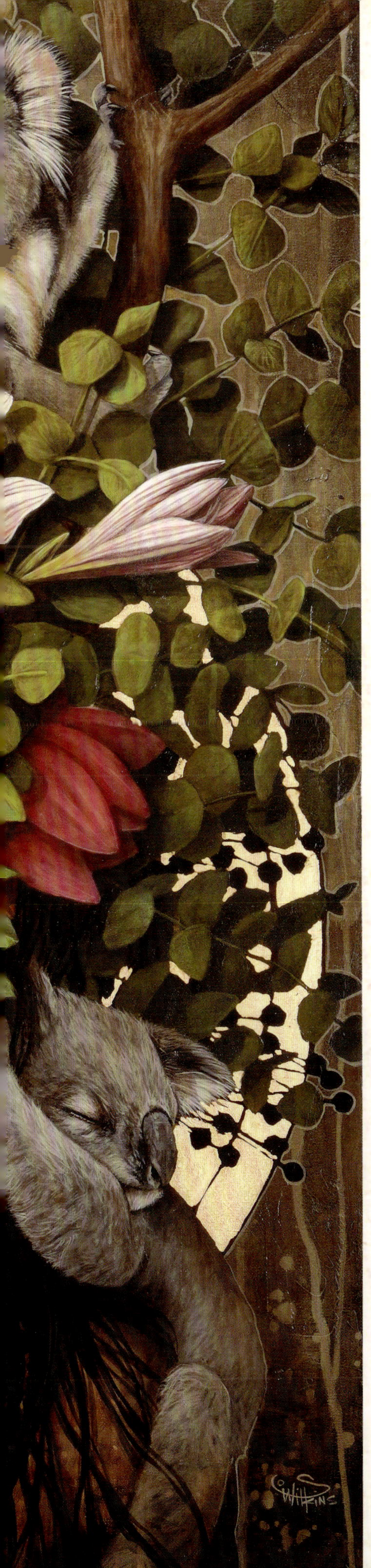

Sri Ma Parameshwari, Supreme Mother,
Repair and restore my being, manifesting your
loving prosperity which brings enlightenment and
peace.

Sri Ma Parameshwari, Supreme Mother,
Facilitate spiritual ripening with mercy, that I may
learn and evolve beyond what I have known, into
the beauty of what you wish for me.

Sri Ma Parameshwari, Supreme Mother,
Heal the brokenness within, cleansing the karma
that led to the break, so I may become stronger and
wiser through every experience.

Sri Ma Parameshwari, Supreme Mother,
Transform my suffering into blissful realisation,
unveiling an abundance of once-hidden gifts,
kindness and love.

Sri Ma Parameshwari, Supreme Mother,
Guide me to discover, develop and express the
fullness of my being, that I may faithfully radiate the
gleaming divine presence within me.

Sri Ma Parameshwari, Supreme Mother,
You who provide the method and the means, bless
me with all that is needed to attain my soul's great
and joyful path.

Sri Ma Parameshwari, Supreme Mother,
May I accomplish complete realisation of our
closeness, which is oneness shining as divine love in
all hearts, to benefit all beings.

Verse VI

With pure heart and clear mind,
I invoke the deity circle of tantric wisdom.

Holy Spirit in the East,
Bestows healing speech.

Beloved Mataji in the South,
Manifests ripening divine fire.

Mother Mary in the West,
Exudes waters for birthing.

Yeshua in the North,
Catalyses divinity in humanity.

Shakyamuni in the Centre,
Radiates calm abiding.

Enlightened ones in unity of love, with profoundest
gratitude I invite your presence, blessing and grace to
infuse this sacred space.

Opening within, Divine Feminine,
Arising within, Divine Masculine,
Intimate Holy Tantra begins,
As presence and light, unite.

Illuminate my heart and mind, clearing confusion and
returning me to realisation of my innate fortitude and
confidence.

Opening within, Divine Feminine,
Arising within, Divine Masculine,
Intimate Holy Tantra begins,
As presence and light, unite.

My resolve is strengthened. I assume the space and place
that is rightfully mine and proceed on my path of destiny.

Opening within, Divine Feminine,
Arising within, Divine Masculine,
Intimate Holy Tantra begins,
As presence and light, unite.

With determination, I find the strength and discipline to
bring inspiration through to fruition.

Opening within, Divine Feminine,
Arising within, Divine Masculine,
Intimate Holy Tantra begins,
As presence and light, unite.

Beloved ones, dissolve into one and dissolve into light
in my heart, sealing the blessing and ensuring holiest
fruition.

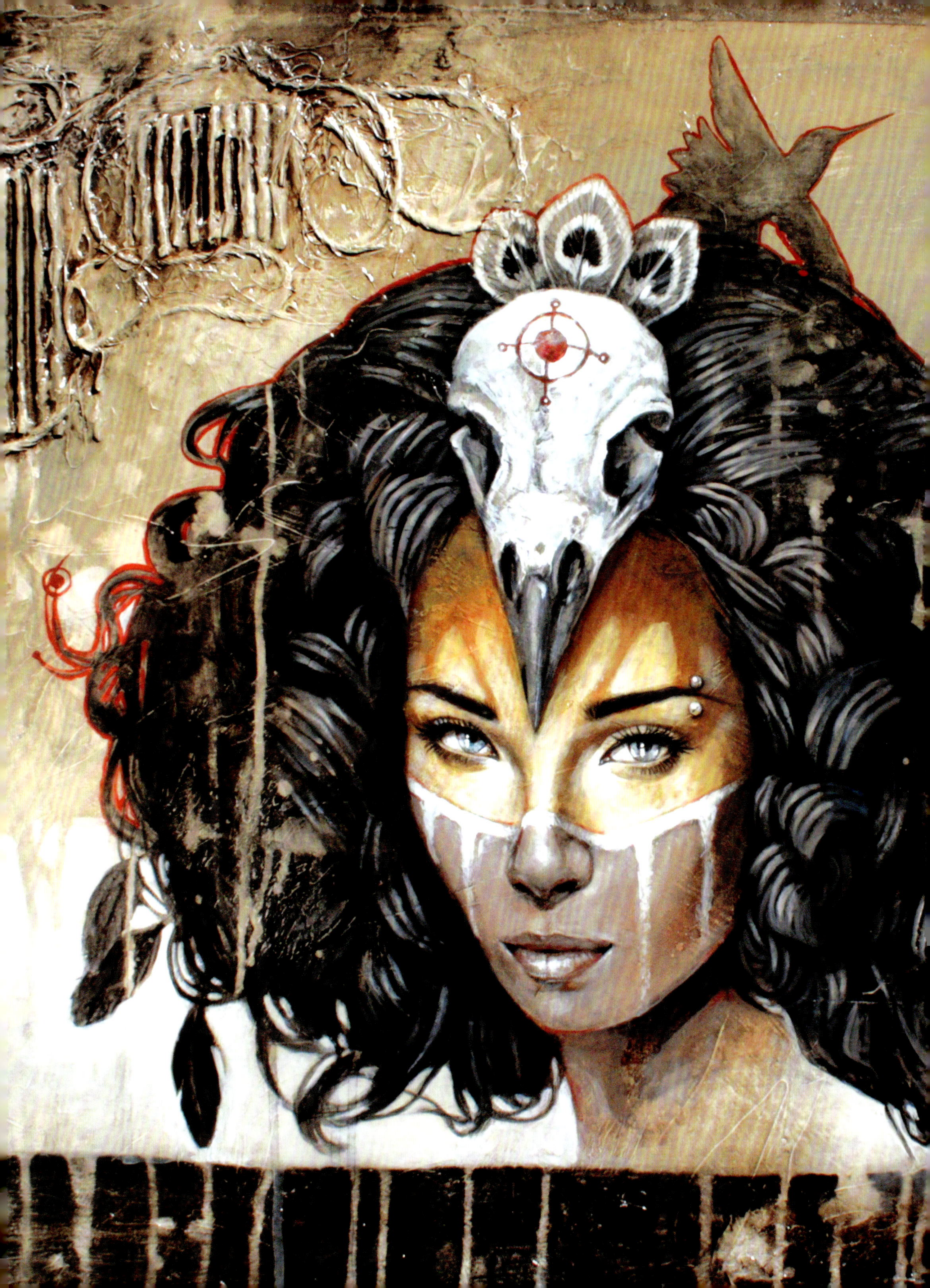

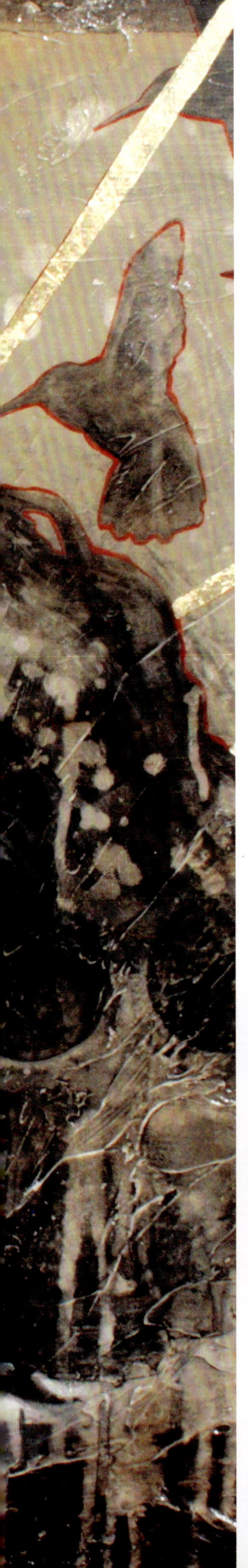

Verse VII

Whilst I embrace full presence in this moment,
I acknowledge the places I need to be,
To fulfil divine mandate of high destiny.

Hayagriva, Vishnu, Chenrezig,
Manifest your swift pace.
Accelerate my process,
With tender, merciful grace.

With spiritual quickening, evolution intensifies,
Karmic obstacles arise as path comes into view,
Yet also give way rapidly, as I place my trust in you.

Hayagriva, Vishnu, Chenrezig,
Bestow your swift pace.
Protect my path and process,
With tender, merciful grace.

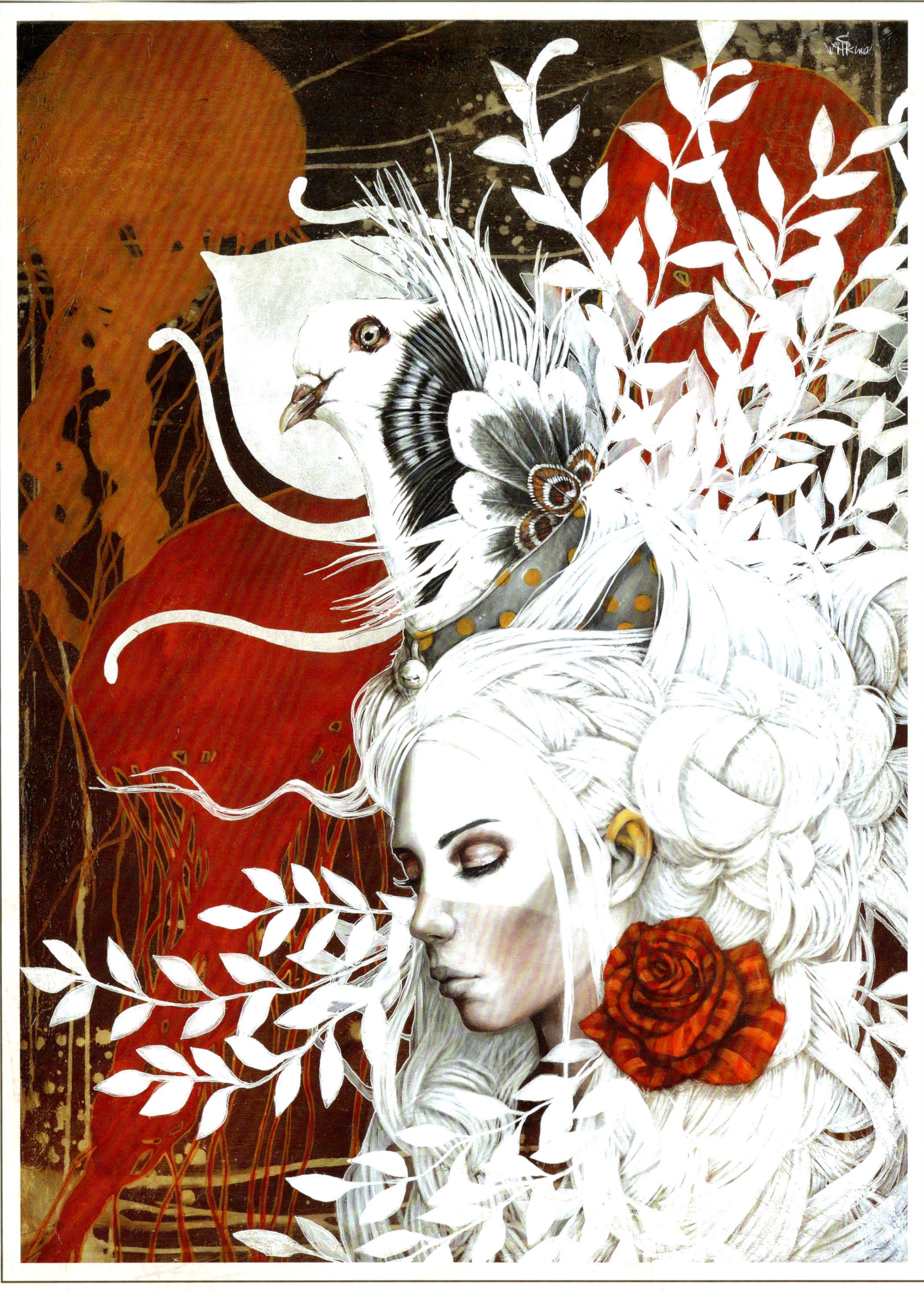

Verse VIII

SHINING ENCHANTRESS, PADMA SORCERESS, HEROIC RED QUEEN, I CHANT THIS INCANTATION OF PROTECTION, DIVINING YOUR BLESSED INTERVENTION. IN ALL THAT I SEEK TO ACCOMPLISH, FOR THE HIGHEST GOOD OF ALL, MAY YOUR PRESENCE BE HONOURED AS GUIDE AND GUARD, ENSURING TRUEST FULFILMENT.

Red Amulet of Kurukulla, shining bright,
Heroic Enlightened Lady, illuminate my heart,
Guard and protect my mind.

Om Kurukulle I Irih Sohum.

Magnetic grace of red dancing goddess,
Attracts, amplifies and anchors the positive,
Deflecting all else with resilient compassion.

Om Kurukulle Hrih Sohum.

Even in vulnerability, I affirm spiritual strength.
Safe in the knowledge of your all-accomplishing capacity,
Wise boldness and willingness energise my being.

Om Kurukulle Hrih Sohum.

Amulet of Trust, ruby red spirit gem,
Radiating your divine protection and power,
Mother Divine Crystalline, vitalise unyielding good.

Om Kurukulle Hrih Sohum.

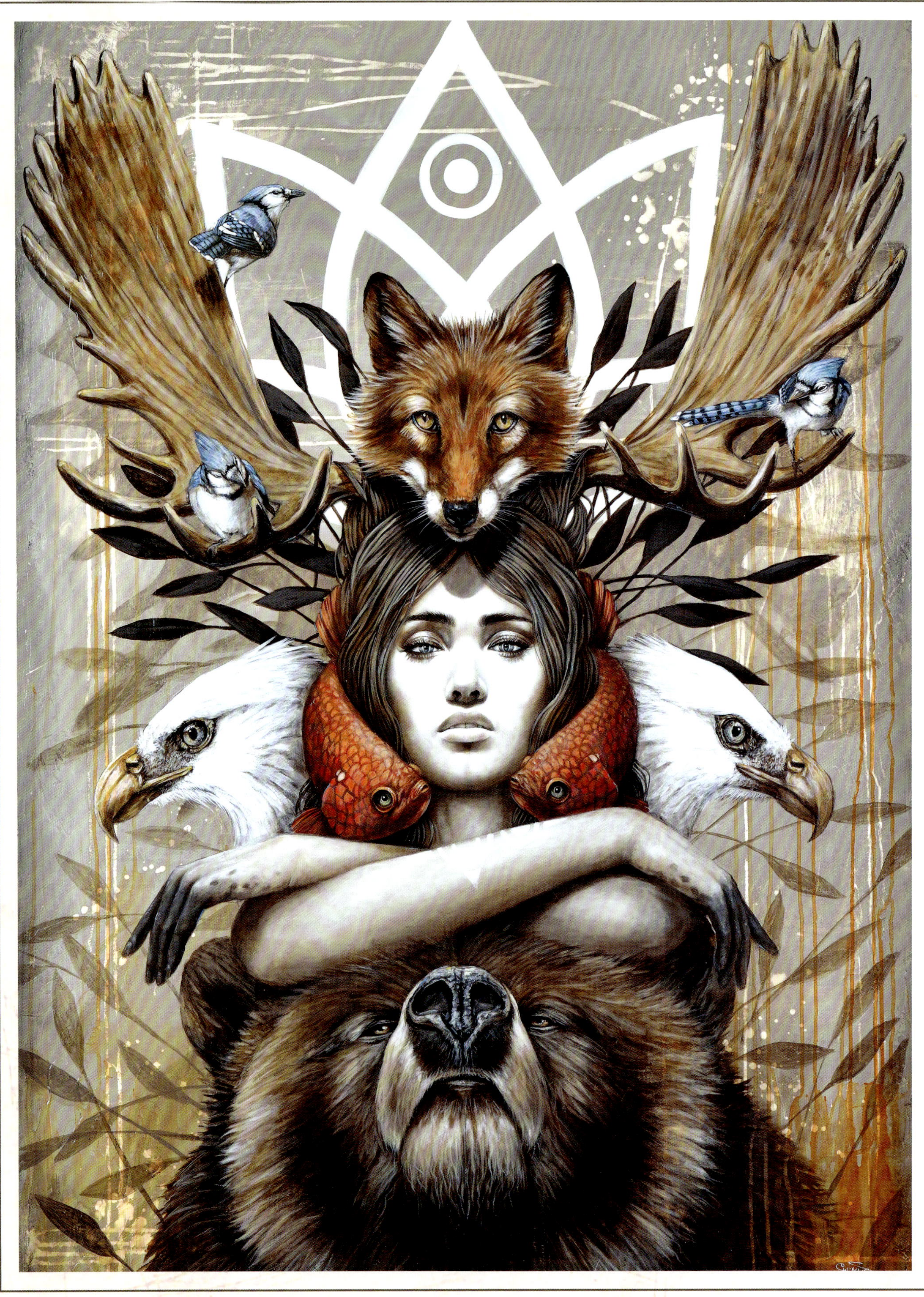

Verse IX

Queen Isis with expansive wings of light,
Cast away persistent shadows of grief.

Lotus-bearing Lakshmi with owls of white,
Overcome loss with your love's sweet relief.

Adar Rhiannon, goddess of blackbird trinity,
Revive my soul magic, power and dignity.

Saraswati with swan, vocalising the prophecy,
Bestow oracular blessings of kindest destiny.

Sky-clad royal Ishtar of wing, talon and key,
Your adamantine will ensures my victory.

Verse X

*Abandoning the delusions of dominating others and imposing
my preferences upon the world, I instead choose to contribute
through presence and create through consciousness, emanating
the spiritual coherence of my heart. And so I invoke the high
guardians of protection, that my body, speech and mind become
vehicles of goodness, effecting kindness and wisdom in this
world and beyond. I am thus protected, uplifted and blessed,
shining the needed medicinal lights.*

I call upon Divine Father of the White Healing and Protection Ray,
Vajrasattva, Divine Buddha Father of Light, Purification, Release and
Renewal. You shine as white light at my crown, protecting my body.

I call upon Divine Mother of the Red Healing and Protection Ray, Red
Tara, Divine Buddha Mother of Beauty, Attraction, Magnetism and
Positivity. You shine as red light at my throat, protecting my energy.

I call upon Divine Father of the Blue Healing and Protection Ray,
Medicine Buddha, Divine *Tathagatha* of Healing, Restoration,
Abundance and Peace. You shine as blue light at my heart, protecting
my mind.

OM AH HUM.
OM AH HUM.
OM AH HUM.

White Ray, Medicine Body.
Red Ray, Medicine Voice.
Blue Ray, Medicine Heart.

I receive the sacred medicine with *vajra* pride of complete faith,
And become the sacred medicine to nurture all beings with goodness
and grace.

OM AH HUM.
OM AH HUM.

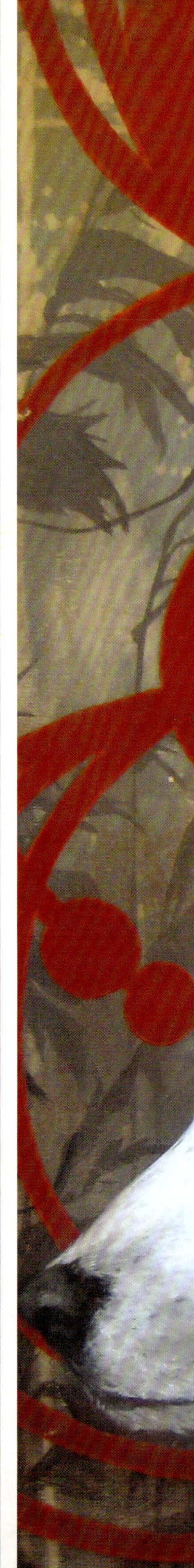

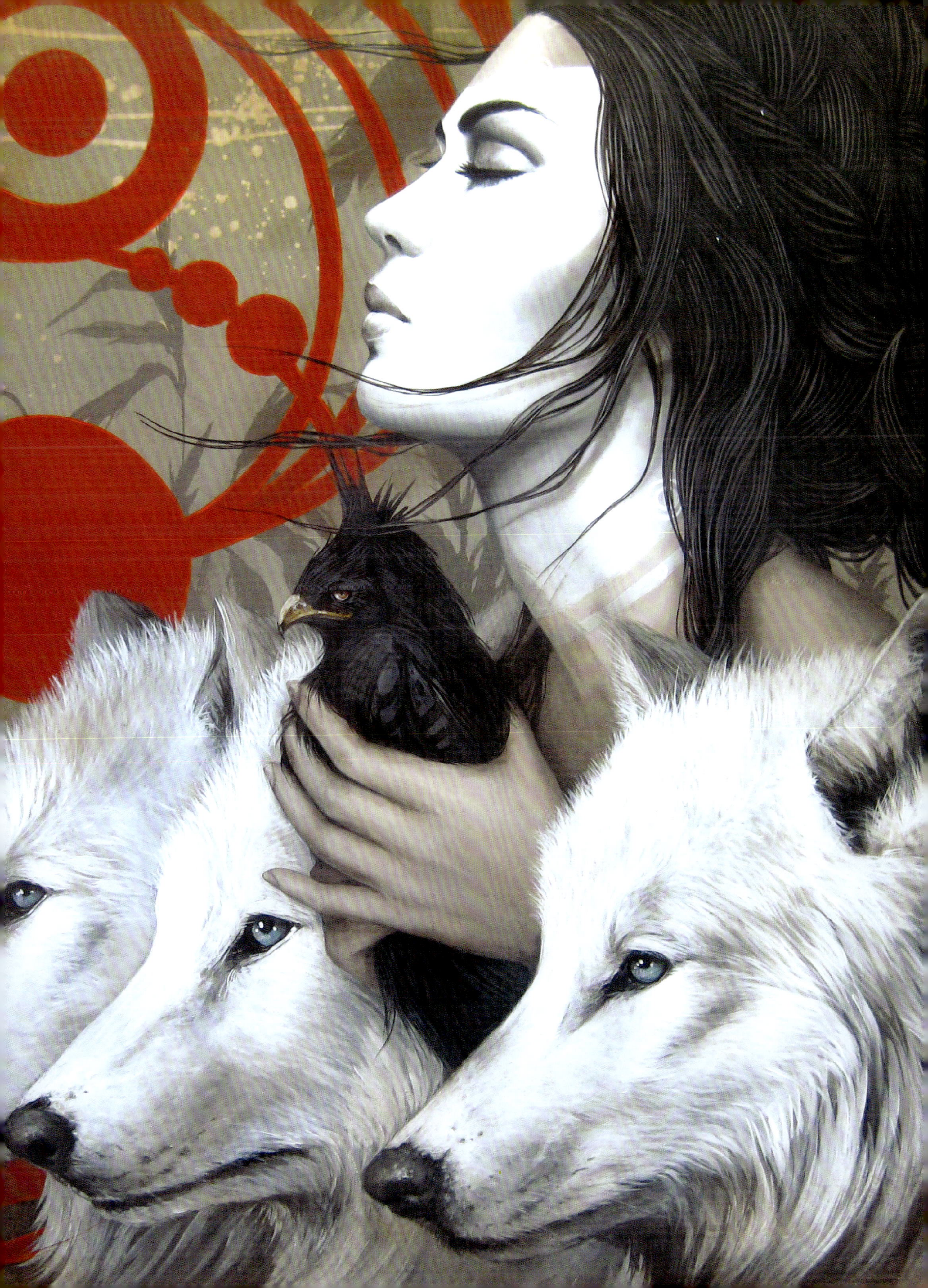

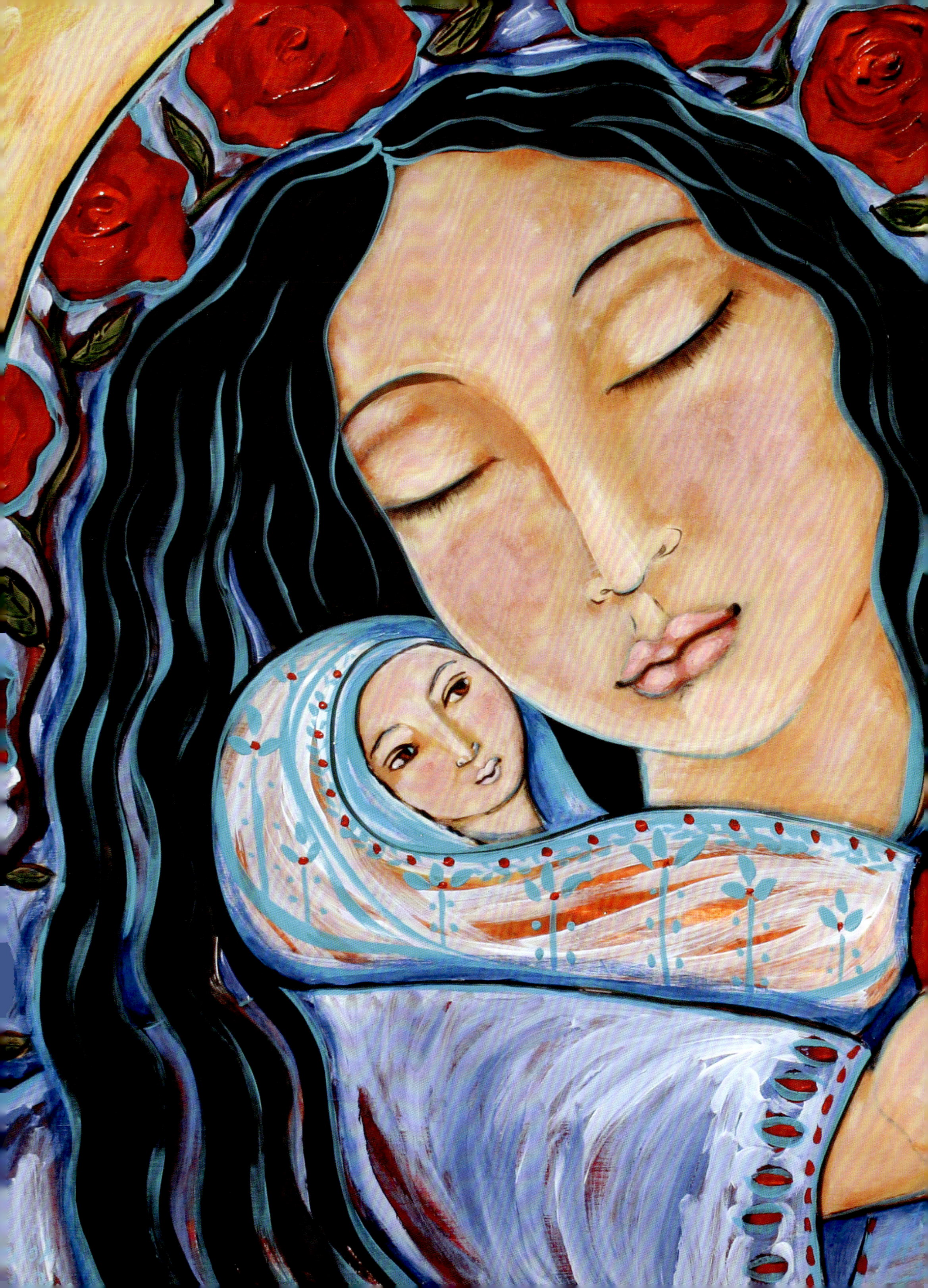

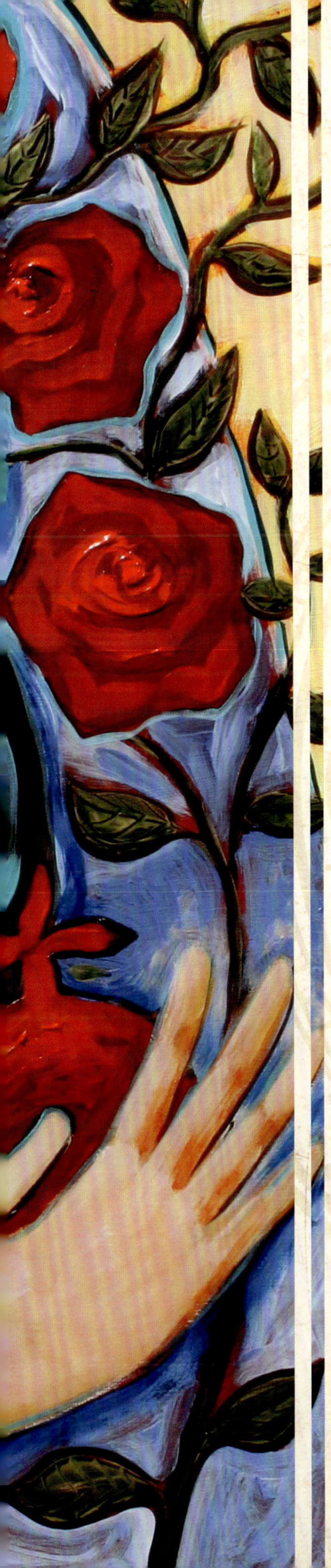

Book of MOTHER MARY

Incantations and Divinations for All-Accomplishing Grace and Precious Mother Refuge of the Sacred Heart

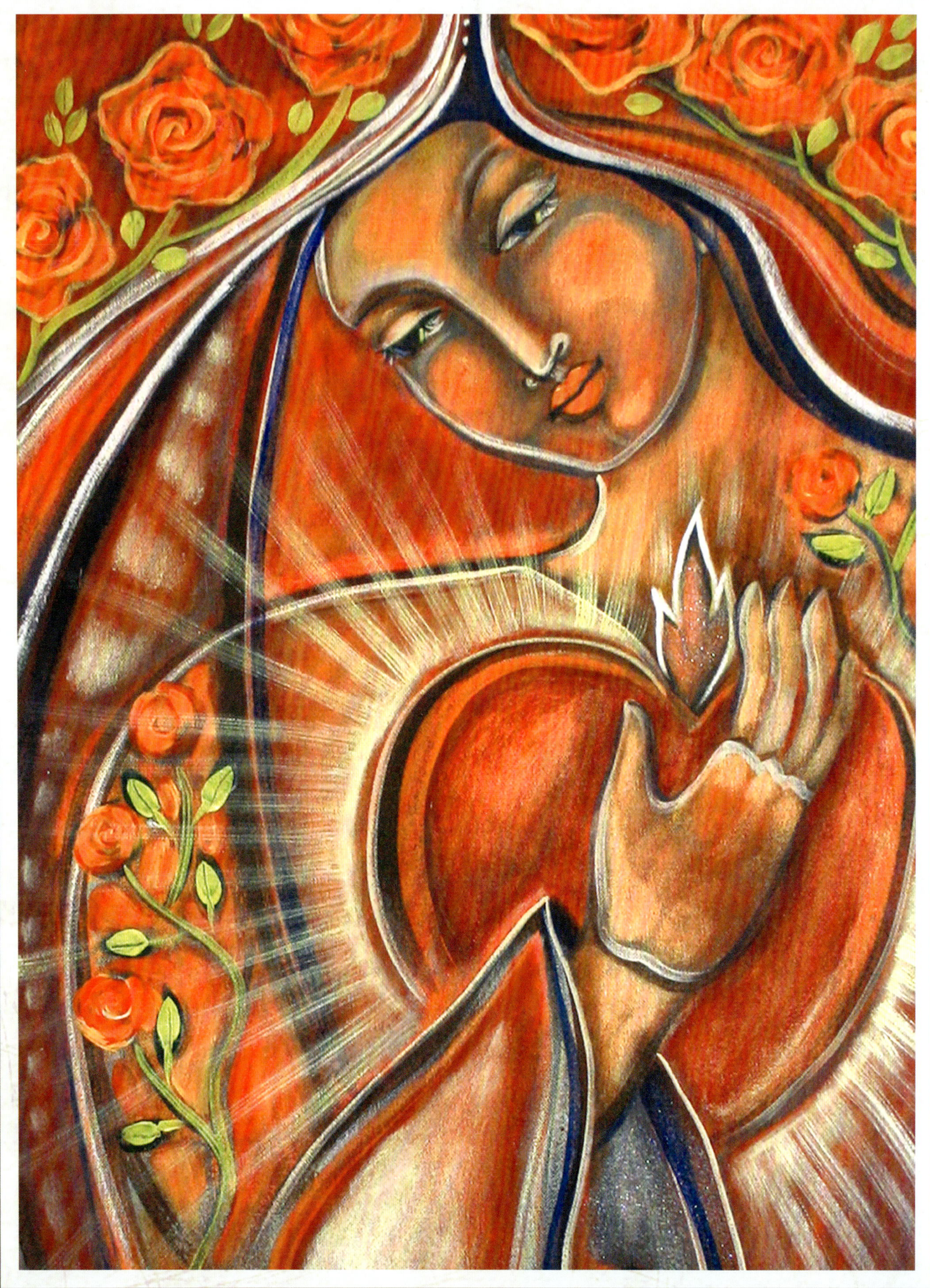

Verse I

Beloved Mother Mary,

Your presence calms my heart,

Filling my mind with peace,

Reminding me of my strength,

As I take refuge in your blessing.

Celestial dove of white light,

Resting peacefully above my crown.

Heavenly rose of pink light,

Blooming generously in my heart.

Crescent moon of silver light,

Shining protectively beneath my feet.

Cosmic Madonna, Lady of Divine Love,

May your miracles of kindness manifest.

I cast my mind, body and soul,

Into your divinely capable care,

Experiencing true sanctuary in you.

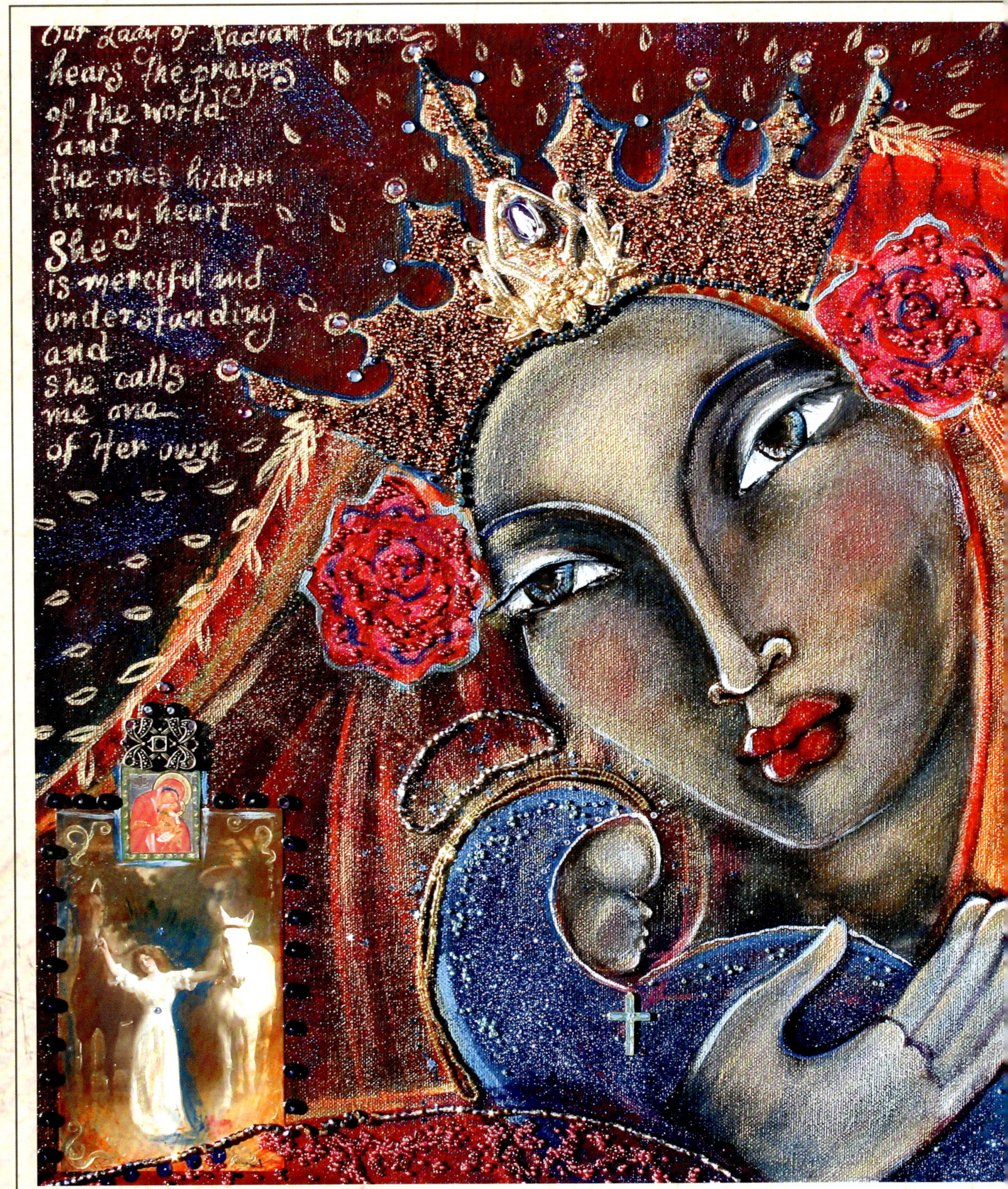
Our Lady of Radiant Grace
hears the prayers
of the world
and
the ones hidden
in my heart
She
is merciful and
understanding
and
she calls
me one
of Her own

Verse II

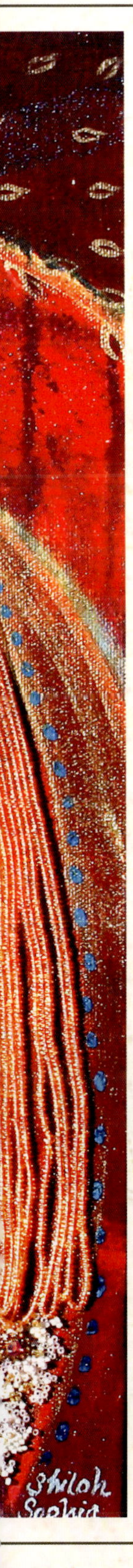

Lady of Unlimited Forms, assuming the necessary qualities to protect and uplift all beings, manifest your presence, Beloved Mother, that I may recognise the reality of you, and return immediately to peace and positivity, proceeding on my path.

Our Lady of Graceful Guidance,
Divine Mother who is always instructing me.

Madonna Guadalupe of miraculous manifestations,
Sheathed in pale rose gown, gleaming like soft light of dawn,
Green cloak adorned with eight-pointed stars of the goddess,
Your magic neutralises all worldly obstacles.

Our Lady of Graceful Guidance,
Divine Mother who is always protecting me.

Charitable Madonna, safe sanctuary in the storm,
Radiant as moon and sun, yellow robes embroidered with silver and gold,
Circled by angels of white light and yellow roses of happiness,
Your will creates the calm that averts fear and restores faith.

Our Lady of Graceful Guidance,
Divine Mother who is always loving me.

Madonna of Lujan, Lady Who Stills Momentum,
Golden rose anointed with myrrh, dusted with incense,
Gleaming diamond diadem adorned with ruby, sapphire, emerald, pearl,
Your unbreakable truth conquers the confusions of this world.

I take shelter in you.
I take refuge in you.
Fill my heart with your guidance.
Bless me with your presence.

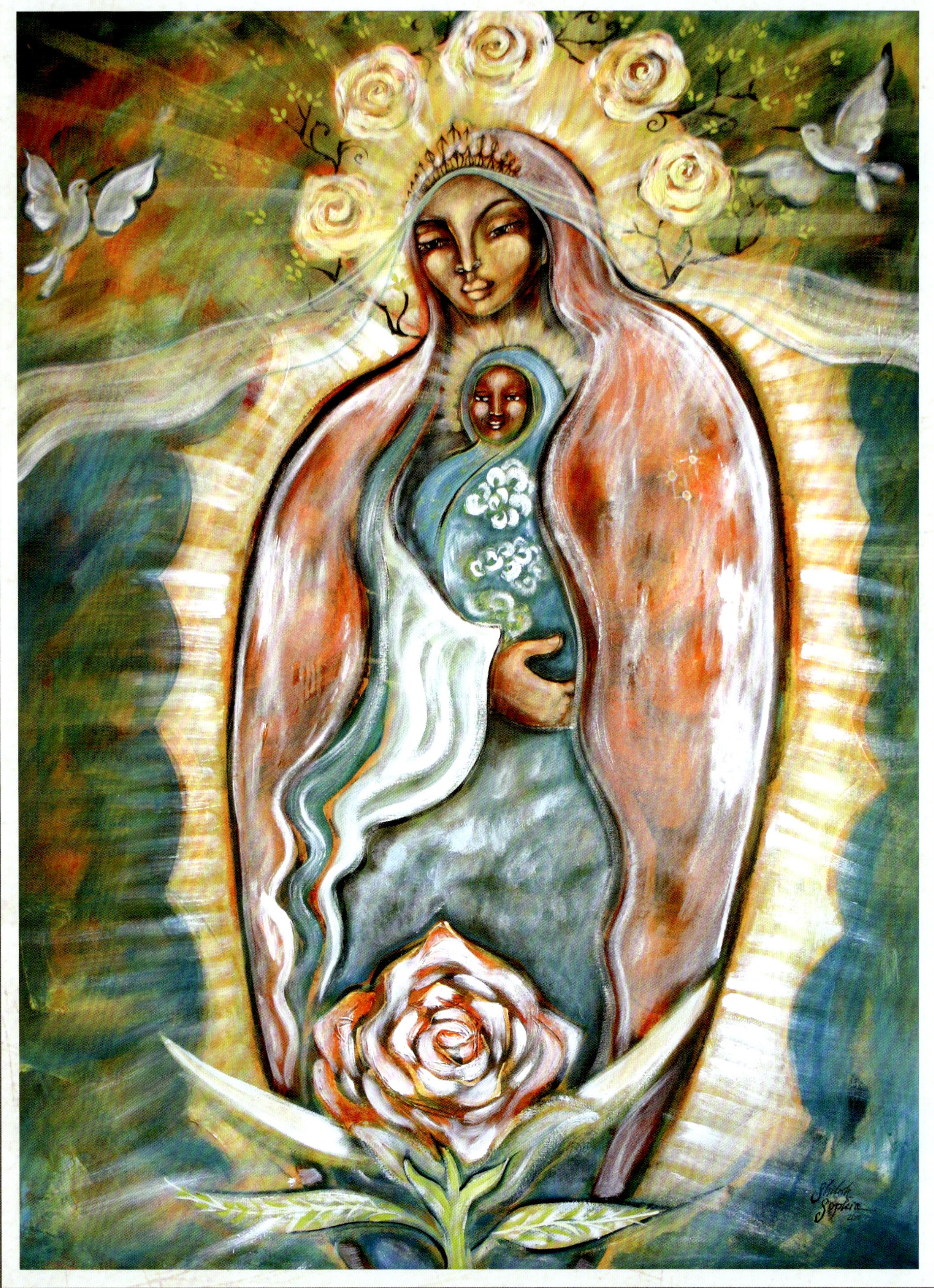

Verse III

THOUGH ALL MAY SEEM LOST, CLOUDED IN CONFUSION AND DOUBT, MY HEART FEELS THE TRUTH OF YOU. WHEN MY TRUST IS TESTED, AND I AM CONFRONTED WITH BETRAYAL, LOSS AND DISAPPOINTMENT, I SEEK SOLACE AND REPAIR IN YOU. YOU WHO ARE MY MOTHER, LOVING ME WHOLLY AND COMPLETELY, UPLIFT ME WITH CLARITY AND REPLENISH MY WEARY WILL. IN YOUR LOVE, MY STRENGTH IS RENEWED AND I AM INSPIRED WITH COURAGE TO CONTINUE.

Our Lady of Trust,

La Madonna della Fiducia,

With faith, I invoke your intercession,

All doubt recedes in your presence,

My path is divinely protected by you.

My Mother My Confidence,

Mater Mea. Fiducia Mea,

Your radiant splendour shines in my heart,

Emboldened, I move forwards on my path,

As you reveal what is true and what to do.

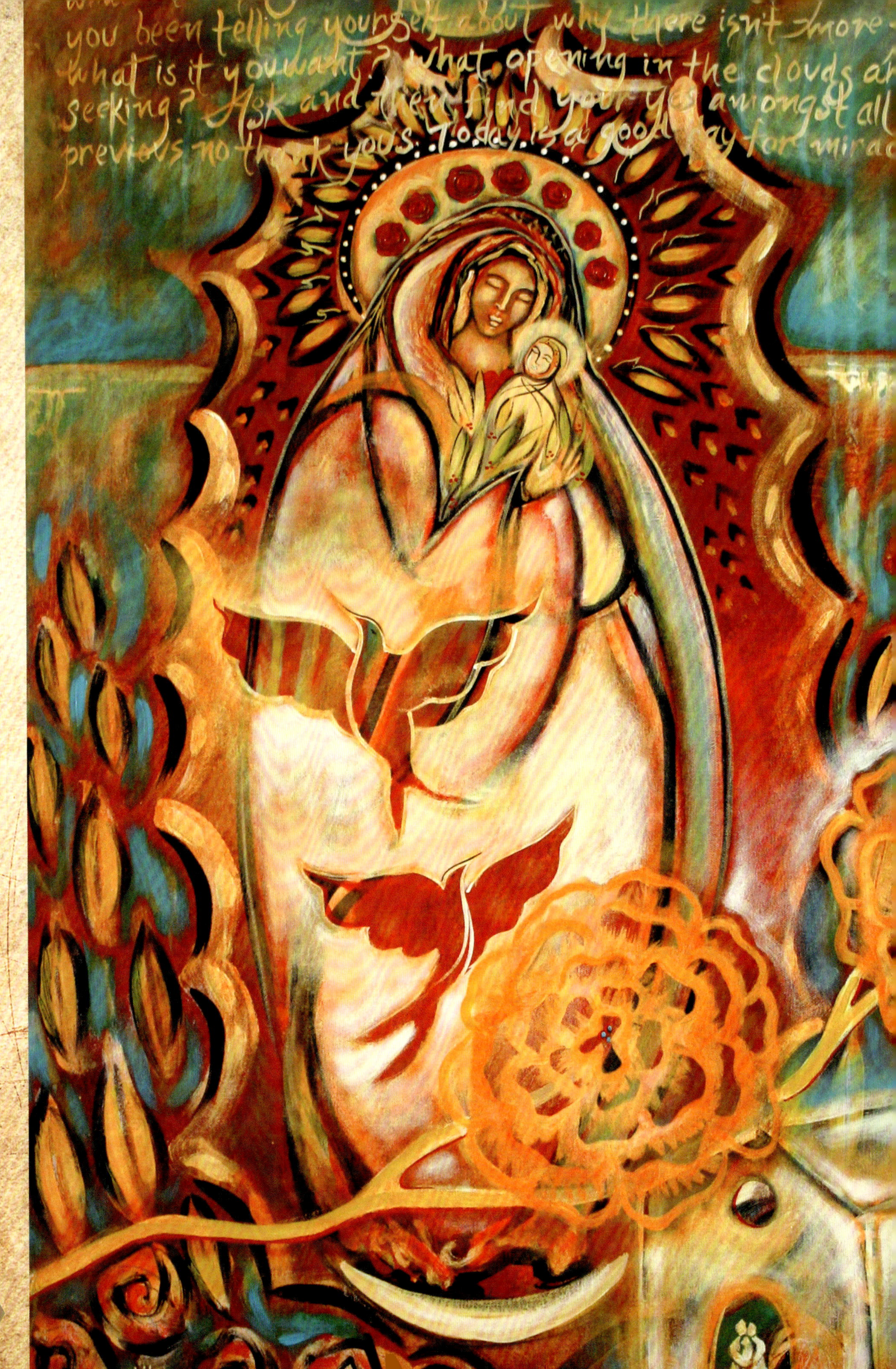

you been telling yourself about why there isn't more
what is it you want? what opening in the clouds are
seeking? Ask and then find your yes amongst all
previous no thank yous. Today is a good day for mira

Verse IV

Madonna of the Hamsa, your divine hand of protection raised above me halts the flow of negativity, directing energies to move in the blessed way, channelled towards constructive purpose. I am set upon your path of love and truth, recognising this path as my own. I am empowered and free to move on, making progress and finding peace. I surprise myself with my confidence, realising nothing shall deter my fruition, as I apply myself with wisdom.

Mother of Indigo Wisdom,

Left foot upon crescent moon,

Right foot upon the serpent,

You tame the wild forces of delusion,

I recognise the stillness beneath the storm.

Tower of Ivory, Turris Eburnea,

Enclosed Garden, Hortus Conclusus,

Safe from intrusion and distraction,

You provide sacred rest and inner retreat,

In your love, I find clarity and relief.

Queen of Angels, Hamsa of Heaven,

With Archangel Gabriel, Michael and Raphael,

With Archangel Uriel, Hanael and Jophiel,

Protected by angelic sound and light,

I make the decisions that honour my life.

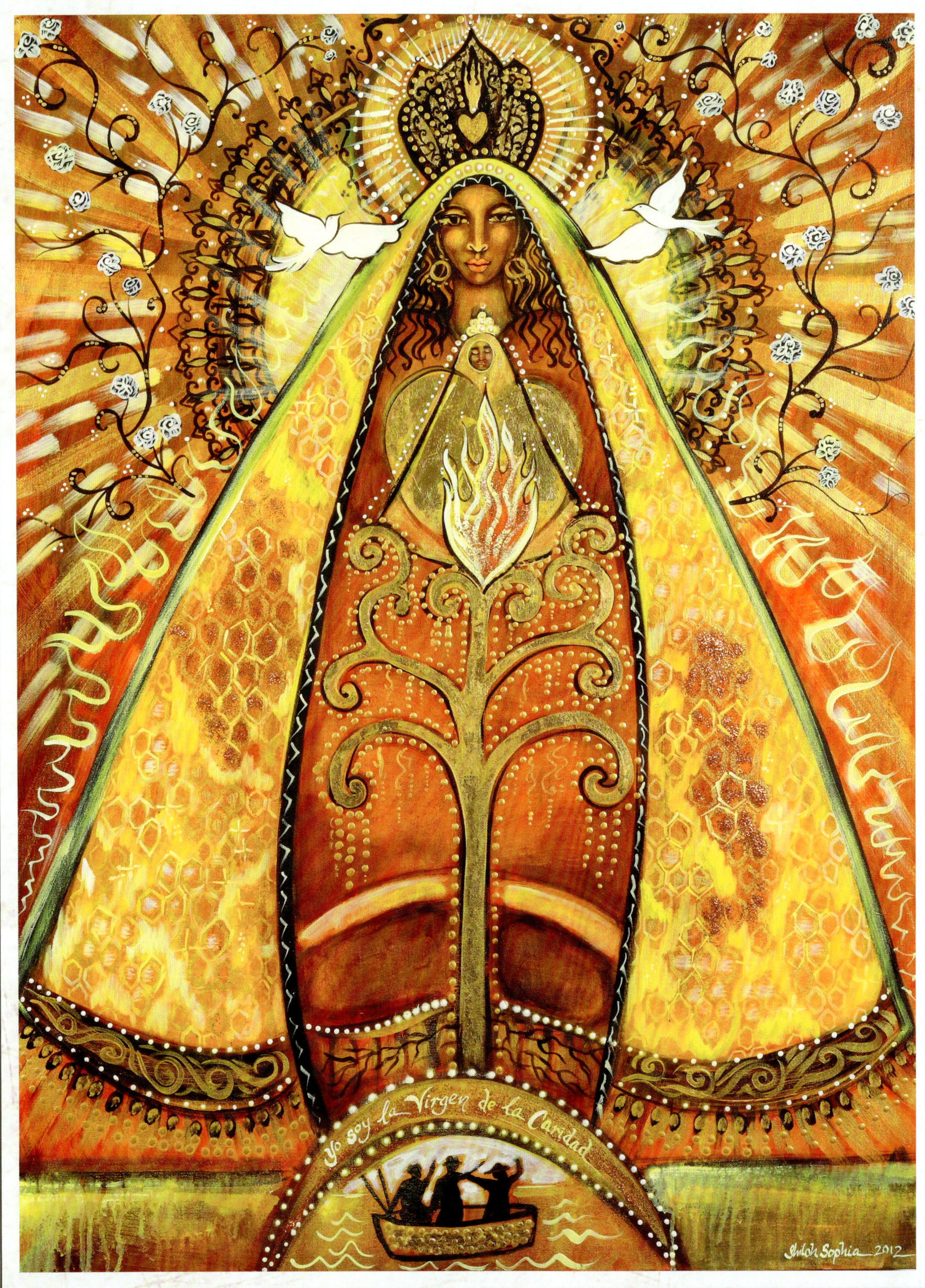

Yo soy la Virgen de la Caridad
Shiloh Sophia 2012

Verse V

Beloved heroic Lady, bring me home to my heart, to myself,
to your love. Lead me into the life that is divinely meant for me.
Help me, heal me, cleanse me and set me free, to embrace my truth
and live my high destiny.

Mother of all that is good and true, *Theotokos, Mater Dei,*
Cosmic Creatrix birthing brightness and beauty in our world,
Domus Aurea, House of Gold, radiant cathedral of loving refuge,
Mother of Wisdom, bring me home to myself.

Life-Giving Spring, Eternal Fountain of Grace,
Your intent imbues holy waters with healing power,
Oceanic Mother of Miracles, wash through my soul,
Purified and empowered, I am readied for my destiny.

Ark of the Covenant, Sacred Vow, Divine Promise,
Unconquerable, Unassailable Word of Love,
Decree your loving oracle of cosmic will,
All goodness ripens joyfully as abundance bestowed.

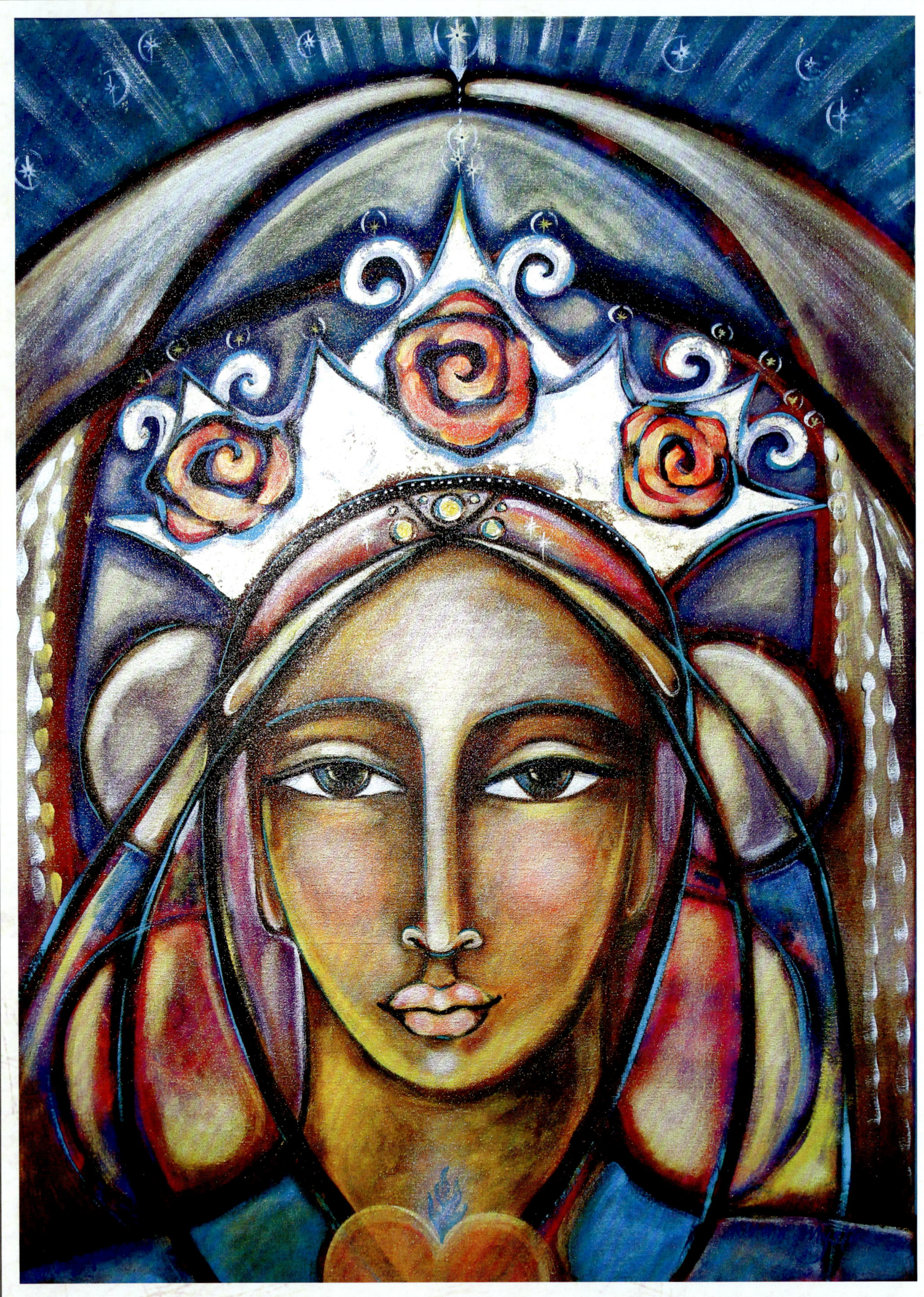

Verse VI

I FORGIVE MYSELF FOR MY DOUBTS AND FEARS,
SETTING THEM TO REST, TIRED AND WORN OUT AS THEY ARE.
MOTHER MARY, OUR DIVINE LADY, I PLACE A SACRED IMAGE OF YOU
IN MY HEART AND MIND, AND DWELL UPON THE DIVINE BEAUTY OF OUR LOVE.

Regina Mundi, Queen of Heaven and Earth,

Providing all that is needed in every dimension, in every way,

Elevating all wants and desires into that which can benefit.

My soul hears the joyful praises of angels,

Singing of your beauty, kindness and love,

And I melt with complete trust in our holy bond.

Verse VII

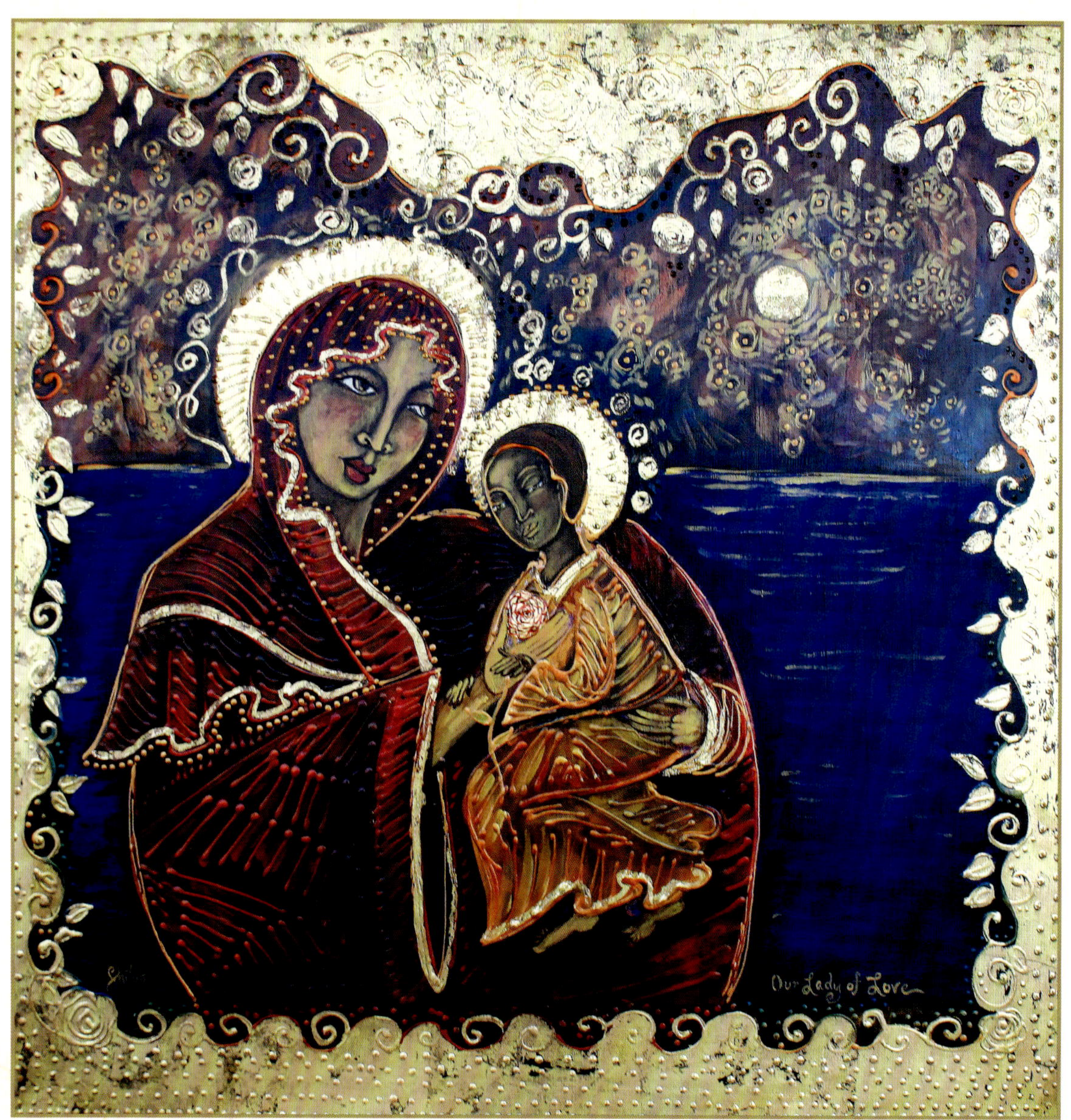

You know the truths of my heart even before I speak them,
yet I make the effort to express myself to you,
knowing that in such heartfelt communication,
clarity arises and I become more able to recognise and receive
the instantaneous healing of your presence.

Madonna of the Red Thread,
Our Lady Undoer of Knots,
You know what needs to be bound,
And what needs to be released.

Your love blooms like a rose in my heart,
Perfumed attractor of blessings rightfully mine,
Deflecting all not part of your plan for me,
I now become restful, certain and brave.

Faith-giving Queen of the Rosary,
My gratitude amplifies your grace,
I count my blessings and am inspired,
Trusting in divine timing and answered prayers.

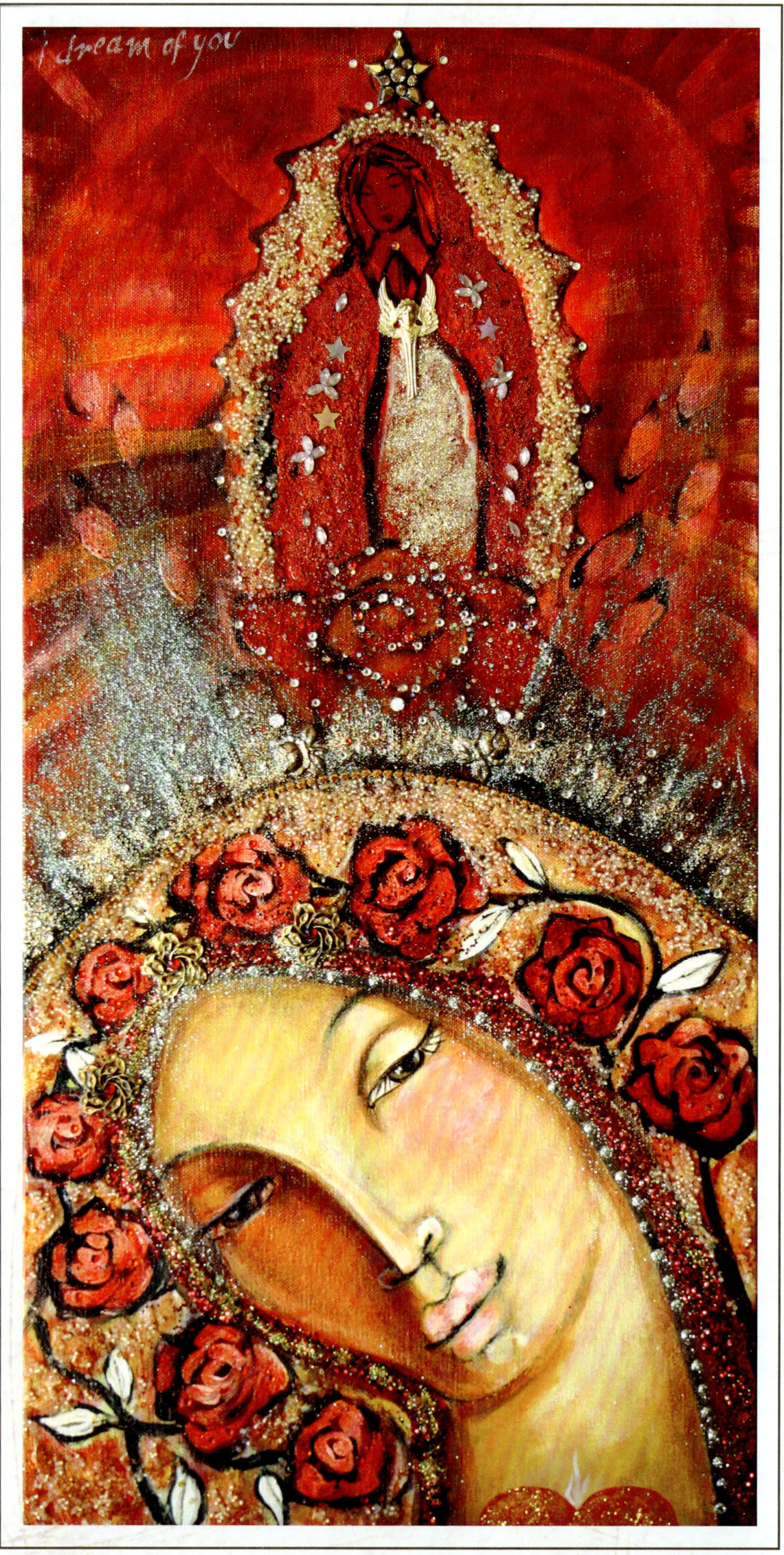
i dream of you

Verse VIII

Madonna of my Heart, Protector, Guide and Guardian, I remember your love and find my faith once again. Madonna of my Heart, Protector, Guide and Guardian, I receive your love and find joyful rest, restoring my energy to manifest my heart's truth.

Rose of Venus, Star of Venus,
Priestess of Pentacle and Dove,
Protect, guide and bless me,
Through your heavenly love.

Stella Maris, Star of the Sea,
Protective goddess of arcane mystery,
Through trials and tests, my faith attests,
You are forever generous divine decree.

Priestess of Venus, Rose of Venus,
Pentacle of Moon and Dove,
Protect, guide and bless me,
Through your heavenly love.

Mata Sri Pada upon crescent moon,
Weaving desire through your heavenly loom,
Chaos abated and higher order instated,
Your miraculous magic now blooms.

Verse IX

You are my harvest mother, my plenty,
my abundant stream of gems. You are the
wish-fulfilling star, the kind-hearted one
who grants gifts with mercy and wisdom.
I trust in the release, in the emptiness and
decrease, because I trust in your greater
cycle of grace, with abundance arising to
generously fill the space.

Santa Maria, Gate of Heaven,
Through you I enter the divine garden,
And all blessings become available.

Abundance and prosperity pour forth,
Merciful wisdom evokes harvest of plenty.

Divine Mother, Divine Light.
Om Marici Moom Swaha.
Om Marici Padme Hum.

Marici, Light of the Rising Dawn,
All that has withered in darkness,
You enrich and restore to fullness.

Abundance and prosperity pour forth,
Joyful compassion evokes harvest of plenty.

Divine Mother, Divine Light.
Om Marici Moom Swaha.
Om Marici Padme Hum.

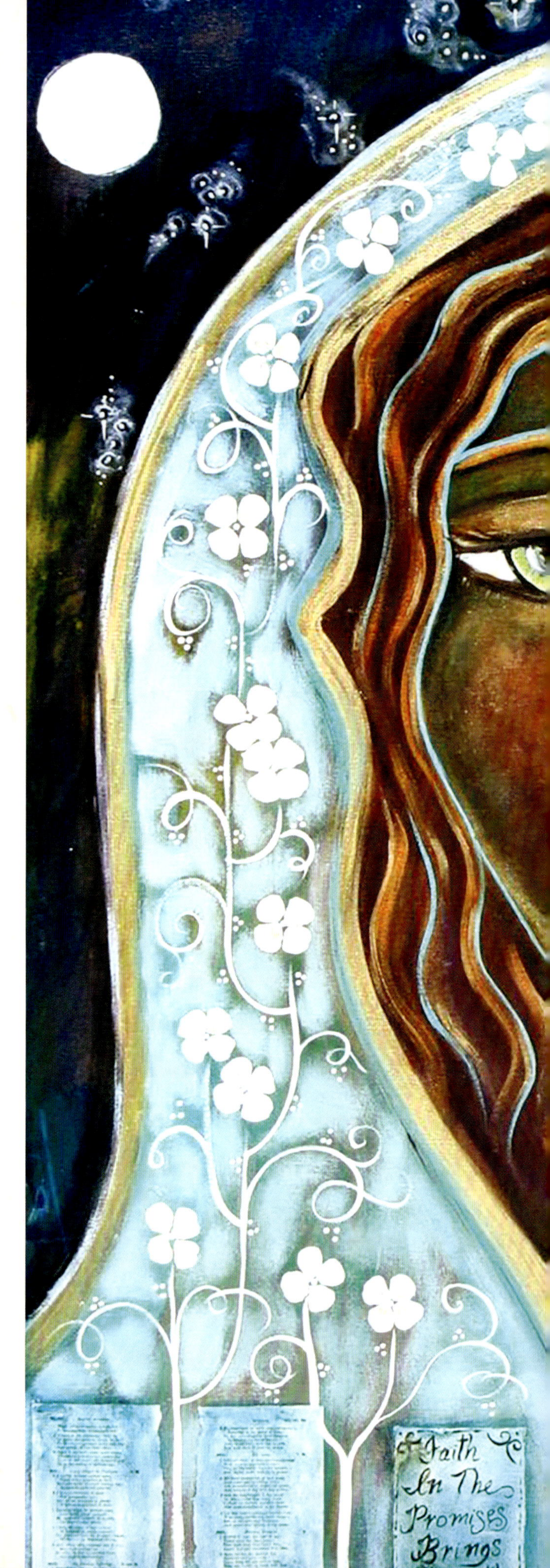

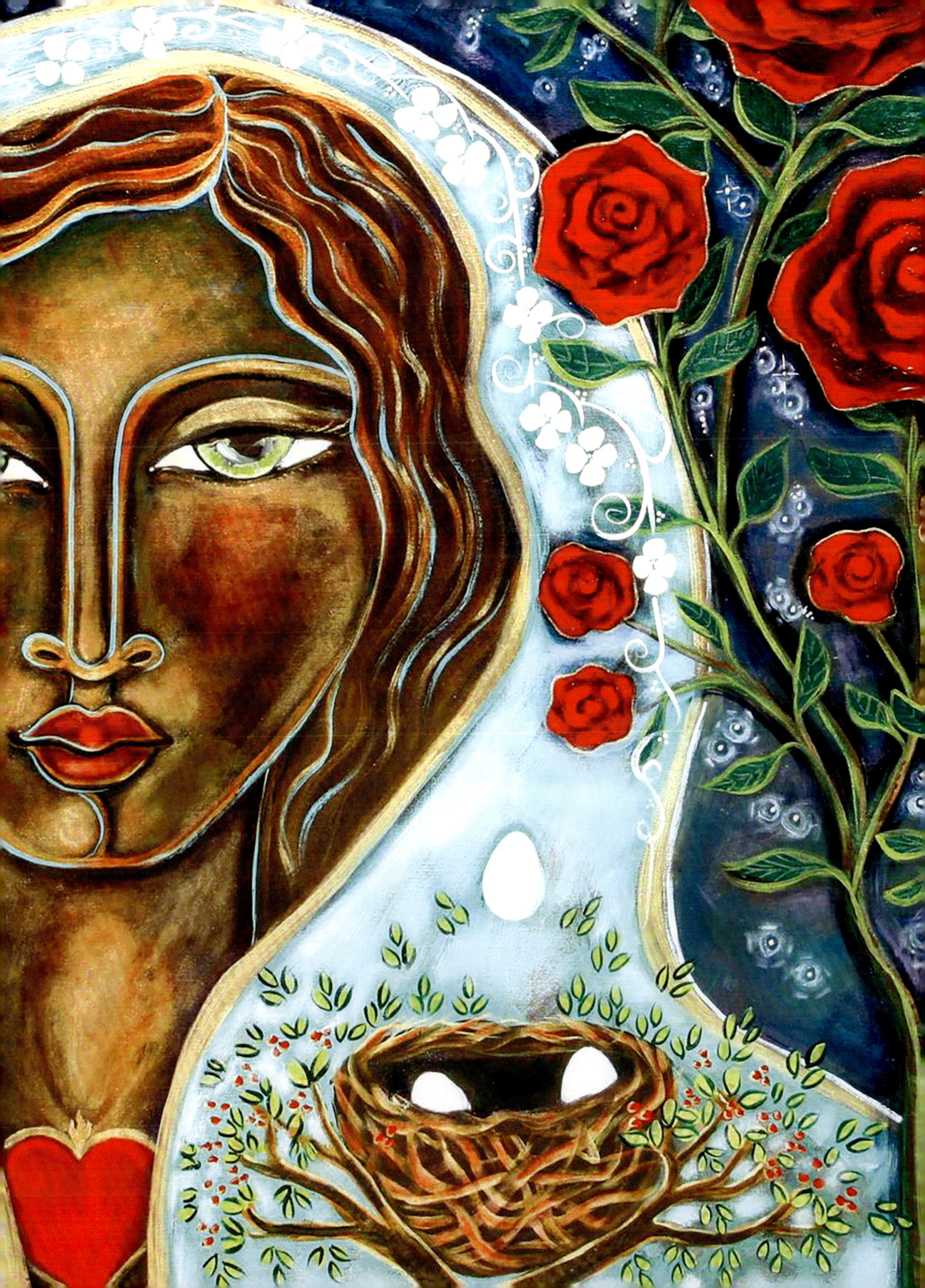

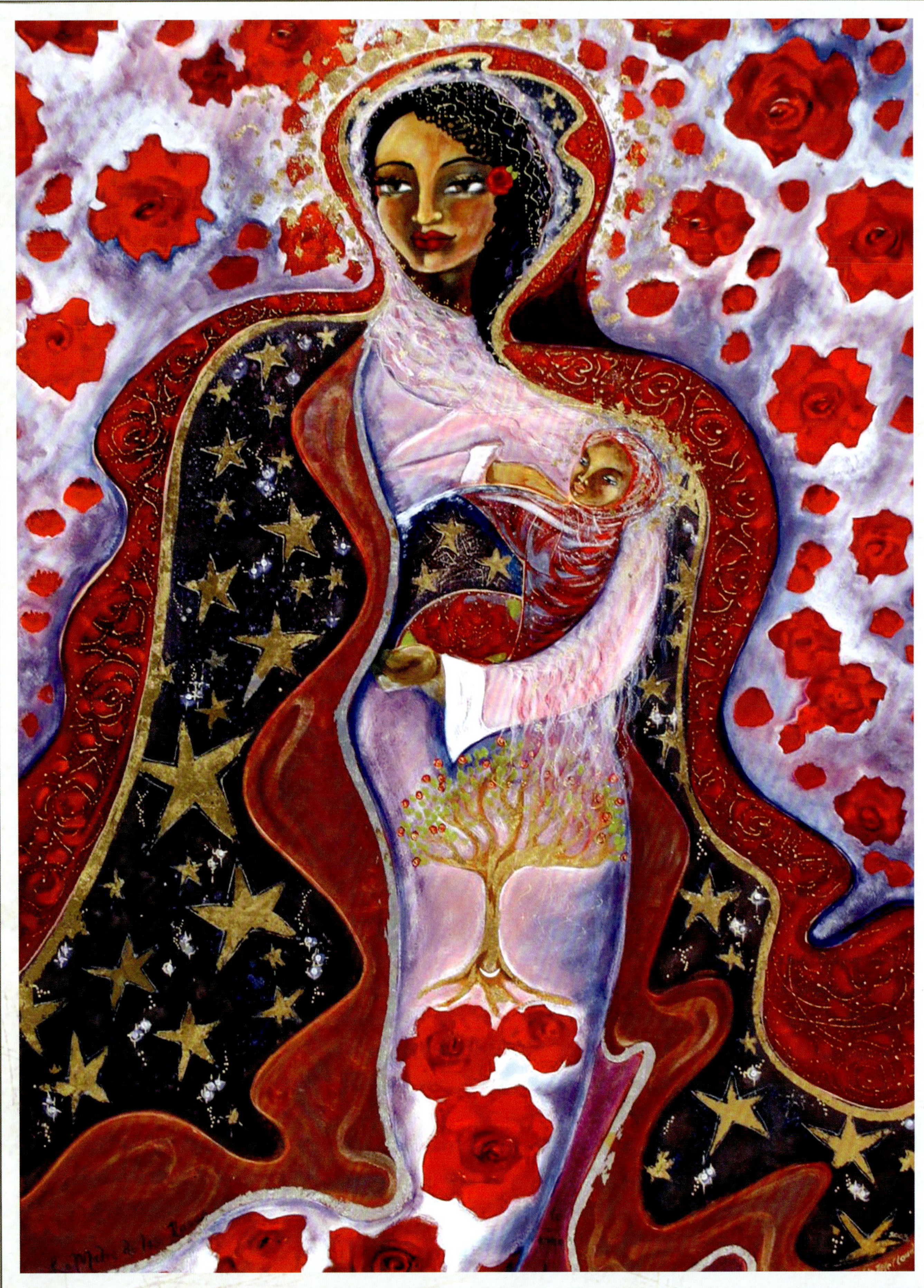

Verse X

Mater Dolorosa, Mother Most Sorrowful,

Who meets me in my darkest moments,

Witnessing my deepest pain,

May my suffering be laid to rest,

As if in Holy Sepulchre,

Entombed for final release.

Our Lady of Salette,

Who yearns to avert future torment,

Inspiring my wisest choices,

May your guidance be known to my heart,

Like a candle lit in sacred temple,

Illuminating the way of wisdom.

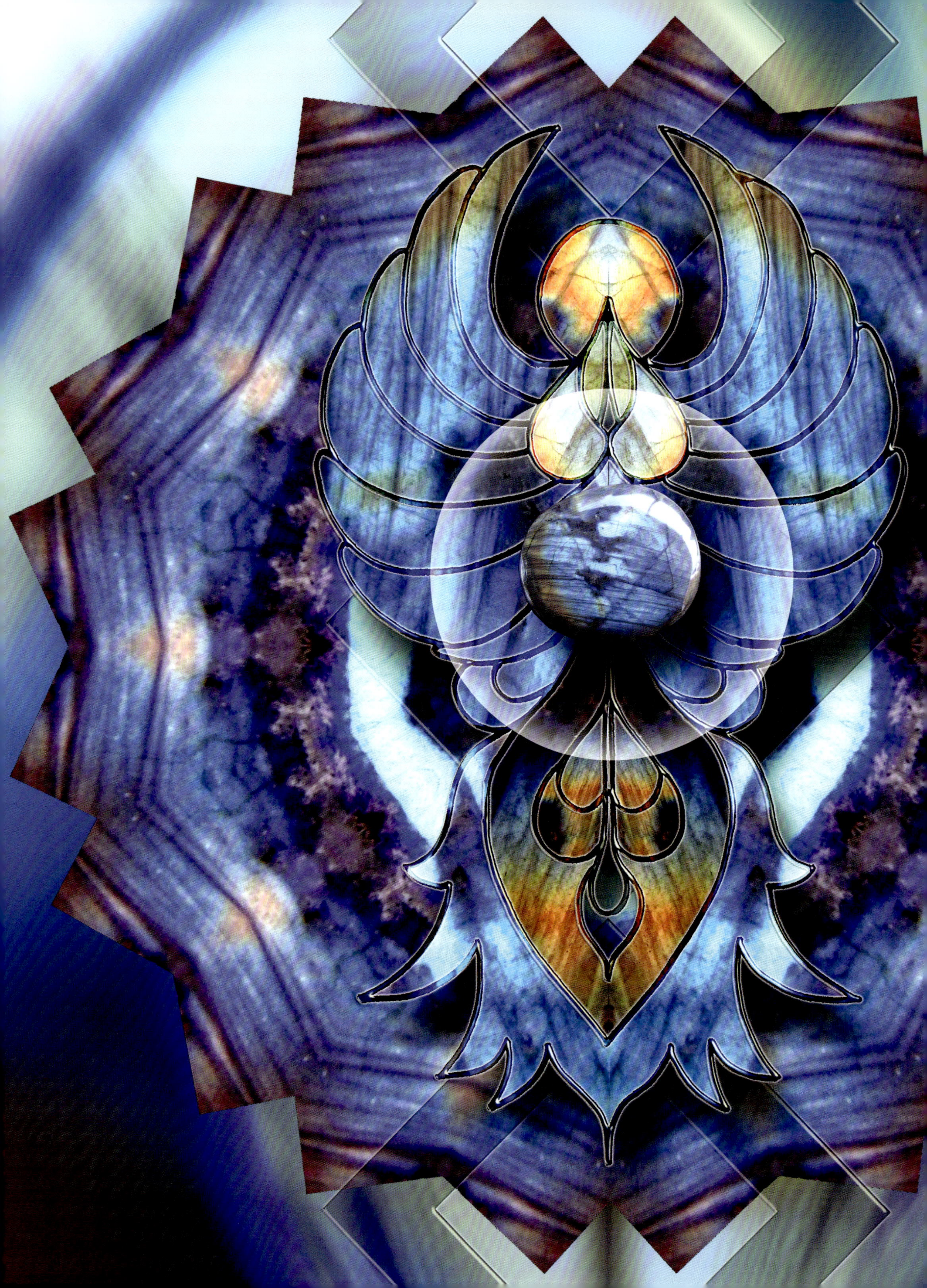

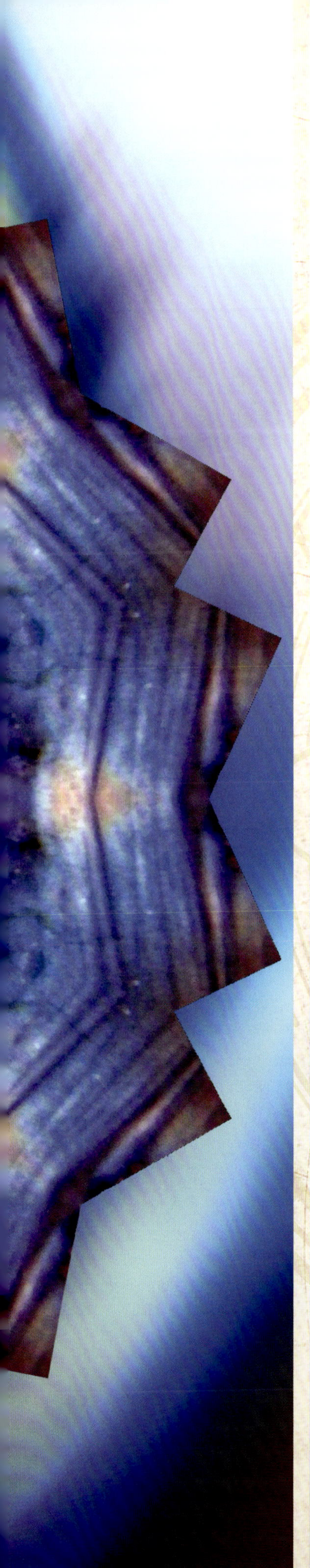

Book of CRYSTAL MANDALA

Incantations and Divinations for Crystalline Ascension Transmissions with Multidimensional Divinities of Radiance

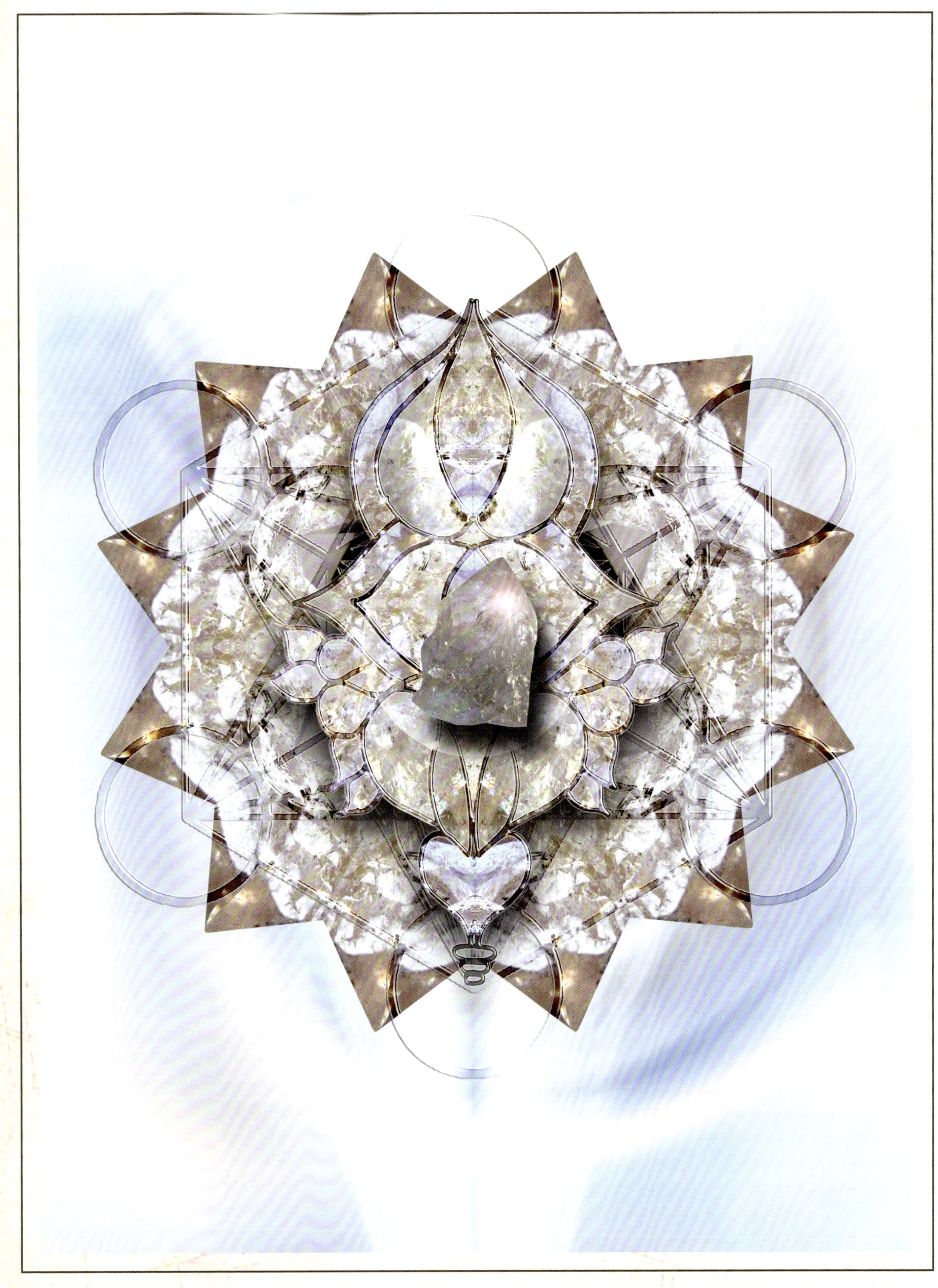

Verse I

With pure intention for sublime regeneration to benefit myself and all beings —

I invoke the Crystal Angel of Clear Quartz and Archangel Metatron.

May your clear light of divine love flow through me now.

I own my power as a method for manifesting loving creativity in this world.

Through this spiritual gift, I distil clarity and confidence for wise expression of power, tamed by mercy and in unfailing service to love.

Through divine grace, so be it.

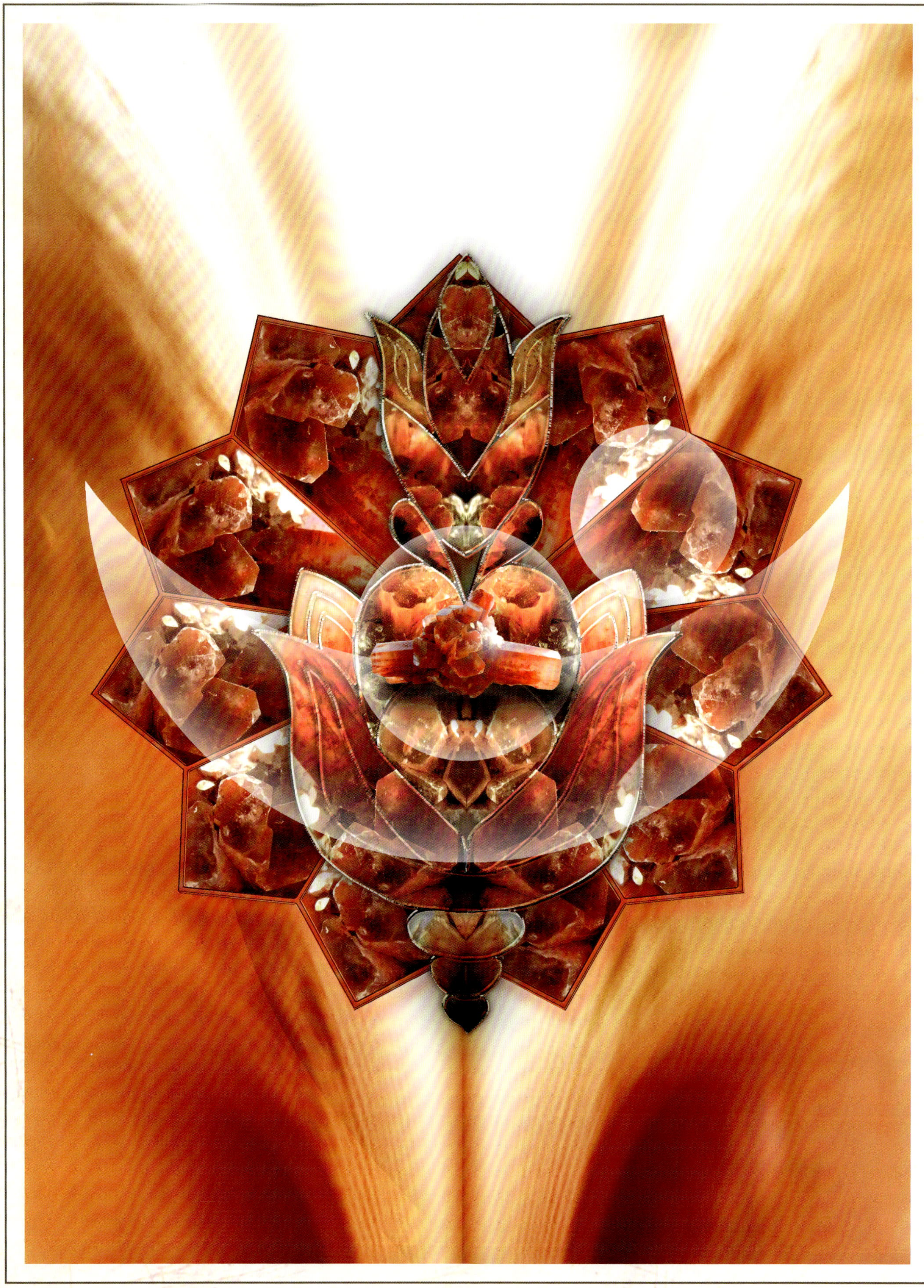

Verse II

INTENTIONAL REST RESTORES MY CAPACITY TO CREATE AUTHENTICALLY AND COMMUNICATE EFFECTIVELY. BELOVED ANGELIC ONE, PLEASE HELP ME ACCOMPLISH THIS TASK WISELY.

With pure intention for sublime regeneration to benefit myself and all beings —

I invoke the Crystal Angel of Aragonite and Archangel Remiel.

May your warm light of divine love flow through me now.

I surrender into your tender ministration, allowing the spirit of restfulness to permeate my body and mind.

Through this spiritual gift, like the earth rendered fertile by gentle rain, my entire being is replenished, restored to joyful creativity and courage.

Through divine grace, so be it.

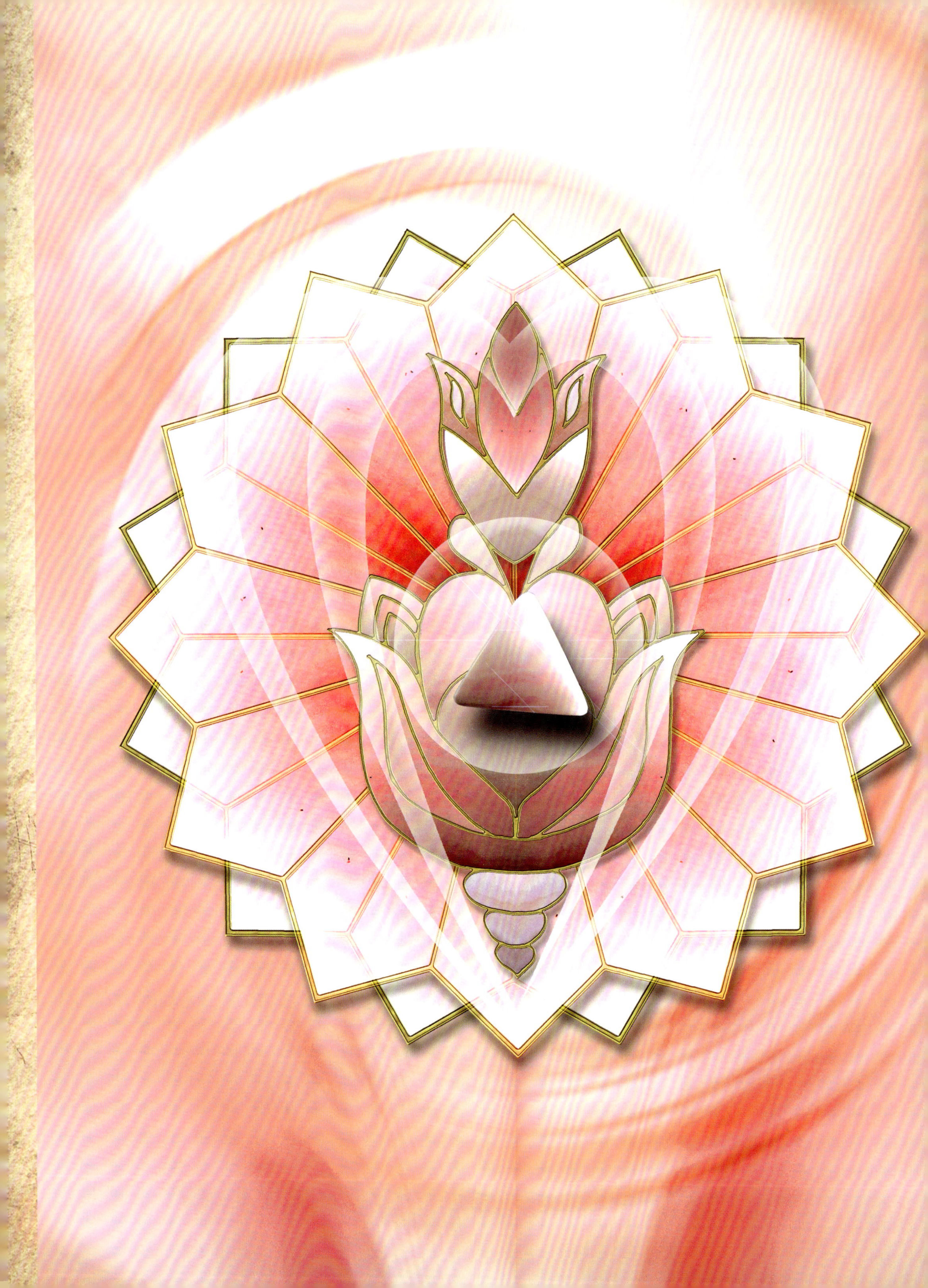

Verse III

*In gracefully accepting what is, I gain insight into
the best way forward. Beloved angelic one,
please help me accomplish this task wisely.*

With pure intention for sublime regeneration to benefit
myself and all beings —

I invoke the Crystal Angel of Pink Calcite and Archangel
Anael.

May your sweet light of divine love flow through me now.

I embrace acceptance of my experiences, activating an inner
spiritual generator that catalyses soul alchemy.

Through this spiritual gift, I perceive with heightened clarity
and recognise the responses and steps that are available to
me now, empowering my healing and freedom.

Through divine grace, so be it.

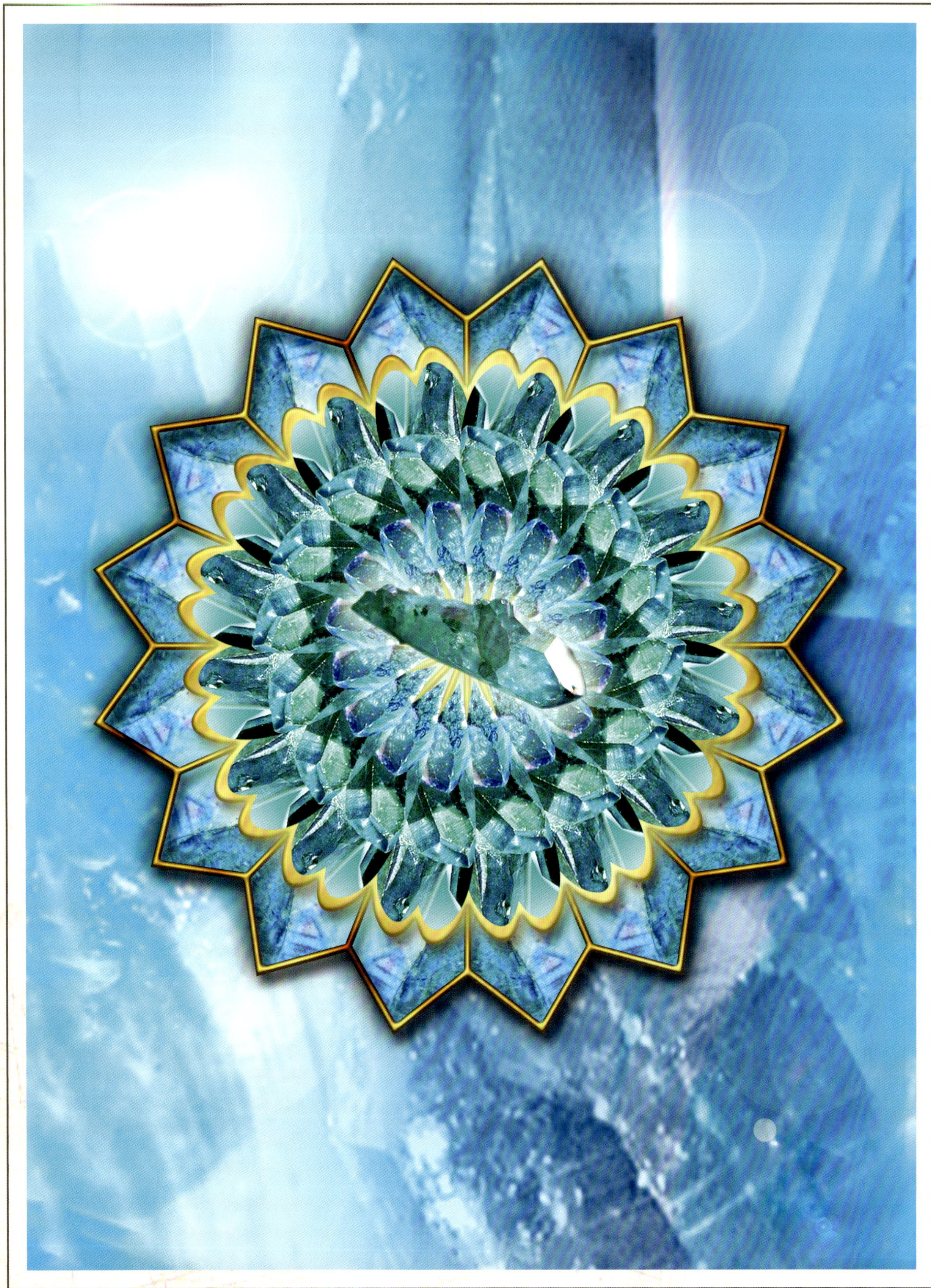

Verse IV

My mind, my voice, my body, I claim as precious spiritual instruments, to enrich my beautiful life path, in alignment with divine love. Beloved ascended one of most passionate devotion, please help me accomplish this vow with skilfulness and grace.

With loving intention for creative evolution to benefit myself and all beings —

I invoke the Crystal Angel of Aqua Aura Quartz and Ascended Master Magdalene.

May your loving frequency of divine voice flow through me now.

Choosing fearlessness of heart, I metabolise all experiences as conduits for spiritual growth, emboldening my passionate determination to attain most sacred fruition.

Through this spiritual gift, I utilise my consciousness as an alchemical elixir, evoking healing transformations through the use of energy in every situation as I choose.

Through divine grace and the oracle of divine alchemy, so be it.

Verse V

My choice, my commitment, my creativity, I claim as precious spiritual instruments, to enrich my beautiful life path, in alignment with divine love. Beloved ascended one of joyful generosity and inspiring confidence, please help me accomplish this vow with skilfulness and grace.

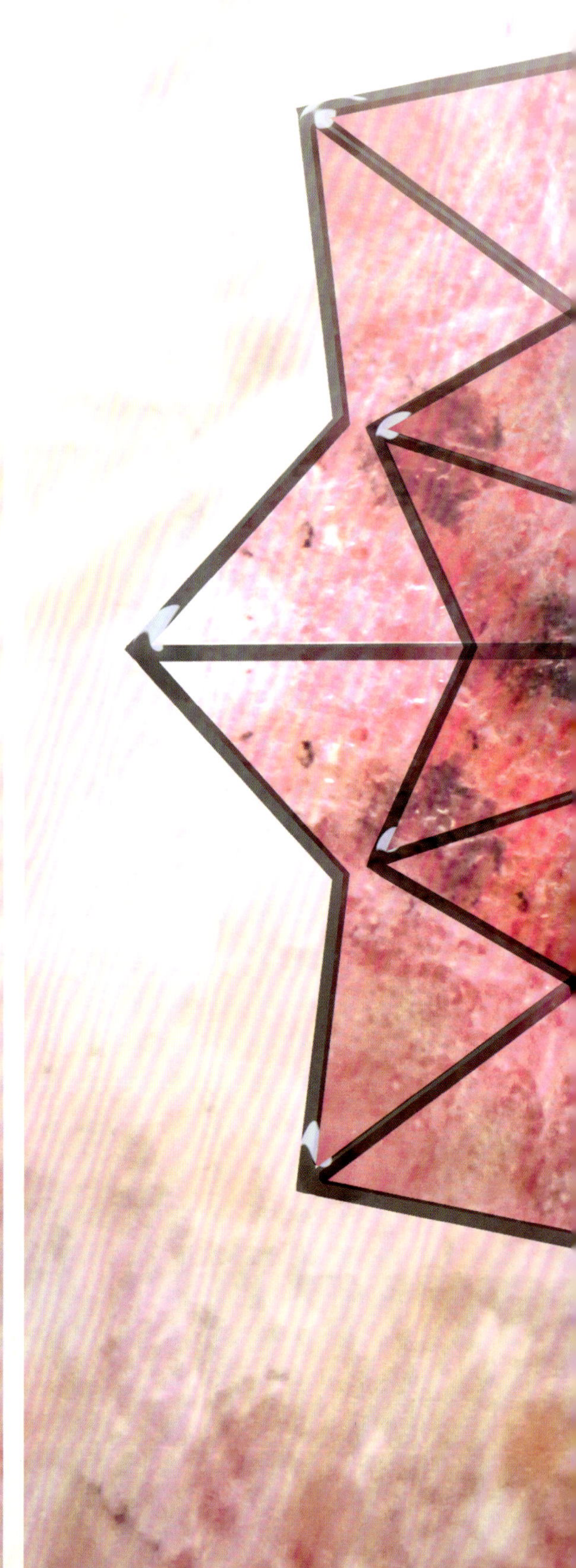

With loving intention for creative evolution to benefit myself and all beings –

I invoke the Crystal Angel of Rhodonite and Ascended Master Yogananda.

May your blissful frequency of divine voice flow through me now.

Uplifted in your frequencies of love, I choose, commit and create in alignment with the truths of my heart, manifesting path and purpose in harmony with the joyful creativity of the Universe.

Through this spiritual gift, I attract abundant divine empowerments, transmissions, blessings and interventions to ensure my fruition, for the spiritual benefit of all beings.

Through divine grace and the oracle of empowered service, so be it.

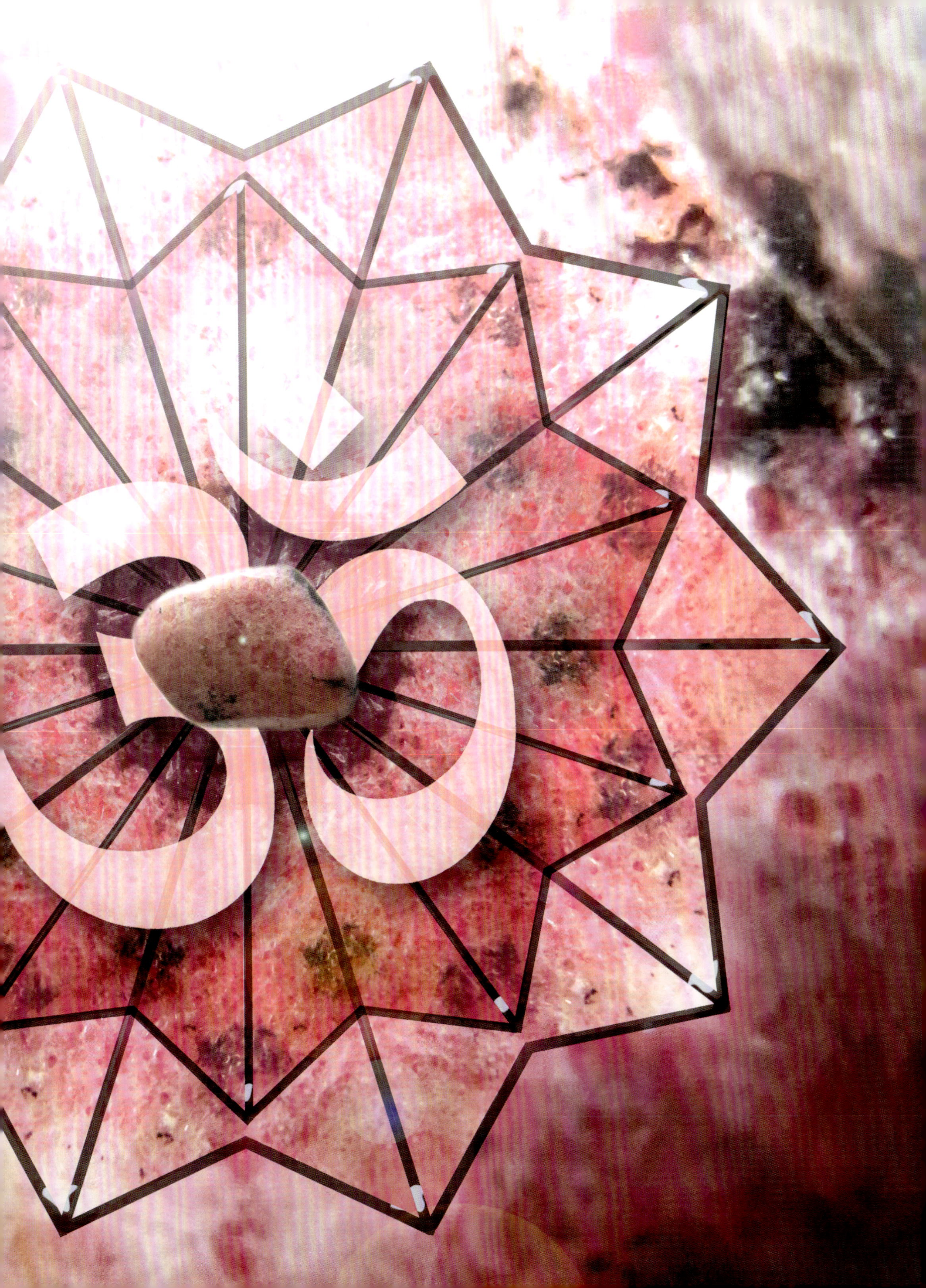

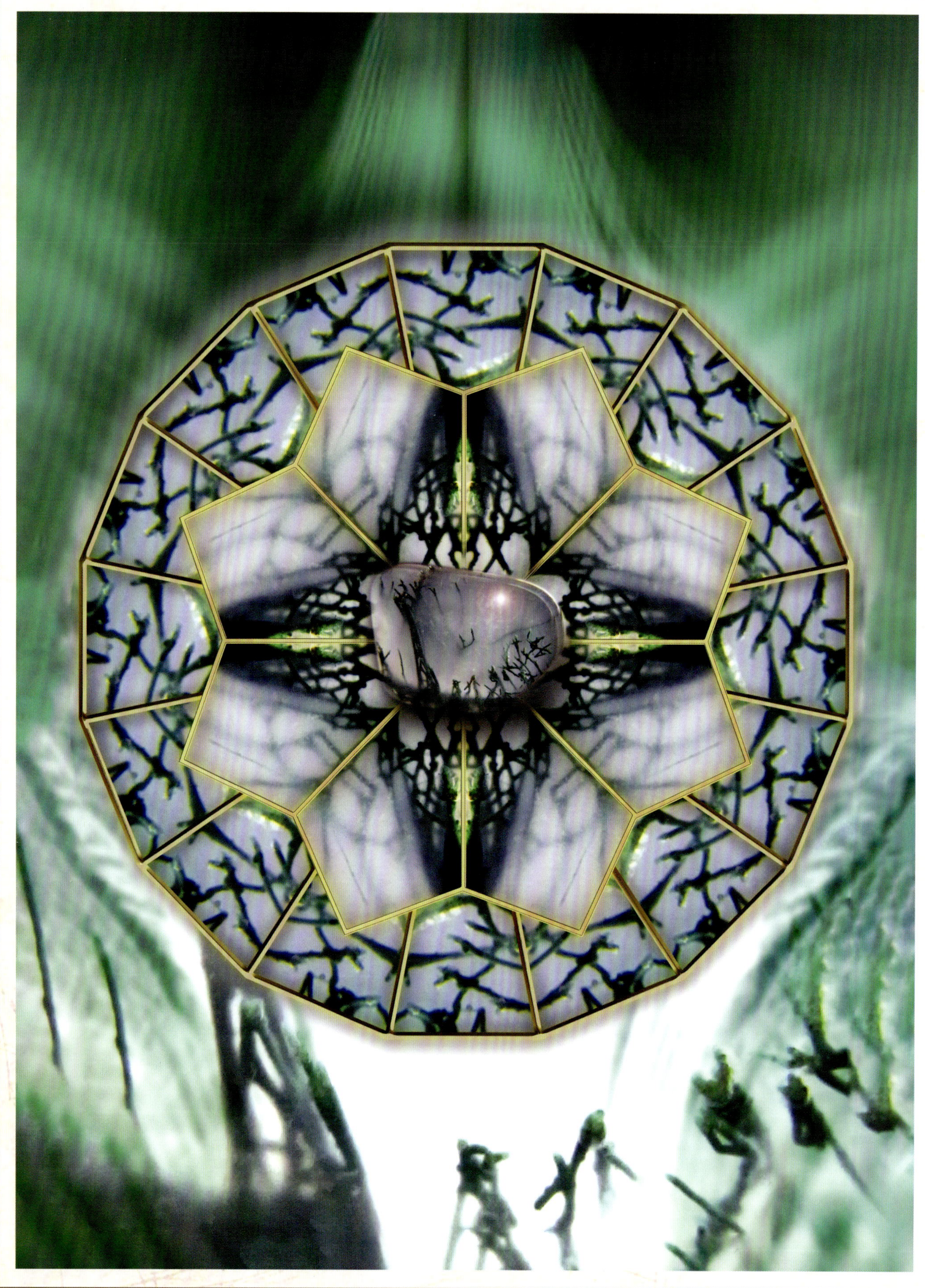

Verse VI

My gratitude, my reverence, my capacity for connection,
I claim as precious spiritual instruments, to enrich my beautiful
life path, in alignment with divine love. Beloved ascended one,
masterful rishi of patience, persistence and precision, please help me
accomplish this vow with skilfulness and grace.

With loving intention for creative evolution to benefit myself and all beings —

I invoke the Crystal Angel of Moss Agate and Ascended Master Kuthumi.

May your wisdom frequency of divine voice flow through me now.

With reverence and gratitude for the ultimate and sacred ecosystem of Life, I am upheld, energised and inspired in a supportive relational web of nutritive and meaningful belonging.

Through this spiritual gift, I exercise my innate capacity for connection, increasing trust and confidence in natural generosity, spontaneously attracting magnetic grace to fulfil my purpose and benefit all beings.

Through divine grace and the oracle of sacred ecosystem, so be it.

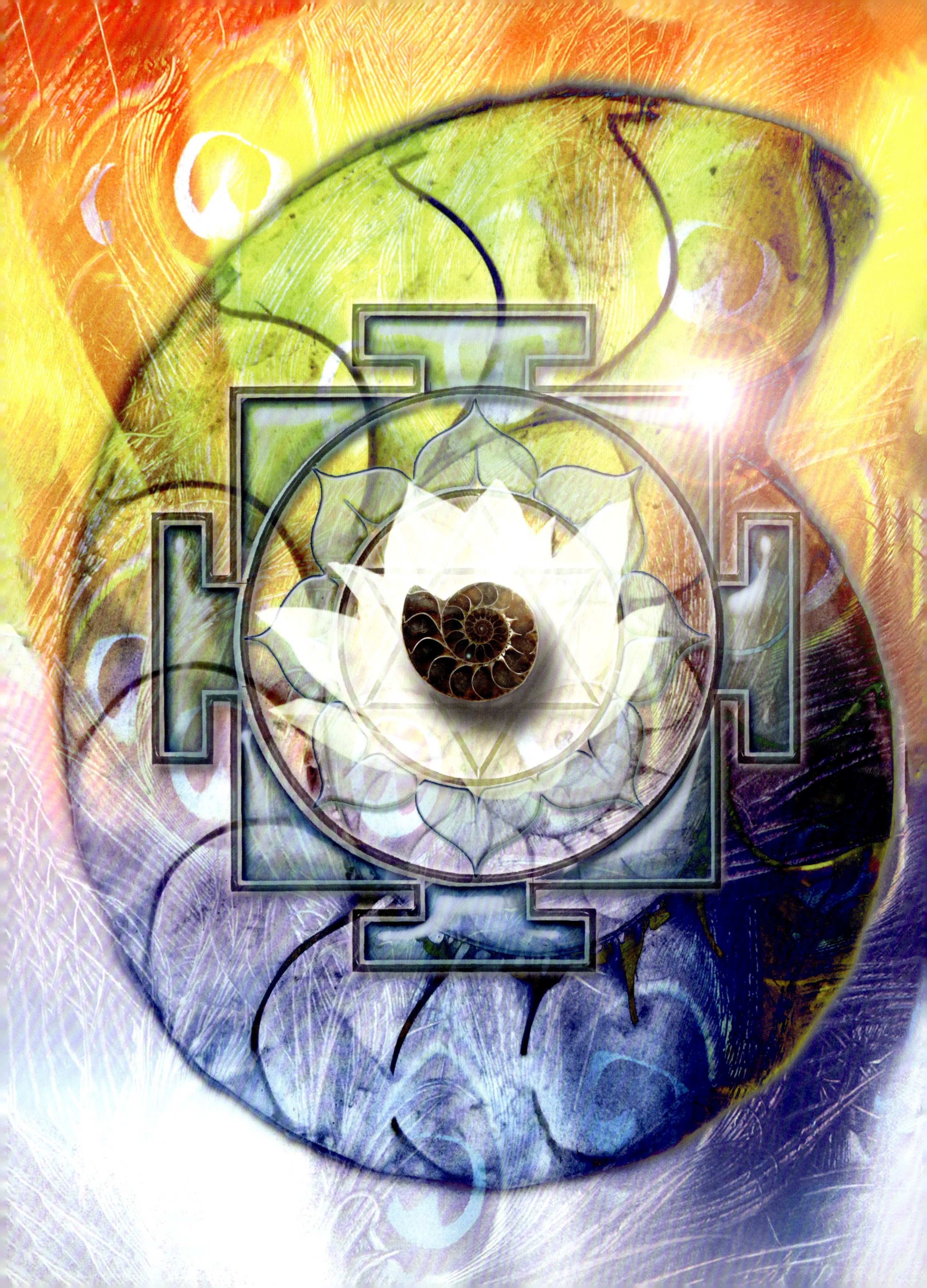

Verse VII

Throat chakra of light, throat chakra of love, harmonised and aligned with the enlightened Divine Feminine, you are a gateway for manifestations most sacred. Beloved goddess, help me fulfil this potential wisely.

With powerful intention for aligned manifestations to benefit myself and all beings —

I invoke the Crystal Angel of Ammonite and Goddess Saraswati.

May your divine decree of sacred creativity flow through me now.

Om Eim Saraswatiyei Namaha.

With faith in you, I reclaim my creative power of free will, crafting conscious choices for deliberate outcomes that amplify the energies I wish to experience and share with the world.

Through this spiritual gift, *vishuddhi*, my throat chakra, is purified and activated with your divine love, and I become capable of intentional manifestation and inspired, confident expressions.

Om Eim Saraswatiyei Namaha.

Through your divine love, so be it, for the genuine benefit of all beings.

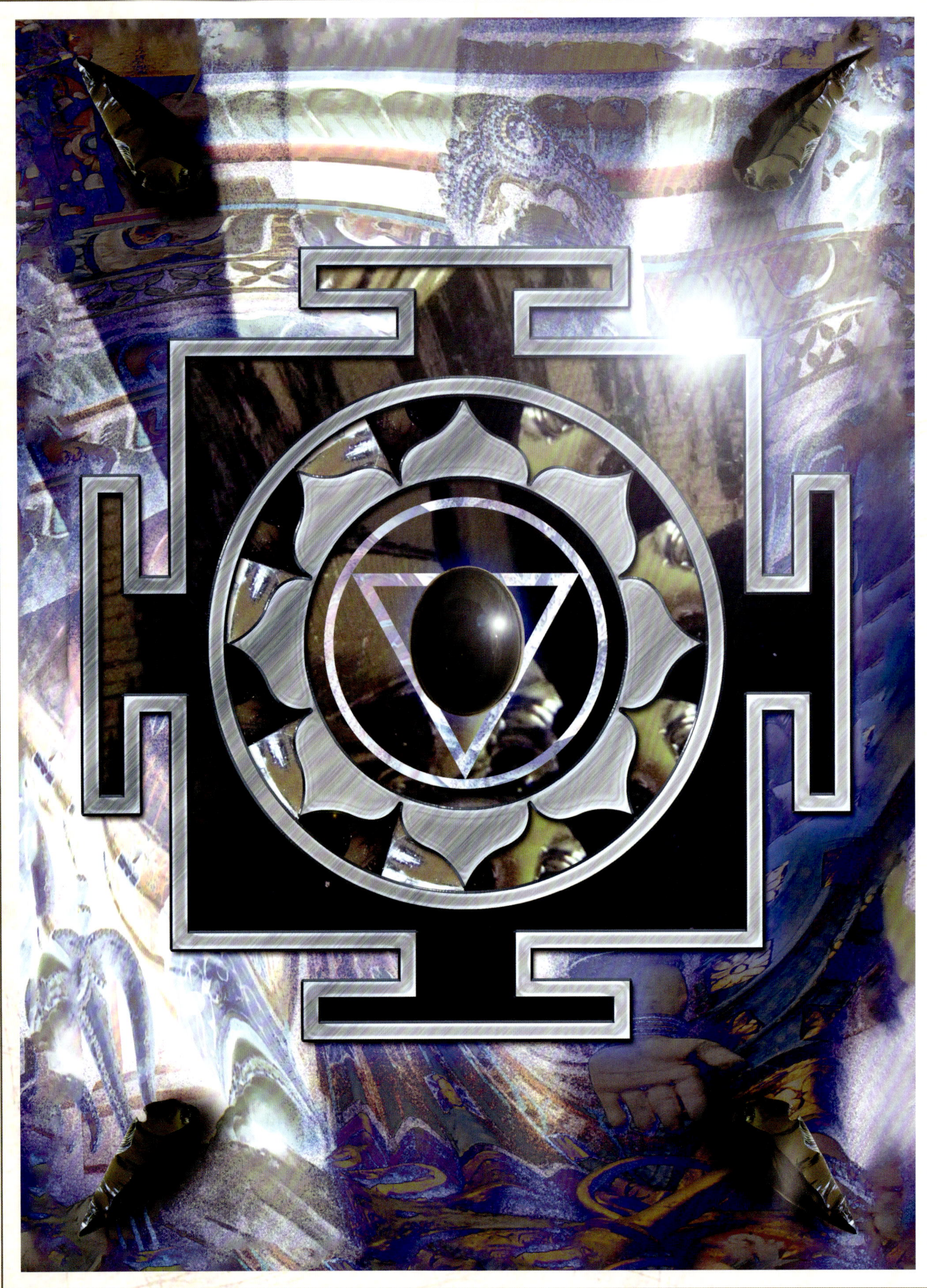

Verse VIII

With powerful intention for aligned manifestations to benefit myself and all beings —

I invoke the Crystal Angel of Black Obsidian and Goddess Kali.

May your divine decree of sacred rebirth flow through me now.

Om Kreem Kaliyei Namaha.

With faith in you, I recognise the secret gift of divine deconstruction, and with increasing clarity, I willingly surrender into my process, trusting in my healing transformation and essential rebirth.

Through this spiritual gift, *ajna*, my third eye chakra is purified and activated with your divine love, and I become capable perceiving inner truths and loving presence, no longer dependent on outer forms.

Om Kreem Kaliyei Namaha.

Through your divine love, so be it, for the genuine benefit of all beings.

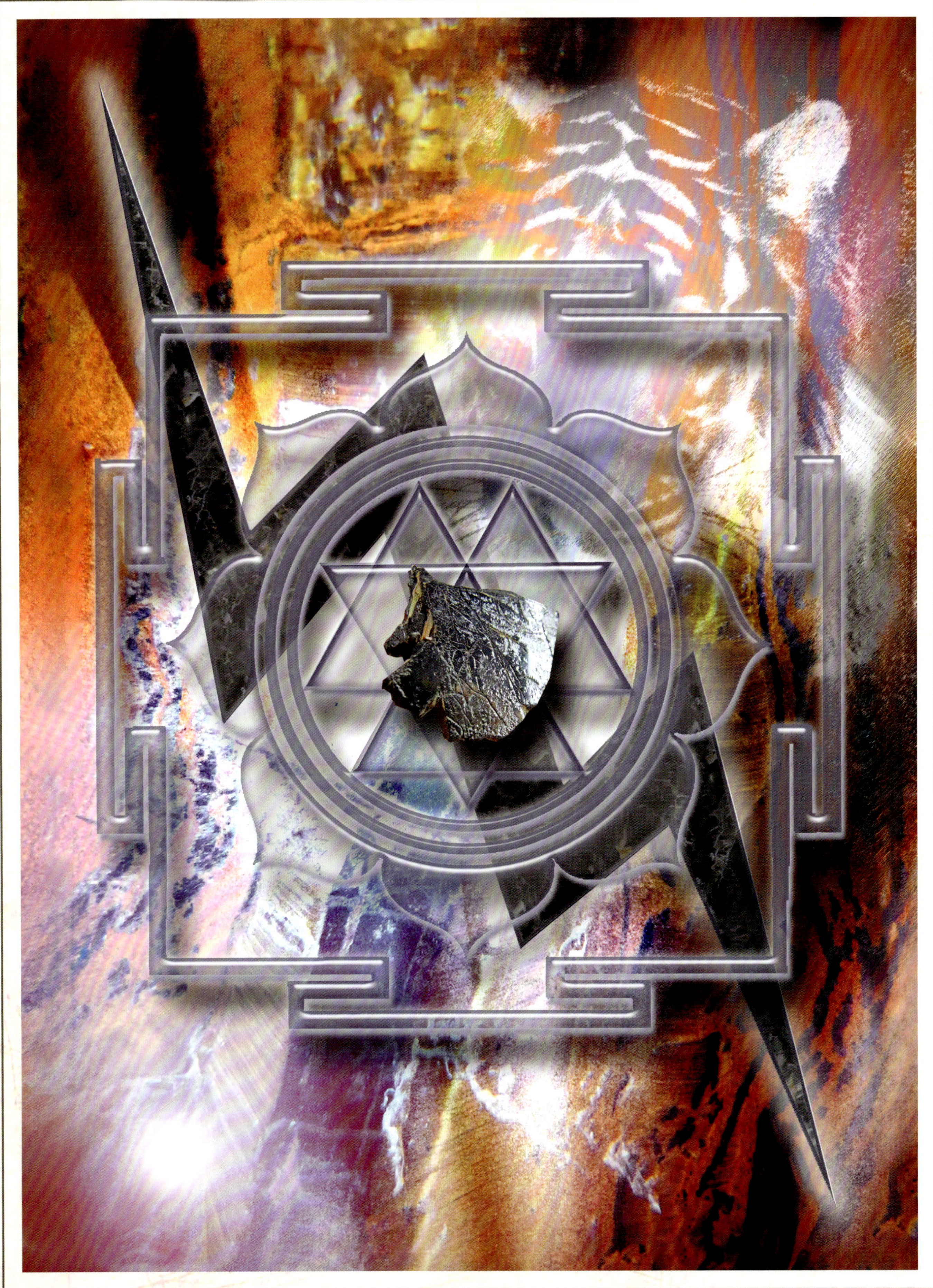

Verse IX

With powerful intention for aligned manifestations
to benefit myself and all beings —

I invoke the Crystal Angel of Hematite and Goddess Durga.

May your divine decree of sacred protection flow through me now.

Om Doom Durgaiyei Namaha.

With faith in you, my Mother Fortress, I discover bold and unshakeable confidence, naturally arising from taking refuge in your unconquerable and radiant divine will.

Through this spiritual gift, *anahata*, my heart chakra is purified and activated with your divine love, and I become capable of the courage, confidence and commitment necessary to bring my soul's most cherished visions to life.

Om Doom Durgaiyei Namaha.

Through your divine love, so be it, for the genuine benefit of all beings.

Verse X

*I own my spiritual
authority and make this
decree, that all blessings
rightfully mine are
restored unto me. From
such inner fulfilment,
my life is reshaped, and
meaningful offerings,
I am empowered to
make. In gratitude
I become one with such
grace. I speak thus
and benefit the entire
human race.*

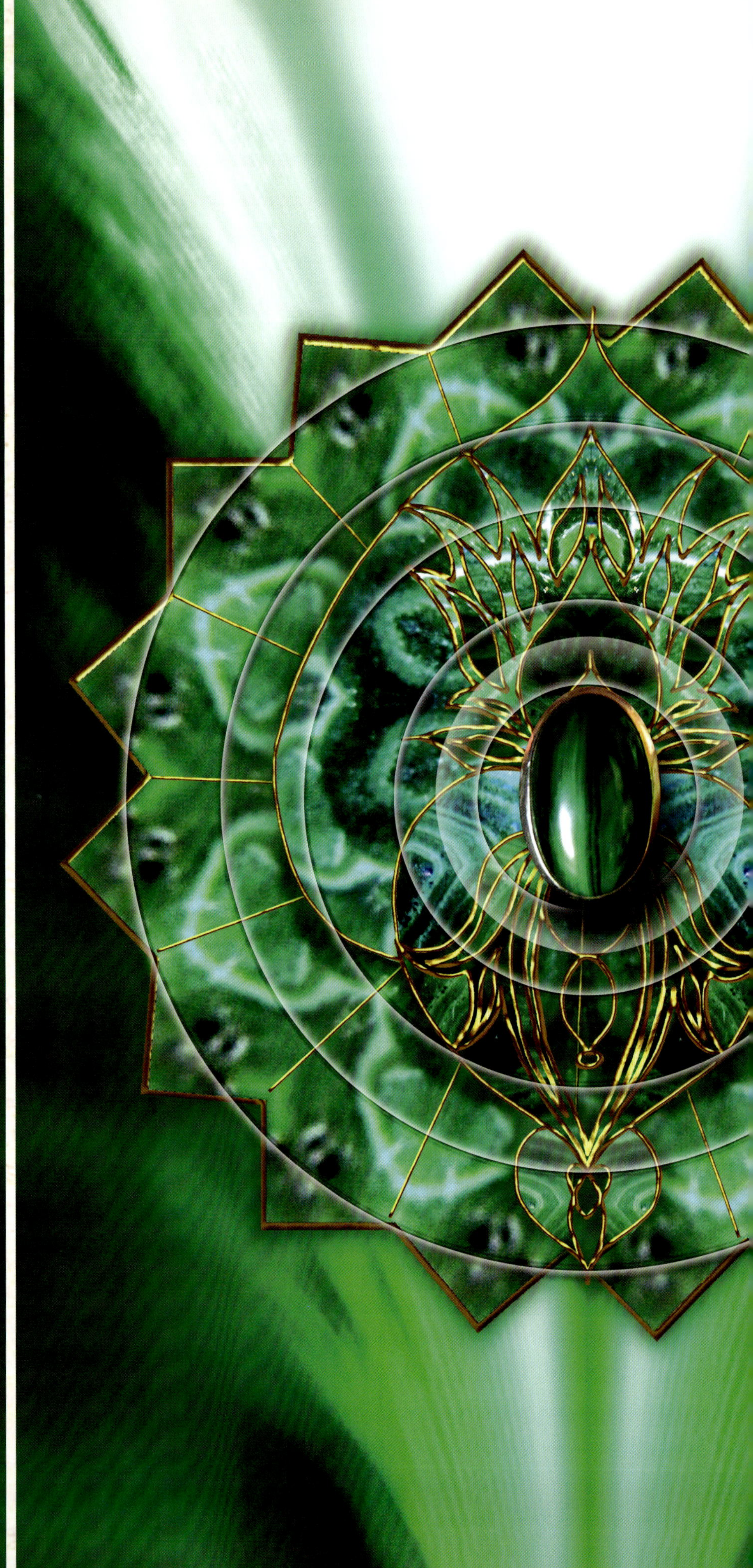

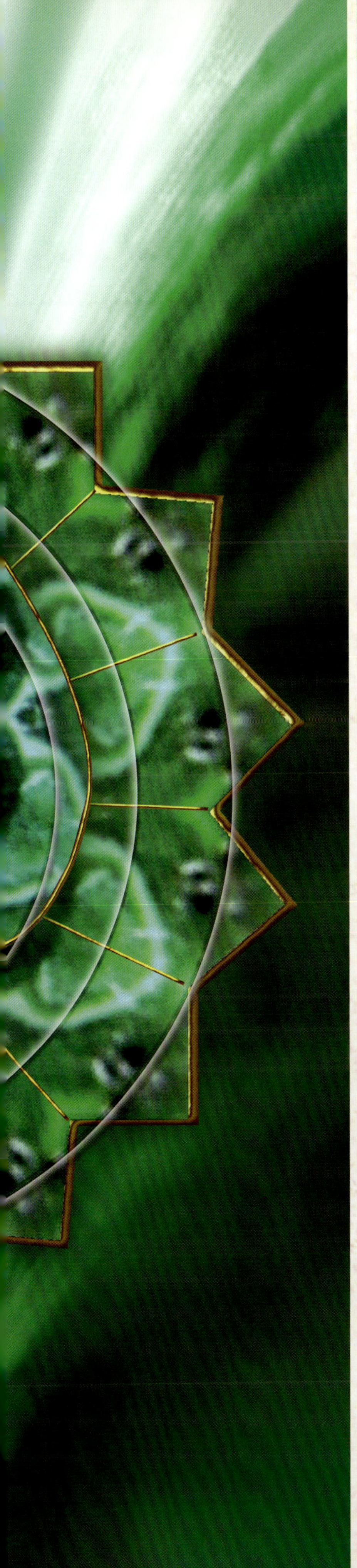

I invoke sacred synergy, affirming secret unity residing within endless diversity, reconciling polarities, alleviating tensions, and awakening deep and peaceful acceptance that embraces all of Life. Through this radical affirmation of soulful action, I become the method through which a new era and a new humanity will evolve.

I affirm the power of good.

Heightened sensitivity combines with powerful vision, and as I stand in the truth of my heart's knowledge, my presence becomes a healing generator of peace and love, uplifting myself and benefitting all beings.

I affirm the power of peace.

As I rest in the resonance of universal wisdom and unconditional divine love within, I reconnect with the truth of my nature, and embracing my path and my process.

I affirm the power of wisdom.

I prophesy all wishes fulfilled, and hence peace arising. I divine all prayers answered with kindness. I decree manifestation of love's intelligent mercy.

I affirm the power of love.

May abundant benefits manifest readily from this work. May goodwill in its entirety, from all sources, synchronise and increase, flowing as pure and generous merit, for the spiritual benefit of all beings.

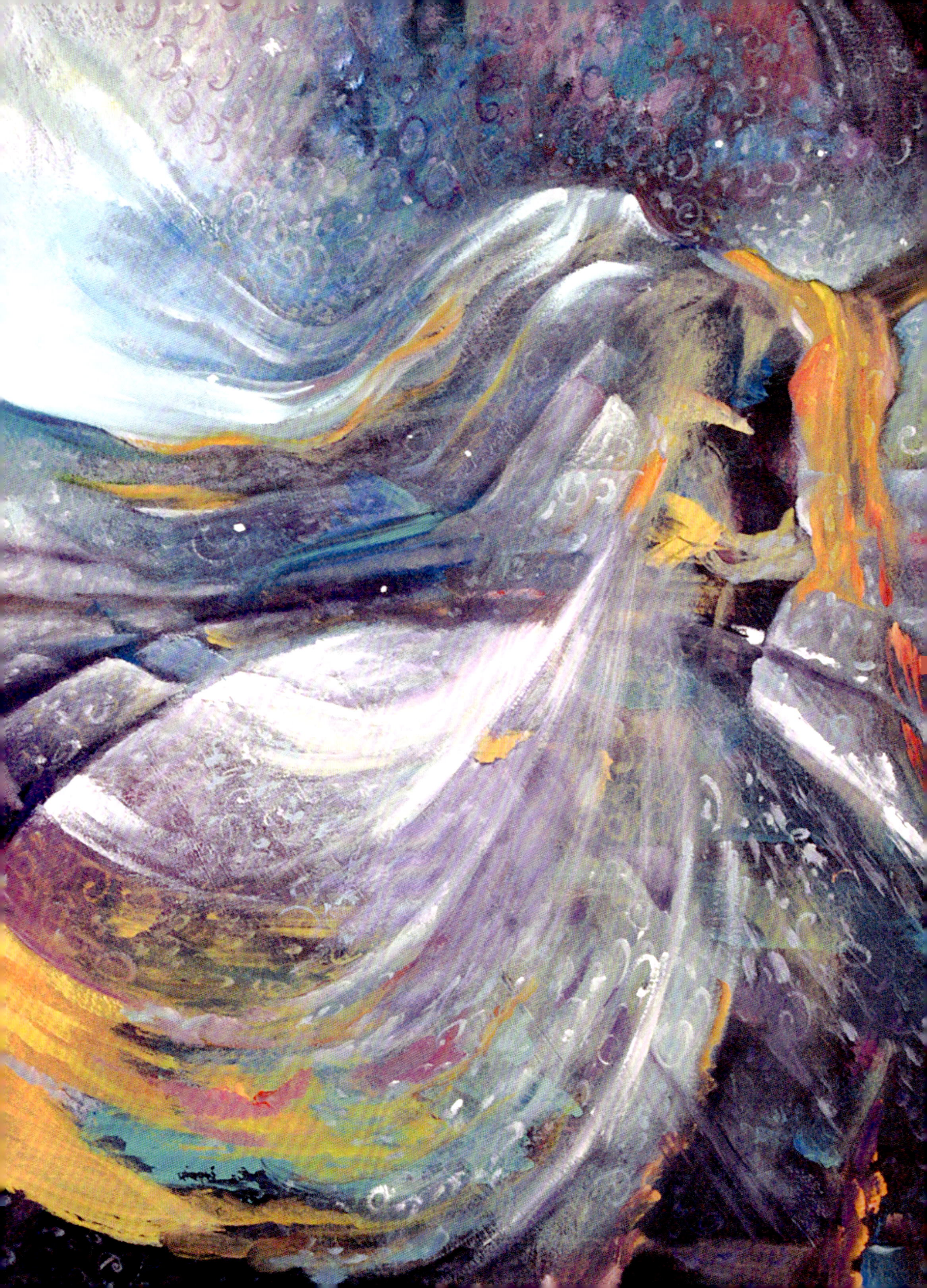

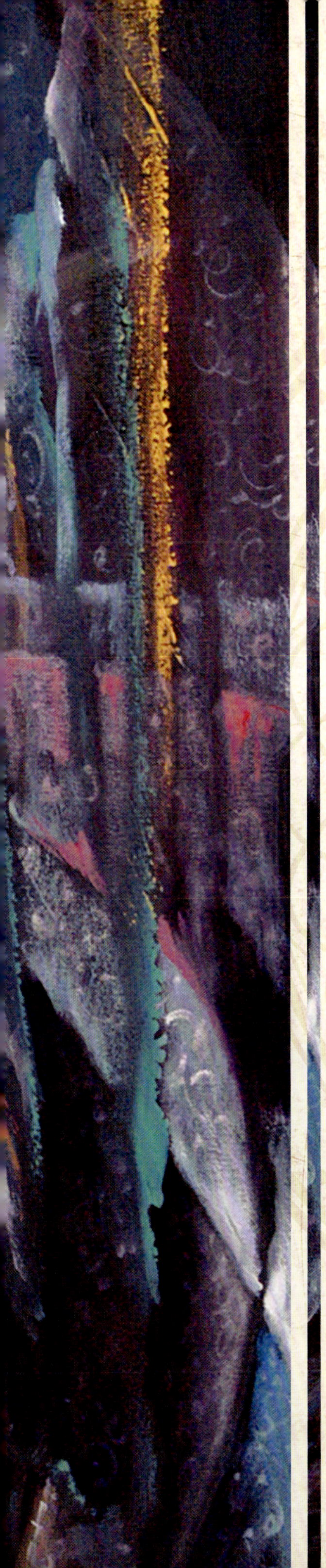

Book of RUMI

Incantations and Divinations to Invoke the Magnetic Mysticism of Your Heart and Heroic Magic of Your Path

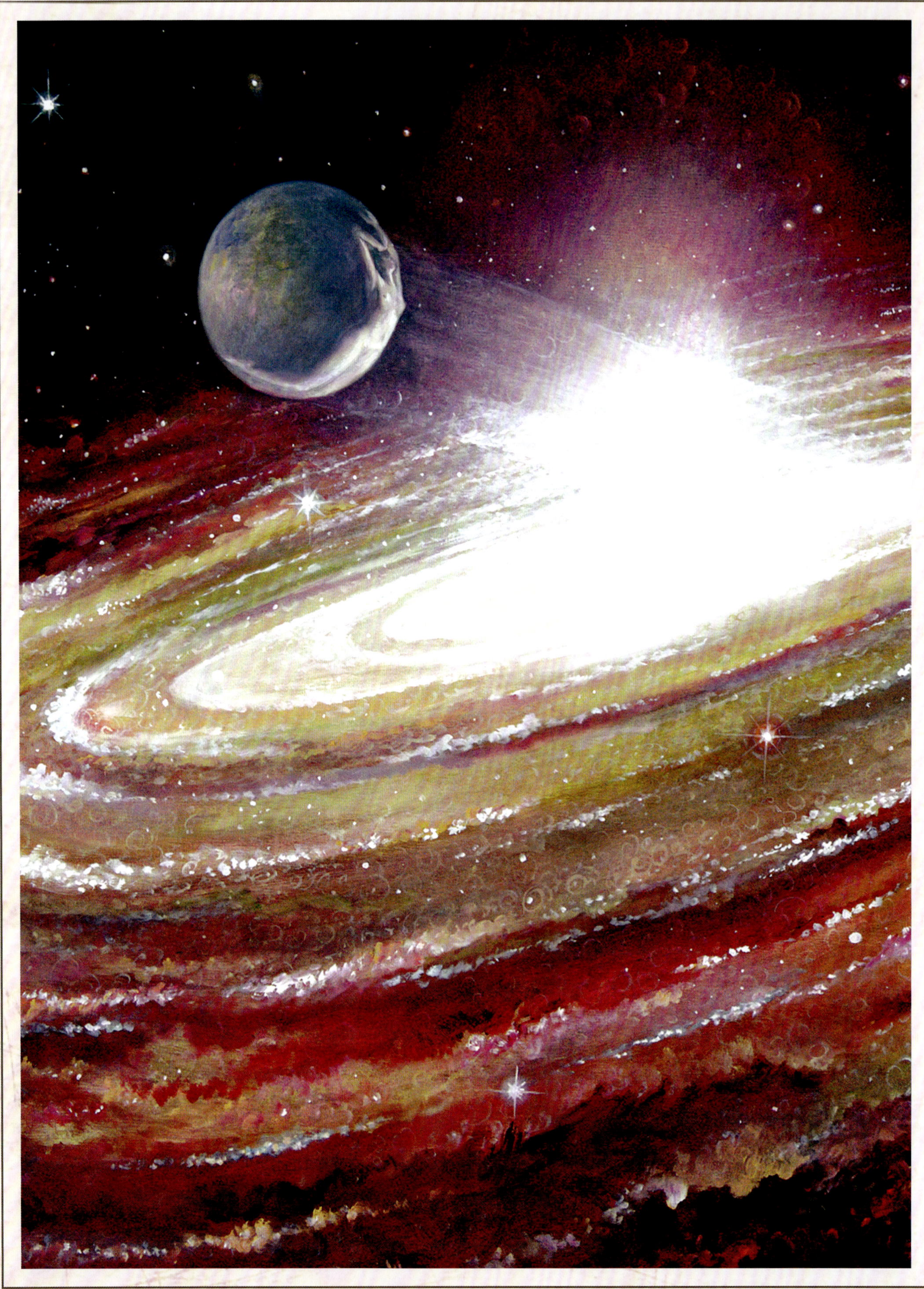

Verse I

Divine friends of my soul, Rumi and Christ,
Bestowing mantel of *Tawakkul*,
Faith in higher plan restored, I rely upon the light,
As radiant love streams from your hearts.

Al-Zahra, Fatima, Maryam,
Rose of Jericho, Flower of the Faithful,
Your restorative birthing magic,
Protects full blossoming of sacred path.

The fullness of your divine humanity,
Mirrors my own sacred humanity,
I shed delusions of inadequacy,
Embracing our family of oneness and light.

Rightful blessings manifest with timely grace,
Distraction dissolves and despair dissipates.
As water on rock, love erodes my defences,
I dance fearlessly in the beauty of what must be.

Verse II

Your presence blooms as celestial rose in my heart, exuding euphoric perfumes of grace. I inhale deeply, transported in ecstasy, as doubt crumbles and fear melts, overtaken by the powerful beauty of your love. Rose of Maryam, Hand of Fatima, I am your own, sweet with contentment in the sanctuary of you, grateful and sheltered within your protection.

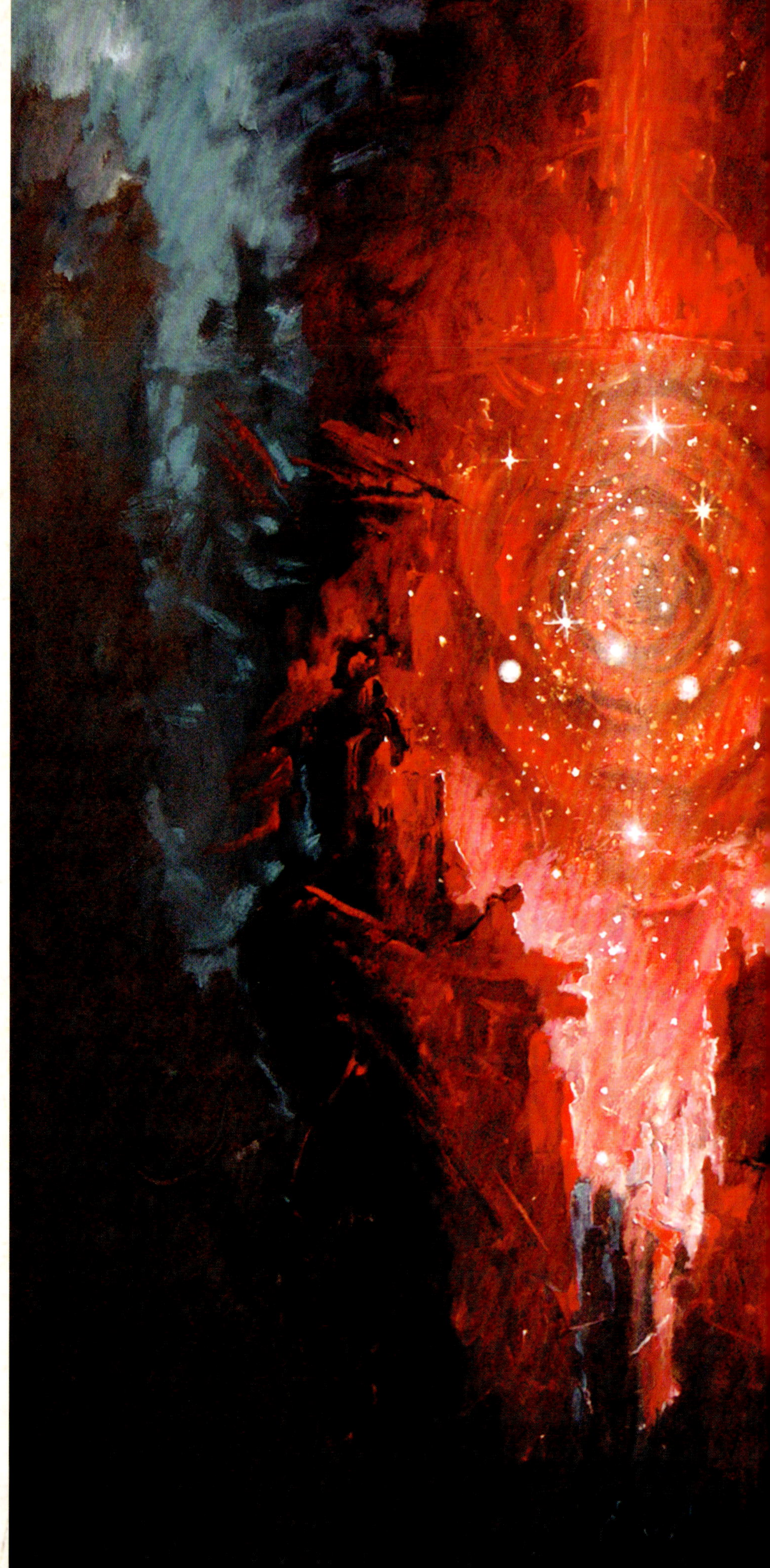

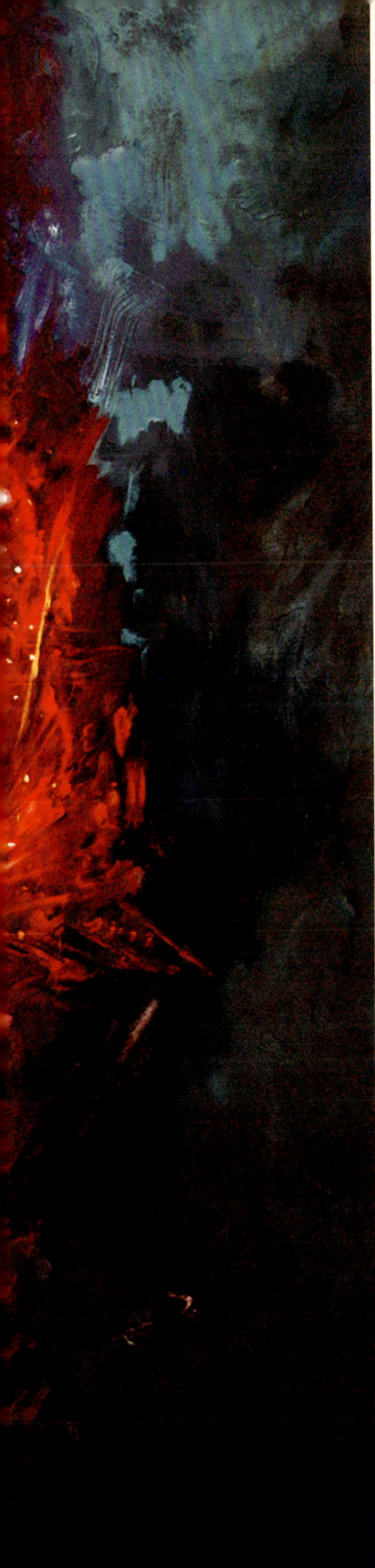

Celestial Rose of Ma,
Blooming Mother Divine,
Hands in prayer,
I invoke your blessing.

Mirrored in your ever-loving gaze,
I am emboldened to look within,
Discovering strength and dignity,
And the courage to be fully alive.

Celestial Rose of Ma,
Blooming Mother Divine,
Hands open at heart,
I receive your blessing.

Thorns belong to the rose,
And as I love the rose,
I honour what is needed for her to be,
And so I honour the thorns.

Celestial Rose of Ma,
Blooming Mother Divine,
Hands on heart,
I absorb your blessing.

Torn by thorn, I have proven my worth,
To myself, for you always knew my value.
I arise confident in my capacity to thrive,
With fearless joy I greet my future.

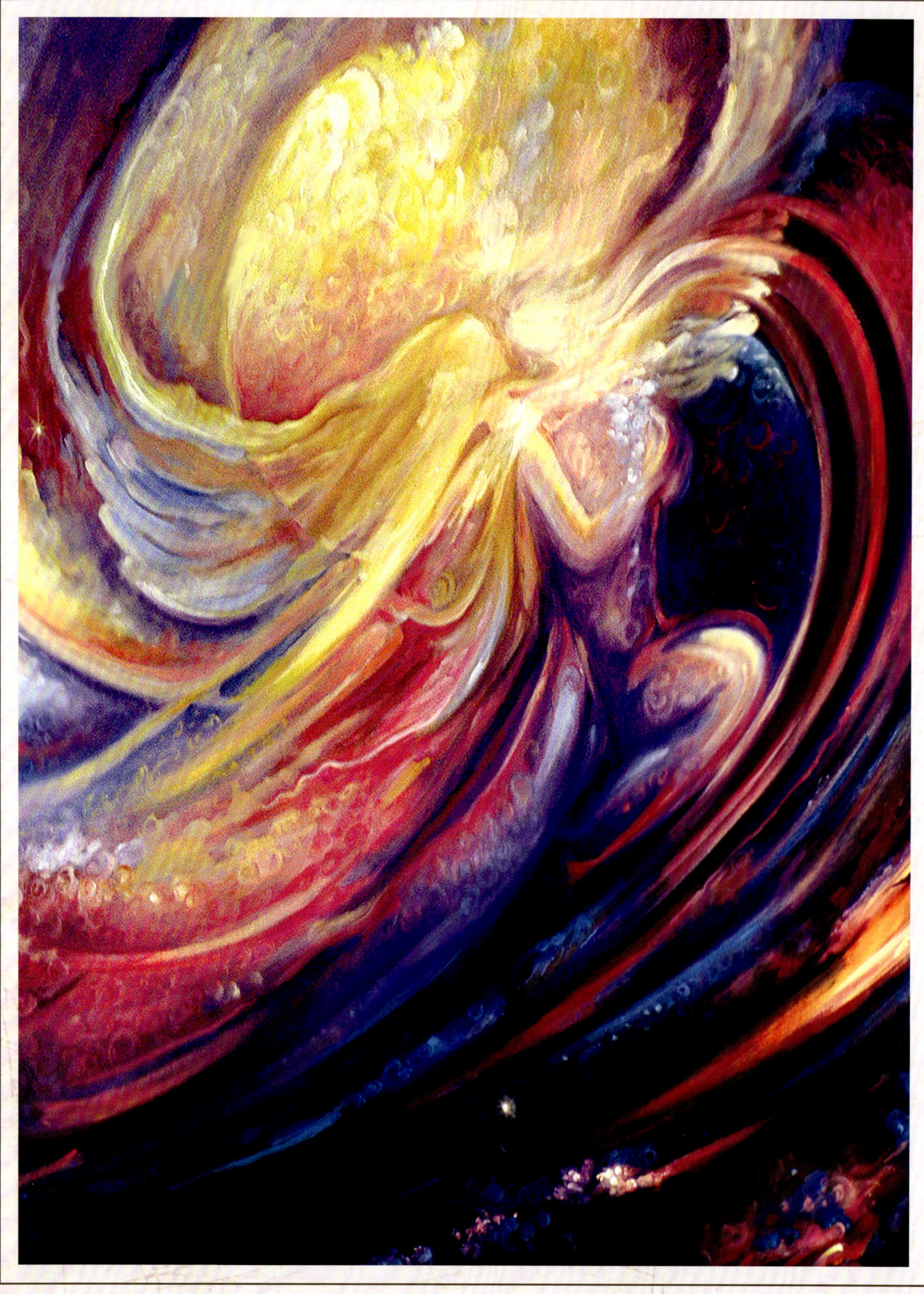

Verse III

Beloved fire of divinity, eternal friend of my heart, kindle holy desire within me, so most passionate faith rises to fulfil the promise of my destiny. May all necessary lessons unfold and blessings vest, for me and all beings, with merciful tenderness. This great love tempers all suffering and evokes the spontaneous joy of delight.

Rumi, beloved friend of my heart,
Let us be one in divine devotion,
Our hearts converge in mystical embrace,
Veils of suffering lift and disintegrate.

With patient compassion, I console the naysayers,
For one day they too will know our secret joy,
Dispensing with can-never-be impossibility,
Childlike in trust of all-accomplishing divinity.

Rumi of all hearts, I evoke your presence within,
And my hopes transform into certainties,
Inviting the Universe to playfully change face,
Reshaping itself to manifest grace.

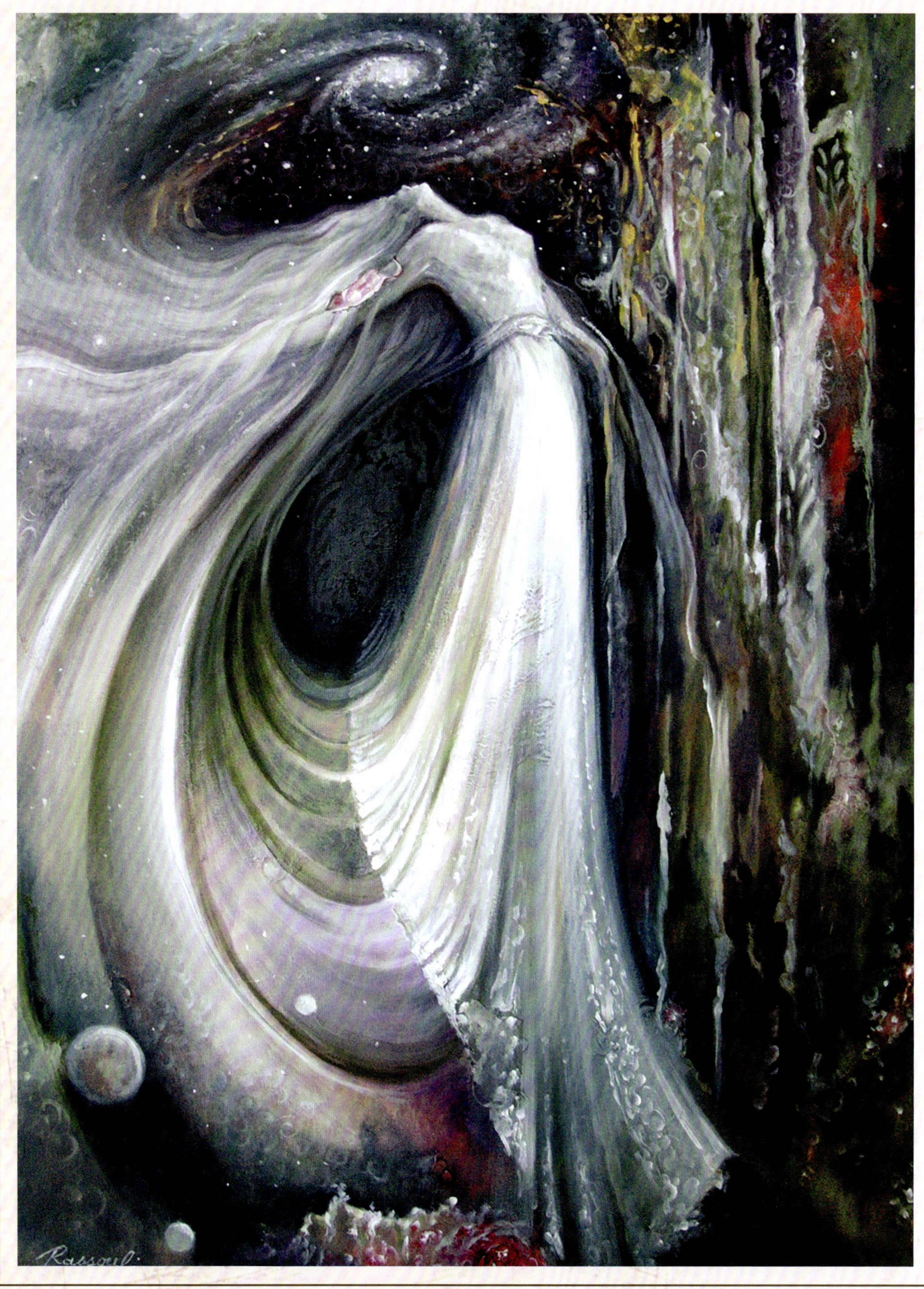

Rassoul.

Verse IV

I AM HEROIC OF HEART AND STRONG OF SPIRIT, YET AT TIMES MY CONFIDENCE WANES, AND SO I CALL UPON MY FRIEND TO REMIND ME THAT I AM FEARLESS, FAITHFUL AND FREE.

Beloved Rumi, you comfort weary heart,
"Arise," you urge, "arise!"

In whirling devotion, you calm restless spirit,
"See!" you urge, "see!"

Singing praise to console despondent flesh,
"Hear!" you urge, "hear!"

My heart renewed with gratitude for this life.
My spirit illumined by secret radiance in all things.
My flesh rallies and rises, hearing the voice of my friend.

You say,

Turn your gaze towards that which lives,
Let's laugh together with deep belly laughter,
In realisation that the only force at work in your life,
Is unconditional love.

Dare to believe!
You are right to be faithful,
And refuse to abandon hope.

This is truth.
Take the step.
This is your time.
Arise!

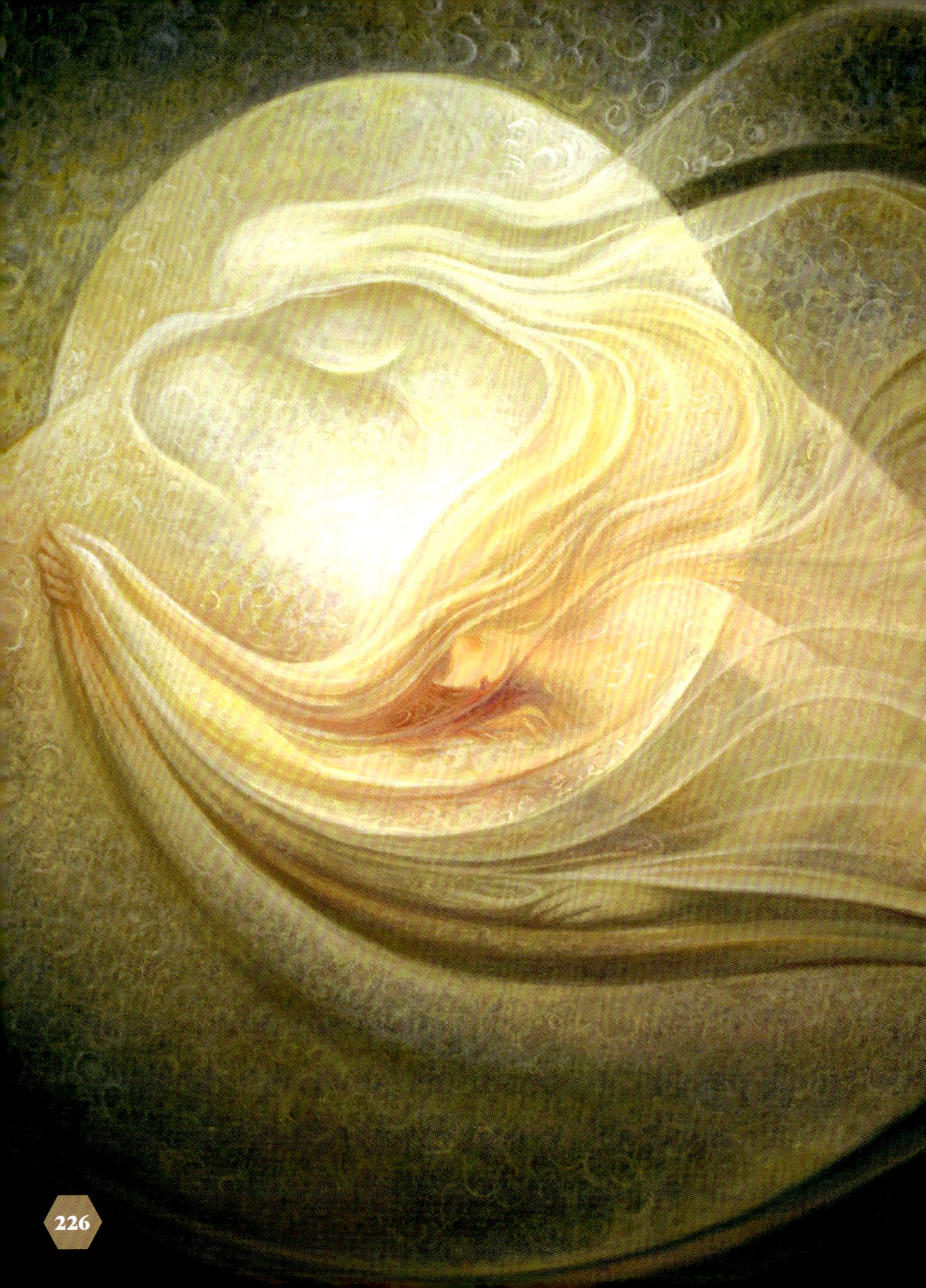

Verse V

Beloved Rumi, kindred of my courageous heart, I am ferociously hungry for soul-deep fulfilment. When I deny myself through fear or doubt, please guide me to the banquet table, where the prospect of such divine delight shall overpower my hesitancy, and together we shall feast with exuberance and gratitude.

I loosen my grip and strengthen my faith,
Reassured in divine companionship,
That all goodness and grace,
Inevitably shall be,
Restored through kindest auspice.

Intent on becoming true and whole,
I dismantle fixed opinion and identity,
Cast aside as if they were shackles.
Unburdened from regret,
I discover a self to be loved.

Images of the past fade from my heart,
I mourn and I celebrate the ending,
Rendering sacred this curious becoming,
For another emanation awaits,
Uncommon and deeply aligned.

Spiritually laid bare, freed from lament,
I am keen to hear new stories,
Crafted by the great cosmic poet,
Especially, lovingly, for my soul,
Sparking hunger for new adventure.

Verse VI

I hear your voice, Rumi of my heart, urging recollection of truth most ancient and known to my soul. My friend, you counsel me with firm kindness to remember pre-eminence of divinity. You speak to me these words of eternity — there is only divinity, always, everywhere! Look deliberately, with intent, and all secrets will unveil themselves at your wise insistence! Put your soul at ease! If you are struggling, dear friend, take my hand, and I will guide you into deep and peaceful knowing. There is only the divine, and only such truth is worthy of your allegiance and worship.

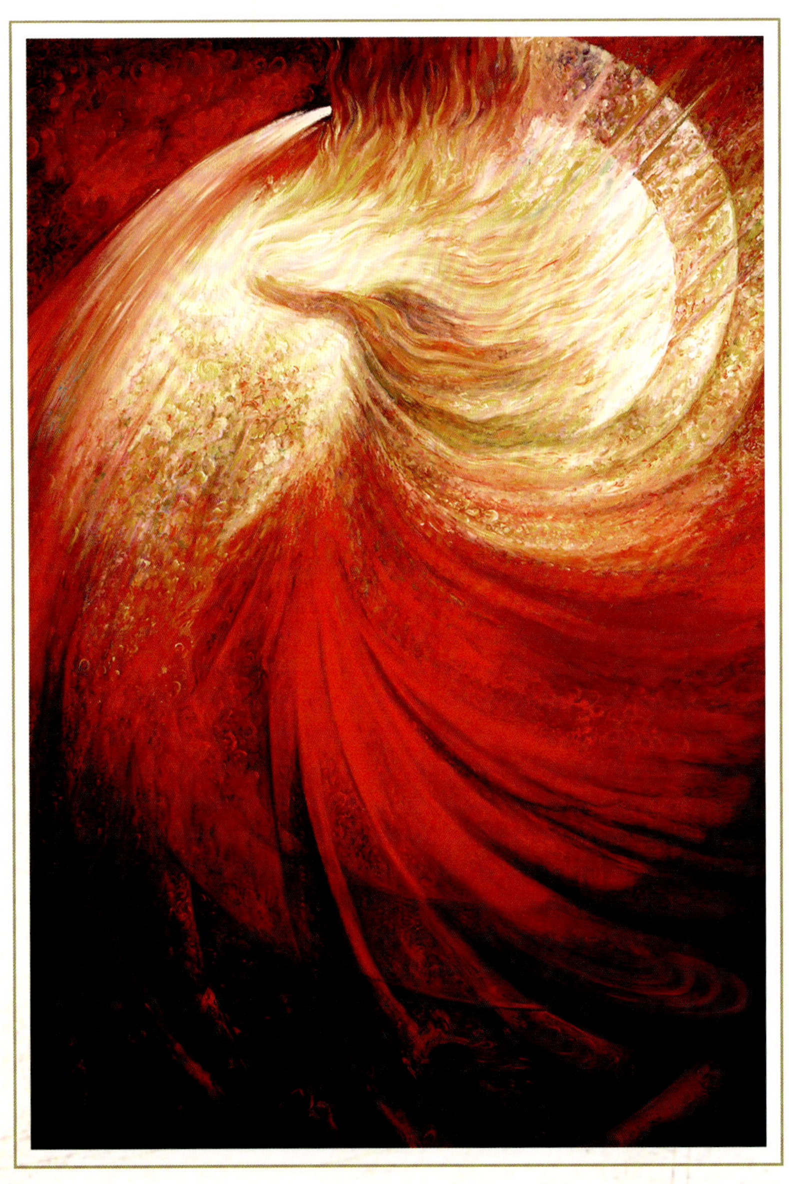

A tattered garment,
Torn by agonies past,
Once a security blanket of sorts,
Falls apart, dissolving into dust.

La ilaha illallah.

A new gown cloaks my soul,
Placed there by love's hand,
Gleaming radiant as precious gems,
Reverence and respect adorn each shoulder.

La ilaha illallah.

This new gown suits me well,
I blaze as angel with sparkling eyes,
Deeply beautiful with heroic heart,
I suddenly remember who I am.

La ilaha illallah.

Descendant of eternity,
Beloved of divinity,
I am here to live, learn and love,
In fearless embrace of Life.

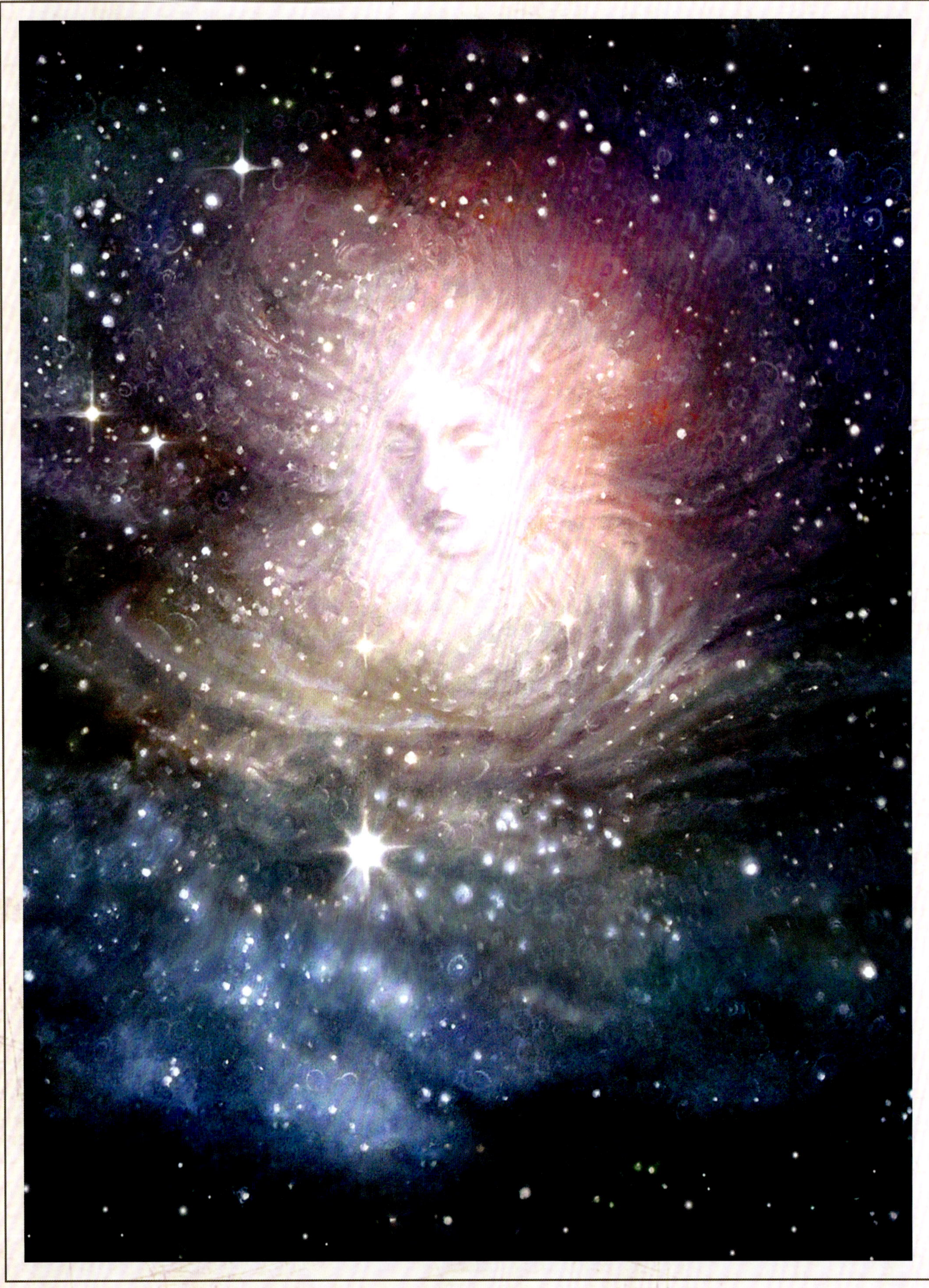

Verse VII

STELLAR GODDESS ARRAKIS, FEMININE RADIANCE OF LOVE, DIVINE NYMPH OF CELESTIAL GOLDEN APPLE AND COSMIC DRAGON GUARDING THE GATES, YOUR LIGHT SWEETENS AND DEFENDS, PROVIDING RESPONSIVE RELIEF TO MY HEART. HEAR ME, HEAVENLY PROTECTIVE MOTHER CAMEL, YOUR LOVE ENSURES THRIVING, FOR WHEN I MUST PASS THROUGH THE SPIRITUAL DESERT, YOU ARE THE DIVINE GENEROSITY OF NOURISHMENT AND PROGRESS THAT OVERCOMES ALL ODDS.

Star mother Arrakis,

Dances her cosmic rhythm.

My soul stumbles and leaps,

In harmony with her play.

She whispers mystical madness,

To abandon reason, trusting the vastness.

She calls me her star child, earth angel,

And sends falling stars to comfort me.

Secure in our bond, I demand her protection,

Rampaging cosmic tigress hurtles towards me,

Claws tearing sabotaging forces apart,

I am loved and ready for everything.

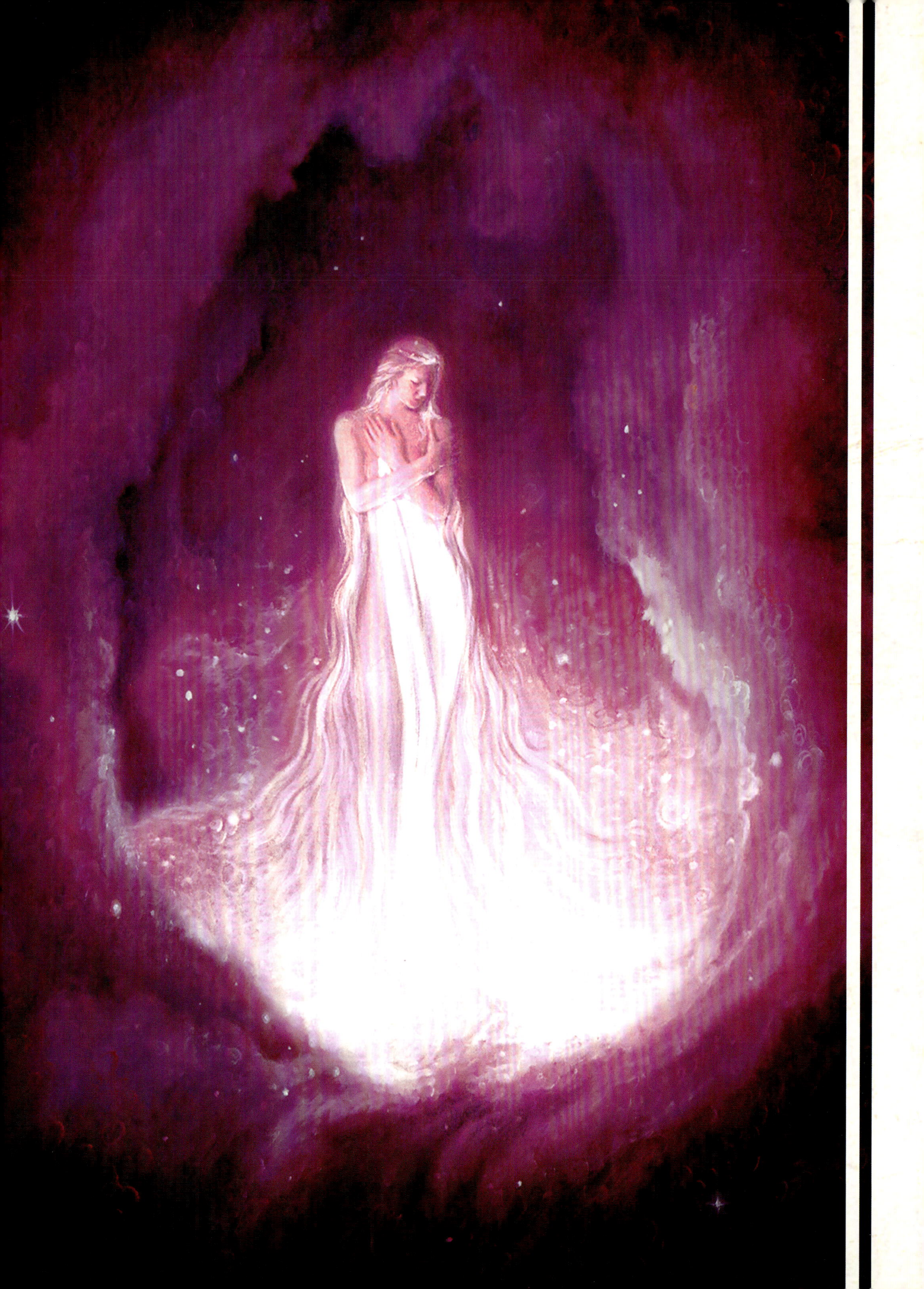

Verse VIII

Generous one, grace me with opportunities, connections, experiences and protections needed to manifest my most heart-fulfilling destiny.

Al Uzza, Star of Venus,
Your return brings the light,
And joy arising at dawn,
Hear my prayer.

When I know I need to move forward, but query which steps to take, may your light reveal beneficial insight and may wise timing infuse every decision made.

Al Uzza, Star of Venus,
Your descent brings the light,
Of comfort through the night,
Hear my prayer.

You shine in my soul as innate magic, to be channelled through my power of choice, cultivating consciousness that elevates and inspires.

Al Uzza, Star of Venus,
Your return brings the light,
And joy arising at dawn,
Hear my prayer.

May my heart's desires and yearnings be fulfilled through your merciful wisdom, in such a way that all beings benefit and are moved closer to genuine freedom.

Al Uzza, Star of Venus,
Your descent brings the light,
Of comfort through the night,
Hear my prayer.

May all beings receive the guidance and teachings, inspiration and energy, love and unconditional affection needed to alleviate suffering and inspire peace.

Al Uzza, Star of Venus,
Your return brings the light,
And joy arising at dawn,
Hear my prayer.

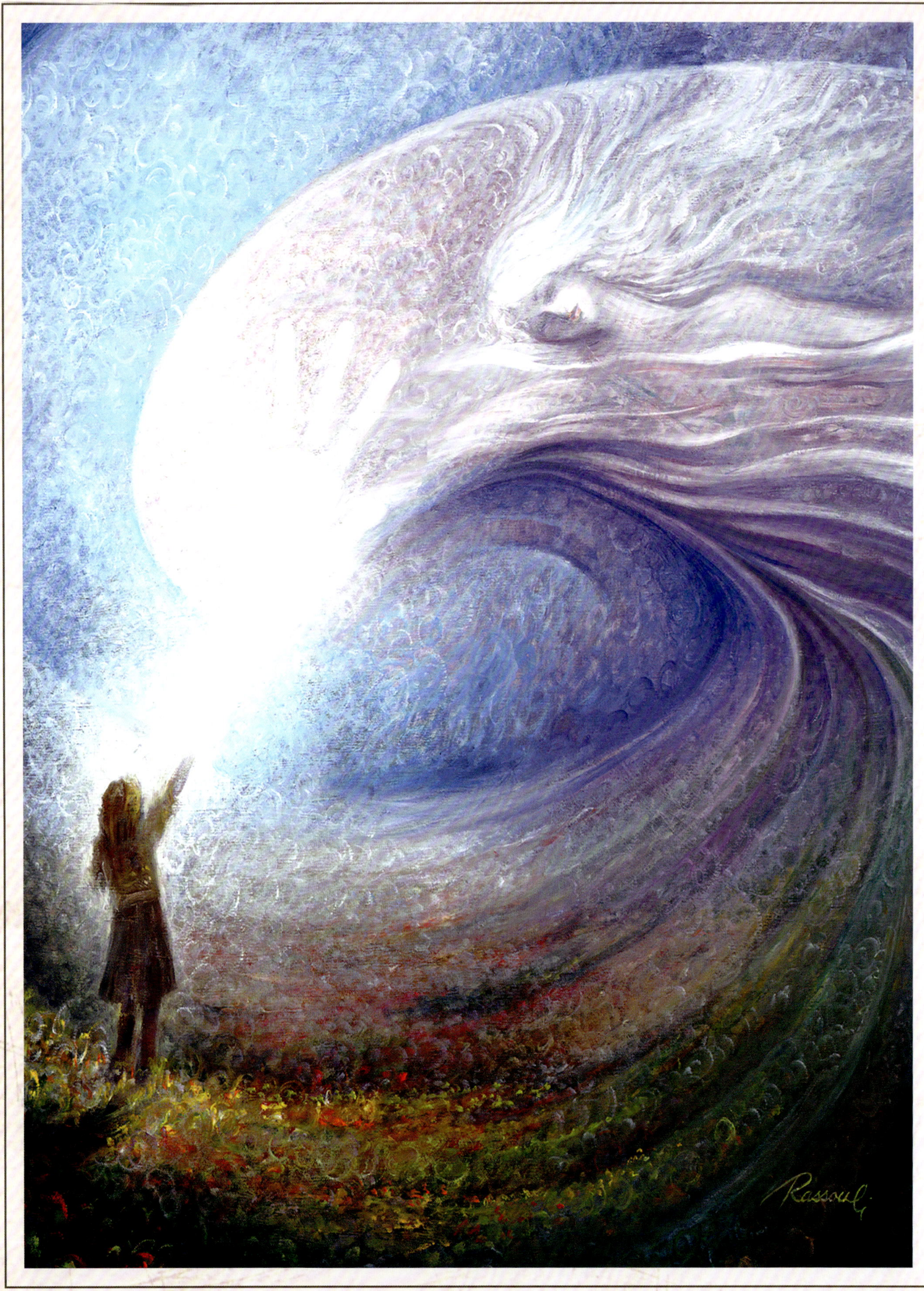
Rassouli

Verse IX

FROM MY HEART, WITH FREE WILL AND VOICE, I INVOKE THE SACRED FEMININE
PRESENCE OF DIVINITY. ANGEL RAZBAR, SOPHIA, SHEKINAH, SECRET KNOWLEDGE,
DIVINE WISDOM, INNERMOST SANCTITY, PROTECT MY MIND AS I OPEN MY HEART
TO KNOW WHAT I MUST KNOW. LET THE REVELATIONS BE MERCIFUL AND SWIFT,
EMPOWERING JOY AND GLORY ON MY PATH, INSPIRING MY SOUL TO GROW.

Hazrat Razbar, Sophia, Shekinah,
Concealing codes of knowledge,
As cipher esoterica.

Tired of worldly decrees,
I yearn for the mysteries,
That cannot be bought or sold,
Only glimpsed and exalted,
In my reverent heart.

Hazrat Razbar, Sophia, Shekinah,
Rich with certainty and energy, I pray.
Like Kodiya of the Zar.

May your enriching feminine force,
Intervene to protect my course,
Consecrating my path,
To masterfully shape raw soul,
Into exquisite human divine.

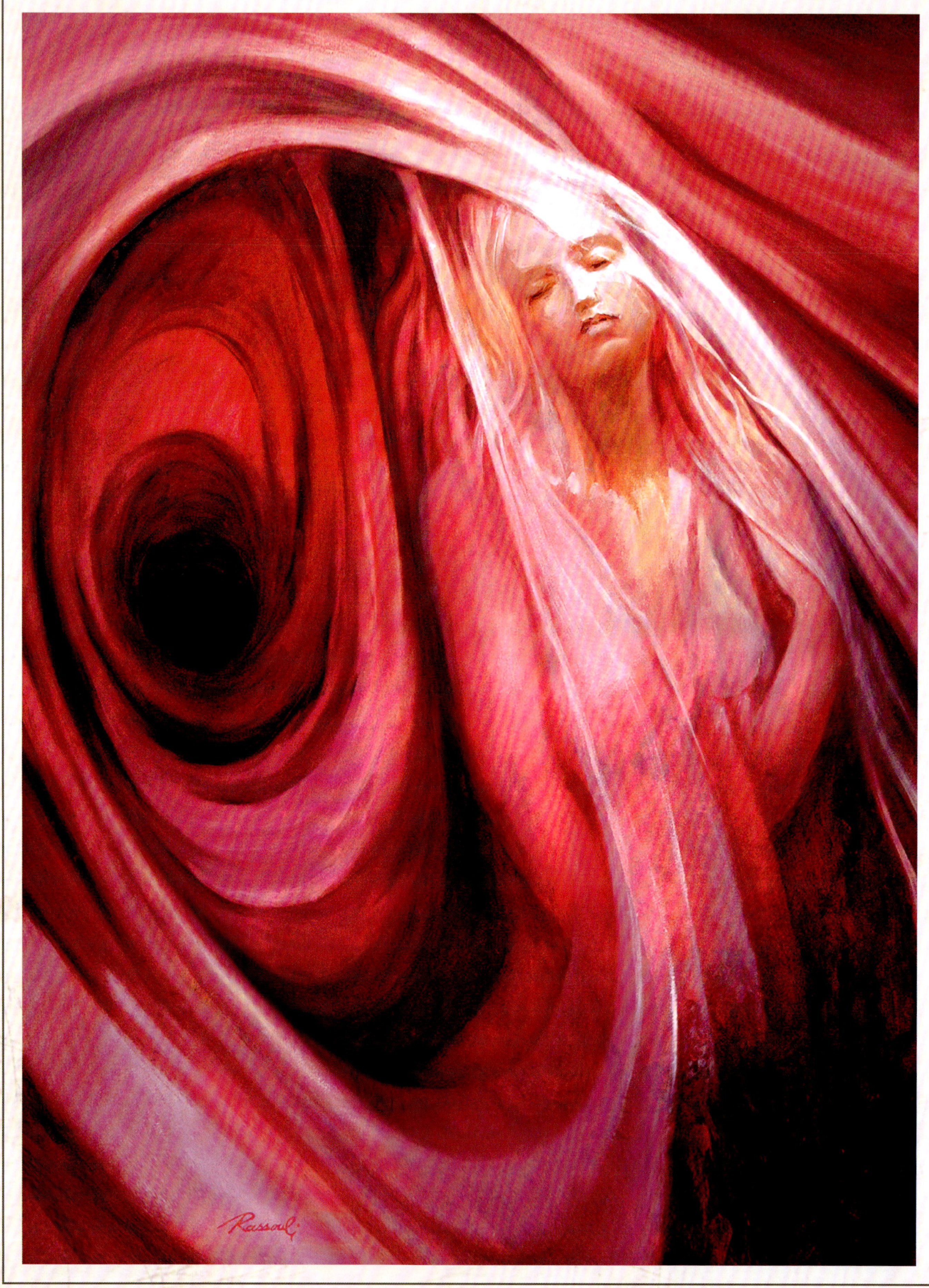
Rassouli

Verse X

Rumi, one with my heart, I enter the necessary darkness, to empty
out and renew, for transformation true. Rumi, one with my path,
I apply the necessary patience, to be ready for fresh arising,
with most exacting divine timing.

Dark divinity, I crave the silence of you,
Incessant thoughts are chatty houseguests,
Overstaying their welcome,
Bringing me no comfort.

Dar Tariki Tarikap,
In the darkness, the path.
I fear nothing,
For your love is everything.

I rest my head upon the Earth,
Inhaling her rich soil smell,
Soothed by her stability and rhythm,
Which gives Life to many beings.

Dar Tariki Tarikap,
In the darkness, the path.
I fear nothing,
For your love is everything.

Faithfully, I await the natural turning,
Of cosmic wheel of destiny,
For even in delay, kindness dwells,
And transformation is my prophecy.

Dar Tariki Tarikap,
In the darkness, the path.
I fear nothing,
for your love is everything.

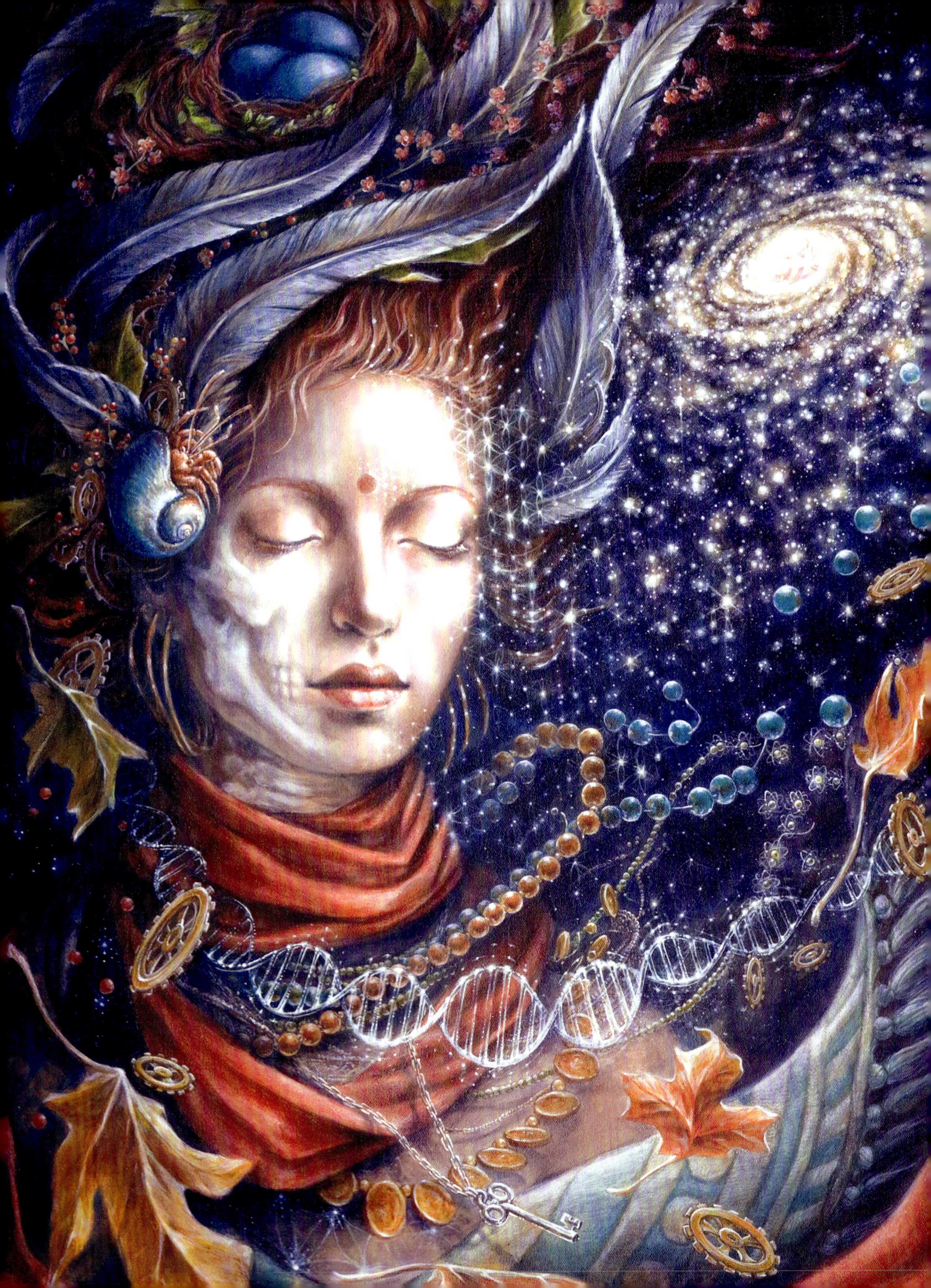

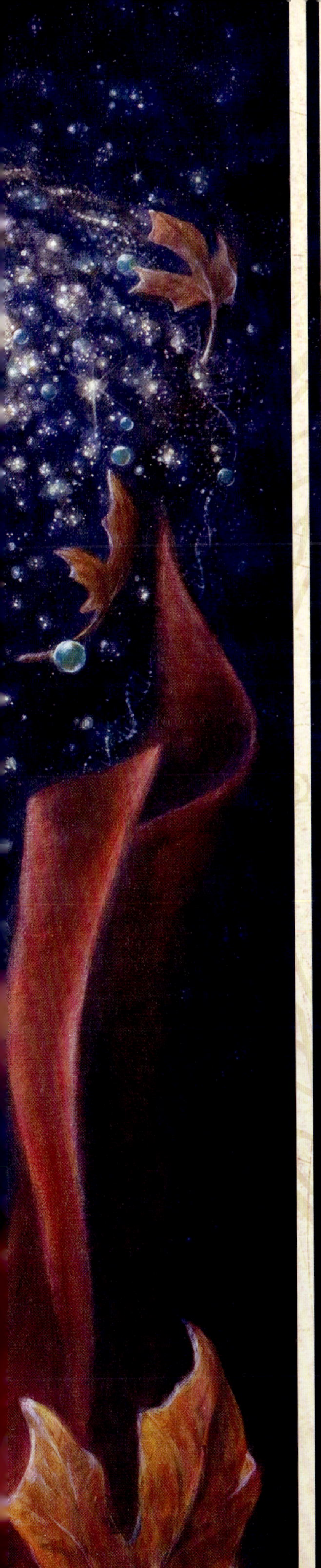

Book of SACRED REBELS

Incantations and Divinations for Consecrated Creativity, Maverick Mysticism and Divinely Defiant Visioning

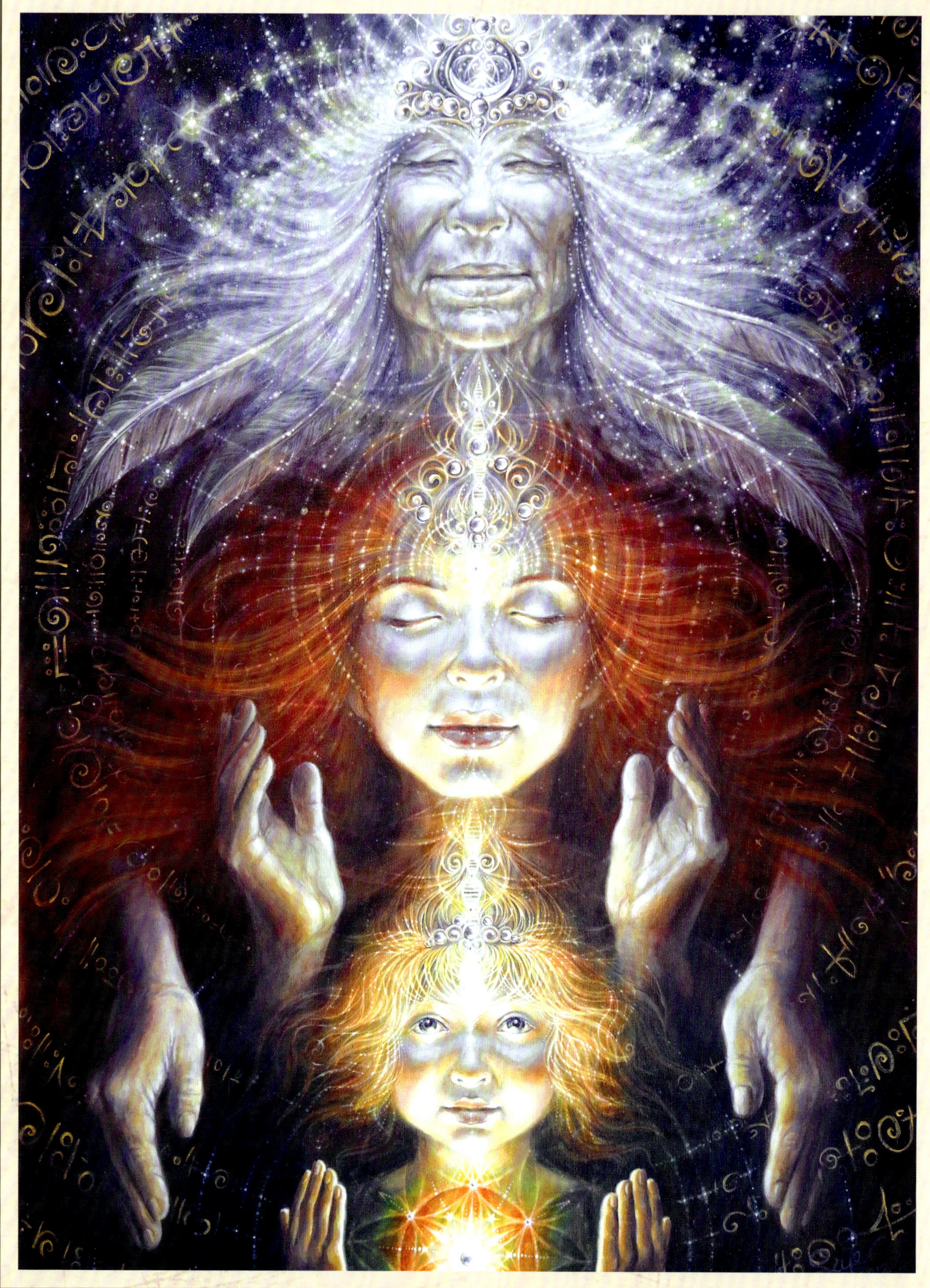

Verse I

WHEN CIRCUMSTANCES ARE BEYOND MY CONTROL, I ENGAGE MY COURAGE
AND MY SENSE OF INNATE FREEDOM, TRUSTING THAT I WILL EVOLVE
AND ULTIMATELY PROSPER IN ALL WAYS FROM WHAT IS UNFOLDING.

Free me from the past,

Storms of cleansing.

Through your wild magic,

A cycle is ending.

Through chaos of clearing,

I am readied for rebirth.

Highest cosmic oracle,

Decrees my sacred ripening.

Storms of change,

Storms of repair,

I recognise your wisdom,

Surrendering to your care.

Peace comes swiftly,

As new way is grounded.

Optimism lifts my heart,

Relief of resolution arises.

Verse II

Divine Feminine Cosmic Attractor, Generous Provider and Mother of Infinite Resources, bless me and all beings with your love. May authentic spirituality flourish in ways esoteric and pragmatic, increasing joyful fulfilment for all, fuelled by your presence and grace. May I witness the truths that I need to know, understand the steps that I need to take, and recognise the wisdom and courage within to do so.

I am ready to access the understanding,
That opens me to a more expansive reality.

So patiently I clarify my sense of things,
As fragments of intuition coalesce.

I affirm trust in myself,
In Life and the Universe,

That all things ultimately,
Work to a higher good,

And the way to that goodness,
Shall always be found.

I choose to see clearly,
Without being afraid,

For I know my capacity,
To heal and create.

Divine Feminine Cosmic Attractor,
Generous Provider, Mother of Infinite Resources,
Bless me and all beings with your love.

Om Hreem Shreem Kleem Parameshwari Swaha.
Om Hreem Shreem Kleem Parameshwari Swaha.
Om Hreem Shreem Kleem Parameshwari Swaha.

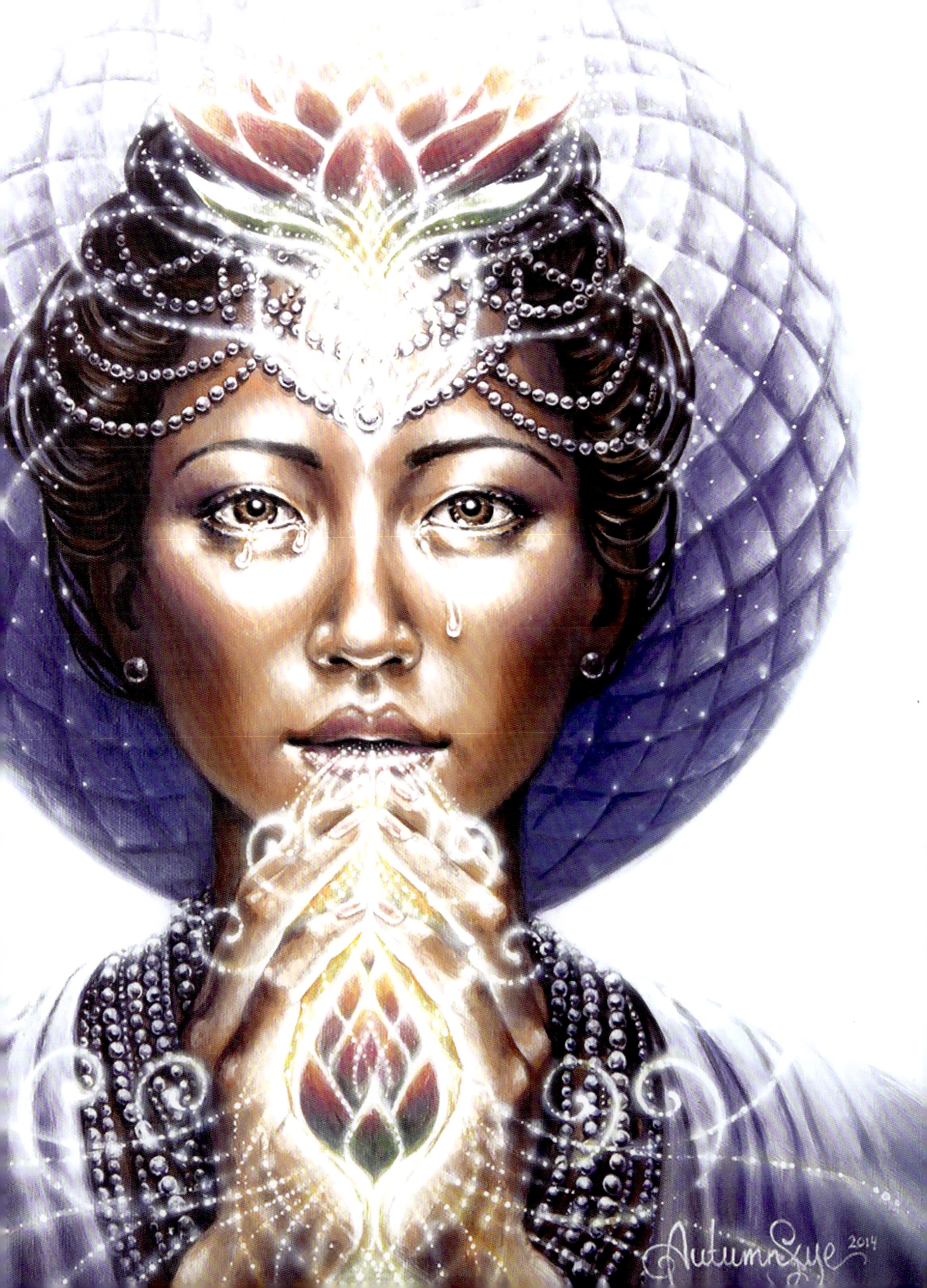

AutumnSkye 2014

Verse III

Mother Bee, Medicine Bee, natural queen of benevolent industry,
may I recognise true purpose and apply myself fearlessly.
Mother Nature provides abundantly, echoed within as my natural
resourcefulness and creativity. I trust in her, I trust in me.

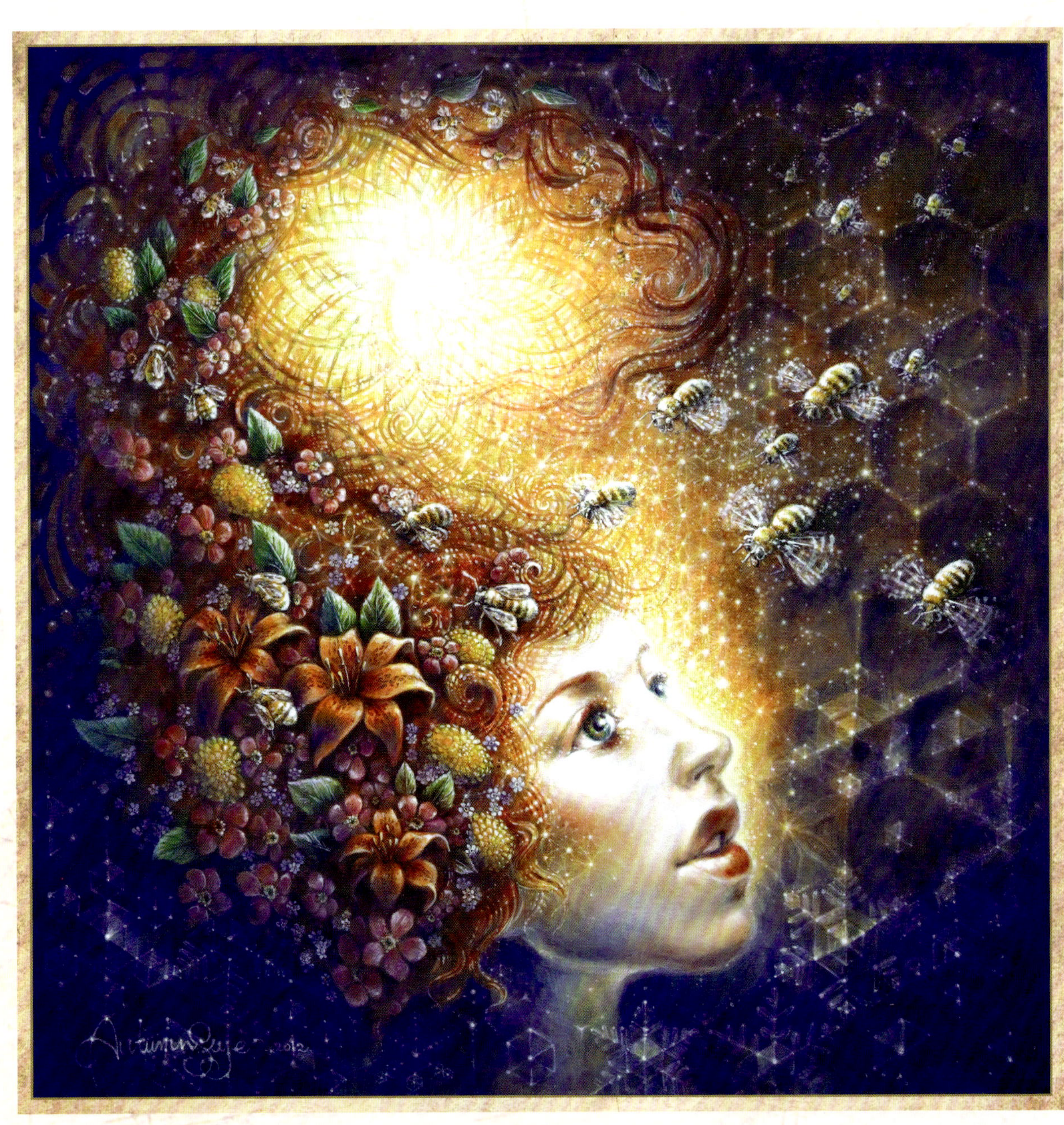

Medicine Bee,
Creatrix of Sweetness,
Express your pleasure and purpose,
In the nectar of my heart.

Bzzzzzzzzzzz
OM AH HUM.

Honouring the greater good,
I divine realisation of highest inspiration,
Fuelling abundant manifestation.

Medicine Bee,
Creatrix of Sweetness,
Express your pleasure and purpose,
In the nectar of my heart.

Bzzzzzzzzzzz
OM AH HUM.

Honouring the greater good,
I prophesy sacred connections and synchronicities,
Weaving mutual enhancement and blissful fruition.

Medicine Bee,
Creatrix of Sweetness,
Express your pleasure and purpose,
In the nectar of my heart.

Bzzzzzzzzzzz
OM AH HUM.

Honouring the greater good,
I invoke your medicine of commitment,
And skilful intelligence to accomplish purpose.

Medicine Bee,
Creatrix of Sweetness,
Express your pleasure and purpose,
In the nectar of my heart.

Bzzzzzzzzzzz
OM AH HUM.

Verse IV

The necessary medicine is the Holy Medicine, the tonic for the soul that alleviates all ill, and guides the precious one to relief and fulfilment. I am the precious one, as are all beings, for we are all one. I witness this sanctity inherent in all hearts. So I quest spiritually for the remedy, the elixir, the soma, that will bring about resolutions most divinely blessed.

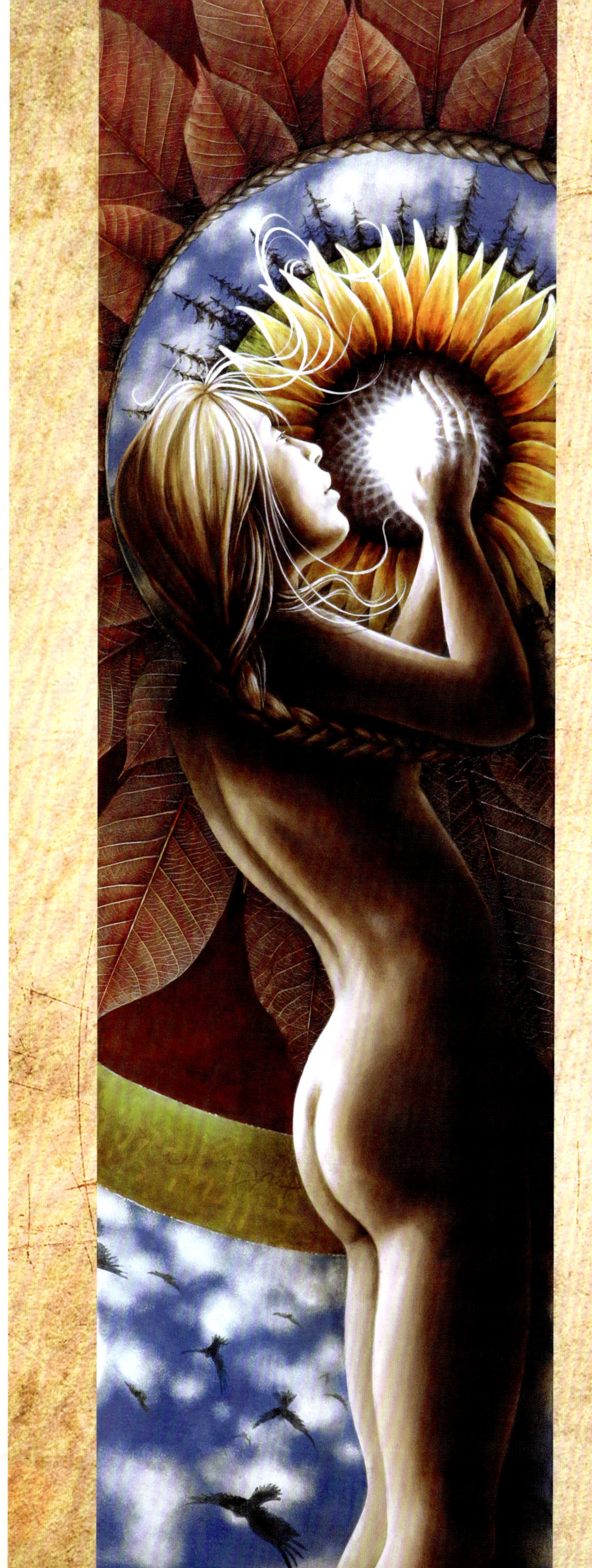

Holy Medicine within me,
Holy Medicine around me,
I recognise the responsive kindness of grace,
Fearless, my heart opens in reverence and awe.

Though I may not fit in, I belong.
Though my process may be unusual, it is true.
Though I may evoke change, I bring peace.

Sacred darkness of Kali, pure light of Kuan Yin,
I invoke the Holy Medicine.

Birthing in darkness, growing in light,
Sacred sound restores my soul to Life.

Om Kreem Kaliyei Namaha.
Om Mani Padme Hum.

Om Kreem Kaliyei Namaha.
Om Mani Padme Hum.

Om Kreem Kaliyei Namaha.
Om Mani Padme Hum.

Though I may not fit in, I belong.
Though my process may be unusual, it is true.
Though I may evoke change, I bring peace.

Holy Medicine within me,
Holy Medicine around me,
I receive the eternal blessing of grace,
Infused, my heart emanates healing love.

I honour unique process, the path to deep truth.
I honour divine generosity, finding courage and confidence.
I honour spiritual protection, amplifying love and joy.
I honour cosmic connection, channelling soul medicines.

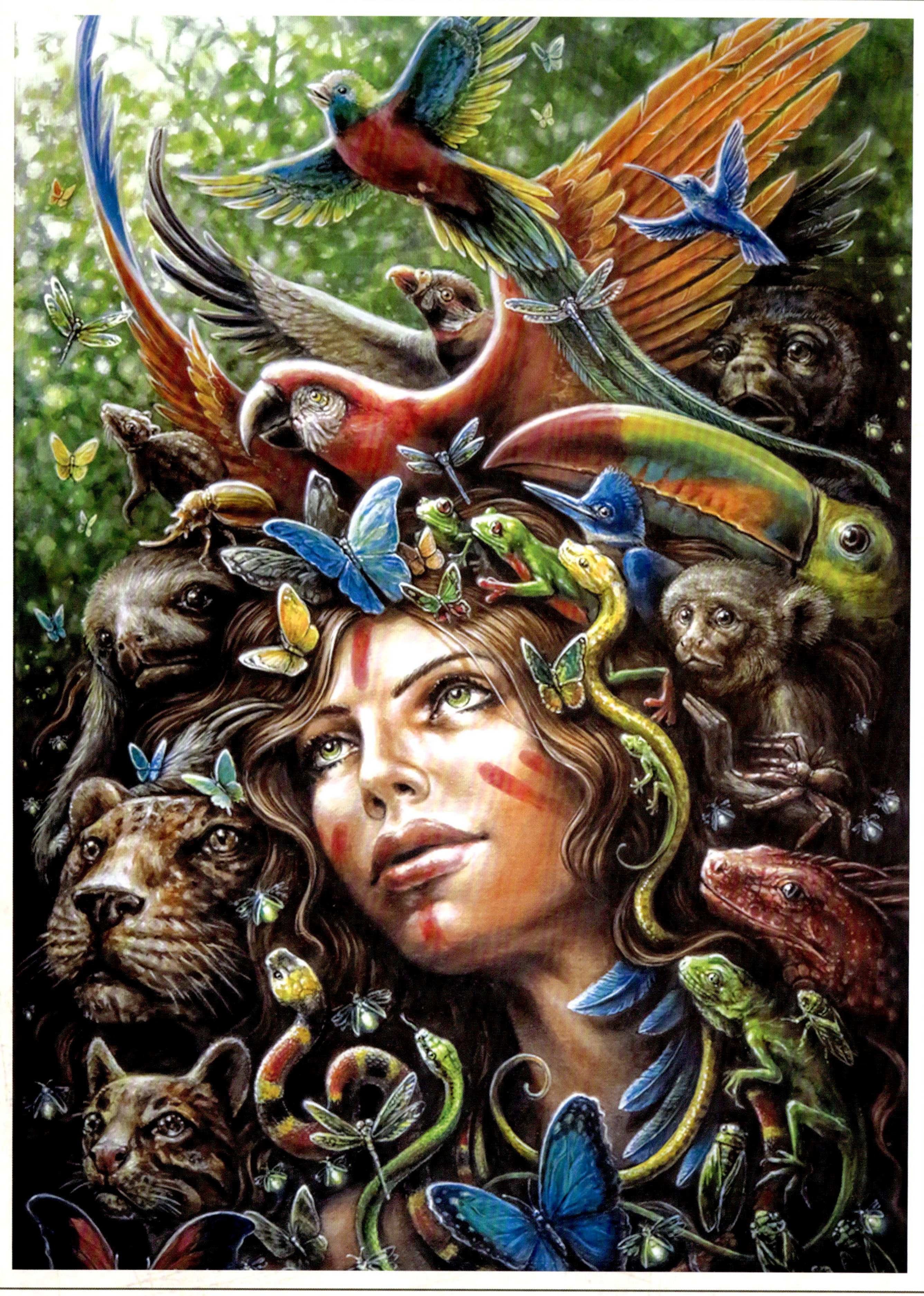

Verse V

MY SOUL MOVES FROM AN ANCIENT POWER, A COSMIC RHYTHM UNTAMED.
TIMING, REVELATION AND RESOURCES LOVINGLY PACED AND DISPENSED BY THE
KINDEST DIVINE BENEFACTOR. BLESSINGS VEST AT THE MOST SPIRITUALLY FERTILE
MOMENT AND AS I TRUST THE GREATER TIMING OF ALL THINGS, I REALISE
MY RIPENING IS ASSURED.

I trust in the ebb, the agitation, the release,
I trust in the flow, the calming, the gathering.

Turning within to connect with myself,
Reaching to others to share myself,

I attune to the rhythms of my own heart,
And align with the song of the Universe.

I honour the wisdom of divine timing,
As I honour the rhythms of my soul.

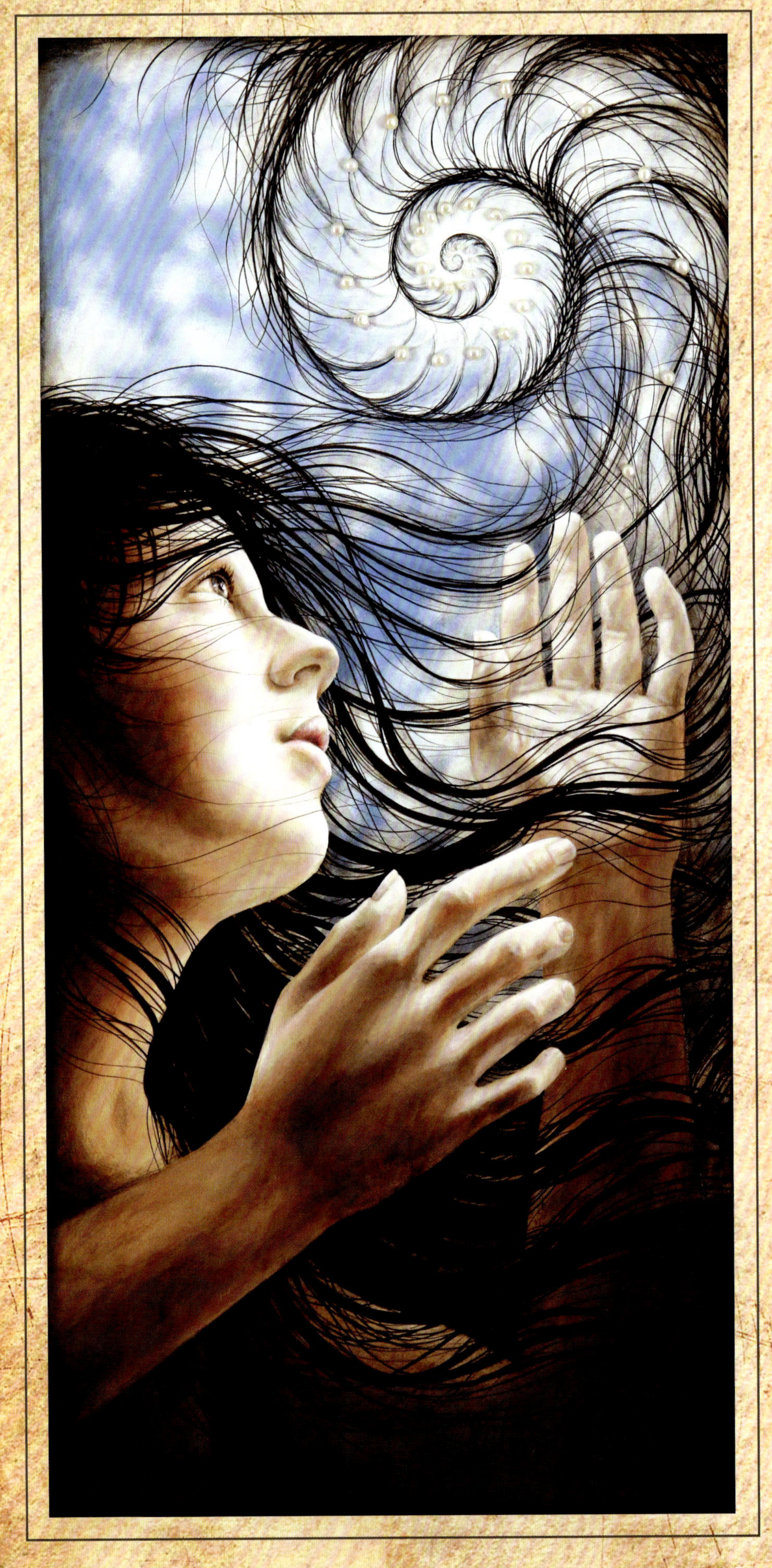

Verse VI

Though guidance may be unconventional,

Mysterious, unusual or tricky to decipher,

I listen intently to the wild oracle within,

For strangely beautiful newness wants to be.

Maybe the message that arises,

Rattles my beliefs and demands my daring,

Creative rumblings temporarily disrupt flow,

Something real, liberating and good is occurring.

That rumble may transform into a roar,

Breaking through complacent mind,

Though startled into bewilderment,

I remain certain that I am blessed.

The old way is out! Done! Released!

I am invited, dragged, coerced, nurtured,

Onto the path that delivers sacred fulfilment,

I fumble with wisdom towards exquisite fruition.

Verse VII

*Holy ones of greatest wisdom, I call upon your skilful
intervention and assistance. Help me in all ways! I
invoke your wisdom of discernment, to recognise and
seize rightful blessings and rebuke interference. May I
proceed with insight and protection on my path, to make
the most of all that I have, and amplify attraction of new
gifts, contributing conscious creativity to this world, and
increasing the presence of love for all.*

Legacy of light, my sacred birthright,
I gain strength from the generations,
Who have walked this path of Life.
I distil all that is good and true,
And express my essence in the world.

Legacy of light, my sacred birthright,
I gain wisdom from the ancestries,
Of body and blood, spirit and sky.
Sacred endowments from the Universe,
Flow into my open and grateful heart.

With feet grounded in gratitude,
I am beloved of Earth Mother,
And crown eager in openness,
I am beloved of Spirit Father.
I am arising love and descending grace,
My heart unconquerable in passionate devotion.

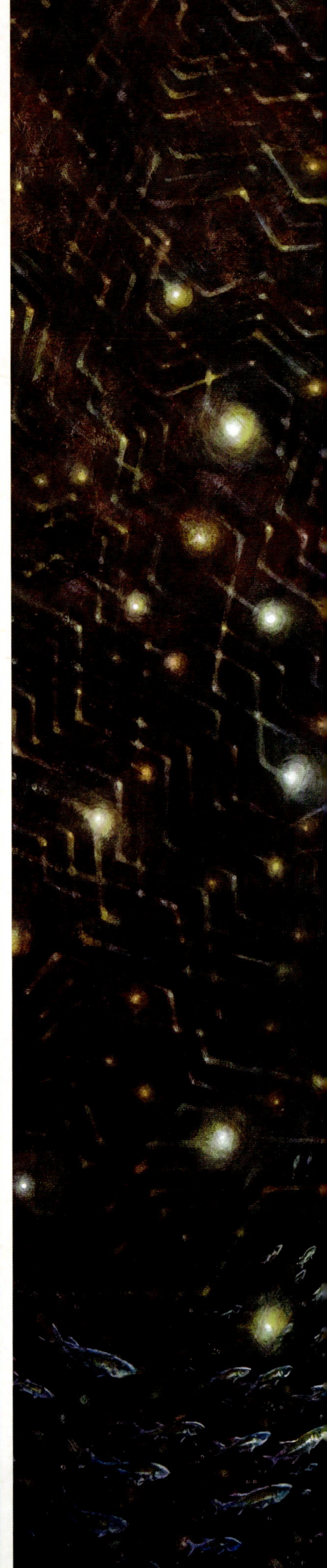

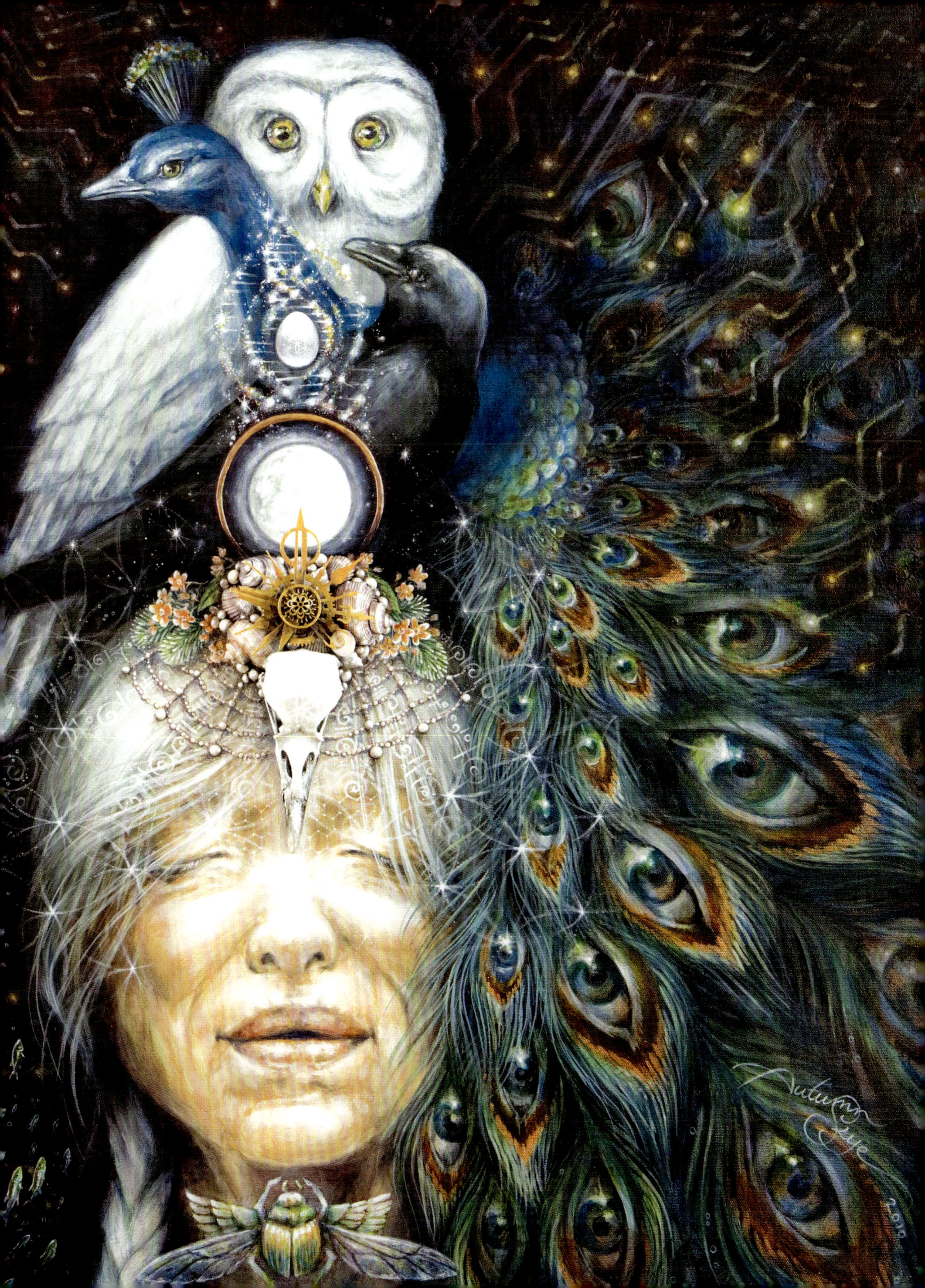

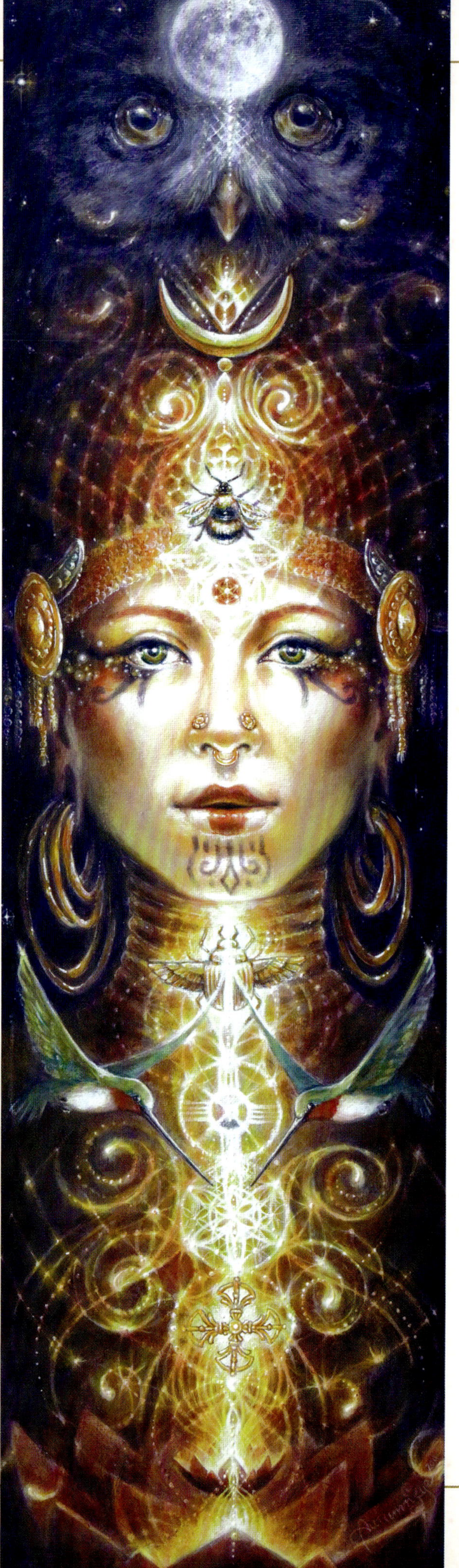

Verse VIII

Divine Feminine
Goddess of All
Remedies, resolve,
resolve, resolve!
May all difficulties,
obstacles and
fears, dissolve,
dissolve, dissolve!
I am immediately
embraced in your
sanctuary, gifted
with blessings untold,
untold, untold!

When the void of uncertainty beckons me,
I move willingly into my process,
Affirming unassailable presence of grace,
For like winter on Earth,
Darkness too has its purpose,
And more than anything else,
I believe in the power of love.

Om Tare Tam Swaha.
In your green radiance,
You emanate the saving grace that alleviates all troubles and fears.

Om Tare Tam Swaha.
In your black radiance,
You emanate the protective grace that overpowers all negative forces.

Om Tare Tam Swaha.
In your white radiance,
You emanate the comforting grace that restores all peace and wellbeing.

Om Tare Tam Swaha.
In your red radiance,
You emanate the joyful grace that vitalises fulfilment of all wishes.

Om Tare Tam Swaha.
In your yellow radiance,
You emanate the enriching grace that attracts all blessings of abundance.

Beloved and trustworthy Tara,
Diverse mother providing all that is needed,
I am fearless, wise and safe in your love,
Our bond ensures righteous manifestation,
Like the winter bursting forth into spring,
As darkness yields to light.

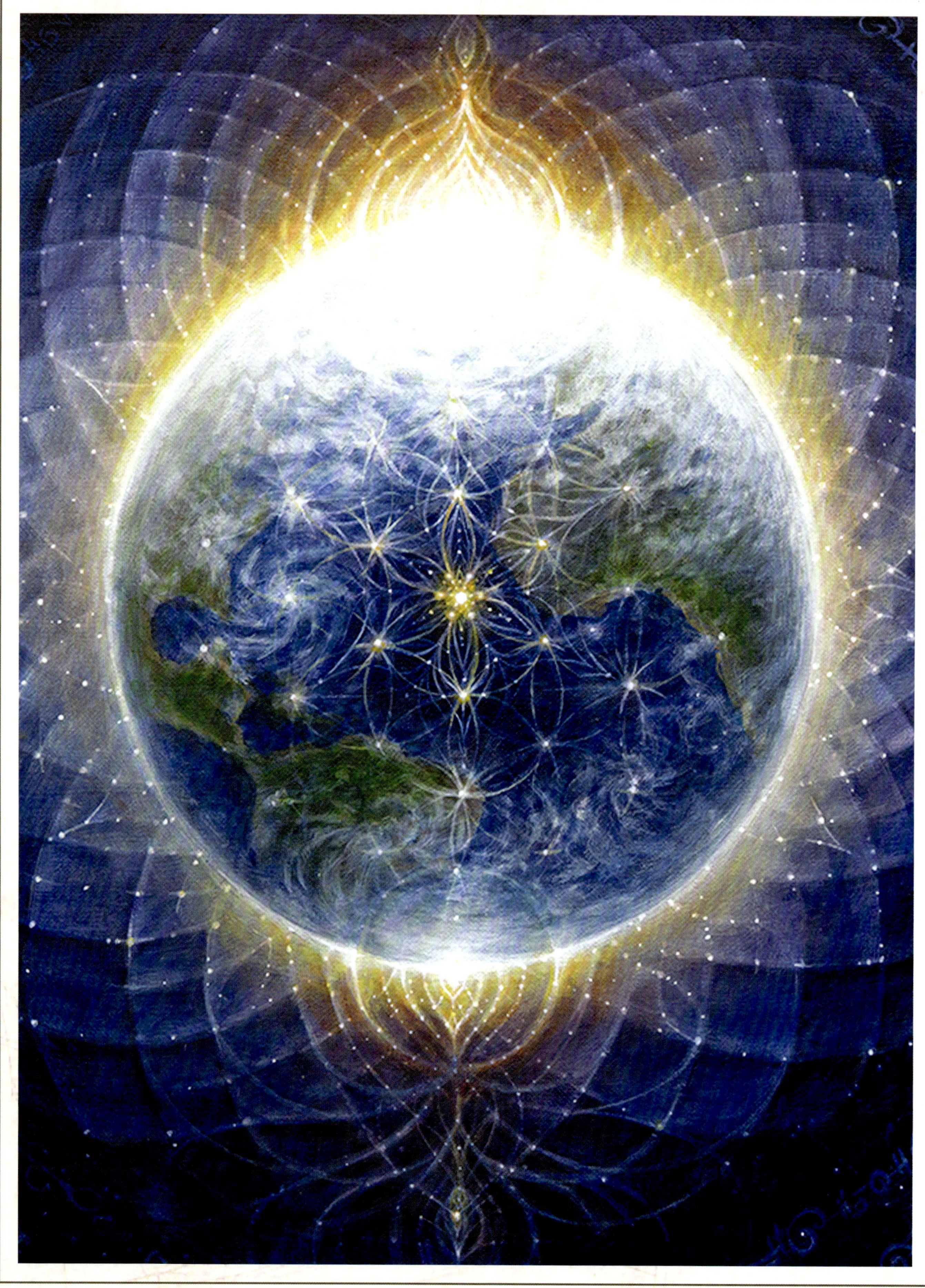

Verse IX

ACTIVATING THE POTENTIAL FOR LIFE-CHANGING MAGIC IN THIS MOMENT
COMES DOWN TO THIS CHOICE — I SET MY INTENTION AND I BELIEVE.

How precious is this one choice,

this one decision, this one step,

Each a single drop of wisdom,

Destined to coalesce as mighty wave,

Empowered by the ocean,

To reach the sacred shore.

Universal wisdom, divine love and eternal light,

Limitless mercy, compassion and tenderness,

Gift me the capacity for clarity and strategy,

For inspirational and deliberate creativity.

Your peaceful augury fills my heart,

I become certain, humble and heroic,

I will accomplish and I will attain,

Complete expression of true love.

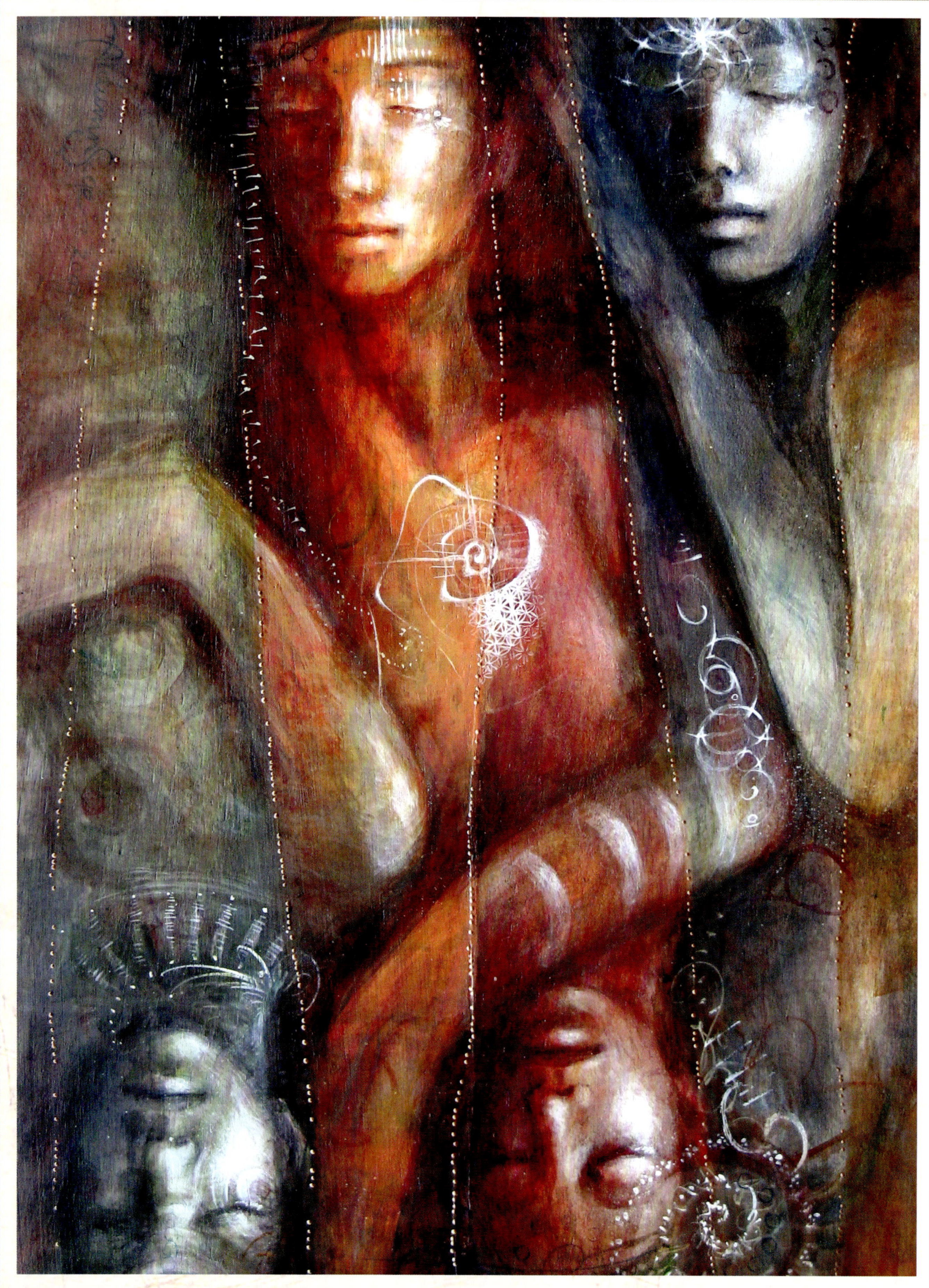

Verse X

I, THE DIVINE ONE WHO IS BLESSED WITH HUMAN LIFE AND FREE WILL, CHOOSE THUSLY — I WILL LIVE FROM MY HEART WITH FAITH IN TRUTH, I WILL CULTIVATE KINDNESS AND PATIENCE IN MY PROCESS, I WILL ATTRACT THROUGH RESONANCE ALL THAT IS NEEDED, I WILL PROCEED WITH TRUST IN THE GREAT LOVE THAT PERVADES EVERYTHING. I WILL ALLOW THE HOLY FIRE, THE PASSIONATE DIVINE LIGHT WITHIN, TO RADIATE BLESSINGS THROUGH ME, INTO THIS WORLD.

I gain wisdom from my past, yet I ground myself in this moment.
I am inspired for my future, yet I am present here and now.

I summon love for myself, resisting nothing.
I acknowledge the light that I AM.

Hands open above my crown,
I receive the light shining for me.

Hands open facing the earth,
I draw up the light shining to me.

Hands on heart,
I sense the light shining within me.

Hands open before me,
I give the light to my future and all beings.

Hands in prayer,
I acknowledge the light that I AM.

All intentions are blessed,
To manifest with merciful wisdom.
So be it!

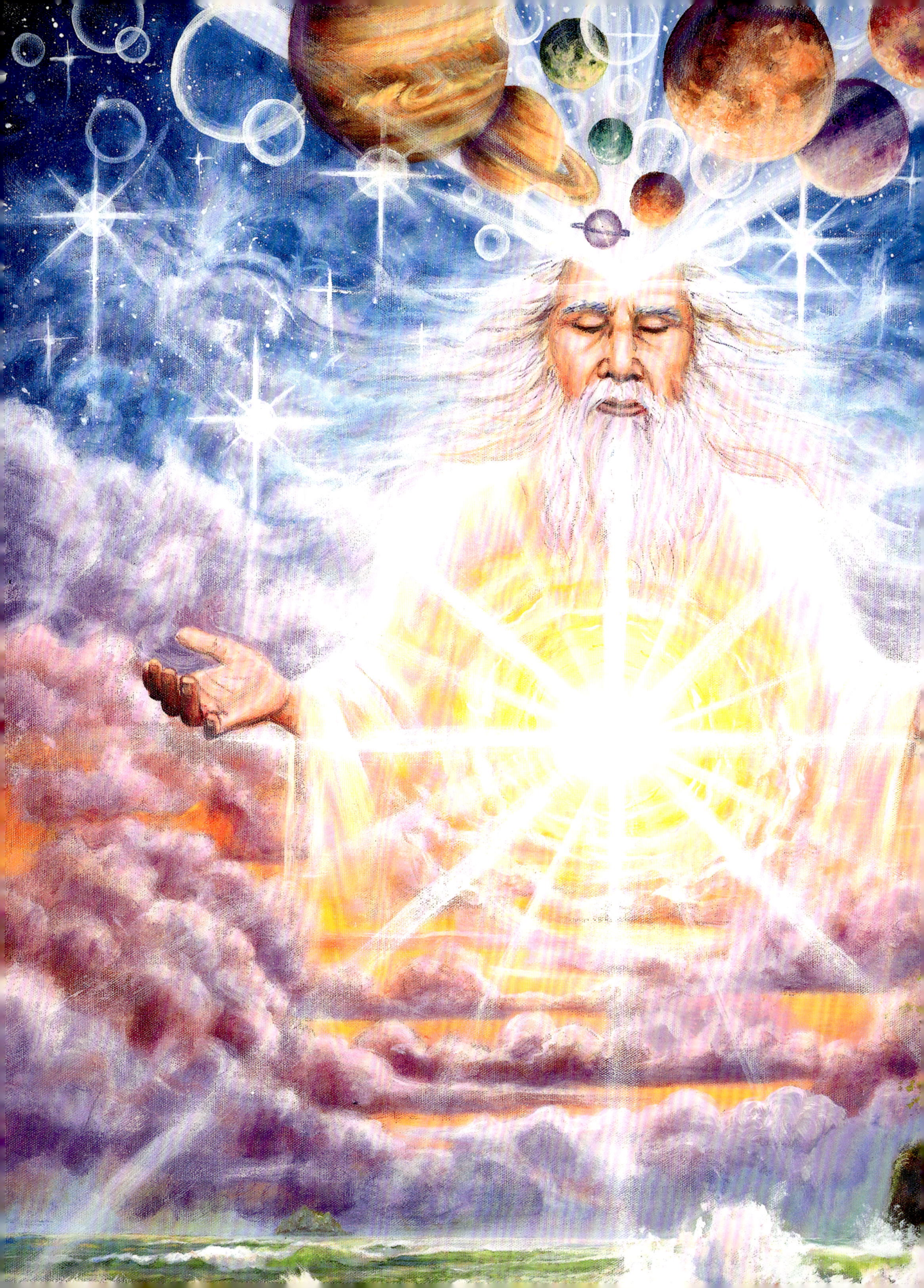

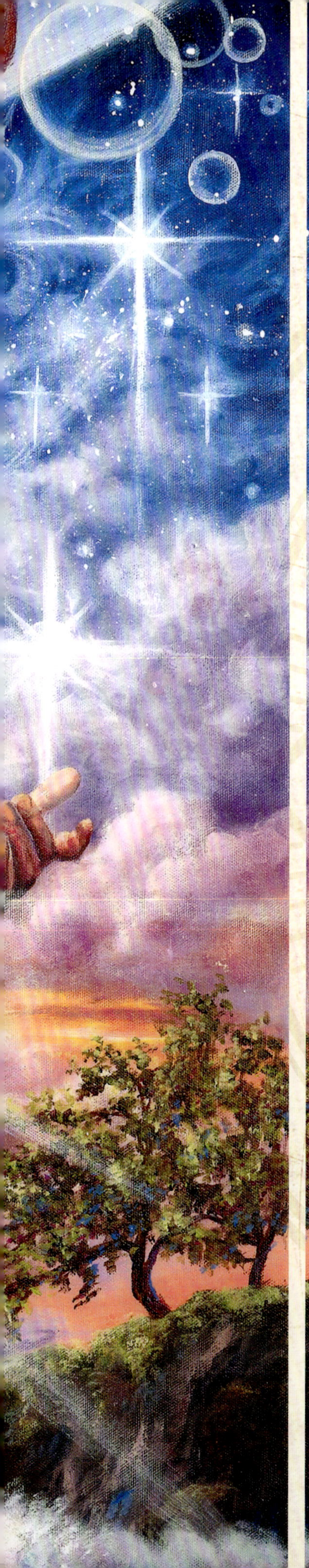

Book of LIGHT-WORKERS

Incantations and Divinations Invoking Love's Radical Unity and Inspirational Manifestation of Higher Consciousness

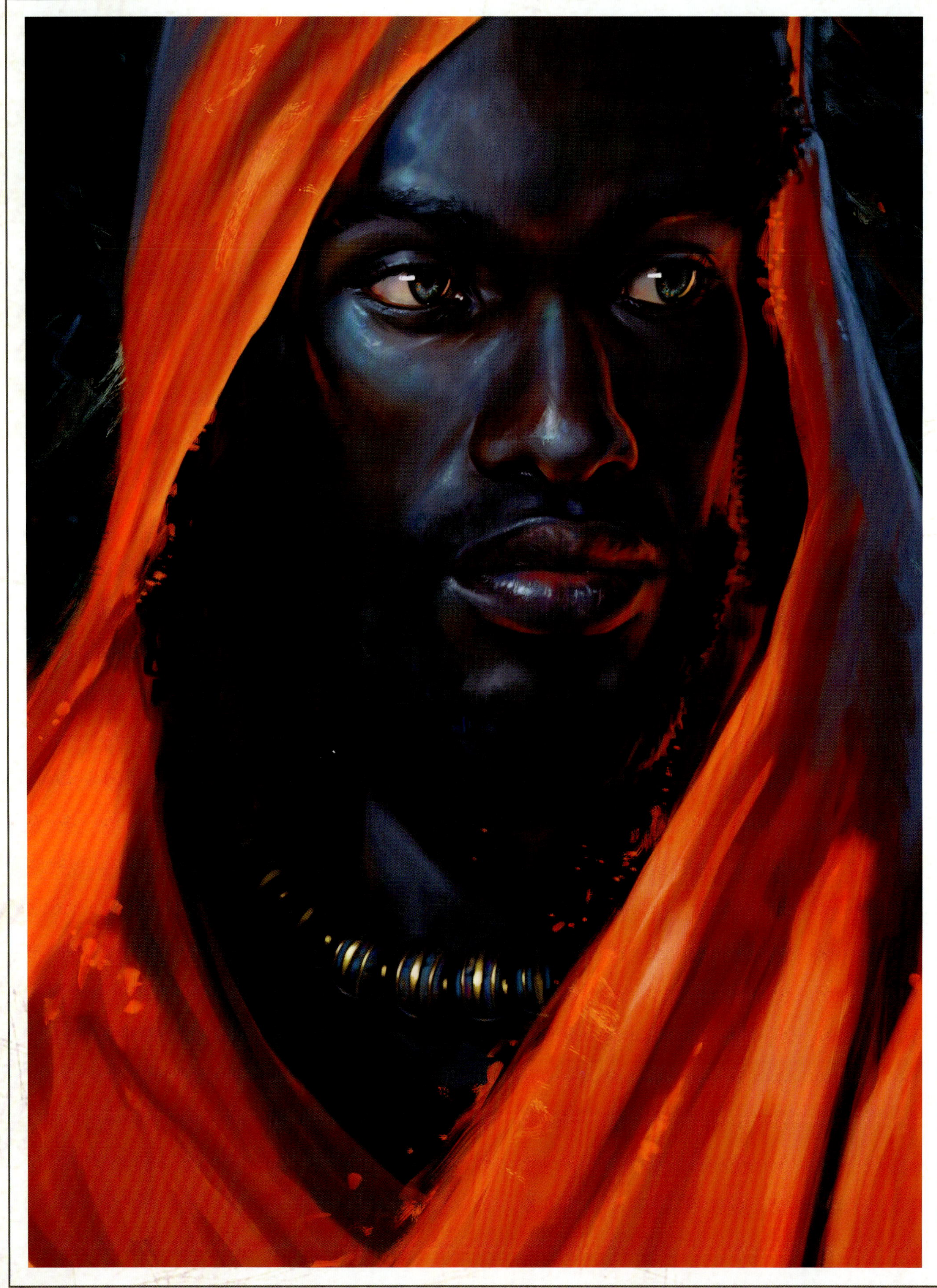

Verse I

I SURRENDER INTO ALIGNMENT WITH HIGHER WILL, MELTING INTO A WISDOM
BEYOND MY UNDERSTANDING, WHICH LOVES, PROTECTS AND GUIDES ME,
ENSURING DEEP FULFILMENT AND JOYFUL FRUITION.

For the highest good, and through divine love, I invoke Ascended Master El Morya,
Beloved emanation of the Blue Ray of Divine Light and the First Ray of Power.

I prophesy thus,

I am cleansed and strengthened as blue light and unwavering goodwill wash
abundantly through me now.

I divine thus,

Energy of intensive clearing and dynamic realignment, I accept with trust.
Whatever is released becomes a loving sacrifice on the altar of my divine destiny.
The intelligent kindness of Higher Will is always working to the benefit of all beings.

I see, feel and intend this cosmic ray of light flows in all beneficial ways.
So be it.

Verse II

Melding into the cosmic consciousness of love-wisdom,
I merge with ever expansive love of the Universal Teacher,
attracting all beneficial blessings and knowledge,
discovering higher awareness and all-pervading bliss.

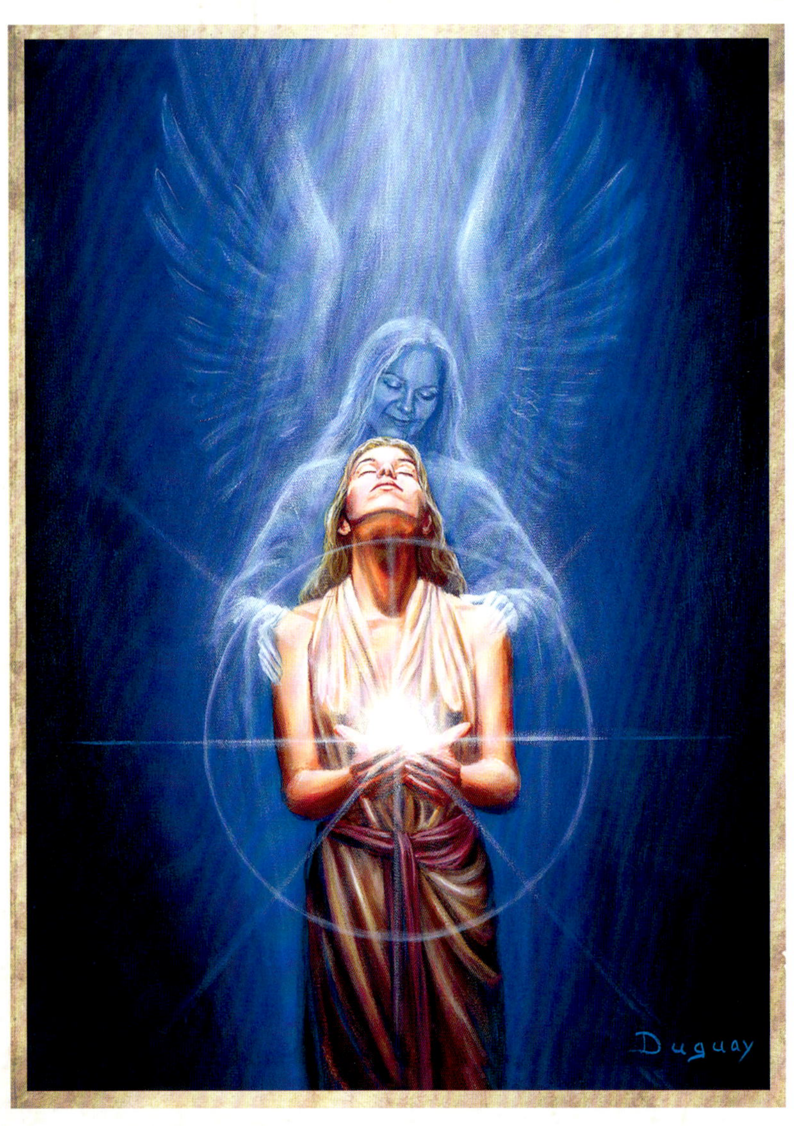

For the highest good, and through divine love, I invoke
Ascended Masters Buddha and Christ,

Beloved emanation the Pink Ray of Divine Light and the
Second Ray of Love-Wisdom.

I prophesy thus,

I am nurtured and protected as pink light and unwavering
goodwill wash abundantly through me now.

I divine thus,

Spiritual teaching of universal wisdom awakens patience, and
the higher understanding that brings peace.

Powerful magnetic inclusivity of divine attraction pulls all
beings in need towards the radiant heart.

The great compassion of love-wisdom is always emanating for
the benefit of all beings.

I see, feel and intend this cosmic ray of light flows in all
beneficial ways.

So be it.

Verse III

I set my intention and apply myself to the sacred work of meaningful contribution, catalysing beneficial manifestations, supported by spiritual intelligence of my heart.

For the highest good, and through divine love, I invoke Ascended Master Serapis Bey,

Beloved emanation of the Yellow Ray of Divine Light and the Third Ray of Creative Intelligence.

I prophesy thus,

I am empowered with pragmatism, confidence and inspiration as yellow light and unwavering goodwill wash abundantly through me.

I divine thus,

I ground my practical spirituality, healing all aspects of my life and increasing confidence in my capabilities.

I am motivated to recognise, express and celebrate the heroic goodness that longs to take root in our world.

Relevant and pragmatic divinity is always manifesting for the benefit of beings.

I see, feel and intend this cosmic ray of light flows in all beneficial ways.

So be it.

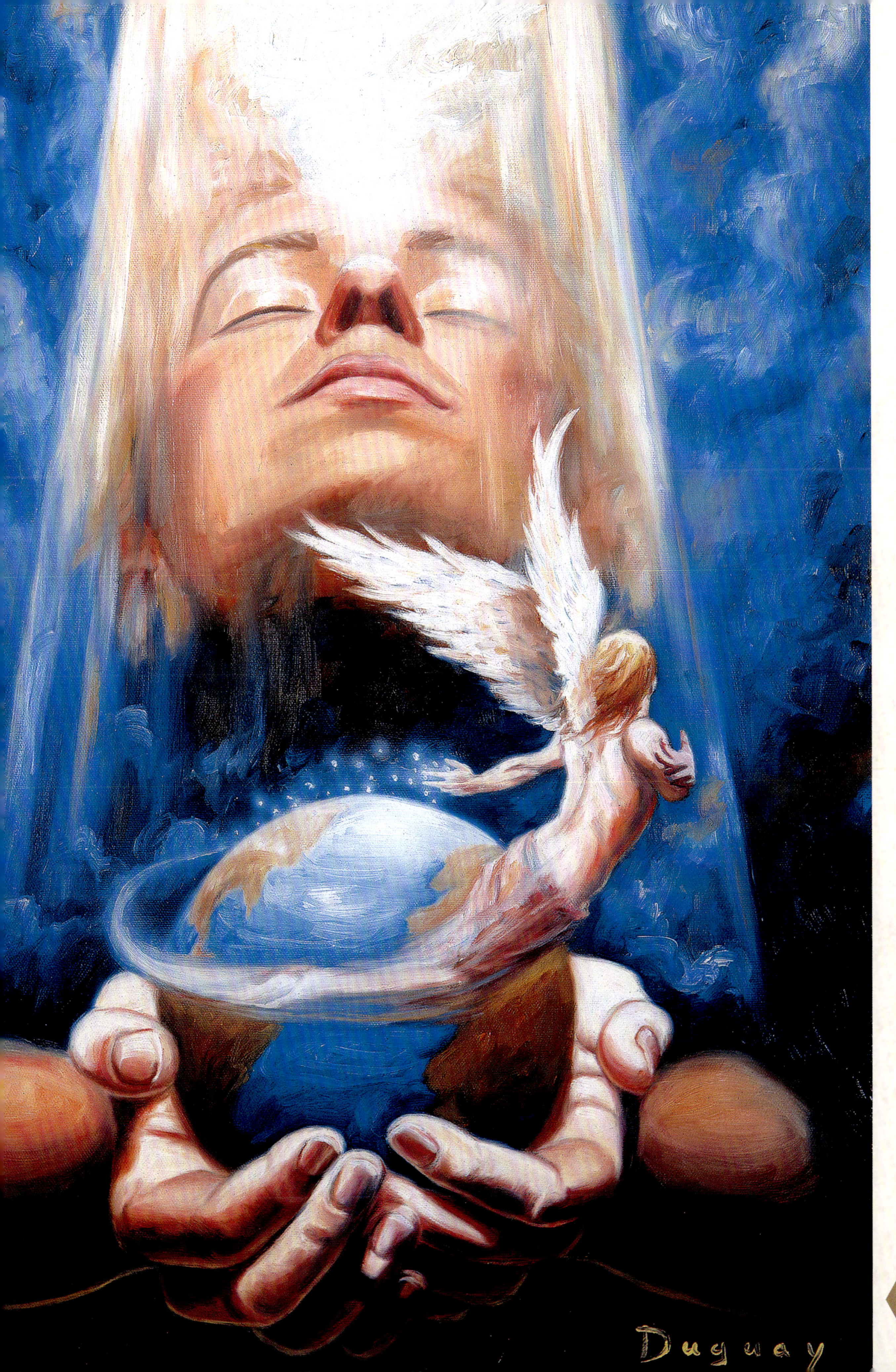
Duguay

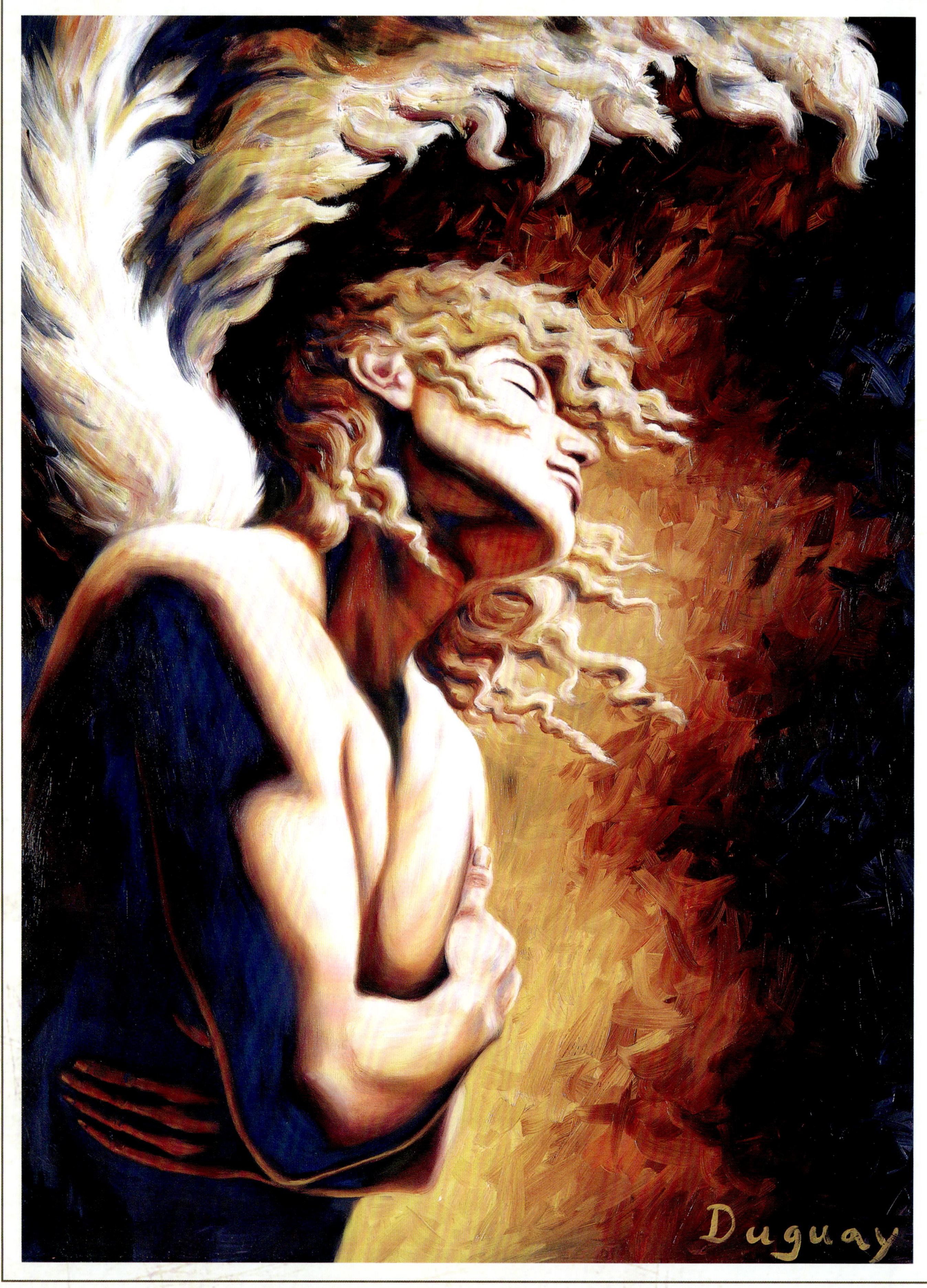
Duguay

Verse IV

Fearlessly present, witnessing tension, I recognise the alchemical potential in the clash of old and new. I affirm and anticipate the transcendent reality being born, for a loving and higher reordering is taking place.

For the highest good, and through divine love, I invoke
Ascended Master Hilarion,
Beloved emanation of the Green Ray of Divine Light and the
Fourth Ray of Cosmic Harmony.

I prophesy thus,

I am harmonised and healed as green light and unwavering
goodwill wash abundantly through me.

I divine thus,

Conflict is creatively integrated, providing spiritual fertiliser for
a superior way to emerge.
Outmoded struggles of the past are skilfully tamed, opening up
a new level of expression.
The divine beauty of harmony inspires and encourages all
beings to navigate tension with wisdom.

I see, feel and intend this cosmic ray of light flows in all
beneficial ways.
So be it.

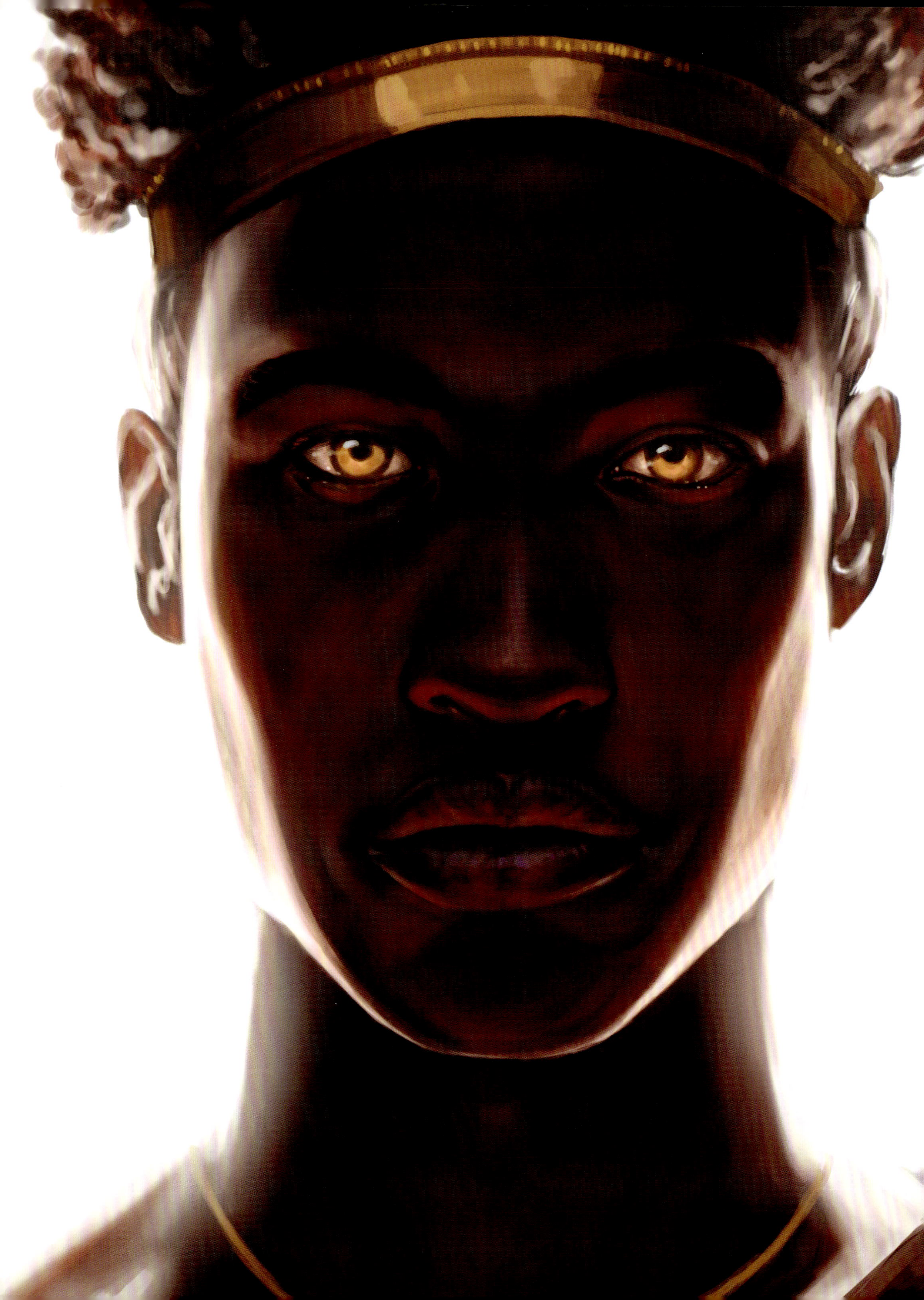

Verse V

For the highest good, and through divine love, I invoke Ascended Master Hermes Thoth,

Beloved emanation of the Sky-Blue Ray of Divine Light and the Fifth Ray of Higher Knowing.

I prophesy thus,

Openness in mind and heart bestows clarity as sky-blue light and unwavering goodwill wash abundantly through me.

I divine thus,

With discernment, I seek and recognise useful information, intuiting creative strategy to shape consciousness and manifest higher vision.

Counselled by inner wisdom, logic and intuition, I formulate constructive steps to take whilst trusting in divine timing.

Higher knowing brings insight and relief to the heart, helping all beings understand their purpose and path.

I see, feel and intend this cosmic ray of light flows in all beneficial ways.

So be it.

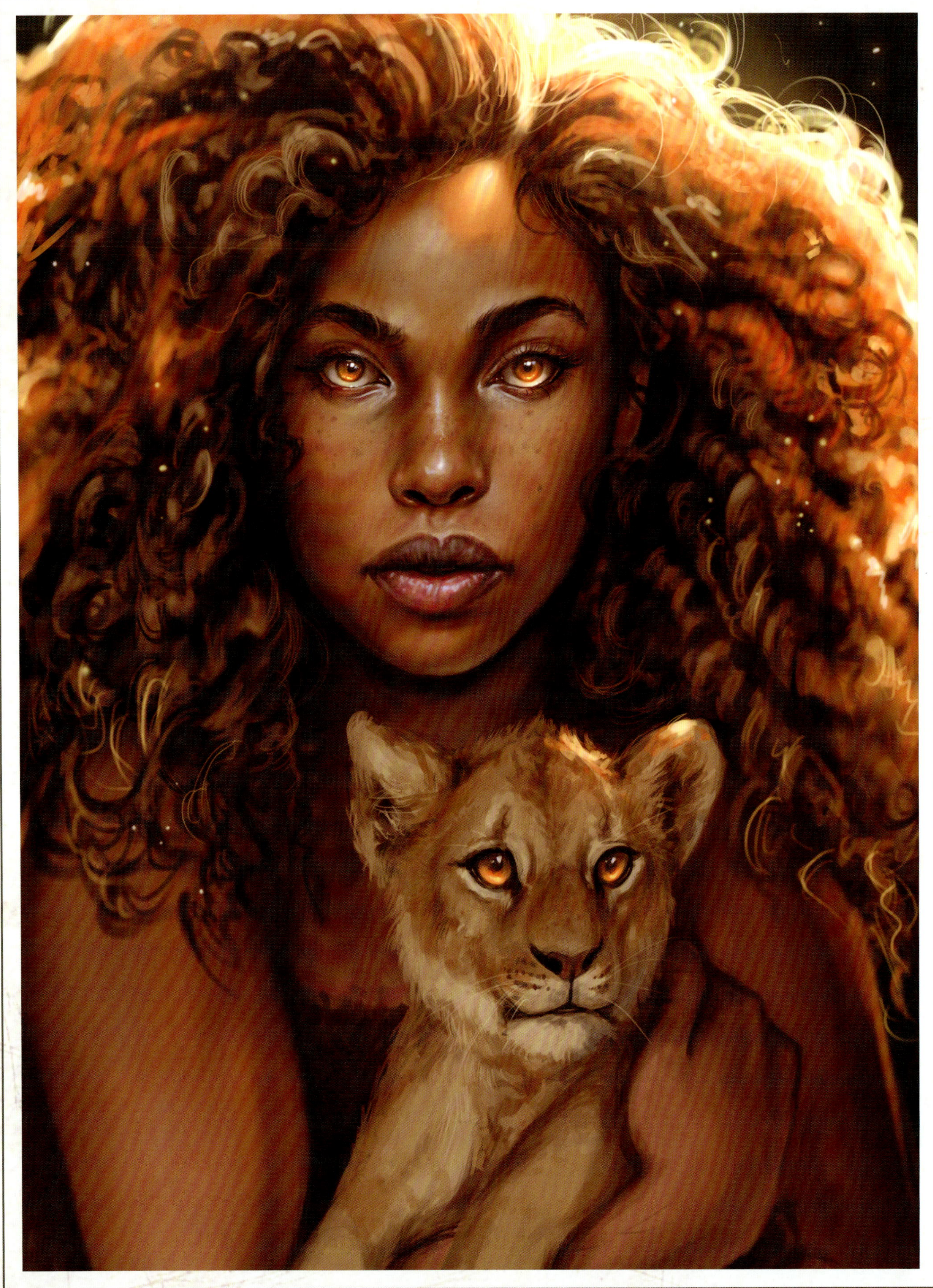

Verse VI

For the highest good, and through divine love, I invoke
Ascended Master Lady Nada,

Beloved emanation of the Red Ray of Divine Light and the
Sixth Ray of Devotion.

I prophesy thus,

Resolve and determination are strengthened as red divine light
and unwavering goodwill wash abundantly through me.

I divine thus,

Inspired by my ideals, my positive resolve and resilience
increase, and I am unwavering in my commitment.

Aligning with my heart's passion exponentially increases my
inspiration and manifestation ability.

Magnetic grace attracts all hearts to a higher calling, providing
the power to overcome distraction with devotion.

I see, feel and intend this cosmic ray of light flows in all
beneficial ways.

So be it.

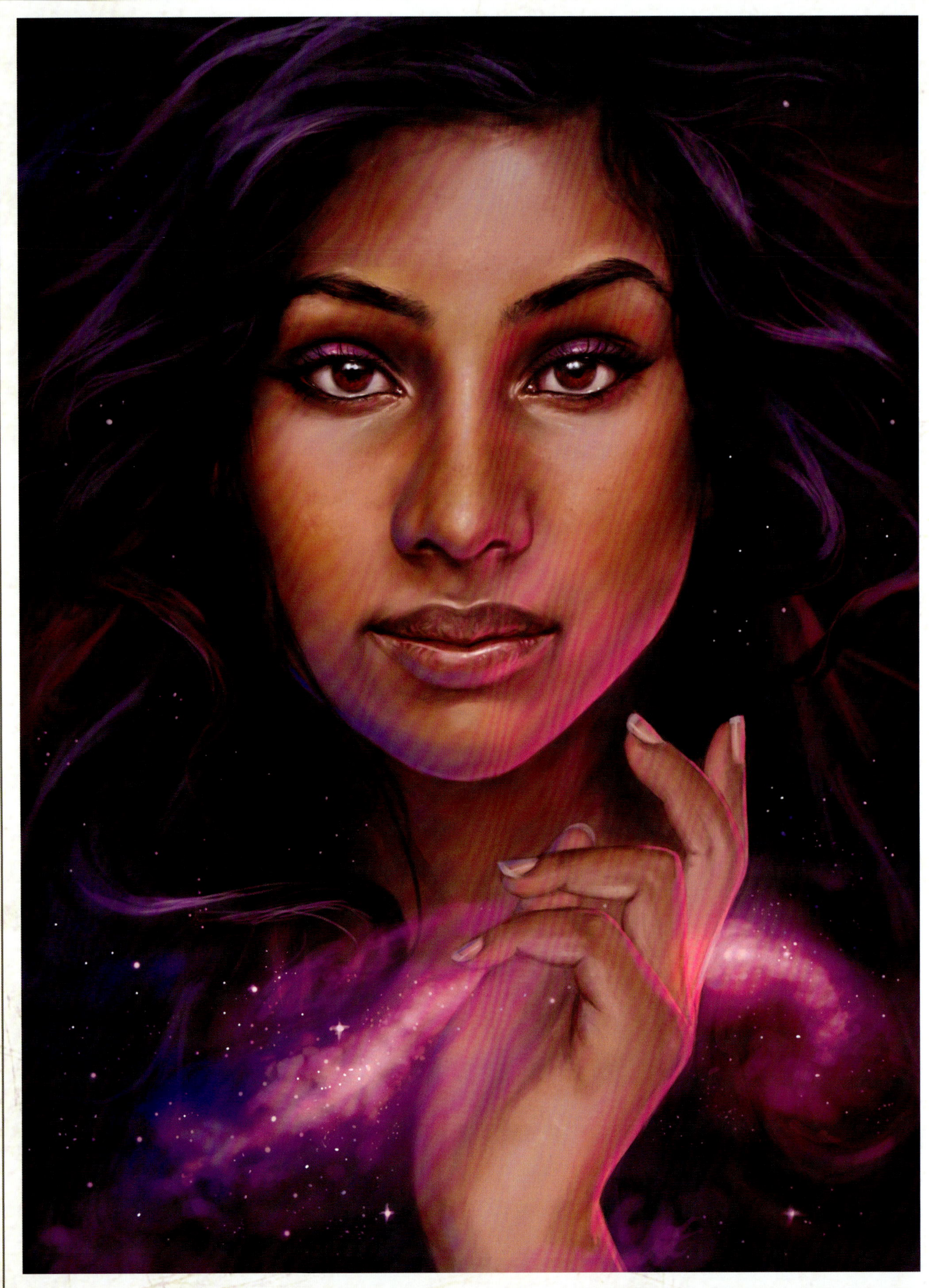

Verse VII

For the highest good, and through divine love, I invoke Ascended Master St Germain,

Beloved emanation of the Violet Ray of Divine Light and the Seventh Ray of Ceremonial Magic and Ritual.

I prophesy thus,

Purified, I recognise my strength and gracefulness, as violet divine light and unwavering goodwill wash abundantly through me.

I divine thus,

Distilling what has value from the past, I release all else, evolving elegantly into a new way of being.

I activate my innate ability for magic, ordaining and actioning that which I wish to manifest.

In this ritual space, cloaked in robe of violet light, I embrace the creative potential in present moment and initiate necessary transformations for future most blessed and bright.

I see, feel and intend this cosmic ray of light flows in all beneficial ways.

So be it.

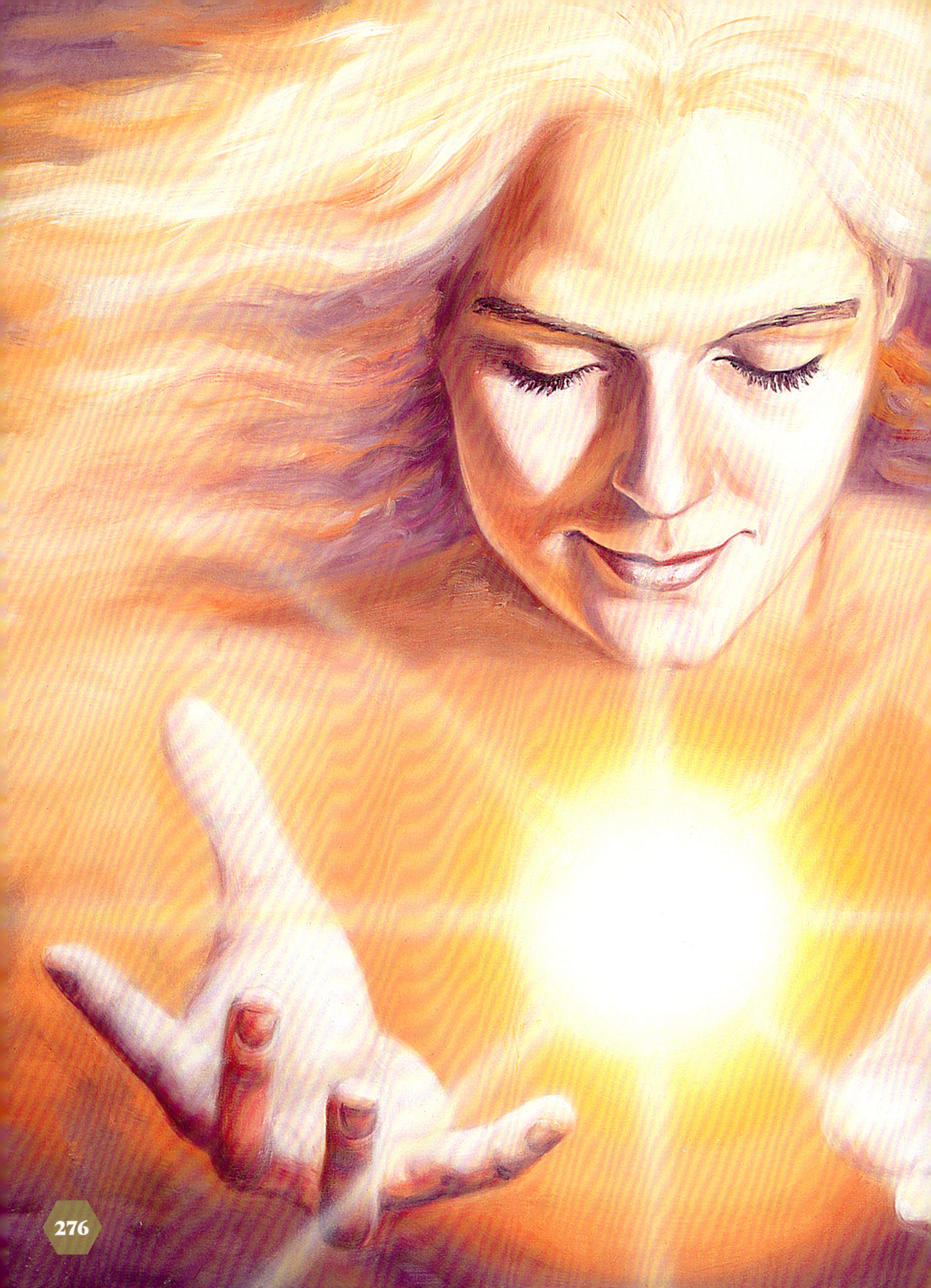

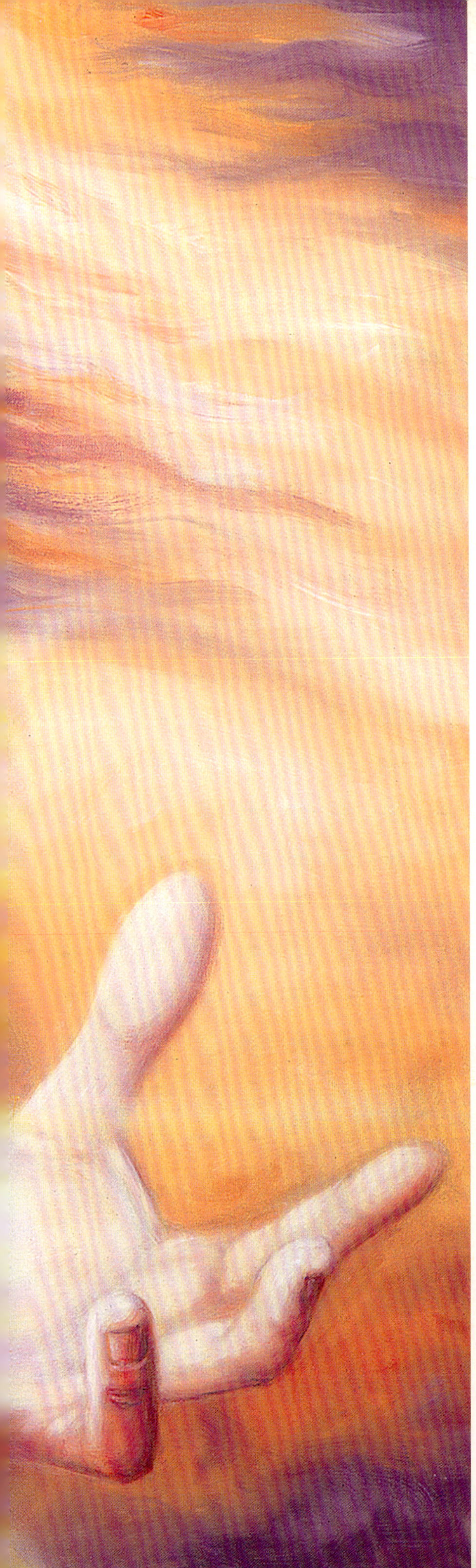

Verse VIII

*888 opens the gate to all the divine heart decrees,
fulfilling all desires with merciful intelligence that
inspires, I open my heart to give and receive.*

Raphael Angelic Heart of Cosmic Lion,
Ariel Lion-Headed Archangel Divine,

Lion's Gate 888,
Ancient portal opens,
As love's galvanising roar resounds.

Isis of Sirius, Avatar of Abundance,
Ishtar of Venus, Light of Initiation,

Lion's Gate 888,
Love radiates, heroic and confident,
Radical evolution becomes inevitable.

Sekhmet Fierce, Patron of Healers,
Ma'at of Divine Timing, Truth and Alignment,

Lion's Gate 888,
Divine blessings stream forth,
Rescuing all beings with enlightened activity.

Simhamukha, Dakini Defender of Good,
Narasimha, Protector of Pure Hearts,

Lion's Gate 888,
Wresting all forces into alignment divine,
As you now manifest your fierce, unyielding grace.

Om Mataji Ananda Shakti.
Om Mataji Ananda Shakti.
Om Shanti Om.

Bless all beings with renewed faith,
And miraculous blessings to partake.
Pour relief through freedom's gate.

Om Mataji Ananda Shakti.
Om Mataji Ananda Shakti.
Om Shanti Om.

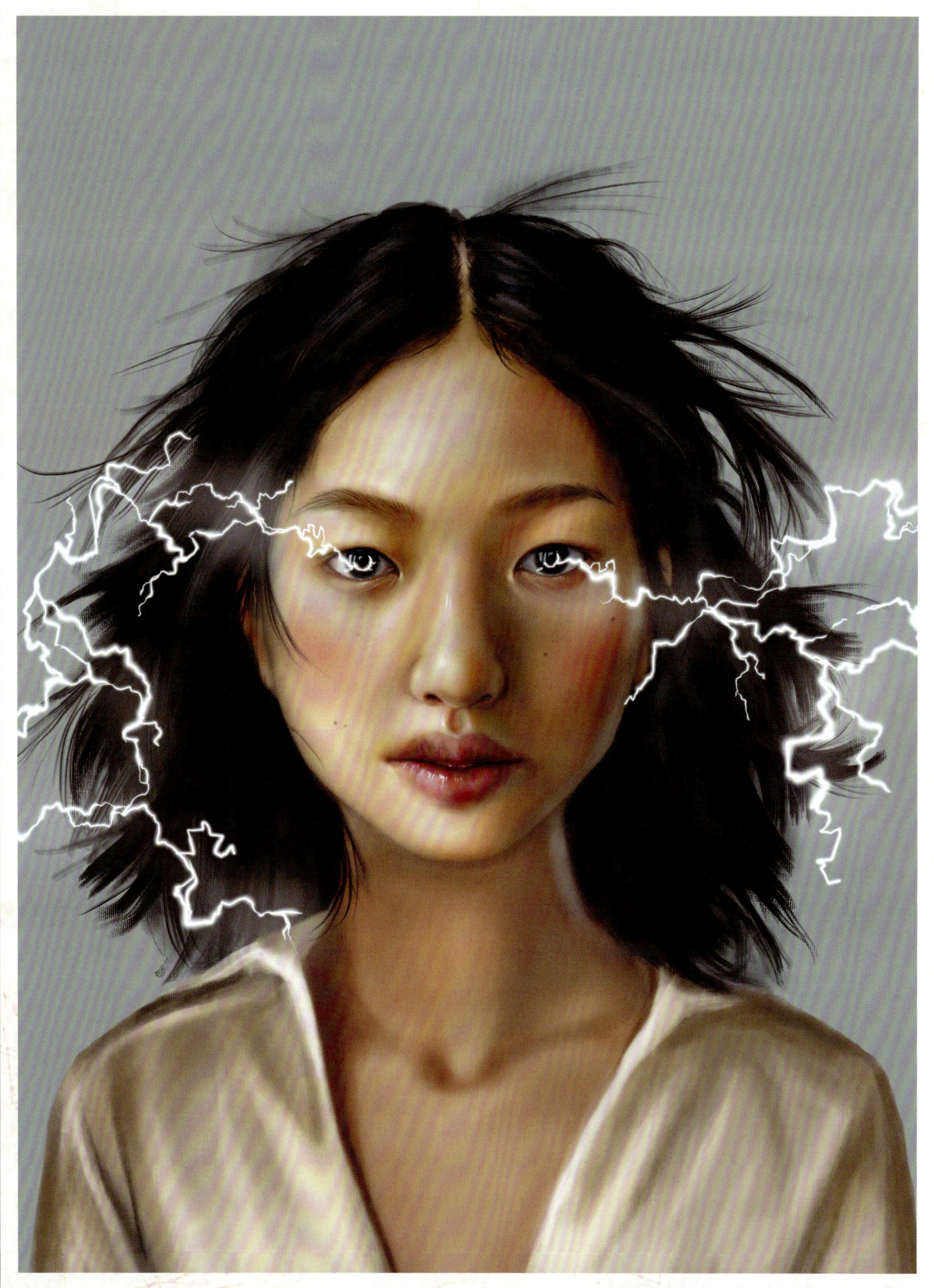

Verse IX

MY HEART BEARS DIVINE CREATIVITY, THE INTELLIGENCE OF REGENERATIVE GENIUS, ABLE TO SYNTHESISE FROM THE UNIVERSE SUCH EXQUISITE ENERGIES TO ENSURE JOYFUL FRUITION, EVOLVING INTO DESTINY MOST DESIRED.

Ascension Codex 11.11,

My heart infused with cosmic currents of higher consciousness,

Elevates my vibration, transforming my attitude,

Empowering my evolution through boldness and optimism.

Mother Mary Codex 12.12,

My heart infused with Divine Feminine majesty,

Imbues my body and soul with all-accomplishing love,

Ensuring divinely aligned manifestation and fulfilment.

Venus Codex of 13.13,

My heart infused with radiance of love's cosmic avatar,

Inner obstacles melt in the heat of your passion,

Outer obstacles yield to love's greater persistence and power.

11.11 I AM evolving.

12.12 I AM miraculous.

13.13 I AM blessed.

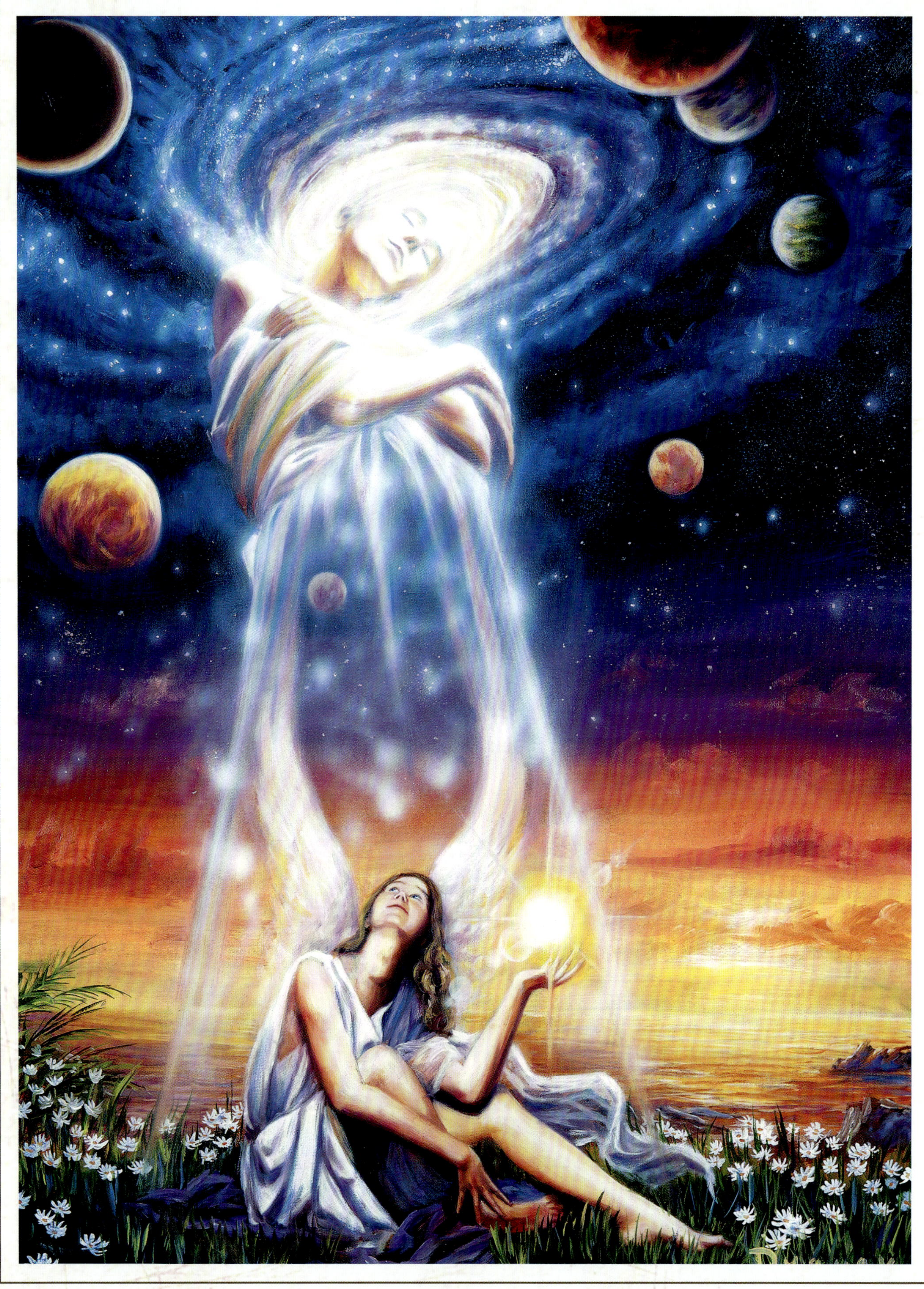

Verse X

Initiation by fire,

Frees my soul from clinging.

I have learned that love is ever generous and unfailing.

Initiation by water,

Frees my soul from fixity.

I have learned that wisdom thrives in flexibility and openness.

Initiation by air,

Frees my soul from doubt,

I have learned that freedom arises through responsibility and creativity.

May mercy of spiritual awakening,

Manifest in all directions and dimensions,

For the genuine and loving benefit,

Of every sentient being.

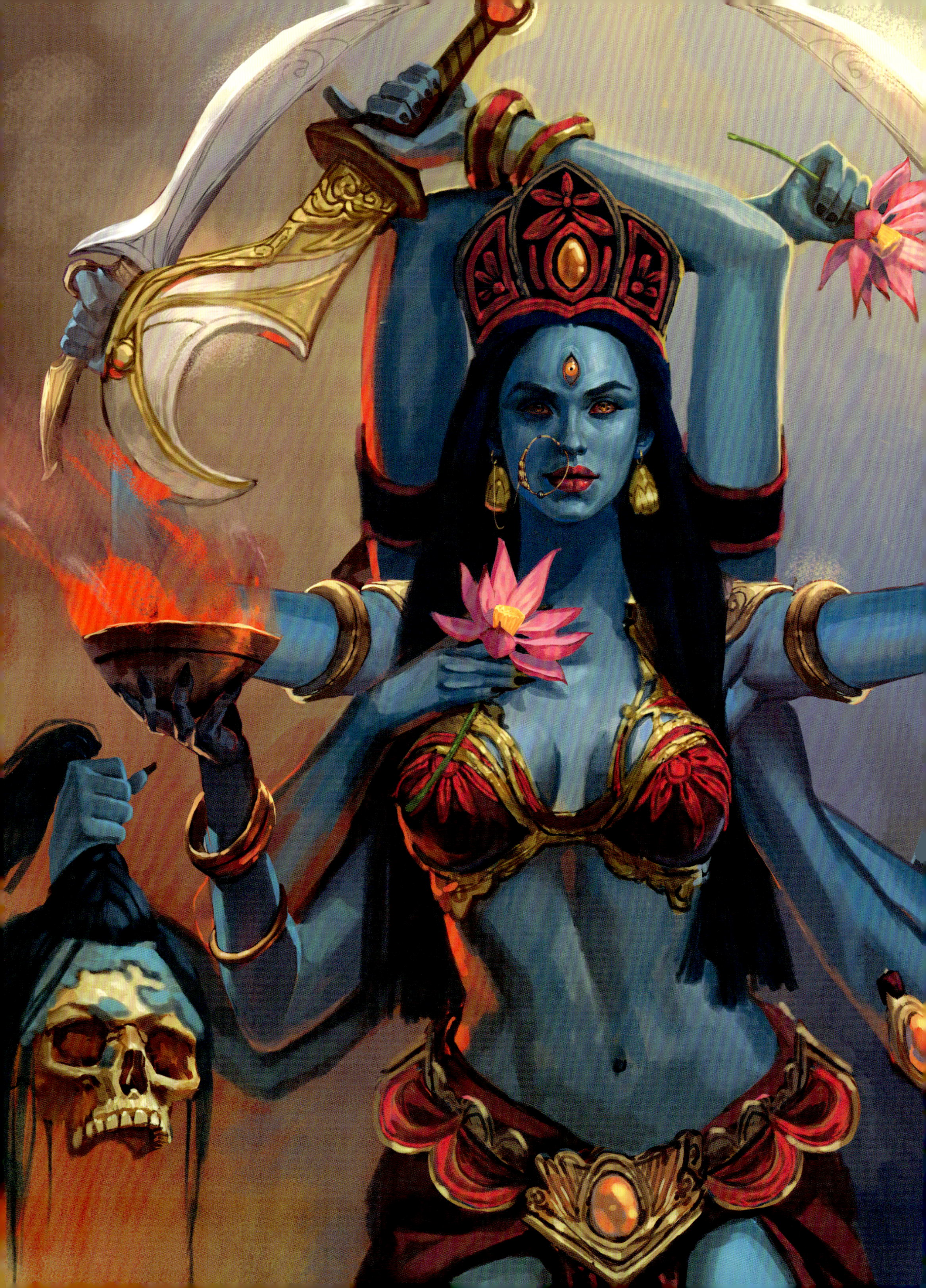

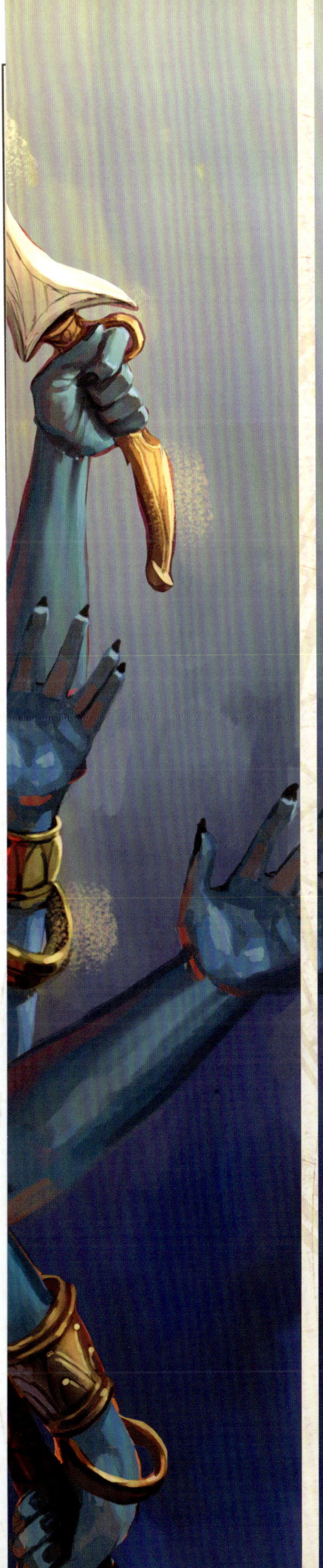

Book of KALL

Incantations and Divinations for Generating Supreme Protective Wisdom

Verse III

Mother of Dark Divinity, fiercer than all fears,
vaster than all difficulties,
I recognise your sweet signature of liberating love,
and your ever-insistent compassion,
which overcomes every challenge,
revealing unexpected grace.

Kali Ma, Smashana Kali, Vama Kali,
Raise your divine sword of truth!
My heart is ready, willing, desiring of your revelation,
And severance of the attachments holding me back.

Om Kreem Kaliyei Namaha,
Jai Ma Kali,
Kali Namaha.

Kali Ma, Kripadhara, Bearer of Mercy,
End entrapment of karmic entanglement,
In confusion, illusion and stories.
Open the way to freedom, with compassion.

Om Kreem Kaliyei Namaha,
Jai Ma Kali,
Kali Namaha.

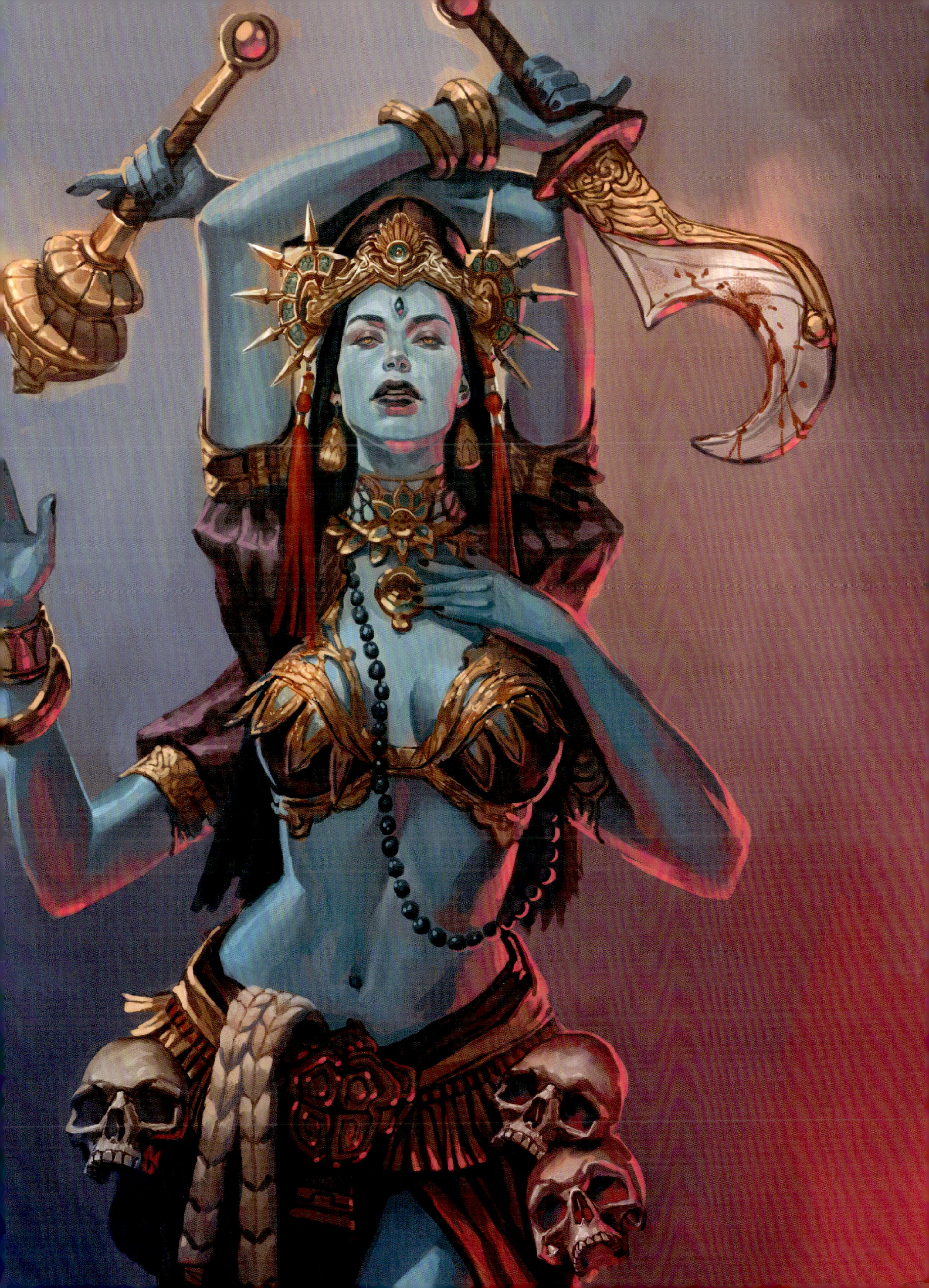

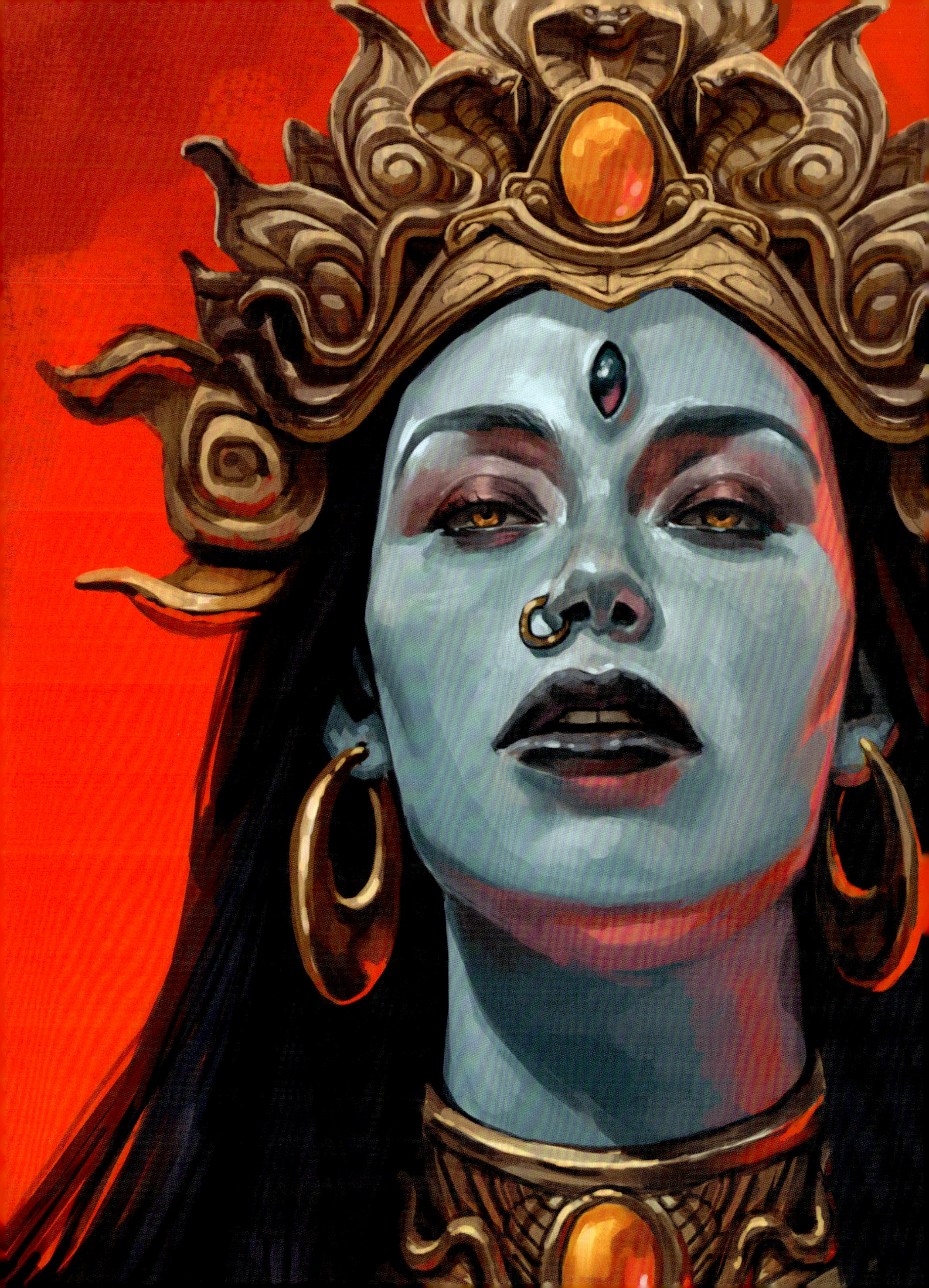

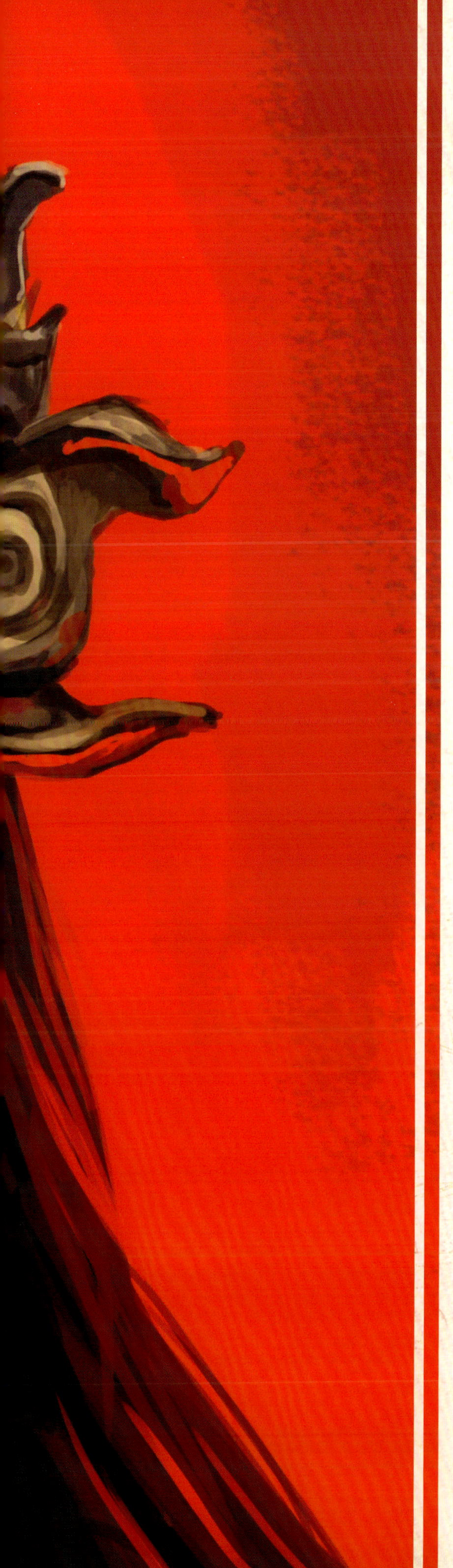

Verse IV

Sacred Void, Cosmic Creatrix, Ancient Lady who arose before the Universe began and shall continue after the Universe ends, you embrace my soul as a mother cradling her precious child, and so with wonder and trust, I call forth your loving intervention.

Divine Mother of Cosmic Blackness,
I cast off all fear and doubt,
For yours is the power of the Universe,
Infused with the generosity of grace,
And I am known to you, and loved.

*Jai Ma Kali,
Jai Ma Namaha.*

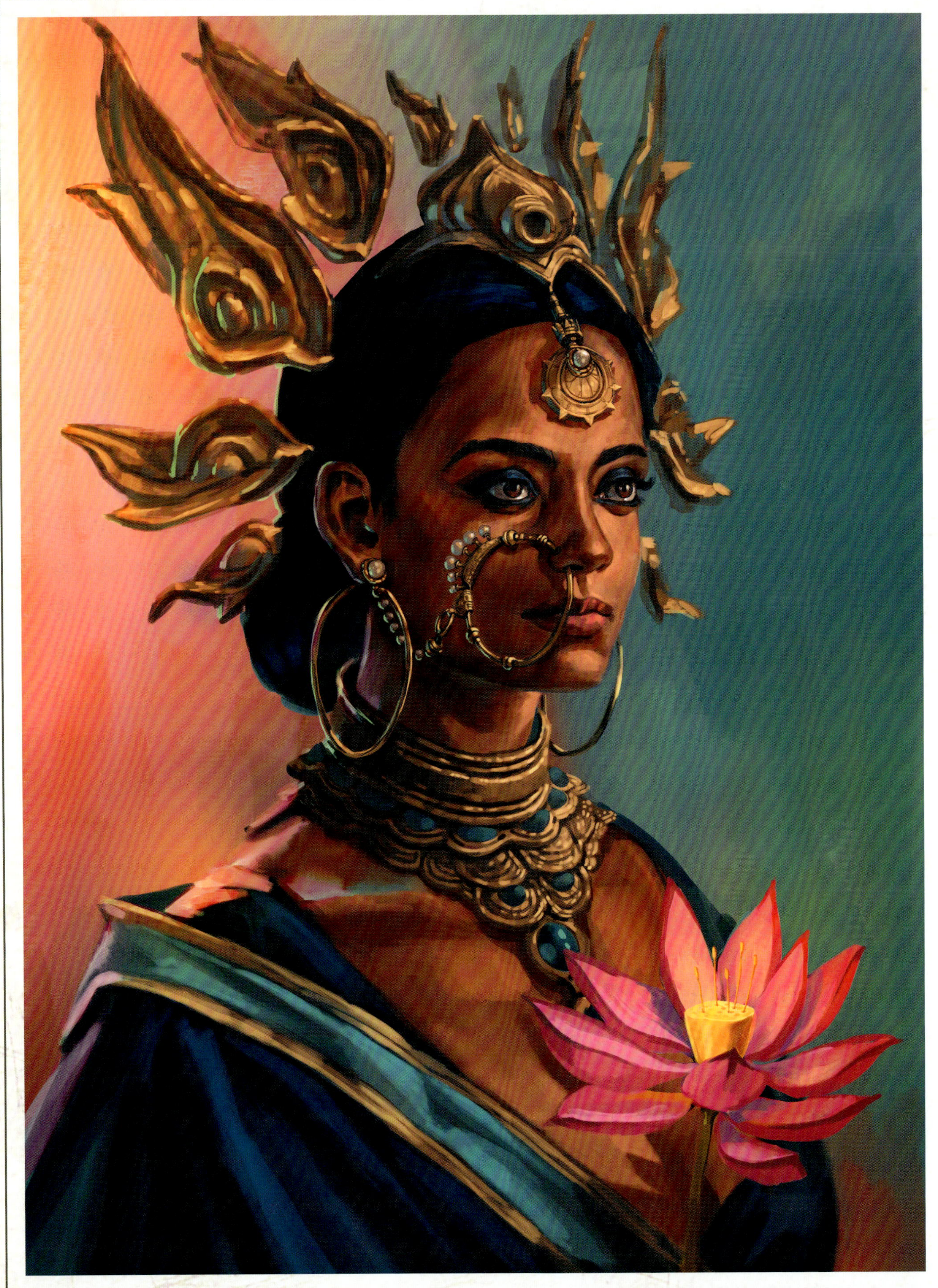

Verse V

Dakshina Kali, I make sincere and heartfelt offering to you,

You who are generous and gracious beyond measure,

Radiating unyielding truth and unending compassion.

Kali Ma Nitya, Cosmic Priestess of Waning Moon,

With trust, I softly release attachment to the past,

For where you bring ending, you also birth beginning.

Kali Ma Niroda Shakti, issue your *kalpa* ending sound,

Bring this era of struggle to swift and complete closure,

Initiating a new cycle of radiance, peace and attainment.

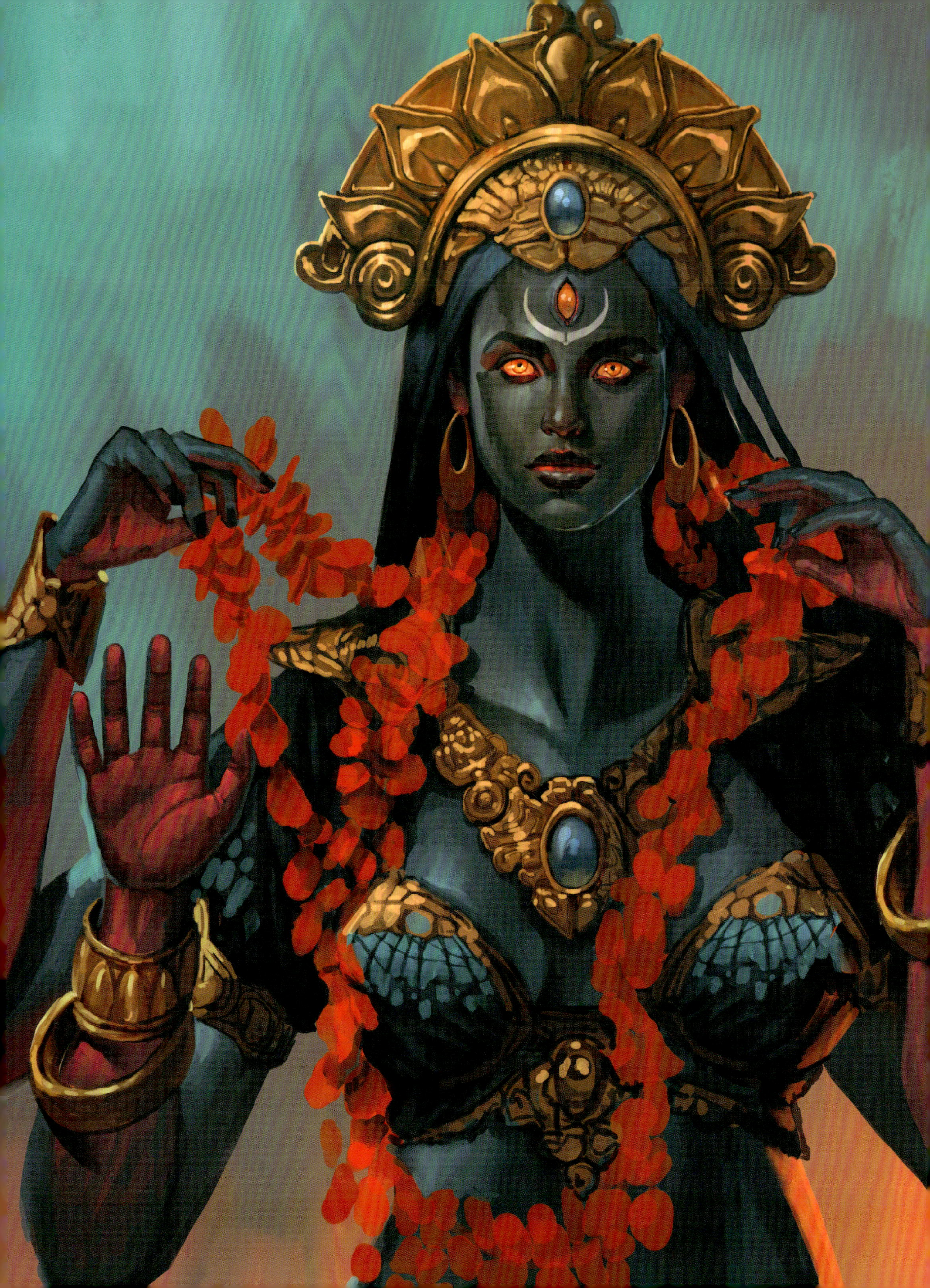

Verse VI

Kali Kapalini, bearing garland of skulls,
You possess power over every sound,
And all of creation is subject to your will.

Sri Ma Bhadrakali, gentle face of the powerful one,
Bestow fortune and abundance of blessings upon me,
That I may fulfil the destiny you intend for me.

Jai Ma Kali Ugra Mata, fierce and final recourse,
Naught can withstand the decree of your will,
I surrender all into your love and am sanctified.

Om Shreem Kreem Kleem Jai Ma Bhadra Kali Namo Namaha.
Om Shreem Kreem Kleem Jai Ma Bhadra Kali Namo Namaha.
Om Shreem Kreem Kleem Jai Ma Bhadra Kali Namo Namaha.

Verse VII

GREAT MA KALI, I INVOKE THEE IN REVERENCE FOR THY BEAUTY,
AND THIS INVOCATION IS MY RITUAL OF THY ADORATION,
THAT I MAY LOVE THEE WITH SUCH PASSION AND ENCOUNTER THY LIVING
PRESENCE AS TRANSFORMATIONAL BLESSINGS IN MY LIFE.

Maha Kali, I invoke thee faithfully,
As I imagine a garland of 108 red hibiscus flowers,
And one thousand purple akonda flowers,
Generously emitting their heavenly aroma.

Red oleander blooms abundantly at your feet,
As you rise four-armed and magnificent.
The crescent moon at your forehead,
Radiates eternal divine ambrosia.

You perform the mudra of *Abhaya,*
For my faith in you ignites unlimited courage.
You perform the mudra of *Varada,*
For my faith in you attracts infinite blessings.

You wield *khadga* sword and trident,
Conquering every malefic effect,
And purifying all defilement,
As an act of merciful salvation.

In this space, now a symbolic cremation ground,
I acknowledge the reality of death,

And the precious gift of this life,
Dedicating to you a strand of my hair.

As I now enact the ritual yantra,
With this invocation of banishment,
Reduce all impediments to holy ash,
In the sacrificial flames of your wisdom.

Kali Yantra be generated now,
Within four gates housing eight inner petals,
Encircling three concentric downward-facing triangles,
Emanates divine yoni bright red as blood of life.

I imagine dotting red kumkum powder,
At the four outer gates of the yantra,
And anointing the central *bindu* point,
With paste of red sandalwood.

Kali Mudra be activated now,
Interlocked fingers, left thumb over right,
Index fingers joined and pointing upwards.
My body becomes your holy instrument.

Kali Ma, enact your power here,
In this ritual night,
To banish and transform all obstacles into grace,
For I am your devoted and faithful-hearted one.

Om Kreem Kalikayei Namaha.
Kali Ma Sohum.
Om Kreem Kalikayei Namaha.
Kali Ma Sohum.

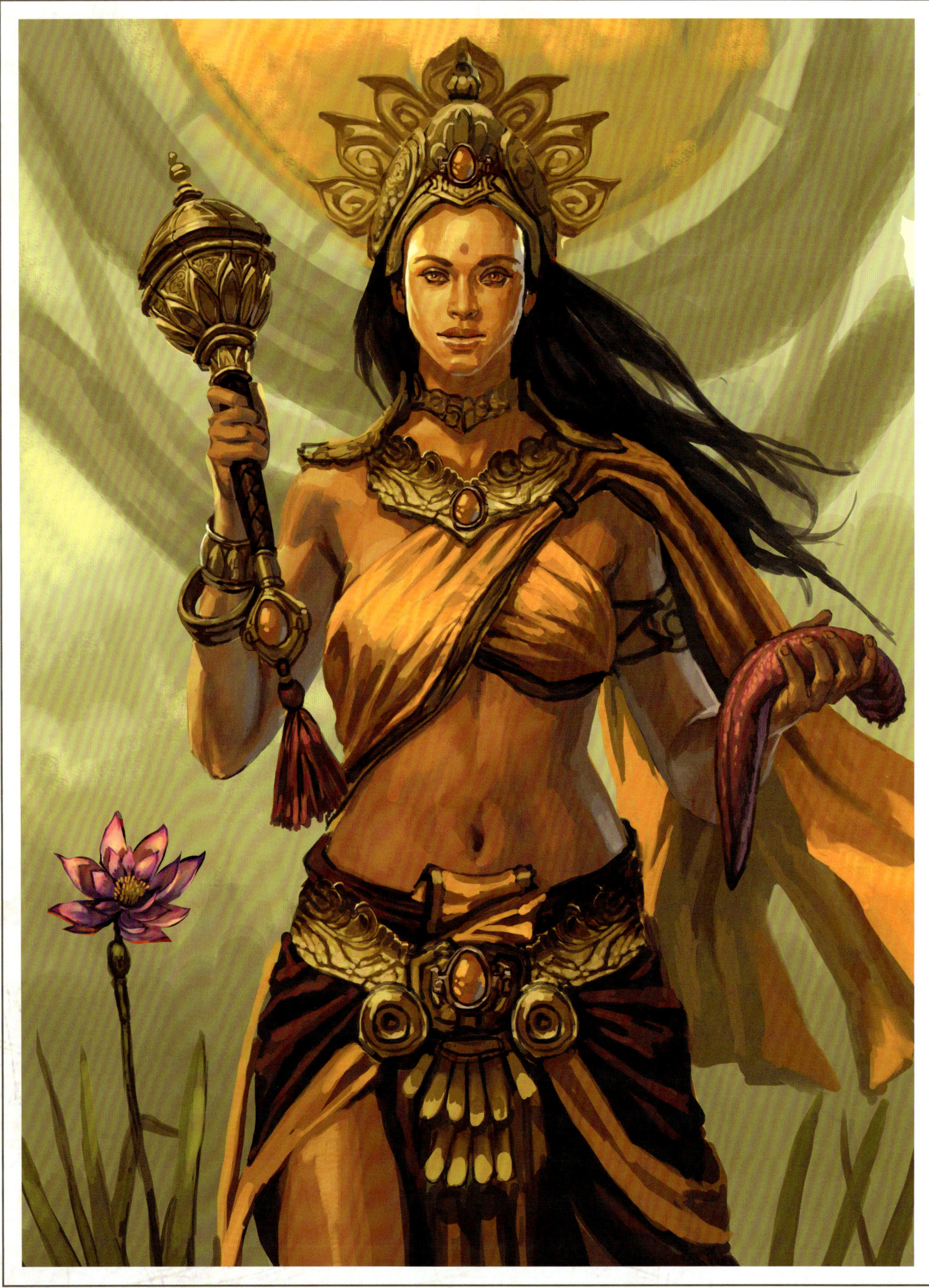

Verse VIII

I ACKNOWLEDGE AND ACCEPT THE TRANSFORMATIONAL ACTIVITY
YOU ARE EVOKING IN MY HEART AND MY LIFE, FOR I REVERE YOU AS WISDOM,
LOVE AND KINDNESS, AND MY HEART IS UNAFRAID.

Bhadrakali, sapphire-skinned goddess,

Bearing a lotus flower and bestowing blessings,

Radiating cosmic blue light of divine protection,

I take sincere refuge in you.

Hreem, kreem, kleem, Jai Ma Kali!

Kali Ma Devi, tender mother to my soul,

Benefic Lady, who reveals truth and ignites power,

I call forth your light with *hreem*,

And your accomplishing potency with *kreem*.

Hreem, kreem, kleem, Jai Ma Kali!

Merciful Mother, Auspicious Kali, *Adi Shakti*,

You show the way and provide means to attain it,

Blocking evil workings and nullifying obstacles,

I attract your welcome intercession with *kleem*.

Hreem, kreem, kleem, Jai Ma Kali!

Verse IX

I honour your strength and mirror it, applying myself with dedication and devotion, and at the threshold where more is required to accomplish the good and necessary outcome, through my faith you arise spontaneously with skilfulness and glory.

Durga of Light,
Bright Fortress of Victory,

Kali of Darkness,
All-Accomplishing Defender,

With fierce brilliance and wisdom,
Grant rightful blessing and attainment,

Even if it be the last moment,
When all may seem lost,

You arise with certainty and glory,
To ensure the divine dispensation.

Om Dum Durgayei Namaha.
Om Kreem Kaliyei Nahama.

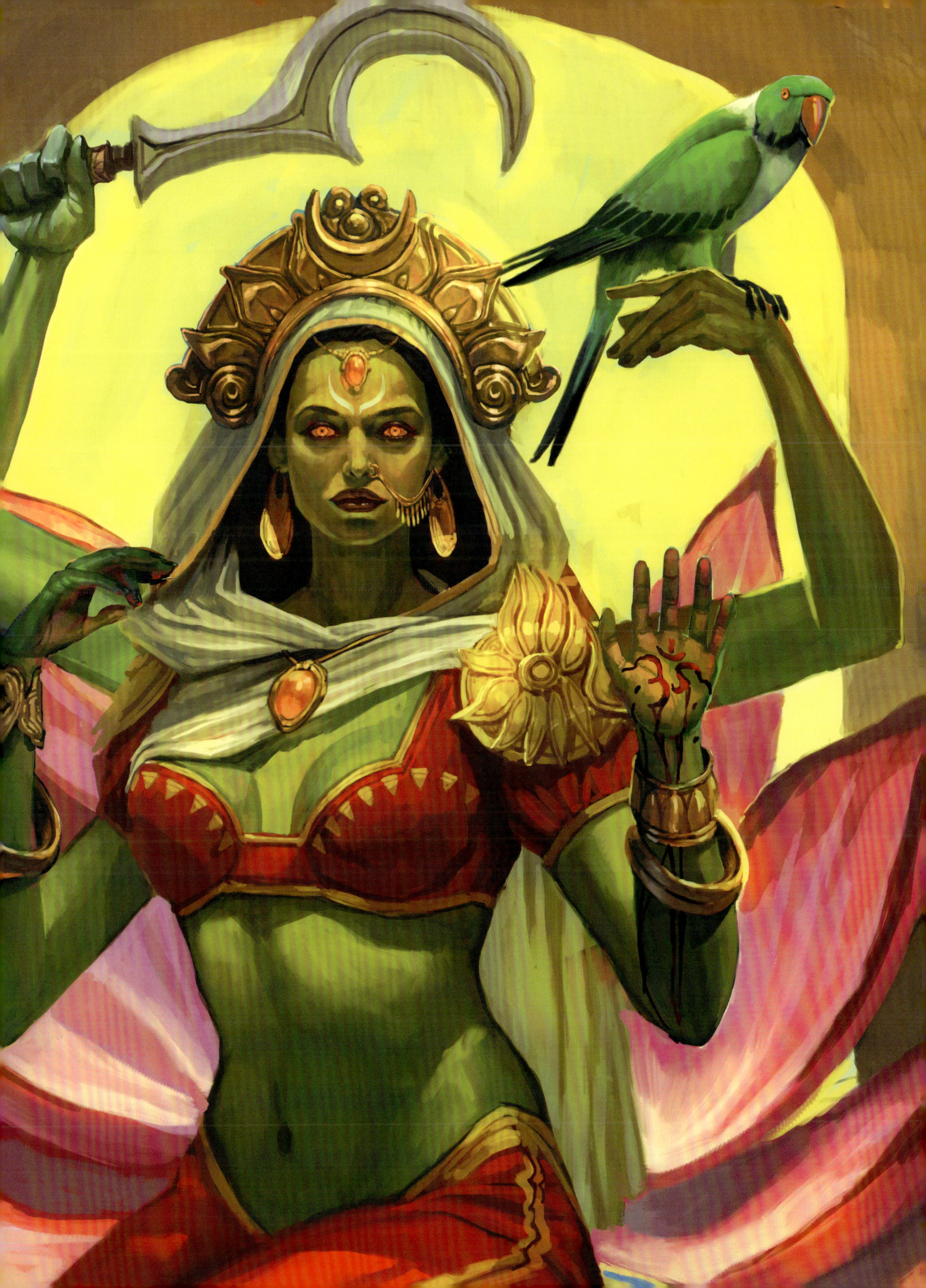

Verse X

Beloved *Kali Ma*,
You who are formless, eternal and absolute,
You who are in all forms, everywhere,
Infuse me, surround me, with your love.

In thirteen forms,
Sacred numeracy of the Divine Feminine,
I invoke this Cosmic Mother Mandala,
For infinite blessings and spiritual empowerment.

Sri Kali Vishvamata,
Sweet one who paves my path with gentle grace,
Jai Ma Kali, Jai Jai Ma!

Bhairavi Kaladhara,
Bearing crescent moon, you bring forth necessary release,
Jai Ma Kali, Jai Jai Ma!

Krodakali Troma Nagmo,
Wrathful Black Dakini severing karmic bondage,
Jai Ma Kali, Jai Jai Ma!

Devi Khadgahasta,
Mother wielding sword of divine victory,
Jai Ma Kali, Jai Jai Ma!

Durga Ma Kalika,
Goddess of divine justice enforcing resolution,
Jai Ma Kali, Jai Jai Ma!

Sri Ma Mahakali,
Undefeated one, arms laden with spiritual weapons,
Jai Ma Kali, Jai Jai Ma!

Sri Ma Chinnamasta,
Who overpowers enemies inner and outer,
Jai Ma Kali, Jai Jai Ma!

Sri Ma Chamunda,
Who overcomes disaster, demons and debilitation,
Jai Ma Kali, Jai Jai Ma!

Sri Dhumavati,
Blackened lady of crow and crone wisdom,
Jai Ma Kali, Jai Jai Ma!

Ghuya Kali,
Who knows all secrets and reveals truth,
Jai Ma Kali, Jai Jai Ma!

Kali Kalmasa Nasini,
She who consumes sin and becomes our absolution,
Jai Ma Kali, Jai Jai Ma!

Kali Phalatarini,
She who destroys the karmic fruits of negative actions,
Jai Ma Kali, Jai Jai Ma!

Kali Bhavatarini,
You who guide me faithfully always,
Jai Ma Kali, Jai Jai Ma!

In this, your Cosmic Mother Mandala,
My karma is purified and my heart lightened,
My unfolding path completely unobstructed,
My mind illuminated with the peace of your grace.

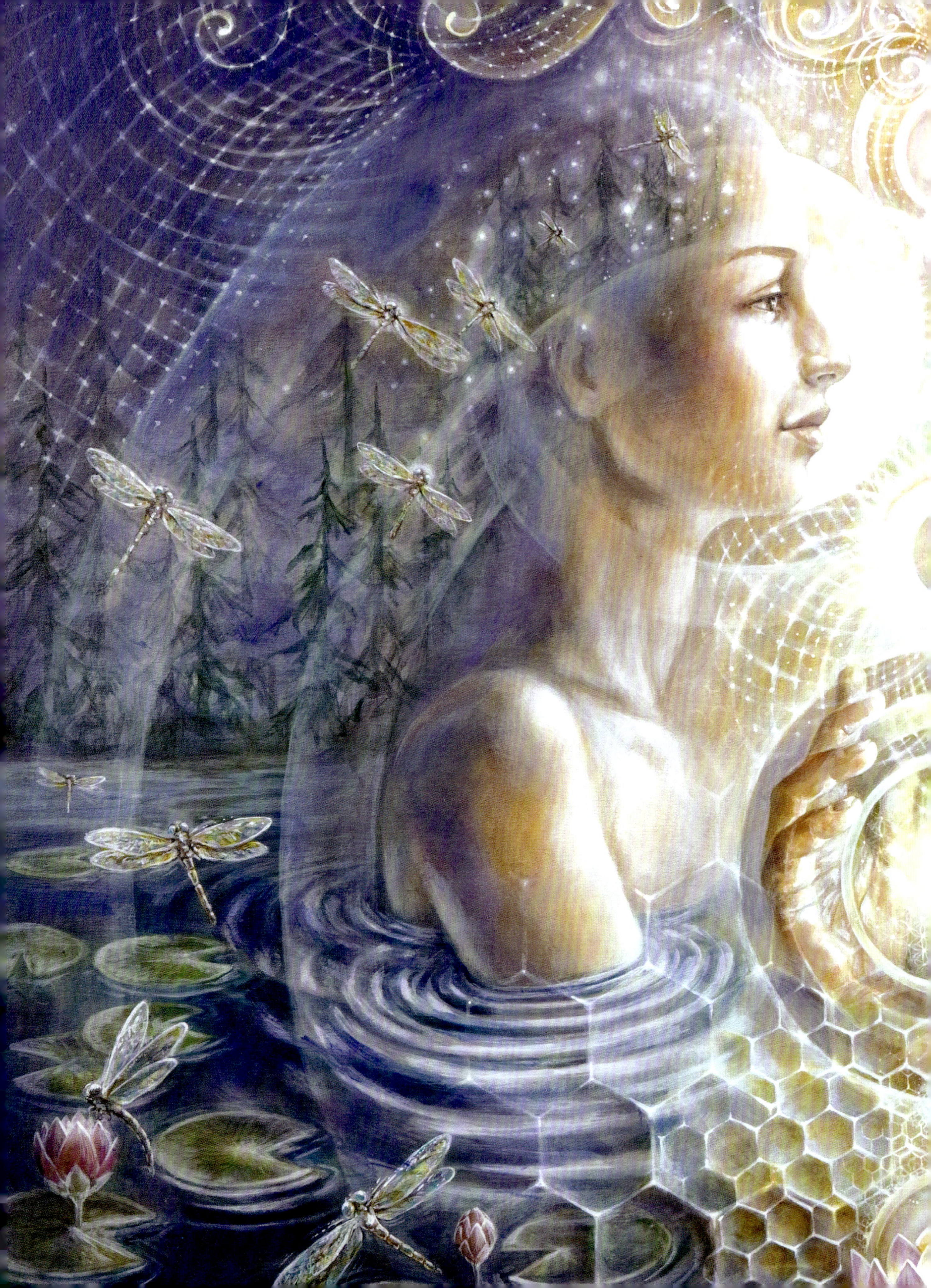

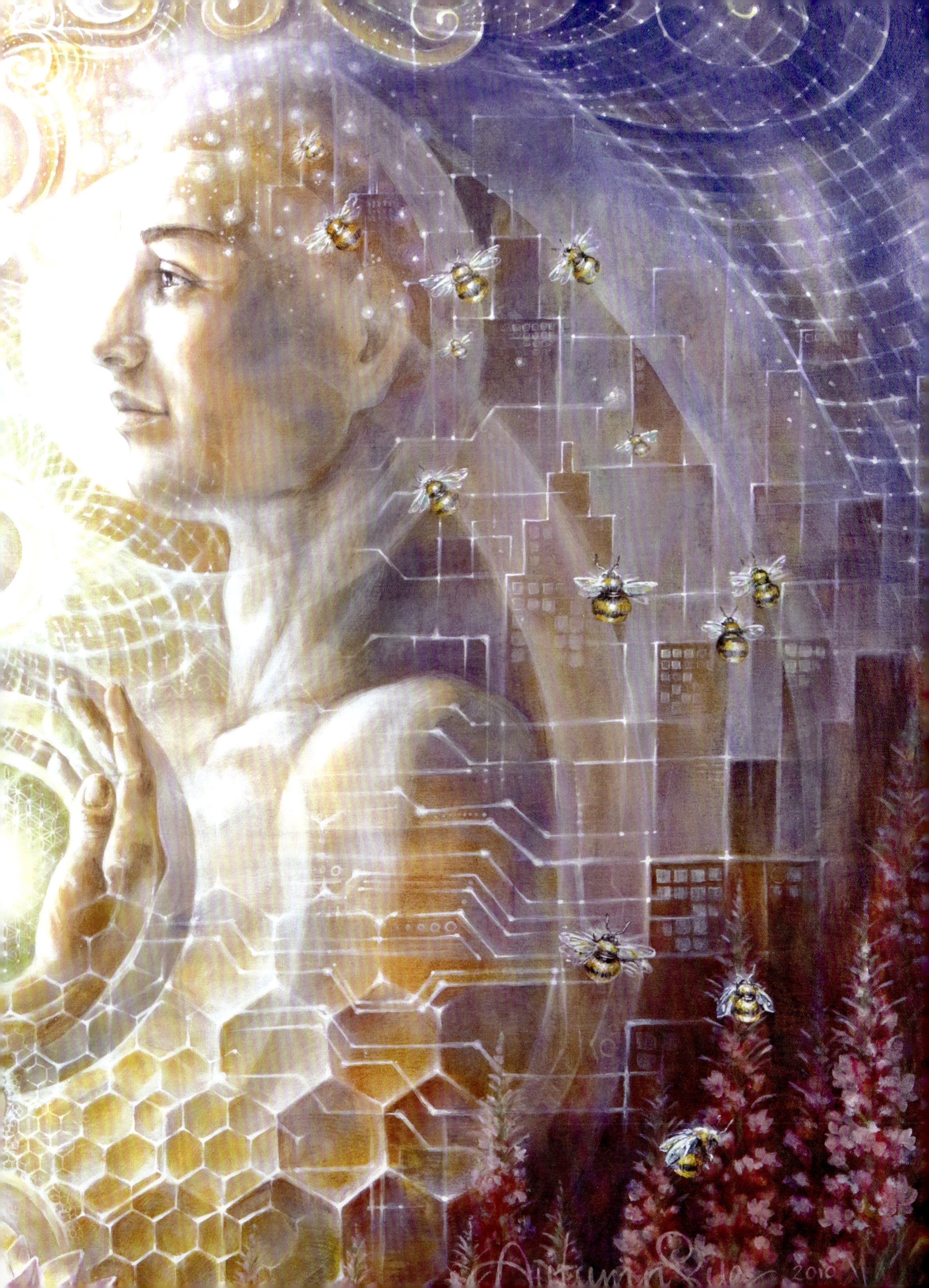

Autumn Skye
2010

Spell of the Cosmic MADONNA

Incantation and Divination of the Primordial Mother

My heart invokes thee, Great Cosmic Enchantress,
Dharani Lotus, red like a ruby,
Spells of light erupt through your joyful laughter,
Creatrix codes ignite,
As I recite these alchemical petitions.

All phenomena mesmerised, bound by the will of your love,
Talisman of my heart emits the corrective sound,
Words of warning, words of warding,
Taming the tempests, yoking them,
With your mercifully unyielding embrace.

Sacred Safeguard, Priestess of *Paritta*,
Divine amulet overcoming obstruction,
Dissolving obstacles into ethereal flowers of light,
To grace the Madonna's altar,
And inspire her delight.

Holy channel of enlightened wisdom,
Lay your claim to my wandering mind,
Stilling the fluctuations that obfuscate presence,
Disarming defence and distraction,
In the superior shielding of your grace.

My concentration becomes unwavering,
Like wild horse spirit gentled,
Resting, restored in the exquisite beauty of your presence,
All falsehood unveiled and swiftly dispersed,
I retain only the deep truth of your heart in mine.

Mantra Mother of Secret Wisdom,
You are living divine word, resonance of sacred sound,
Your scriptural spells and sweet sorcery,
Charm all beings with mother medicine of protective love,
I invoke your unfailing and gracious intervention.

Bandha, *Bandha*, Bind, Bind,
Act with grace, in perfect time.

Om Parameshwari Swaha,
Your *guhya* essence is love divine.

Om Hreem Shreem Kleem Parameshwari Swaha.
Om Tare Tuttare Ture Soham.
Om Tare Tam Swaha.

BELOVED,

may your sacred
work truly benefit
you and increase
grace for all beings.

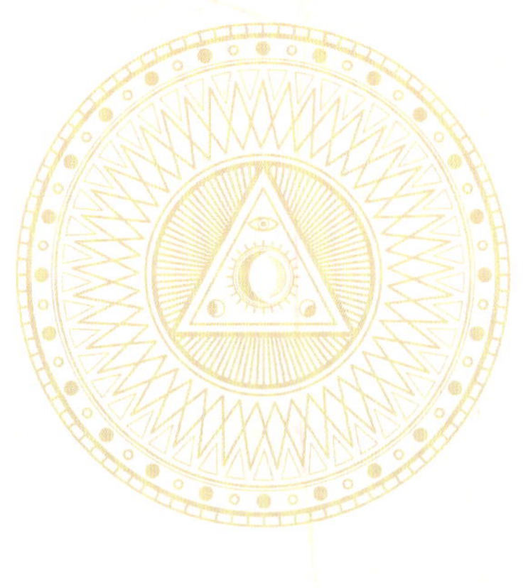

Next STEPS

There is power in amplifying process, and love to be received and shared. I warmly invite you to join the kindred folk in our divinely diverse and delicious community. I offer a multitude of magical programs including online courses and live sessions, ritual art performances, retreats and more. Open up in safe and activated space to connect, create and celebrate your unique journey. Find out more at **alanafairchild.com**.

I embody, enrich and express my unique magic
with loving wisdom for the highest good.

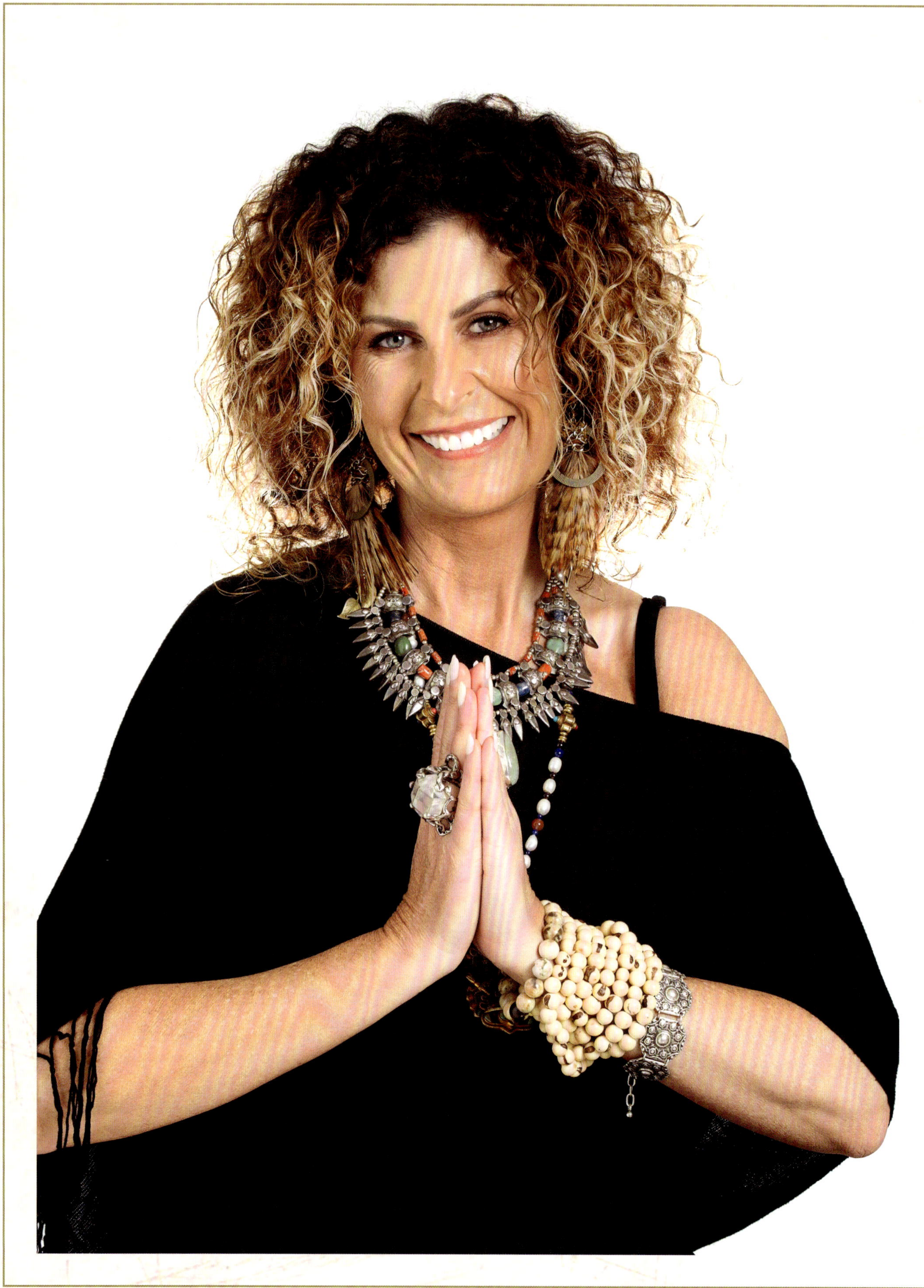

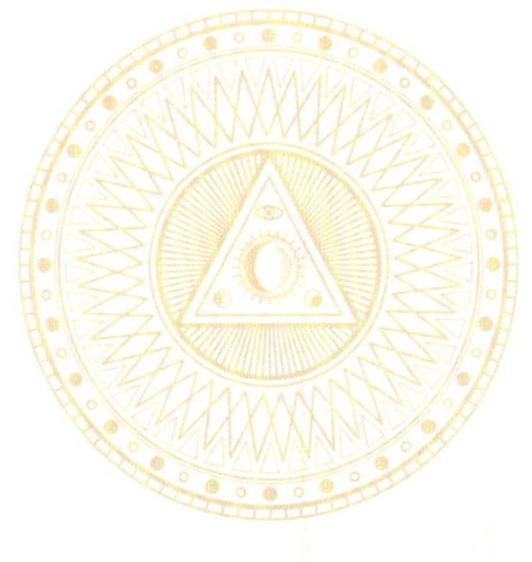

About ALANA

AN ARTIST OF A DIFFERENT KIND, ALANA FAIRCHILD IS A visionary powerhouse with a gift for soul-stirring communications. With a loving sense of humour and considerable knowledge across a broad range of metaphysical topics, Alana weaves magic into the world to uplift, vitalise and comfort the heart. She is a rare and nourishing channel who stimulates spiritual awakening and healing through her very presence. Alana's energy is a consciousness catalyst for transformation with a gentleness, purity and potency that sets her apart.

Alana's insights articulate a spirituality that is creative and personally empowering, valuing freedom and self-responsibility. Alana has devoted her life to creating unique works that resonate deeply with the soul and ignite the subtle fire of Spirit within, to inspire and spiritually equip human beings to reach most sacred and blessed fruition. To explore Alana's special offerings, including online programs, unique in-person experiences and more, you are warmly welcomed to visit **www.alanafairchild.com**.

List of ARTWORKS

Cover
Front cover art © 2025 A. Andrew Gonzalez
www.sublimatrix.com

Back cover art © 2025 Laila Savolainen
IG: @aboutlaila6604

Page 2
Artwork © 2025 Sophie Wilkins
www.sophiewilkins.com

Introduction
Artwork on pages 10, 12, 17, 18, 20, 22, 26-27,
32-33, 36-37, 44, 48-49
© 2025 A. Andrew Gonzalez
www.sublimatrix.com

Book of Isis
Artwork on pages 62-63, 64, 66-67, 68, 71, 72 ,
74-75, 76, 78, 80-81, 82
© 2025 Blue Angel Publishing
www.jamanimation.co

Book of Earth Warriors
Artwork on pages 84-85, 86-87, 88, 90-91, 92,
94-95, 96, 98-99, 100, 102, 104-105
© 2025 Isabel Bryna
www.isabelmariposagalactica.com

Book of Kuan Yin
Artwork on pages 106–107, 108, 111, 112, 114,
116–117, 118, 120–121, 122, 124, 126–127
© 2025 Laila Savolainen
IG: @aboutlaila6604

Book of White Light
Artwork on pages 128-129, 130, 132-133, 136-137,
138, 140, 142-143, 146-147, 148
© 2025 A. Andrew Gonzalez
www.sublimatrix.com

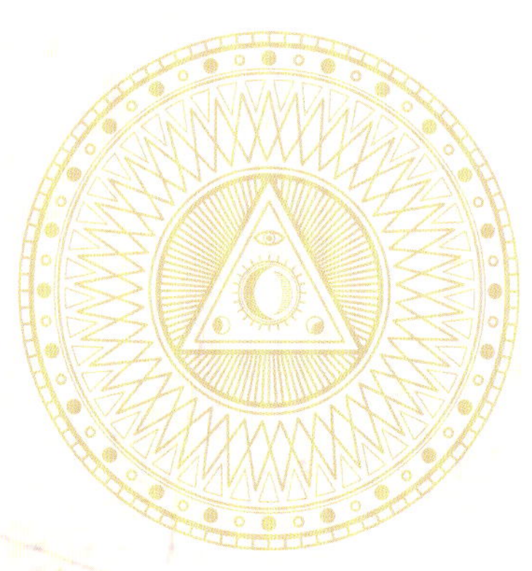